The Popes on Air

World War II: The Global, Human, and Ethical Dimension
G. Kurt Piehler, *series editor*

The Popes on Air

The History of Vatican Radio from Its Origins to World War II

Raffaella Perin

Fordham University Press | New York 2024

Copyright © 2024 Fordham University Press

Università Cattolica del Sacro Cuore contributed to the funding for the translation of this publication.

Front cover photo: Copyright © Vatican Media

All rights reserved. No part of this publication may be reproduced, stored in a retrieval system, or transmitted in any form or by any means—electronic, mechanical, photocopy, recording, or any other—except for brief quotations in printed reviews, without the prior permission of the publisher.

Fordham University Press has no responsibility for the persistence or accuracy of URLs for external or third-party Internet websites referred to in this publication and does not guarantee that any content on such websites is, or will remain, accurate or appropriate.

Fordham University Press also publishes its books in a variety of electronic formats. Some content that appears in print may not be available in electronic books.

Visit us online at www.fordhampress.com.

Library of Congress Cataloging-in-Publication Data available online at https://catalog.loc.gov.

Printed in the United States of America
26 25 24   5 4 3 2 1
First edition

For Sergio

Contents

List of Abbreviations ix

Introduction 1

1 **The Popes and the Media: The Origins of Vatican Radio (1931–1939)** 9

2 **Vatican Radio and the Outbreak of the War (1939–1940)** 33

3 **Vatican Radio, National Socialism, and Communism** 68

4 **Vatican Radio, Racism, Antisemitism, and the Shoah** 110

5 **Toward the Axis Defeat: Vatican Radio, the Occupation of Rome, and the End of the War** 142

Epilogue: The 1950s 177

Acknowledgments 183
Notes 185
Index 253

Abbreviations

AAV	Archivio Apostolico Vaticano
ACA	Assemblée de cardinaux et archévêques de France
ACS	Archivio Centrale dello Stato
ACUA	Archive of the Catholic University of America
ADSS	*Actes et documents du Saint-Siège relatifs à la Seconde Guerre Mondiale*
AN	Archives Nationales de France
ARSI	Archivum Romanum Societatis Iesu
ASDMAE	Archivio Storico Diplomatico, Ministero degli Affari Esteri
ASRS, *AA.EE.SS.*	Città del Vaticano, Archivio Storico della Segreteria di Stato—Sezione per i Rapporti con gli Stati e le Organizzazioni Internazionali, *Congregazione degli Affari Ecclesiastici Straordinari*
ASRV	Archivio Storico Radio Vaticana
BA	Bundesarchiv
BCIR	Bureau Catholique International de Radiodiffusion
CAD	Centre des Archives Diplomatiques de La Courneuve
DDI	Documenti Diplomatici Italiani
FBIS	Foreign Broadcast Information Service
IBU	International Broadcasting Union
LOC	Library of Congress
NA	The National Archives
NARA	National Archives and Records Administration
NCWC	National Catholic Welfare Council
PAAA	Politisches Archiv des Auswärtigen Amts
RSI	Repubblica Sociale Italiana
STO	Service obligatoire du travail
UI	Ufficio Informazioni Vaticano

The Popes on Air

Introduction

On the morning of March 4, 2019, in the Clementine Hall of the Apostolic Palace, Pope Francis addressed the officials of the Vatican Apostolic Archive,[1] announcing that the archival documentation on the pontificate of Pius XII (1939–1958) was to be opened to researchers for consultation beginning on March 2, 2020.[2] Scholars all over the world had been waiting for this moment for decades.[3] Those who had succeeded in reserving a seat in the study room of one of the various archives of the Holy See on those first days of opening described their emotion at finally being able to lay eyes on the documents of the controversial papacy of Eugenio Pacelli.[4] But only a week later, the COVID-19 pandemic turned the whole world, including the tiny State of the Vatican City, upside down. Following the guidelines of the Italian government, the Vatican archives closed the service of consultation, and scholars who had come to Rome had to quickly return to their home countries before the frontiers were closed for good. After this false start, it was not until the following June that the archives cautiously began to reopen and, albeit with persistent difficulties, it was at last possible to start new research.

This book is one of the results of the contribution of the newly released documents on the papacy of Pius XII. Starting in 2010, I looked for sources to assist in writing this history of Vatican Radio—from its creation to the Second World War. Few scholars have ventured into studying Vatican Radio due to the fundamental lack of resources because of the closed archives and, especially, the absence of recordings and scripts of the programs.[5] It seemed an impossible story to reconstruct, paradoxically in a period when the radio had become an important means of communication and propaganda. In contrast to other political institutions whose history of that period can be reconstructed through the preservation of audio and video recordings, it was as though this chapter in the history of the Catholic Church was destined to be unable to rely on sound sources. The darkest prospects were overturned when a series of archive discoveries led me to not only collect an extraordinary number of documents, but to also realize the global attention that Vatican Radio has received since its creation, especially during the Second

World War. The small broadcaster, with its headquarters located on the highest point of the Vatican gardens, was, at first, only to be used as a means of telegraphic communication between Rome and the peripheries of the Catholic world. However, it became an instrument of propaganda and diplomacy during the war years, gaining the interest of the governments of the belligerent countries, which ordered departments appointed to listen to foreign radios to monitor it systematically.

Thanks to the digests compiled by those in charge of monitoring Vatican Radio in Italy, Germany, France, Britain, and the United States, I have been able to write a book about the contents of the programs that listeners considered to be the *Pope's Radio*.[6] With the opening of the archives, new internal Vatican sources have allowed me, on one hand, to confirm the interpretative structure of my previous research on Vatican Radio, and, on the other, to clarify some aspects concerning relations between the pope, the Secretariat of State, and the management of Vatican Radio, and the exchanges between foreign diplomats and the Holy See. The new archives have also assisted in the clarification of the different positions of people within the Roman Curia or linked to Vatican circles with respect to the war. From this point of view, Vatican Radio can be considered a significant litmus test of the government within the papacy of Pius XII during the Second World War. The attitude of Pius XII toward the radio reflects the doubts, reluctances, and caution in relation to a conflict which highlighted all the contradictions, not only of the international situation between World War I and World War II, but also of the position taken by the Holy See at a time characterized by many unprecedented changes. The indecision, the challenges, the steps backward and forward, the instrumental use, and the programmatic silence which marked the history of Vatican Radio between 1939 and 1945 were the reflection of Pacelli's leadership of the Church—torn between the old and the new, between tradition and modernization.

The management of Vatican Radio seemingly reflected the sensitivity of the Society of Jesus, to which it was entrusted, both in the choice of topics dealt with in the radio conversations and news bulletins, and because it followed the closeness of the Society of Jesus to Pius XII. But in the effort to identify the radio announcers, even though it was not always possible to attribute the exact paternity of all the programs, a multiplicity of positions has emerged among those Jesuits and prelates who made up Pius XII's entourage. The reconstruction of the geographic and linguistic structure of the programs of Vatican Radio has highlighted the existence of different points of view on the war and on what could, or should, have been the policy of the Holy See. Although the employees of the monitoring services were convinced that they were listening to the Pope's Radio and therefore the programs were the direct expression of his positions and will, the new sources shed light on the indecisions and uncertainties of Pius XII in relation to the more defined convictions of the radio announcers, whether they were more pro-fascist (Italians and Spaniards), anti-Nazi (the Pole Ledóchowski, the Belgian Mistiaen, the Swiss Ambord), or pro-Allies (the Americans Hurley and McCormick). If it is true that Pius XII often gave indications on what Vatican Radio could or could not broadcast, the announcers carved out margins of freedom, making Vatican Radio the mirror of the multifarious Catholic world, even in the inner circles of the Vatican.

Vatican Radio, constructed by the inventor of the radio Guglielmo Marconi, and inaugurated in 1931, did not actually begin broadcasting until 1936. But the content of the programs became more interesting during the following years, with the establishment, by the Society of Jesus, of a fully-fledged editorial staff. During the war, thanks to technical improvements, Vatican Radio was able to regularly broadcast in not only Italian, English, French, German, and Spanish, but also in Dutch, Polish, Russian, and Ukrainian, and to use shortwaves to reach countries far from Rome, such as the Americas and India (in 1943 the weekly broadcasts totaled fifty-two in eleven languages).

Little of the content of these programs has been kept in the Vatican archives. However, it has been possible to reconstruct a great deal thanks to the BBC Monitoring Service, created on the request of the British Ministry of Information in 1939 to send the ministries and departments of the British government a daily digest of the information and news broadcast by foreign radios, which would have been used as a source of intelligence for studying enemy propaganda and the positions of the neutral countries, as well as prepare counterpropaganda.[7] Vatican Radio, as the broadcaster of one of the neutral countries, was also monitored on a daily basis beginning in January 1940. The monitors compiled a daily register of the programs in English, at times also noting the tone of voice of the newsreaders which is an important detail in the absence of sound sources.[8] The Overseas Intelligence of the BBC, the Foreign Office, and the Religious Relations Department of the British Ministry of Information acted in synergy to influence public opinion through the use of the Vatican Radio programs, which were quoted in the programs of the BBC and published in the press.[9]

Two monitoring services, similar to the British, were set up in Germany and the United States: the Sonderdienst Seehaus and the Foreign Broadcast Information Service (FBIS). The Sonderdienst, managed jointly by the German Ministry of Propaganda and German Ministry for Foreign Affairs, monitored programs from forty-five countries in thirty-seven different languages every day. Vatican Radio began to be monitored systematically on December 15, 1940.[10] In 1941, the US government set up the Foreign Broadcast Monitoring Service—from 1942 the Foreign Broadcast Information Service—as a unit of the Federal Communications Commission, which monitored American radio. Vatican Radio appeared in the FBIS digest from December 1942 and was monitored until at least the end of the war.[11]

Italy had also set up a monitoring center during the war, but records of the programs were apparently destroyed for security reasons.[12] On the request of the Ministry of Popular Culture, from February to April 1940, the Italian Ministry for Foreign Affairs received copies of the registers in Italian of some of the Vatican Radio programs broadcast in Polish, Spanish, German, English, French, and Italian.[13] From October 1940, the monitoring service of foreign radio printed two editions every day of a radio-telegraphic bulletin which, distributed to the competent ministries, was used to help write the news programs and orient political comments.

The programs in French, spanning the years between 1940 and 1943, form an almost complete corpus, thanks to the discovery of a multiplicity of witnesses which allows the reconstruction of the bulletins read on the radio with a minimal margin of error from a philological point of view. A group of Catholics belonging to the Christian Resistance of the French Free Zone collected the scripts of Vatican Radio programs in French, the work of the Belgian Jesuit Emmanuel Mistiaen, and produced a clandestine newspaper entitled *La Voix du Vatican*.[14]

As can be seen from their summary description, the sources were external to Vatican Radio and the Holy See itself: dependable but selected according to criteria useful to their producers. From the methodological point of view, it has been necessary to work with philological rigor, collate the witnesses where possible, and always bear in mind that the monitors selected and recorded essential information to use in their favor. Nonetheless, the reliability of the digests is confirmed by the fact that they were sources for internal use. Therefore, if we exclude a margin of human error in the translation of the bulletins compiled by the monitors into English or German, or the difficulty in listening clearly because of the jamming of radio stations during the war, there is no reason to believe that the texts were altered.

Looking at the history of the birth of Vatican Radio, it can be inscribed into the controversial relationship of the Catholic Church with modern means of communication. The word *propaganda* was used for the first time during the age of Counter-Reformation and European geographical expansion. Closely linked to the spread of Christianity, Pope Gregory XV created the Congregation of Propaganda Fide in 1622. Evangelization was a preeminent concern of the Catholic Church and consequently the Church has always tried to employ the best methods of conceiving a successful strategy to reaffirm the universal character of its apostolic mission. These means changed over the centuries, following cultural and social evolutions: press, cinema, radio, television, internet, etc.[15] Although, on several occasions, the nineteenth century popes denounced the danger of the freedom of the press as freedom of expression and the dissemination of ideas and doctrines was considered erroneous, from the second half of the 1800s many Catholic newspapers and magazines were founded, including the unofficial newspaper of the Holy See, *L'Osservatore Romano* (est. 1861).[16] In 1878, Leo XIII instructed the Congregation of Extraordinary Ecclesiastical Affairs to work on a draft regulation valid for the entire European Catholic press so that addresses in the social and political spheres would converge, in order to make known "to the adversaries a true commonality of sentiments, of desires and even of intentions in all Catholic peoples, who then could become strong and fearsome in the face not only of the sects, but also of the governments themselves, when they trample the rights of religion and of the Apostolic See."[17] This project foundered. In the 1897 Apostolic Constitution *Officiorum ac munerum*, which revised the criteria for the selection of books to be included in the *Index librorum prohibitorum*, art. 21 prohibited the publication of newspapers, sheets, and periodical pamphlets that attacked religion or good morals, and art. 22 recommended that Catholics, and especially clergymen, should not publish anything in such media except for just and rational cause.[18] Pius X had to address the spread of the periodic press as a medium of apostolate, and while subsidizing some integrist publications to fight the reformist ones, he was never fully convinced that it was an instrument that could be useful for Christianization.[19]

This attitude of initial mistrust and prudence of the Church toward the press, and the concomitant ability to exploit all its potential, reappeared *mutatis mutandis*, after the First World War highlighted the revolutionary resource of the wireless telegraph—both in military and civil context. The wireless network, initially used only in military maritime operations, was employed first by Germany and then by Great Britain to reach the colonies and for communications on the battlefields.[20] At the end of WWI, two major models of radio broadcasting arose: that of the United States, characterized by free competition, and that of the British, then adopted by all of the European powers and based on State monopoly and vigilance. In the 1920s, the competition between the different corporations led to a rapid development of telecommunications, with the establishment of groups that tried to gain control of the programs.²¹ Although it is not possible to determine exactly when radio began to be employed as a medium of propaganda, several countries started radio services in the '20s and '30s:²² in the United States, the Radio Corporation of America (RCA) was founded, which in turn created the National Broadcasting Company (NBC); in the United Kingdom, the British Broadcasting Corporation (BBC); in France the Compagnie générale de TSF; in Italy the Ente Italiano per le Audizioni Radiofoniche (EIAR); and in the Soviet Union, Radio Moscow. In Germany, radio broadcasting was initially hindered by a clause in the Treaty of Versailles and the first program did not go on the air until 1923.²³ While the main radio networks were being set up, a regime of regulation on the spectrum of frequencies was decided, which assigned to each station a specific wavelength.²⁴ In just a few years, the immense power of telecommunications was universally acknowledged as an instrument of social, cultural, and political influence.

The Catholic Church did not remain indifferent to the political repercussions that this international climate of discoveries and innovations had caused. However, as mentioned, the interest aroused in radio broadcasting was accompanied by the traditional mistrust toward modernity. On December 23, 1926, Archbishop of Prague Monsignor František Kordač, addressed to the Congregation of the Holy Office a query regarding the lawfulness of broadcasting the solemn Mass over the radio. In Bohemia, some maintained that this would have incurred a profanation, as non-believers listening to the celebration could have laughed at it; others, on the contrary, found it a way for those who could not go to church to listen to Mass.²⁵ On January 26, 1927, the Holy Office answered this query with a negative opinion, expressing the wishes of Pope Pius XI himself. On February 24, 1928, the ordinary of Prague asked again whether it was possible to broadcast liturgical music and songs as was already being done in other cities, but referring to the answer of the previous year, the Holy Office denied its consent, adding that if elsewhere it was allowed to broadcast liturgical songs over the radio, it was an abuse.²⁶

Nevertheless, following the example of the Jesuits of Radio Barcelona and the religious of Notre Dame, who broadcast from Radio Paris and from Radio Luxemburg, the Holy See had not opposed the active participation of Catholic preachers in Italy, either. In the United States, from the early 1920s, numerous confessions and religious organizations held radio licenses.²⁷ When Catholic culture met mass society, the Church also had to confront social changes, seeking alternatives to the traditional methods of apostolate.²⁸ It was a modernization of proselytism (which inevitably meant updating its technological instruments) marked by ideological conservatism. For example, in Italy, the presence of representatives of Catholic culture was appreciated on the radio, in film production, in the theater, and in music, if the purpose was to cooperate or compete with fascism for popular education. However, as Pius XI warned in the encyclical *Divini illius Magistri* (1929), "the radio" was one of the "powerful means of dissemination, which can be of great utility for instruction and education when directed by sound principles," but which was "too often used as an incentive to evil passions."[29]

The idea of providing the Holy See with a radio station of its own arose from the need to make the communications of the pope, and of the Roman Curia, independent from the Italian authorities through which the telephone and telegraphic traffic of the Vatican had to pass—before the Conciliation (1929).[30] To this end, in 1918, the secretary of state of Benedict XV, Pietro Gasparri, contacted Guglielmo Marconi for the first time. In her memoirs, Marconi's daughter Degna recalls that first conversation which took place in the period when the family had settled in Rome in the Villa Sforza-Cesarini on the Gianicolo hill: "There was great excitement at home on the day when my father announced the visit of Cardinal Gasparri who wanted to have a radio station installed in the Vatican and wanted to discuss it with him. We did not have the faintest idea of the etiquette to follow in such a circumstance and we asked for advice. At the set time, Cardinal Gasparri was welcomed at the front door by my parents and by servants holding large lit candles."[31]

The project was not fulfilled, and a second attempt was made under Pius XI, when Giuseppe Gianfranceschi s.j., then president of the Pontifical Academy of the Sciences, imagined the creation of a scientific radio bulletin spread by a broadcasting station installed in the *Specola*, the Vatican astronomic observatory.[32] On November 24, 1926, Marconi was received by Pius XI, whom he had asked for an audience on the suggestion of Gasparri. As the scientist confided in a letter to his ex-wife Beatrice O'Brien, he was in Rome to give a lecture, which had been listened to by Pius XI on the radio. Presumably, on that occasion, they discussed the construction of the Vatican Radio station.[33]

According to Carlo Confalonieri, private secretary to Pius XI, it was not until June 11, 1929, after another audience with the pope that Marconi made his first inspection of the Vatican Gardens, where, as Gianfranceschi had already imagined, the station was to be installed.[34] In the meantime, with the signature of the Lateran Pacts, relations between the Holy See and the Italian State had been normalized, which was an essential condition for those juridical aspects which would guarantee the connection of telegraphic, telephonic, radiotelegraphic, and postal services to Vatican

City.³⁵ On November 18, 1929, a new, specific convention for communications was signed depending on the Treaty.³⁶ On February 10, 1930, a letter from the Bureau International Télégraphique of Berne confirmed the registration of the Vatican City radio station and its wavelengths.³⁷

There was expectation, interest, and curiosity at an international level for the construction of Vatican Radio. In the Italian magazine, *Radiocorriere*, an advertisement appeared for a radio receiver with the following caption: "Receive the shortwave stations of Rome and of the Vatican City, to open soon."³⁸ German and American newspapers also announced that the Vatican was about to start a radio service and the author of a note to the Secretariat of State commented, "technical radiophonic journals have also got their hands on the news, and have imagined the most unlikely things from this piece of news."³⁹ Toward the end of 1930, the installation was completed and the inauguration ceremony of Vatican Radio was held on February 12, 1931.

1
The Popes and the Media: The Origins of Vatican Radio (1931-1939)

The first steps of Vatican broadcasting

On February 12, 1931, Pope Pius XI inaugurated Vatican Radio. For the occasion, he made a speech in Latin written by his own hand: he greeted and blessed religious and laypeople, "the infidels and the dissidents," the governors and their subjects, the rich and the poor.[1] As Marconi emphasized, it was the first time that the voice of the pontiff could "be heard simultaneously over the whole surface of the earth."[2] The radio broke down the physical barriers of communication, and even the confessional ones, allowing the pope to reach the non-Catholic world, as well.

From the beginning, a close bond was established between Vatican Radio and the Pontifical Academy of the Sciences, the Vatican scientific institution *par excellence*, particularly indicated in this first phase of experimentation in which the academy supervised the main activity of the radio, consisting of radiotelegraph and radiotelephone programs. Vatican Radio was to act, essentially, as a medium of communication between Rome and the periphery.

On March 9, 1931, experimental radio programs began to be broadcast in several languages with the aim of registering the reception of Vatican Radio in the different countries and to get listeners used to its presence on the air. During the practice runs, articles from *L'Osservatore Romano* would be read out in Italian and, for the other languages, news items from the Fides Agency would be included. The International Fides Agency, created by the Pontifical Society for the Propagation of the Faith, began its activity in December 1927 with the purpose of providing news (in English, French, Italian, Spanish, and German), photos, and studies of missionary interest. Vatican Radio reserved special attention to the missionary world, conveying the traditional Catholic missionary impulse. From October 1931, it was customary on Missionary Day for Vatican Radio to broadcast a message from the prefect of Propaganda Fide, translated into the various "missionary" languages.[3]

The newsreaders were Fr. Giuseppe Gianfranceschi, the first director of Vatican Radio,[4] Monsignor Richard Lorenz Smith, deputy rector of the English College, and Fr. Jean Delaire, a lecturer at the French Seminary in Rome.[5] From April 19, 1931 to January 30, 1936, the *Scientiarum Nuncius Radiophonicus* was broadcast, which consisted of reading scientific articles that had been published in the *Atti Lincei* of the Academy.[6] At the inauguration of the *Nuncios Radiophonicus*, Pius XI gave a speech in which he stressed the harmony between science and faith, always in the traditional horizon of subordination of the former to the latter, as the apostolic constitution *Deus scientiarum dominus* (May 24, 1931) confirmed shortly afterward.[7] Gianfranceschi himself, during some practice runs of programs and the reception of ultra-shortwaves by Marconi, and in the presence of Pius XI, said: "It is science at the service of faith and it cannot aspire to a higher service; nor can men of science ask for a more coveted prize for their work."[8]

Meanwhile, discussions had begun about the opportunity for a fully-fledged radio service. At an audience on May 29, 1931, Pius XI asked for information about the times when Russian Catholics would be able to listen to Vatican Radio and asked Gianfranceschi to include programs destined for the Soviet Union.[9] There was a project to build a Catholic radio corporation of religious propaganda for the moralization of the world, connected with the newborn Vatican Radio, and which would operate through agreements with the individual concessionary companies in the different countries. The need to give the Holy See a medium that would make it capable of competing with the propaganda of other States was beginning to be realized.

Fr. Gianfranceschi died on July 9, 1931, and in August Pius XI appointed Fr. Filippo Soccorsi as the new director of Vatican Radio. It was under his management, which lasted until 1953, that the broadcaster developed and became, to all effects, a radio station.[10] Pius XI answered the criticisms that were raised concerning the public's apparent disinterest in the practice radio broadcasts by inviting Soccorsi to make improvements. However, there remained hesitation, indicating a persistently cautious attitude toward radio broadcasting, as well as the need to clarify what the purpose of Vatican Radio was, its degree of officialness, and what type of programs should be put on the air. The medium of the radio also brought up completely new fears. Emblematic in this sense is the letter of July 14, 1932, from the patriarch of Venice, Pietro La Fontaine, to the Secretariat of State seeking advice on the measures to take when, as in the case which he presented, during transmission, mass was heard on the radio at an inn, patrons started to talk irreverently and make obscene parodies.[11] In June 1929, Pius XI had already raised the problem when the Congregation of Rites had asked the Holy Office for instructions on the use of the radio in churches and during ecclesiastical functions.[12] Pius XI responded: "It is to be borne in mind that any sacred radio broadcasts naturally penetrate all places, and therefore they could easily be subject, in some hostile environments, to ridicule and contempt."[13] What was to be done in these cases? How to remedy the inconveniences produced by a medium which, by its very nature, transcended any frontier and could penetrate any place, even where it was not wanted? Any control could only be held in the content of the broadcasts. The type and degree of worldwide exposure of Vatican Radio in its infancy required a meticulous study.

An exceptional witness to the period when Vatican Radio began its effective broadcasting, who helps to clarify how the first real programs were created, is the German Jesuit Friedrich Muckermann.[14] An important Catholic freelance journalist, he was and is known, above all, for his anti-communist and anti-National Socialist campaigns conducted from 1934, while in exile from a homeland where the Nazi government, as early as the day following the signature of the Concordat (1933), had begun to vex Catholics. During his Roman period (1936–1937) one of Muckermann's most important roles was that of editor of the "Lettres de Rome sur l'athéisme moderne," the journal of the *Secretariatus defensionis contra atheismum*, published by the Jesuit Joseph Ledit from 1935 to 1939.[15] In 1936, while he was a guest of the Pontifical Oriental Institute, the general of the Jesuits wrote to him: "I am very pleased that you have been able to begin your services for the Vatican radio station. If you proceed with wise moderation, very soon you will be able to sow fertile seeds in the hearts of very many."[16] Muckermann's memoirs, written between 1941 and 1942 when he was hiding from the Gestapo in Vichy, France, provide some information on his collaboration with Vatican Radio, which is a lesser-known aspect of his biography. As an editor of much experience in the field—he had been editor of the journal *Der Gral* and of the news agency Katholischen Korrespondenz that would be suppressed in 1936 by the Gestapo, and from Netherlands he continued his battle against National Socialism through his journal *Der Deutsche Weg*—Muckermann gave Soccorsi some advice on how to make the radio programs more attractive for listeners, in particular suggesting taking great care with the news bulletins and the lectures.[17]

The new organization of Vatican Radio, after the change of management in 1934 and the arrival of Muckermann, had an internal hierarchy in the editorial staff which gave Soccorsi the responsibility for contact with the Vatican and the superior general of the Society of Jesus, and assigned the radio and telegraphic management to a technician. There were at least two announcers for each language in order to alternate the voices and guarantee a "more conscientious preparation of the programs," allowing one of them to occasionally go to the country of his audience, make contact with competent personalities, and give lectures on the radio. The number of programs was to stand at three per day, a quarter of an hour each. Mass would have been broadcast daily with the exclusion of Sundays when there was a special schedule. As for the content, there were three main subjects: religious thoughts, news bulletins, and lectures. In the morning, there could be religious formation through meditation and fervorini, or short sermons; at midday, a news bulletin; and in the evening, the lectures that were to be "well worked out, in a spoken, modern style" and "spoken into the microphone with a certain perfection." An unsigned and undated typescript specified:

> To avoid clashes once and for all, it has to be communicated to the world that Vatican Radio has an official nature in two cases only: 1) When the text of papal documents (and only the text, not the commentaries) are read. 2) When the announcer says: It is officially communicated. All the rest is unofficial and private in nature. Vatican Radio must be a tool of apostolate and not a diplomatic organ.[18]

During the World War II, the question of the official nature of Vatican Radio was to become a major problem in the relations between the Holy See and the embassies of the belligerent countries, especially Germany, the UK, and to a lesser extent, Italy. As will be seen, declaring (in the context of war) that Vatican Radio was not the official organ of the Holy See was essentially a way to defend itself from complaints and attacks by the diplomatic representatives regarding the content of the programs. However, the problem was evident from the very beginning of Vatican Radio and refers back to the question of the responsibility for the content of the programs. The medium of the radio was more difficult to control compared to printed medium. Having admitted the hierarchization of the functions, who supervised the texts read in the different languages? Who wrote, edited, and revised them before they went on the air? The document reveals that there was still uncertainty in the face of the great potential of this new medium. The uncertain and potentially counterproductive consequences suggested that the radio managers adopt a profile that would safeguard the Holy See on the international level.

Despite his doubts, Pius XI understood the potential of the radio. He defined it as "such an impressive apostolate, which every day takes on great and profound importance, operating in the midst of humanity."[19] Radio encouraged the work of evangelization, and took the word of the pope in real time to regions far away from Rome. The pope now had a voice which could be heard, as well as a face and a body, thanks to photography and emerging cinema, acquiring a more human aspect in the eyes of the faithful. All of this boosted the pontifical sovereignty and the consensus around the figure of the pope, two dynamics which had their roots in the centralization intelligently woven by the predecessors of Pius XI, but which now found a completely new development in the new medium of global communication. The gradual rationalization of the use of the technological instrument started from an unquestionable awareness of Pius XI: "There are no terms of comparison for the radio: the radio, in itself alone, is without rivals."[20]

The anti-communist campaign as an incentive for developing Vatican Radio

The decision to make Vatican Radio a means of propaganda is closely linked to the intention of the Holy See to promote and defend Catholic interests at an international level through radio broadcasting.

Despite the violence and the abuse of power, to the detriment of the faithful and the Catholic institutions, by the Nazis in Germany, in the second half of the 1930s the Church still considered communism the greatest evil of political modernity. Soviet propaganda was the Holy See's major concern, to the extent where it was considered one of the greatest incentives for the development of Vatican Radio. The recognition of the unbounded power of radio broadcasting guaranteed the possibility of defending the interests of the Church and strengthening Catholic anti-communist counterpropaganda.

In spring 1936, news arrived at the Vatican that in May a "Congress of Atheists" was to be held in Moscow. Monsignor Giuseppe Pizzardo, secretary of the Congregation for Extraordinary Ecclesiastical Affairs, asked Fr. Soccorsi to look into this and, if he deemed it opportune, to prepare counterpropaganda through Vatican Radio. The director advised writing to the nuncios and contacting the Catholic members of the International Broadcasting Union (IBU) to gain their support.[21] The IBU was founded in the mid-1920s with the purpose of bringing together the radio corporations present in the different countries, and to discuss the preparatory outlines of the international regulations. In March 1936, Vatican Radio, as it did not broadcast in its own State, was accepted into the IBU as a member in a special capacity: from then on it was recognized as having the right to exercise radio broadcasting without any geographical limitation.

On April 30, Vatican Secretary of State Eugenio Pacelli informed the apostolic nuncios that the Moscow Congress was to have made "intense non-religious propaganda, including through [...] radio broadcasts in different languages."[22] Pacelli hoped that the governments of the countries where the nuncios were delegates would prohibit the retransmission of these programs on the national stations and organize counterpropaganda. He also hoped that, through a formal agreement, the members of the IBU would be able to prohibit "radio transmissions that were offensive to religion," also in order to influence the World Conference of the Society of Nations, which was to be held in Geneva in September to promote a "project of an international convention concerning the use of radio broadcasting in the interest of peace." The draft of this convention was circulating to be approved by the various member States, and the Holy See was working on an article that prevented the broadcasting of anti-religious content: the main interest was obviously that of preventing "antireligious and subversive Russian propaganda."[23] The proposed article was not included in the convention, despite the attempt to influence some representatives of the member States of the Society of Nations by the nuncios, to support the requests of the Holy See.[24]

In a similar occasion occurring two years later, Monsignor Giovanni Battista Montini, substitute of the Secretariat of State, wrote to Soccorsi that it was necessary to take "precautionary measures" through radio broadcasting "as the unfortunate event of the Congress of Atheists to be celebrated in London next September was growing nearer."[25] Montini asked if it were possible to interest the radio corporations of the various countries so that they would contact the BBC and ask them not to give international resonance to the event. The Foreign Office, though, contacted by the Dutch Minister for Foreign Affairs, communicated that "given the reputation of the fact and the principles of freedom and tolerance of the British people, it was not possible to obtain from the BBC to not talk about it."[26]

In May 1936, the twelfth congress of the Bureau Catholique International de Radiodiffusion (BCIR) was held in Prague, to which Soccorsi was also invited. The BCIR was made up of the heads of religious programs in the various countries to "serve the efforts of Catholics for the radio and through it to serve their civilizing cause" and to neutralize "the programs that hurt the feelings of the Catholic population."[27] The director of Vatican Radio then wrote to Augusto Ciriaci, president of Italian Catholic Action, to inform him that he hoped that the lay association would also take part.²⁸ He explained that it could not "fail to take an interest in one of the most powerful and irresistible means in good and evil" that was "unfortunately widely used by the enemies of the Church." Soccorsi envisaged a sort of "indirect penetration with people and production of certain morality, to prevent the state radio lending itself to questionable or reprehensible programs" and a "direct assertion through programs of an openly Catholic nature and also of such high value that they impose themselves on the attention of the huge audience." This was evidence of how the Church could have used and exploited the radio in the best way possible.

On November 10, 1936, in a speech to the members of the BCIR who were meeting in Rome, Pius XI said that the activity of the radio was "immensely great and therefore beneficial if put at the disposal of truth and good" and therefore it came within the field of Catholic Action. The apostolate of laypeople which was put at the service of the Church since "*in omnem terram exivit sonus eorum*" (their sound has gone out into all lands), could not fail to include the "current apostolate of the radio," as it was capable of broadcasting all over the world.²⁹

Fr. Maurice Hankart, secretary of Belgian Catholic Radio, in an article published in *L'Osservatore Romano*, and in a lecture he gave at the Gregorian University, hoped that the press and the radio, "these two powerful spreaders of thought, can be mutually supportive and together form a rampart [. . .] against the assaults by the enemies of the Catholic faith; a magnificent platform for the spread of the kingdom of Christ."³⁰ Vatican Radio was to represent this rampart and it was given the mission as it was a "powerful medium of education and moral elevation."³¹

Demonstrations of interest in Vatican Radio, in order to "neutralize the threatening voice of Moscow and Berlin," also reached Rome from other parts of the world, above all from South America and, in particular, from Argentina, Uruguay, and Colombia.³² From India, Monsignor Ludovico Mathias, the archbishop of Madras (today Chennai), recommended creating a Catholic agency for the press in his diocese, and the Jesuit Anton De Staercke suggested that Vatican Radio become an instrument to spread news as an aid for the Catholic press in India.³³ The idea of making Vatican Radio become a sort of "papal agency" which, like the great agencies Wolffs and Reuters could serve the whole press, had been conceived by a group of German publishers who, in the 1920s and 1930s had faced a problem that was widely felt by the editors: the need to have, directly from the Holy See, a more exhaustive account of the news they could publish in their papers.³⁴

A memo drawn up in the Curia, dated December 1936, "on the possibility of broadcasting on the radio against communism and for the Catholic cause," and containing some proposals on the activities that Vatican Radio could have done, represents, in a way, the answer to these requests.[35] The project envisaged that Vatican Radio would make direct and daily contact with the main Catholic agencies in America and Europe, such as KIPA (Katholische Internationale Presseagentur), and that it would set up an information office with the task of circulating the news exclusively collected to subscribed newspapers: the income from the subscriptions would have borne all the expenses. This service would also have completed one of the radio broadcasts, because by collecting Catholic news from all over the world, there would have been sufficient material to enrich the news bulletins, and these, in turn (although presented already directly to the public) would have provided the press with further news, denials, or rectifications.[36]

On March 14, 1937, the initiative was proposed to Pius XI who answered: "Study the matter thoroughly so that we can implement the program." On July 18, Fr. Edward Coffey[37] was authorized by Pius XI to travel to the United States to make contact with the American centers of the Catholic press, and in May of the following year the project, essentially complete, was presented to the pope. Fr. John P. Delaney,[38] in charge of the English-language broadcasts, became director of the center of collection, selection, and circulation of the news in Rome. He traveled in Europe to find correspondents and contributors, as did Fr. Ortiz de Urbina in Spain.[39] The radio programs were perfected and the broadcasts in the main languages were changed from weekly to bi-weekly. The material for the announcers was provided by Delaney, while for the German programs, "which had particular requirements, Fr. Alfred Lutterbeck was called with the explicit approval of the Holy Father."[40]

The content of the programs of Vatican Radio, between September 21, 1936 and December 1, 1937, were documented by the monitoring service organized by the fascist regime, which controlled the Vatican broadcaster.[41] Perhaps the latter was involved in an anti-communist campaign coordinated by the Church and the regime together. In fact, whereas up until the outbreak of the Spanish Civil War, a certain distinction had been made in Italian fascism between communist ideology and the Soviet State,[42] after a pro-Russian phase which led to political and economic agreements, in 1936 the opposition to bolshevism became central to fascist propaganda. In that very same year, Fr. Joseph Ledit, head of the Secretariat against Atheism, met with Guido Leto, a member of the General Directorate of Public Security.[43] We do not know the content of their conversation but, considering that the

Secretariat provided material for the programs of Vatican Radio, there may be a connection between the meeting, the start of radio broadcasting, and fascist anti-communism. It is probable that the control of the regime was not conducted so much out of suspicion for Vatican Radio but to collect information and news to use in support of its own anti-communist propaganda. After all, communism was a common enemy of both the Church and the fascist regime.

The programs aired from 4:30 p.m. to 8:00 p.m. and lasted fifteen to twenty minutes each. The characteristic signals were the ticktock of the clock in the five minutes before transmission, the words "Laudetur Jesus Christus" (Praised be Jesus Christ) pronounced at the beginning and at the end of the broadcast, and the bells of St. Peter's Basilica that rang the hour.[44] The news bulletins were in Italian, English, French, German, and Spanish. These first programs had, in their infancy, characteristics which would be further developed in the following years, such as the possibility of spreading the Christian message in different languages, thus connecting distant regions, and boosting inter-ecclesiastical communication.

Communism was indeed the main subject of the programs. The Catholic anti-communism campaign had taken on (in those years) unprecedented scope and the Vatican Radio programs were a means to reinforce it via cross-referencing information from Europe, Australia, and the Philippines. Some constants can be identified in the discussion of the issue: extensive accounts on how the Spanish Civil War was progressing, with the annexed denunciation of the massacres perpetrated by the "reds"; the daily bulletin of the abuse against the religious by the Soviet regime in Russia; and the anti-Catholic measures in Mexico. The "triangle of sorrow," referencing the expression used by Pius XI,[45] fueled the fear of the spread of communist ideology in the world, presenting opposing programs which offered an alternative solution to Marxism and liberalism to meet the economic and social distress of the world population. A conspicuous number of news bulletins were, in fact, devoted to the presentation of the Catholic social doctrine.

As far as Spain was concerned, Vatican Radio broadcast the speech pronounced on September 14, 1936, by Pius XI to Spanish refugees, and it was then read in Spanish, French, German, and English. The pope's speech was then rebroadcast by the EIAR, the Austrian stations, the Radio Verkhers Aktiengesellschaft, and the National Broadcasting Company in the United States.[46] Interestingly, this speech was included in the papers that made an "eminent [contribution] to peace and the closeness of peoples" in the questionnaire distributed to the members of the IBU conducting a census on the activities "aimed at fostering reciprocal understanding between people."

The way in which the Spanish Civil War was discussed, and the choice of what news to disseminate by Vatican Radio, can be interpreted in the light of a consolidated historiographic picture. According to the myth of Catholic Spain, the Spanish Catholics were the martyrs of the defense of the Church and Christianity, and therefore the Francoist design of a Catholic State was exalted.[47] In the program in Spanish on February 17, 1937, two ways of operating were compared: "The recent successes of the war in Spain allow us to hope in better times for the Catholic Church. [...] Where the communist wave has passed, it is all destruction [...]. In the Provinces occupied by the Nationalists, Catholic priests are making immense efforts to help thousands of abandoned children."[48] The news of the aid given to orphans by the national government was given again on March 3, in contrast with the "Russian communist party [which] proceeds to collect many children in Spain to take them to Russia, where they will be educated according to the atheist spirit. The Spanish Falange has energetically protested against this tactic."[49]

The difference in attitude with regard to religion was highlighted in the program on April 7: the Easter celebrations were sabotaged in the regions "occupied by the reds" while in those "occupied by the Nationalists, they were held with great solemnity [...] and a significant increase in religious feeling is recorded."[50] In the programs about Spain, as moreover in the Catholic press, there was no political analysis of the conflict, and the news on the outbreak of the conflict was always given through the filter of an ideological interpretation. One of the main sources on Spain was the Secretariat directed by Ledit.[51] The reasons for such a limit must be sought in the attitude of the Jesuits toward communism, often marked by arbitrary generalizations. Like the journal of the Italian Jesuits *La Civiltà Cattolica*, Vatican Radio also saw in the Spanish Civil War the national reflection of the international policies of Soviet communism.[52]

The news bulletins on Russia, which was never called Soviet Union,[53] were almost exclusively denunciations of the persecutions against the Christian churches, at times featuring extensive descriptions of the abuse. Alongside these bulletins, the announcers of Vatican Radio promoted the stigmatization of communism as a political religion, which could only fight the traditional religions to assert itself. In English, for example, it said: "In Russia the new wave of atheist propaganda wants to destroy not only Christianity, but also Buddhism, the religion of Mahomet etc. The only religion allowed in Russia is communism."[54] These programs expressed a conviction that was also present in a document of the Secretariat of State dated April 14, 1932, sent to the nuncios and apostolic delegates. In this circular, it was observed that: "The antireligious effort of the third international focuses in particular on the monotheist religions, so Judaism and Mahometism as well, but above all the Catholic Church."[55] The idea that there was an anti-Jewish and anti-Muslim communism is confirmed in the information collected by the *pro Russia* Pontifical Commission on the effects of the religious policies of the Soviet Union against the Jewish and Muslim communities present in the Russian territory. However, beyond the objective historical data, it is significant that the suggestion made by Nikolaj Berdjaev of communism as a "phenomenon of a religious order,"[56] and upheld by Italian Catholic journals such as *Azione fucina* and *Studium* in the early 1930s,[57] was taken as its own and spread as propaganda by Vatican Radio, as well.

Information was also broadcast about the consequences of the anti-Catholic laws in Mexico, in application of article 130 of the 1917 Constitution approved by the government of Plutarco Elías Calles. The churches no longer had legal status, the priests no longer had the right to vote, and the federal authorities had the power to intervene in religious matters.[58] As the Mexican episcopate had already done, the Catholic press and Vatican Radio described the situation through the interpretative prism of bolshevism. From a program in German, it can be seen that in Mexico "active communist propaganda had set its target on schools."[59] The news was also given in English:

> In Mexico as elsewhere, communism is conducting an intense campaign of propaganda based on literary and photographic material. Photographs of Karl Marx and scenes of communist life in Russia are circulated everywhere. Elementary school teachers are forced to take an oath in which they declare that they are not Catholics, that they do not profess Catholicism even in secret and not to circulate Catholic teachings in schools or outside.[60]

In another, they said: "The persecution against the Catholic religion is accentuated in Mexico, in step with Soviet Russia. The systems are the same and reveal the unity of direction of the movement."[61]

Particular attention was given to India, but there were also programs that warned against the spread of communism in England, the United States, Portugal, Switzerland, Africa, and China. Vatican Radio was the tool employed to counteract the internationalism of communist propaganda, which, moreover, in its anti-colonialist accents, supported the reawakening of national identities and the relative struggles for liberation.[62]

The Catholic Church and the Third Reich:
The first programs directed at Nazi Germany

The prospect of using Vatican Radio in the anti-communist campaign was not the only incentive to consolidate its presence in the field of radio broadcasting. The other important stimulus was the programs for Germany, since they were means of propaganda for the German-speaking area after the suppression of the Catholic press and the exclusion of Catholics from the radio of the regime had practically deprived it of news from the ecclesiastical world.[63]

Fr. Muckermann had begun to speak in German on Vatican Radio with some lessons that took their cue from the encyclicals, so that the authority of Pius XI's words gave them an unquestionable basis. He soon realized, however, that this was not the type of radio program that the public expected. He then decided to abbreviate the lectures and to broadcast more news about Church life. For example, reading bishops' pastoral letters, which the faithful in Germany could not easily know about.

On several occasions, the German episcopate expressed the desire to see the number of broadcasts increase.[64] In a conversation, held in Riedenburg on August 10, 1937, between Fr. Robert Leiber, the private secretary of Pacelli, Conrad Gröber, archbishop of Freiburg, and Albert Hackelsberger, representative of the *Zentrum* political party, the need for Vatican Radio to take an interest in current affairs, not only in religious questions, was underlined. For example, articles from the weekly of the SS *Schwarze Korps* or press releases from some National Socialist minister could be read, without it being necessary to comment on them afterward. To better exploit its potential, Vatican Radio could be used to deny the false information circulating in Germany, or to broadcast music.

The public's interest in Vatican Radio's programs was also noted by the German regime.[65] A report by the head of the Office of Security of the SS dated May–June 1934 observed that German Catholics listened to foreign radios to get news that did not exclusively concern religious context (which the Catholic media in Germany was only allowed to provide), and that they bought shortwave receivers to listen to, in particular, Vatican Radio. The same report reveals the National Socialist government's concern that the Vatican's pretext of broadcasting news of a religious character concealed the intention of spreading propaganda for political Catholicism.[66]

Between 1936 and 1937, Vatican Radio dealt with the persecution of Catholics by the National Socialist regime in a fairly systematic way, especially in the programs in German. But the denunciation of the continuous violations of the Concordat, and of the abuse of the clergy, was not accompanied by news on topics of a political and social nature that did not directly involve the German Catholic Church. By doing so, Vatican Radio may have wanted to make its non-interference on questions considered German domestic policy, such as the discrimination against the Jews, clear.

From the very beginning of its broadcasting activity, Vatican Radio tenaciously addressed the persecution of Catholics by the National Socialist regime. In the months immediately preceding the issue of the encyclical *Mit brennender Sorge* (March 14, 1937), with which the condemnation of some aspects of Hitler's regime would have taken on an official character, in many programs different news was given on the failure to respect the agreements concerning confessional schools,[67] the critical situation of the Catholics "due to neo-pagan theories,"[68] and the violation of their rights.[69] The possibility of a revision of the Concordat—a quite unprecedented threat—was also dreaded:

> In Germany the bishops oppose the antireligious struggle and continue to write pastoral letters. The 1933 Concordat which guarantees full freedom to the Church is a legal contract that must not be violated. The government pays no attention to the commitments it has made and the violations are an everyday occurrence. Priests are arrested [. . .]. A revision of the Concordat is absolutely necessary because the current state of affairs cannot continue. [. . .] The fight against the Church in Germany has taken on vast proportions and it can be said that a general offensive is being organized against the Catholic Church with the aim of destroying the faith by order of free thinkers, and there is the danger that Germany becomes a second Spain.[70]

In a case worthy of note, Vatican Radio underlined the fact that Protestants had joined the Catholics' protests:

> All Germany's Protestants have fraternally joined the Catholics to protest against this policy and this shows the profound solidarity that unites Christians all over the world. This solidarity comes from the absolute faith in the divinity of Christ, a faith which is mocked by the Minister for Propaganda of the Reich. But the illustrious Minister can continue to laugh, if he wants, without realizing that his hilarity will lead to the establishment of a single front by all the Christians who will come together to defend themselves from Nazi paganism.[71]

It is highly probable that the author of the program was Muckermann, who on other occasions had been able to solicit the union of Protestants and Catholics in a single front against Nazism.[72]

In the programs for the United States, Vatican Radio also "dealt with the present religious situation in Germany, and it gave a critical, uncensored picture of conditions there." These programs, according to Thomas E. Delaney, who wrote about this to the secretary general of the NCWC (National Catholic Welfare Council), Monsignor M.J. Ready, "gave to Americans a true picture of current affairs which cannot be gleaned from the newspapers in their reports on the same situation."[73]

The annual report of the *Sicherheitshauptamt* of the SS in spring 1939 confirms that Vatican Radio continued to denounce the situation of Catholicism in Germany. The report also highlights how, in the Catholic *milieux*, the National Socialist and communist ideologies were beginning to be thought of as equivalent:

> Vatican Radio has been heard with a retrospective of the year 1938, describing "the eruption of the forces of evil," as the most important event. The persecution of the faith has spread to all the provinces of Germany, a new heresy has come into being and its influence goes far beyond its country of origin. [. . .] Together with the declarations of the pope, other actions by the Vatican have to be observed, the programs of Vatican Radio, the attacks by "L'Osservatore Romano," the controversy of the international press and the ecclesiastical hierarchy that regularly show that Nazism and bolshevism are equivalent.[74]

At times, the radio announcer left the job of noticing the similarities in the anti-religious policy to the listener, only reading news that concerned Germany and the Soviet Union, one after the other. For example, the news of the condemnation to death of nine Russian Orthodox priests, falsely accused of spying, was followed by the news of a Catholic priest on trial in Germany.[75]

In spring 1938, Vatican Radio was at the center of a diplomatic incident caused by a program that followed the solemn declaration of appreciation of the Austrian episcopate for the results obtained by National Socialism, and in which Austrian Catholics were invited to vote in favor of annexation (*Anschluss*) in the referendum that was to be held on April 10, 1938.[76] In addition to the note published on April 1 in *L'Osservatore Romano*, with which the Holy See had distanced themselves from the positions declared by the bishops,[77] Vatican Radio broadcast a program in German in response to an article in *Schwarze Korps*. The article maintained that political Catholicism, the "most infamous of all political systems has now undergone the greatest collapse on Austrian soil and in the hearts of the Germans and, by our will, its final defeat."[78]

"Political Catholicism" refers to the engagement of Catholics in politics to defend the rights and interests of the Church in Germany since the time of the *Kulturkampf*. By 1870, the Zentrum had been founded, the political party that was officially nondenominational but brought together Catholics who, with reference to the Catholic *Weltanschauung*, pointed to the Church's social teachings as the basis on which the State was to be governed. After World War I, the Holy See had supported the Weimar Republic, during which Catholics gained cultural and political legitimacy that they had not had under the Hohenzollern monarchy. German political Catholicism supported and defended the Weimar Republic, obtaining from the Weimar Constitution the first full recognition of its political, legal, and religious existence. After January 30, 1933, when Hitler was given the task of forming the new government, the future Führer launched an attack on political Catholicism which he blamed for the lack of understanding in the initial consultations and the general ruin of the country. Hitler accused the Zentrum of having gone "for years at arm's length with Social Democracy."[79] Nonetheless, on March 23, the Zentrum voted on the Full Powers to Hitler Act. Crucial for Hitler was the elimination of competition from the Catholic parties of the Zentrum and the Bayerische Volkspartei from the political scene. It was to bring about the end of political Catholicism as had happened in Italy. The Zentrum was disbanded on March 5, 1933.[80]

In response to the *Schwarze Korps* attack on Austrian political Catholicism, the presenter of Vatican Radio accused National Socialism of putting itself on the "same doctrinal line" as the ideologies that it said it was fighting, i.e., communism."[81] But the part of the talk that greatly indisposed the German government, because of the clear reference to the pro-Nazi position of the Austrian episcopate, was the following:

> Naturally there also exists a false political Catholicism. [. . .] There can be no doubt that this false political Catholicism has already brought very serious damage over the course of history to the honor and the austerity of the Church [. . .]. The damage was and is even greater when even those who are assigned to political Catholicism or let themselves in some way be impressed by the triumphers of the day. Then, the eyes of these Shepherds may no longer recognize, as their duty should be, the wolf in lamb's clothing and they believe the promises of men, in front of whom they should be alert, both because of the sad experience of others, and the words of the Supreme Shepherd. [. . .]

> For example they use their moral religious authority of teaching to convince the faithful of the truth of certain statements on things that exclusively concern political and social life, even when those statements and the facts underlying them are judged otherwise and by many judicious men. For example, it is outside the competence of the Church authorities to make, as such, declarations that measure and appreciate the purely economic, political, social and popular successes of a government. No worshipper is obliged in their conscience to give their approval of these opinions, as opinions of the teaching Church, and to orient the use of their political rights according to them.[82]

The author of the program's text was the Jesuit Gustav Gundlach, although he likely did not read it aloud on Vatican Radio.[83] The program caused complaints by the German and Italian ambassadors. In a note, Monsignor Domenico Tardini, secretary of the Congregation of Extraordinary Ecclesiastical Affairs, talked about a telephone conversation with Italian ambassador Pignatti, who threatened that if *L'Osservatore Romano* did not deny the authorization of the Secretariat of State for the radio program, everyone would think that it was responsible for it and, indeed, that Pius XI had written it himself.[84] In the afternoon of the same day, the advisor to the Italian Embassy at the Holy See had also asked for explanations. He was told that "this broadcast had no official or unofficial nature; and that the Secretariat of State was so extraneous from it that it had no knowledge of the text."[85] The existence of a connection between the note in *L'Osservatore Romano* of April 1 and the Vatican Radio program was denied after the latter was widely circulated in the foreign press. It was stressed that "the radio's initiative was purely private," and that "the Secretariat of State was completely extraneous to what had been broadcast."[86] However, the content of the program had caused different reactions in the Roman Curia. After the repeated complaints of Ambassador Pignatti, Tardini wrote to him, confidentially, that the radio had acted "as always, on its own initiative":[87]

> I can never remember one case in which the Secretariat of State has directly used the radio for official communications, only "L'Osservatore Romano" has been used. The radio has never received direct news from the Secretariat. It takes it from "L'Osservatore." It may seem strange, but this is how it is. Until now, I had been informed that the programs of Vatican Radio were terribly boring. This did not surprise me greatly and I attributed it, at least in part, to the criteria, to the temperament and to the voice of the excellent director, Father Soccorsi. Today, for the first time, I am told of a radio program which

has produced a very great impression. I can only repeat that it is something that does not depend on this Secretariat.

Tardini's criticism of Vatican Radio was also put down in black and white in an internal note in which he wrote that, while the statement from *L'Osservatore Romano* kept the Holy See "equally far from the two extremes, saved what could be saved and did not hasten the irreparable," the program contained "a great confusion of ideas and inaccuracies of words." The same detachment was expressed by the nuncio in Berlin, Cesare Orsenigo, who wrote to Pacelli about the "deleterious effect [of the program], because it increased panic on the one hand and the propositions of vendetta on the other, where a marked coldness can already be perceived."[88] On April 4, the denial published by *L'Osservatore Romano* arrived. The program "was a theoretical study and of a private initiative and therefore neither official, unofficial or inspired, for which, as all the others of a similar kind, the Holy See does not intend to take on any responsibility."[89]

However, Pius XI had not found it so inaccurate. In Pacelli's *taccuini*, the secretary of state wrote that the pope, although he had given the order to publish the aforementioned denial in *L'Osservatore Romano*, did not retract or rectify any of the content of the program.[90] In a note Gundlach had even maintained that "the Cardinal Secretary of State Pacelli, who had corrected and approved the text, was covered in full by Pius XI."[91]

A new pope: Pius XII and the radio

In the last year of the papacy of Pius XI, between 1938 and 1939, Vatican Radio gradually started moving toward broadcasting daily in different languages in order to meet the concerns of the ecclesiastical hierarchies and foreign editors who wanted more and prompter news on the Catholic world. The occupation of the airwaves with daily programs had also become necessary to prevent countries with numerous radio stations such as Britain, Germany, the Soviet Union, and the United States, from demanding the use of airwaves assigned to other stations, if they were not being effectively used throughout the whole day.[92]

On July 6, 1938, the Secretariat of State wrote to the Italian Embassy at the Holy See that "the demands for international radio broadcasting require more circuits, so that the Vatican Radio Station can make connections that are simultaneous and independent from the EIAR but also from the radio broadcasting Stations of other States."[93] For this purpose, technical modifications were made, and on April 5, 1939, the Additional Agreement between the Holy See and Italy regarding the use of radio services was signed by Ambassador Bonifacio Pignatti Morano di Custoza and Secretary of State Luigi Maglione.

In the meantime, the service of information collection coordinated by Fr. Delaney found the collaboration of other Jesuits. During the XXVIII General Congregation of the Society of Jesus, which took place from March 12 to May 9, 1938, a questionnaire and a memorandum were distributed to organize the new editorial board and the news service. The recipient of the questionnaire was Fr. Delaney, who oversaw the planning and coordination of Vatican Radio's activity for the coming year.[94] The memorandum spoke of a news service project with the aim of collecting and distributing Catholic news through Vatican Radio to the countries farthest from Rome—the ancient idea to supply countries that do not have Catholic service of their own.[95] The programs were of two types: news bulletins and talks. The *nuncios de vita catholica* (the news bulletins) were necessary above all, according to the typescript, due to the radio's characteristic of being fast to circulate; it could quickly serve the most distant regions and could deny or correct the news given in the press, as well as becoming material for the newspapers themselves. As far as the *apologetica* (conversations) were concerned, they were to deal with social and moral questions, catechetical and liturgical matters, and were to give historical and artistic descriptions or commentaries on current affairs and celebrated centenaries. The subjects depended on the region which was to receive the programs, and political controversies were, in all cases, to be avoided. The goal would be making the talks given in different countries contain the spirit of each country. Delaney also specified that "a rule of anonymity is being insisted upon, so that we may not announce that this or that broadcast was prepared by so and so."[96]

In October, regular programs had begun being broadcast to the different countries and a special weekly program for the United States had also started.[97] The schedule for Vatican Radio included programs lasting from fifteen to thirty minutes for Europe, the Americas, the Philippines, India, and Africa. In order to reach the countries at various latitudes, the programming went from 2:00 a.m. until 10:00 p.m. (Rome time). The special US broadcasts began on October 9, and continued every Sunday afternoon at 1:00 p.m. (US time), transmitting news, music, and talks. Two reports received indicated very good reception. There were other English news broadcasts weekly, on Tuesdays at 4:30 p.m. and 8:00 p.m., directed respectively to India and the British Isles, and on Fridays, at the same hour, a talk was broadcast to the British Isles. Numbers of English listeners sent in flattering reports, especially regarding the Sunday afternoon US program.[98]

On February 10, 1939, on the eve of the tenth anniversary of the Lateran Pacts, Pius XI died. American journalist and war correspondent William Shirer, assisted by Fr. Delaney, covered (for CBS) Ratti's funeral and the conclave, which led to the election of Eugenio Pacelli on March 2.[99]

On April 13, 1939, before leaving for the US, Delaney wrote to Fr. Joseph Murphy that he felt no great regret in leaving Vatican Radio, of which he said: "just at present the station is more or less marking time, waiting new directives from the present Holy Father, hoping that a war will not come along to ruin all that has been going on, trying desperately to make up its mind to organize the whole lay-out as it should be organized to carry on its work with any hope of success and expansion."[100]

Fr. Soccorsi presented the success of Vatican Radio to the new pope, Pius XII.[101] According to the notes of the director, the programs in English were followed with interest in England and Ireland, where, often, the local stations asked to rebroadcast them. Similar requests had been received from the United States and the Philippines. The programs in French and Spanish were listened to regularly, while those in Russian were intentionally interfered with by the Soviet Union, although they avoided every political subject or controversy with the Russian Orthodox Church.[102] As far as the programs in German were concerned, according to the roughly four thousand letters received in answer to a question asked by the radio as a test, the rate of listening was fairly high.

After the outbreak of WWII, the lack of contributors and the difficulties due to the delicate situation induced Soccorsi, through Montini, to ask Pius XII for indications on how to proceed in the new circumstances. Pius XII gave the following order: "Continue everything, as far as possible."[103] Shortly after, a new editorial board, made up solely of Jesuits, had to be reorganized to work at Vatican Radio, alongside their usual activities. In October 1939, the American Jesuit Joseph Louis Vaughn, was summoned to Rome as the first director of programs.[104] A few months later, he was replaced by the Italian Jesuit Luigi Ambruzzi,[105] who continued as director until 1941, the year when he was replaced by the already mentioned Ignacio Ortiz de Urbina, and in 1943 the position went to another Italian father, Salvatore Gallo.[106] For the French programs, Joseph Boubée[107] was thought of initially, but was soon replaced by Emmanuel Mistiaen. For the programs in Polish, provisional aid was used until the return to Rome of the rector of the Polish College, Mons. Josef Młodochowski. He was assisted by Fr. Felix Lason and replaced in 1943 by Fr. Ludwik Semkowski.[108] The German newsreader was the Swiss Beat Ambord; for Britain and Ireland it was Francis Joy; for North America, the already mentioned Edward Coffey, Vincent McCormick, and

George Delannoye followed one another; for the programs in Spanish, Enrique Pérez García[109] and Ortiz de Urbina were used; and for the Italian programs, Francesco Pellegrino,[110] Galileo Venturini, and Carlo Miccinelli.[111] Moreover, in 1940, there also appeared as *scriptores propaganda catholica* (among whom the presenters of Vatican Radio were identified), Johannes Haarselhorst for the programs in Dutch and the Spanish-speaker Mateo Domingo Mayor.[112]

Relations between the management and editorial board of Vatican Radio and the Secretariat of State and Pius XII evolved in just a few years. Initially, the scripts of the programs were not submitted beforehand to the Secretariat of State but checked by the vicar general of the Society of Jesus, the Belgian Maurits Schurmans,[113] and by the superior general Włodzimierz Ledóchowski.[114]

On October 16, 1939, Ledóchowski gave several directives to Fathers Soccorsi, Haarselhorst, Mistiaen, Mayor, Pellegrino, Baumann,[115] Mackone,[116] and Ortiz de Urbina. He recommended, in order to perfect themselves in "the art of speaking," listening to the best radio announcers of other countries, and considering above all, the ways of presenting the programs which would contribute greatly to attracting listeners. A precaution that he repeated several times was that everyone had to know that it was not allowed to add absolutely anything that was not written and approved by the censorship. Besides, he informed them, Pius XII, at least on some occasions, listened to the programs and was very interested in them. Also, they would be listened to by appointed members of the General Curia, who would make their observations.[117]

An undated and unsigned typescript further clears up some aspects:

> Before the Holy Father and the Secretariat of State, Father Soccorsi is responsible for the readings, therefore he must be informed beforehand of what is to be read. Between Father Delaney and Father Soccorsi the understanding can be oral and by making joint revision of the material collected. Special care must be taken on agreeing on the comments and appreciations to be added to the facts. The facts of Germany and Spain must be the subject of careful verification, promptly calling on the authorized revisers. The German- and Spanish-speaking editors must have the approval of the authorized revisers. When presenting social events in general, and in particular those of Germany and Spain, care must be taken in highlighting the aspect that involved the interests of the Church, thus avoiding dangerous opposition or that the Church appears to be opposed for another reason which is not religious, or that in the face of a good cause the attitude of the Church must be

identified with the activity of one side. Speaking in general of national things, care must be taken to speak not as one of the Nation, but from the Roman and Catholic point of view. If the individual editors had added to the material received other news or appreciations or comments, they must inform Father Soccorsi of this, before going on the air. The script (preferably typed) of all the readings must be kept by Father Soccorsi or by Father Delaney. [In pencil]: do not say anything that has not been written and approved.[118]

This long quote defines the rules established for Vatican Radio. First, it tells of the existence of a prior check of the texts of the programs made within the Society of Jesus. The revisers were chosen depending on the language and the degree of monitoring that was to be exercised: it could be Vicar General Schurmans; Delaney, in the period when he occupied the position of director of programs; Pietro Tacchi Venturi, as was the case for the programs in Italian; and even Soccorsi himself, on whose desk the scripts always arrived in the end and who was the final person responsible, before the Secretariat of State. For Germany and Spain, the supervision had to be tighter, to the extent that Soccorsi's memo of March 25, 1939, said: "*In dubiis* say nothing, unless there is explicit approval by the Secretariat of State."[119] No changes were permitted to the news bulletins, but if the speakers had taken the liberty of commenting on some facts, they should have notified their superior. Actually, as it will be shown, this did not always happen. The typescript does not clarify who the authors of the radio conversations were to be. According to what has been observed, working via sources, when the authorship of a script was not explicitly stated, it is likely that the appointed announcers had an active role in the selection of the information with which they made up the news bulletins read in their languages. The Holy See did not seem to have a voice (yet) in the editorial decisions of Vatican Radio, except on special occasions. This demonstrates that, from the very beginning, an attempt was made to control what was broadcast by Vatican Radio, with an awareness of the authority that news broadcast by the Vatican medium could convey to listeners. For the same reason, the Secretariat of State lost no opportunity to reiterate that Vatican Radio broadcasts had no official character. The inextricable complexity of the relationship between the Secretariat of State and the multitude of Jesuits employed makes it difficult to say, once and for all, that Vatican Radio gave voice to the Holy See's official line. On the contrary, and it is the most interesting implication, it shows the multiplicity of positions, even inside the closest religious order to the pontiff.

Things changed in the following years. On October 1, 1940, Monsignor Montini wrote to General Ledóchowski that Pius XII deemed it opportune to pass on to the Secretariat of State all of the scripts of Vatican Radio programs, which had gone on the air the day before, so that the Holy See would always be aware of what was being broadcast.[120] This order was due to the agitated exchanges between the Secretariat of State and the German chargé d'affaires, Fritz Menshausen, about some programs aired on Vatican Radio between 1940 and 1941, which will be discussed later. Cases were also attested to in which Pius XII himself told the broadcaster to circulate some news items or not to broadcast others.[121]

The general line of Vatican Radio was therefore dictated by those who monitored its trends, i.e. Ledóchowski, Soccorsi, and the director of programs in office; from a certain point onward, the supervision of the Secretariat of State and Pius XII himself began, ready to intervene in the event they deemed it necessary. But the content of the programs and of the news bulletins, depending on the language and the countries they targeted, were also left, in part, to the discretion of the speakers. This was the case, for example, for the programs in English, for which, by the very admission of the general of the Jesuits, "he had left the appointed fathers to act a little more freely."[122] It will therefore be a question of gradually understanding which messages were to be broadcast to the different countries involved in the war or that were still neutral for the time being.

Concluding remarks on the early years of Vatican Radio

Pius XI had strongly desired the creation of a radio station in the Vatican to foster apostolate and to oppose anti-Catholic propaganda. To this purpose he engaged the inventor of the radio himself, carrying out the attempts of his predecessor Benedict XV. The Lateran Pacts, which had recognized the Holy See's sovereignty as a State over a small territory called Vatican City, had at the same time broken down the earthly barriers of the very concept of the pope's sovereignty, making the birth of a communication tool that would change the perception of papal power and the figure of the pontiff himself legally possible.

"The Vatican Radio should be a power. Rome should be the place for a Catholic center of news; for a dissemination of worthwhile ideas on topics of the day; and with the right cooperation (and a willingness on the part of the authorities at Rome to spend some money) it can be,"[123] wrote Delaney to his provincial while setting up the restyling of Vatican Radio in 1938. Indeed, the multilingual service that Vatican Radio began to provide, and improved upon in the second half of the 1930s, was in line with that of the major European networks. Radio Bari, an EIAR station broadcasting in Arabic from 1934 to 1943 for the countries of North Africa and the Middle East, is among the first radio stations to host programs in a language other than the one spoken in the country from which it was broadcasting. The USSR had begun a program in Romanian a few years earlier to counter anti-Bolshevik propaganda. The BBC would not inaugurate programs in foreign languages until 1938.[124]

Despite trying to avoid covering political topics, the birth and early broadcasting activity of Vatican Radio had a very close connection with politics. The denunciation of the danger of the spread of communist ideology internationally and the persecution against the Catholic Church, committed by the Nazis or the communists, occupied the early years of the broadcast. Surprisingly, for these years there are no sources concerning Vatican Radio's Italian broadcasts. However, silence on the part of fascist authorities suggests that such broadcasts were of no particular concern.

From the perspective of media history, differences and similarities can be observed between Vatican Radio's broadcasting activity and commercial radio stations—public or private—of other countries. For example, Vatican Radio was not interested in entertainment, except for broadcasting concerts of sacred music, and although the editorial staff tested whether broadcasts were successful or not, in an attempt to adjust the content to the interests of the listeners, audience opinion was not crucial in determining the type of programs that were aired. Broadly speaking, Vatican Radio was run more as a broadcasting monopoly regime.

Pius XII was interested, more than any other pope, in the technical aspects of modernization. He had a natural inclination toward technology (he liked to surround himself with modern objects such as the radio, an electric razor, a car, etc.), and continued along the path drawn out by Pius XI. Meanwhile, the internal editorial organization of the radio station was developed. With regard to content, the division of programs between news bulletins and radio conversations harks back to the discussion that was carried on in those same years about the "radiogenicity" of certain forms of sociability taken from existing cultural reality. In fact, there was not yet an adaptation of talk style to the radio medium.[125] Nonetheless, the strategic use of Vatican Radio, both for propaganda and for diplomatic purposes promoted during World War II, provided an information and cultural service capable of reaching an increasing number of believers and listeners.

There are no estimates as to the number of listeners of Vatican Radio during the period under consideration. By 1939, however, Fr. Filippo Soccorsi, the second director of Vatican Radio, could say that he was satisfied with the success that the station was having in Europe. Some data regarding the diffusion of the radio in the American and European context may be helpful to give an idea. A study by the IBU claims that in 1936 the number of radio sets per country was divided as follows:[126] 22,269,000 in the United States, covering 17.3% of the population; 7,914,506 in Great Britain, covering 17.1%; 8,167,957 in Germany, covering 12.2%; 3,128,541 in France, covering 7.5%; in the Soviet Union, 3,760,400, covering 2.2%; and 625,350 in Italy, covering 1.5%. With differences in timing and modalities in each country's broadcasting history, radio began to enter homes in the 1930s, while listening in public places remained widespread. This means that for every subscriber who was in possession of a receiver device, several other people could be assumed to be listening outside their homes. In the United States, for example, in the first three decades of radio's existence (from the 1920s to World War II), not only did families gather to listen to programs, but neighbors or the population of an entire village could depend on a single device. The owner of a radio in a small town or neighborhood would open doors and windows so that others could also listen.[127] The 1943 IBU general report stated that in Europe, excluding the Soviet Union, the number of radio licenses was 69,986,000, and considering that an average of four people depended on each, the actual number of listeners stood at 280,000,000. In the United States, 28,052,160 households owned a radio set in 1940, a number that rose to 30,600,000 in 1941.[128]

A BBC study on religious broadcasts in 1939 shows that they were widely listened to.[129] Vatican Radio certainly cannot be considered *au pair* with national radio stations (especially when these were engaged in wartime propaganda), nor can it be assumed that it had an audience equal to that of the major European or US networks. Nonetheless, as will be shown in the following chapters, the monitoring carried out on Vatican Radio by the listening services of foreign radios by the countries involved in World War II, the jamming to which the broadcasts were subjected, and their coverage in the international press and by other broadcasters, are all evidence of Vatican Radio's widespread use and effectiveness.

2 Vatican Radio and the Outbreak of the War (1939-1940)

The impartiality of the Holy See and the search for the causes of the conflict

On August 24, 1939, speaking on Vatican Radio, Pius XII launched an appeal to the world powers to protect peace:

> Nothing is lost with peace. Everything can be lost with war. May men once again go back to understanding one another. Let them begin to negotiate again. Negotiating with goodwill and with the respect of the reciprocal rights, they will realize that an honorable success is never precluded to sincere and effective negotiations.[1]

Pius XII did not address the merits of the dispute since he was convinced that he was exercising his precise pastoral duty: to celebrate and foster peace.[2] On behalf of the British government, the British minister at the Holy See, Francis d'Arcy Osborne, put pressure on the pope, hoping that he would have some influence in averting recourse to armed conflict.[3] François Charles-Roux, the French ambassador to the Holy See, told Monsignor Montini that a word or a public gesture in favor of Poland would have been opportune.[4] However, Pius XII said that "this would be too much": the forty million German Catholics could not be exposed to the reprisals that they would have suffered following the Holy See taking up a position in favor of Poland.[5] The fear of worsening the situation of the Catholics in the Third Reich immediately appeared as one of the main concerns and became one of the reasons most frequently put forward to justify the decision of Pius XII to not publicly intervene against Nazi policy.

Cardinal August Hlond, the primate of Poland and archbishop of Poznań and Gniezno, left his homeland, with the Polish government, and arrived in Rome, where on September 21, 1939, he was received for the first time in an audience with Pius XII. Hlond tried to make the pope speak up, but without any success.⁶ To fill the pope's silence, Cardinal Hlond spoke on Vatican Radio on September 28, inviting his countrymen not to despair, despite the catastrophe that had befallen them. The Italian version of the broadcast was published by *L'Osservatore Romano* the day after the audience granted by Pius XII to Poles living in Rome, during which, although showing sincere sadness for the fate of their countrymen, he avoided any explicit condemnation of the German aggression.⁷

In a letter dated October 7, Hlond asked Pius XII to include explicit support for Poland in the first encyclical that he was preparing. In the encyclical *Summi pontificatus*, which was published on October 20, 1939, the requests of the Polish primate were partially upheld⁸ and yet, a few days earlier, *L'Osservatore Romano* had published an article, corrected and approved by Pius XII himself, which explained the position of the Holy See to those who had accused him of indifference to the Polish tragedy.⁹

The "common Father," as the universal father of the Catholic Church, was asked for impartiality in exercising his authority, an attitude which necessarily differed from that of the national ecclesiastical hierarchies. This distinction brought out a contradiction which had already been unsolved throughout World War I. In 1914, Benedict XV had adopted the line of neutrality; the Holy See had to remain *super partes* to keep the unity of the universal Church, in view of the presence of Catholics on both sides of the conflict, and to avoid any retortions on ecclesiastical institutions in each country. Political neutrality would also have allowed the Holy See to be free to bring aid and assistance to soldiers and populations of all of the countries involved and be able to offer mediation through diplomatic channels to reestablish peace.¹⁰ The national churches, on the other hand, had taken sides and had actively taken part in the 1914–1918 war, not only by sending soldier-priests to the front who ensured religious support for the army, but also by taking part in civil events full of religious symbolism, such as the blessing of the flags and those who had fallen for their country.¹¹ In his first encyclical, *Ad beatissimi* (1914), Benedict XV interpreted the outbreak of war as divine punishment, inflicted on contemporary society for having distanced itself from God through secularization that had taken place from the French Revolution onward. Benedict XV recognized the right of each nation to fight for its survival—"nation" meaning the context necessary for peoples to preserve themselves and the adaptation of political frontiers to human diversity—on the condition that men did not demand absolute sovereignty, deciding their political destiny without considering Catholic aspirations.

In 1939, Pius XII, on the model of his predecessor, proposed the pattern according to which the reasons for war were to be sought in distancing man from the Church and in the rejection of the Christian principles in the establishment of the civil consortium.[12] As a consequence, taking up general motivations concerning the outbreak of war induced the Holy See not to take sides, allowing it to keep a line of reserve, but also allowing each of the national churches to legitimize the participation of its faithful in the conflict. Pius XII interpreted the new conflict as a classic war between countries, although the warmongering policy and the military maneuvers of Hitler had shown from the very first months that it was a very different situation. While the Great War had been, above all, a fight to defend frontiers or to claim their recognition, now, with WWII, ideologies, visions of the world, and ideas of civilization were clashing, which, depending on the victory of one side or the other, would have overwhelmed the face of society on a global scale. Although engaged on the diplomatic level (including secretly) to restore peace, Pius XII had not acknowledged that the world faced unprecedented conflict. He maintained the classic categories that belonged to both a theological tradition (the theory of the 'just war') and to pontifical diplomacy.

In the first dramatic months of World War II, the official newspaper of the Holy See *L'Osservatore Romano*, and the fortnightly magazine published by the Italian Jesuits *La Civiltà Cattolica*, followed the suspension of judgment of Pius XII, avoiding indicating Germany as being responsible for the outbreak of the conflict and criticizing its policy in the territories as it gradually occupied them—but with some exceptions and some allusions. The general indication was to only recall obedience to authority, which will be discussed later.

The position of Vatican Radio must certainly be included in the picture just sketched out, but with some significant nuances. For an analysis of the nine months of Italian non-belligerence, we have the unabridged texts of the Italian programs of Fr. Francesco Pellegrino.[13] The Jesuit, a member of the previously mentioned Secretariat against Atheism, was assigned to the programs in Italian during the war.[14] He alternated the news bulletins with conversations on religious subjects, ending with some reference to the current political situation.

On the topic of peace, Pellegrino dedicated a program to Francis of Assisi, who had been proclaimed patron saint of Italy, together with Catherine of Siena, on June 18, 1939. The figure of the saint was exalted by Pellegrino as a symbol of peace in "this period of ours, which, at least in appearance, seems to have lost many of those notions which ought to characterize a world redeemed by Christ."[15] Although the phrase with which St. Francis was usually described, "the most Italian of saints, the saintliest of Italians," was repeated several times, Pellegrino did not use the nationalist narration which was in vogue in Italy at that time. During World War I, many Catholics had attributed a warlike dimension to St. Francis' nationalization. In those years, the Franciscan friar Vittorino Facchinetti, a radio presenter well known for his religious programs on the EIAR, had used the image of St. Francis, presenting him as a symbol of willingness to sacrifice in order to legitimize Italy's participation in the conflict from the religious point of view, and exalting his qualities as an Italian in the nationalistic sense. The "Soldier Francis," "the perfect model of citizen and patriot," an icon for the Italian military virtues to imitate.[16] In 1925, a Royal Decree declared a national holiday on the date that marked the seventh centenary of the death of St. Francis, October 4, 1926. In a message to Italians abroad, Mussolini described the constituent traits of the character of the Italic people, represented by the saint: "simplicity of spirit, the ardor of ideal achievements and, where necessary, the virtues of renunciation and sacrifice."[17] Pius XI, in his encyclical *Rite expiatis* (1926) rebuked those who "by their inordinate love for their nation" used St. Francis as a sign or banner of this heated national love, shrinking the Catholic champion. Pius XI tried to prevent St. Francis from being made an object used by nationalists, although he did not forbid his Italianization.

In his broadcast, Pellegrino highlighted the pacific virtues of St. Francis: "The human side of Francis, although covered by poetry and sentiment, remains organizational will and activity for good and for peace. Without this element of essential importance, the figure of the Saint would be distorted."[18] Pellegrino ended the conversation with an explicit reference to the present time:

> In modern times, nowadays, the Pope wants men and nations to direct their attention increasingly to Francis. Today, humanity has an imperious need for supernatural aspirations, kind words, fraternal gestures, ideals that are other than those incomplete, illusory, and mocking ones that a revived paganism and perhaps more ruthless than the ancient one, would like to impose. Men want immediately and intensely the return of a time of love and peace. We are tired now of this prolonged uncertainty of living.

In tones that are very far from the triumphant ones of the "fascistized" saint of the 1930s, the characteristics of St. Francis exalted here were poverty and humility, which were echoed by a modest declaration of humanity expressed in the hope of "love and peace" and in the weariness caused by the "prolonged uncertainty of living." Pellegrino's speech on St. Francis was in harmony with

Pius XII who, in proclaiming St. Francis patron saint of Italy, emphasized his role as a peacemaker, almost wanting to encourage the Italian government to take up a similar position in the difficult international situation.[19] This way, a religious-devotional support was provided to the Vatican's political line which wanted to make fascist Italy, and Mussolini in particular, an interpreter of the diplomatic negotiations to bring the war to an end. However, with Italy's entrance into the war, the image of St. Francis, at least the one promoted by some Italian bishops from their pulpits, changed. Again, from the point of view of a politicization of sainthood, between 1940 and 1941 there were numerous references to the *Poverello* as the protector of the Italians, who respected and obeyed legitimate authority in the speeches, writings, and sermons of the ecclesiastical hierarchy. There were even those who maintained that Benito Mussolini was a "perfect Franciscan."[20]

In general, through the conversations and news bulletins of Vatican Radio, Pellegrino tried to relay the message, remodulated to a greater or lesser extent, depending on the context, of promoting the need for a restoration of the Christian principles for a return to peace. In the weekly review of October 9, for example, he mentioned, among the movements of a prayer for peace organized abroad, the pilgrimage of the Swiss diocese of Freiburg to Notre-Dame des Marches, led by Bishop Marius Besson. In the public speech, the bishop had said: "If the law of God were generally respected, war would not be possible. The first lesson of war is therefore this one: live like Christians."[21]

The program that was broadcast on October 26, on the celebration of the solemnity of Christ the King, was wholly dedicated to the topic of peace and war. Pellegrino launched the appeal "to seek serenity in Jesus Christ," blurred by the tragic events, as "Jesus is that *Vir Oriens*, [...] who can deviate the distressing route of the human ship."[22] The Church was presented as "an anchor and a lighthouse" and the "solemnity of Christ the King," expressed in Pius XI's encyclical *Quas Primas,* was to be opportunely celebrated "in this October of fire and blood." Pellegrino emphasized some concepts of the 1925 encyclical, stating that "Jesus Christ is the King not only of the supernatural world, and of that mystical one of His Church, but also the Supreme King of our society in this time, as it is up to Him to govern on a more general and complete level the lives of individuals and peoples."[23] Only by recognizing Christ as sovereign, not only of spiritual matters but also of terrestrial ones, could humanity find peace again, especially as "Christ is first of all a peaceful King. And it is such a King that men need above all today. [...] If the Nations, as faithful subjects of the Great Kingdom of Christ had sincerely accepted and observed the laws of Christ, written in simple words in the eternal Gospel, we would certainly be living in better days." "The universal and absolute power" of Christ "over all men, individuals and groups, nations and families" who expected to be governed by Him with a view to the supreme supernatural purposes, was stated.

In his long program (ten sheets of typescript instead of the usual six on average), Pellegrino did not only invite men and nations to grow closer to the Church and its laws again, but also entered into the matter of the war in two distinct ways: by reasserting the impartiality he was bound to, but also going as far as to list some of the causes of the conflict with concrete references to political reality. About his position, he wrote:

> We detach ourselves from the just reasons or not that have caused it [the war]: the need for space to live in awareness of having to honor the word that has been given—fears of freedom under threat. Let's leave to history and to those who will have the job of assigning right or wrong. However, beyond and outside every side, a principle and an experience have constantly shown that war destroys, it does not build, war exasperates and does not bring souls together, war affects mainly innocent victims and generally does not bring the world to an arrangement, on the contrary it opens abysses at the bottom of abysses. It is very difficult to define when it becomes justified: then war would be holy.

Just over a month earlier, *La Civiltà Cattolica* had published an account of the escalation that led to the outbreak of the conflict, reporting on the steps taken by the pontiff to avert war, diplomatic negotiations, and statements and notes from the German, British, Polish, and French governments.[24] Without taking sides, the search for responsibilities for the war was left to the "future historian": the line of the two organs of information run by the Society of Jesus and close to the Holy See, was the same. Except that Pellegrino, although not abandoning the principle of "just war," raised a doubt, without solving it, on which war could be defined as such. It is certain, as he said later, that "the Divine King wants peace in His kingdom but also to defend it and defend His subjects from attack by adversaries."[25]

However, on the causes of the war, without a direct reference to politicians or to countries, Pellegrino gave himself away in the following:

> They [the causes] are, to call them by their name: hatred, ambition, egoisms, injustices, lies, an unbridled thirst for earthly goods, the oppression of the freedom of others and the violation of the rights of others. In modern

language, these crimes against humanity and coexistence take on these other names: exaggerated nationalism, the fever for commercial or political hegemony and the arbitrary breaking of the given word, the monopoly of raw materials, the enslavement of peoples, despotism, the use of violence and the class struggle.[26]

The political ideologies, liberalism, capitalism, and excessive nationalism, which had characterized the last decades of European history, and which had been denounced on several occasions as dangerous by Pius XI (e.g., *Quas primas* against laicism), can be recognized in Pellegrino's words. "Exaggerated nationalism," expressly indicated by him as one of the causes of the outbreak of war, was a syntagma that had been part of the Catholic discourse on nationalism since the articles by Enrico Rosa in *La Civiltà Cattolica*, and taken up by Pius XI in the encyclical *Ubi arcano* (1922).[27] In it, Pius XI distinguished between "patriotism," which is "the stimulus of so many virtues and of so many noble acts of heroism when kept within the bounds of the law of Christ," and "extreme nationalism" which forgets that "other nations have an equal right with us both to life and to prosperity."[28] During the 1930s, though, Pius XI lost confidence that the totalitarian States which referred to nationalistic principles could take a Christian point of view on this. In 1938, he commissioned the encyclical *Humani generis unitas*, which would have condemned nationalism, branding it a real "perversion of the spirit,"[29] but he died, and Pius XII decided not to continue along the path of a final condemnation of the nationalist ideology, avoiding issuing the encyclical.

Nonetheless, other topics of the "hidden encyclical," such as the foundations of the unity of humankind and the concern for the respect of the rights of all men, were taken up in the programmatic encyclical *Summi pontificatus*.[30] Pius XII assured that Christian teachings approved the promotion, by all peoples, of the "prosperity and legitimate interests" of their country on the condition that "legitimate patriotism" did not make them lose sight of the fact that others also had the same right.[31] All the more, since it was religious formation itself that prepared youth "to fulfill with intelligent understanding and pride those offices of a noble patriotism which give to one's earthly fatherland all due measure of love, self-devotion and service." Vatican Radio reserved a great deal of space to the circulation of and commentary on this encyclical. The news bulletin on October 30 stated that it had been published in *L'Osservatore Romano* on October 27 and that in the late afternoon Vatican Radio started reading it in various languages.[32]

Pellegrino dedicated three programs to the *Summi pontificatus*, in each of which he discussed a different topic dealt with in the papal document. In the first, focused on the conception of the State criticized by Pius XII, he tried to explain how war and economic and social difficulties had emerged from "disorder and subversion of human thought," from the absolute autonomy claimed by the civil power, giving up the principles of natural law and a Christian conscience.[33] It was surprising, continued Pellegrino, that "this type of modern State" had needed, to be accepted, "ideological theories such as nationalistic union, the unity of the race and the union of the proletariat." "Agnosticism" was at the basis of the "absolutist" State, but "if men were left free to think, they would see that the modern State has not carried out its natural mission." During the program, Pellegrino also tried to show that the "lay spirit" had given rise to the evils of the time, that the war was the result of "laicism." According to the encyclical, quoted by Pellegrino, the State had to control, aid, and direct the individual activities of the national life, making them converge toward the common good defined according to the harmonious development and the natural perfection of man, provided by society as a means of the Creator.

In the next program, with a learned *excursus* into the philosophy and literature of the late nineteenth century, Pellegrino wanted to highlight other examples of how man had reached the ruinous situation in which he was at present. He dwelled on what Pius XI's encyclical had said about the consecration of humankind to the Sacred Heart, proclaimed by Leo XIII in 1899 in the encyclical *Annum sacrum*, using it as an occasion to criticize what had been done wrong in the last decades of the nineteenth century.[34] A new "lay faith," "Renan's faith," had replaced the true faith, deluding men into believing that trust in science was the only way to solve, not only social problems, but also ethical ones. In literature, Flaubert, Zola, and the Goncourt brothers had attempted to popularize the new dogma of positivism, "but they will be the ones that take humanity by the hand to this complex of moral, social diseases, to this immense apprehension that bursts out from everywhere, from hearts and souls, in this dusk of the century." Leo XIII had offered a handhold to man, consecrating humanity to the Sacred Heart, because he had given it a "model support, a single master, as a response to all the scattered appeals, to the anguish-ridden questions, to the tragic problems that weigh on humanity, the person of Our Lord."

In the third conversation on the *Summi pontificatus*, Pellegrino focused on those passages of the encyclical in which the pope clearly outlined the root of the evils of modern society—traceable to the negation of natural law and the "abandonment of that Christian teaching of which the Chair of Peter is the depository and exponent."[35]

An analysis of these programs show that both Pius XII and Pellegrino, in their reflection on the conflict under way, had extended their condemnation to all of the havens of political modernity: the pope denying that the "absolute autonomy of the State" and the separation of the "right of peoples from the anchor of divine law" could lead to peaceful international relations, and Pellegrino, when he made the ruin of the contemporary period derive from positivism and the laity of the States.[36]

Pellegrino explained this concept even more broadly in an article published a few months later in *La Civiltà Cattolica*.[37] Commenting on the headline that the newspaper *La Prensa* of Buenos Aires had used to present the papal encyclical, *The Catholic Church for the freedom of men and against demagogy and dictatorships*, Pellegrino clarified that Pius XII had not totally condemned the "absolutist State" because, as in Catholic and fascist Italy, at times "a certain prevalence" of "authority" was opportune for a "historical moment of varying duration." In the same way, continued Pellegrino, historically democratic systems, although the offspring of the French Revolution, had been "tamed" to the point that some Catholics exalted them because they had made some social conquests possible. And he concluded:

> Totalitarianism and democracy are living systems, therefore dynamic ones; they can change their content from one day to the next and become, respectively, that absolutism condemned by the Encyclical and that liberalism equally banned by the Church teachings and they can also—admitted the aforementioned reserves—become the most suitable system of a given ethnic character, for a specific historical period.

In his *Summi pontificatus*, Pius XII condemned the degenerate absolutism that had not considered Christian law, but as Pellegrino explained on Vatican Radio and in *La Civiltà Cattolica*, any other system that separated the laws of man from divine law was equally condemnable.

In the Italian programs broadcast in the first months of World War II, Pellegrino seemed to make himself the interpreter and propagator of Pius XII's magisterium, as was often the case with the Italian Jesuits.[38] He reproposed the idea of Catholic civilization as the world's only salvation, a key concept of Pius' pontificates. Suffice it to recall the mottos of Popes Pius X and Pius XI, respectively *instaurare omnia in Christo* and *pax Christi in regno Christi*, and the popes' general endorsement of the intransigent current since the nineteenth century. Through Vatican Radio, Pellegrino was a mouthpiece of Pius XII.

The occupation of Poland: The first testing ground of Vatican Radio

The process of the Germanization of Polish territory, on the one hand, and Sovietization on the other, had an immediate result, leading to the repression of the freedom of worship and the implementation of restrictive measures including the segregation, arrest, and deportation of the Catholic clergy.[39]

The Holy See followed the situation in Poland with apprehension through the reports of the bishops which, not without difficulty, reached Rome, and those of Cesare Orsenigo the nuncio in Berlin. A new reference, again without explicitly criticizing the States involved, was made by Pius XII in his speech at the Sacred College on December 24, 1939. He included the "acts irreconcilable with both the prescriptions of positive international law and with the principles of natural law and with the most elementary feelings of humanity," "the premeditated aggression against a small, laborious and peace-loving people, with the excuse of a threat that did not exist or was wanted or even possible; the atrocities (by whichever side they were committed) and the illegal use of means of destruction even against non-fighters and refugees, against the elderly, women and children." In the five "fundamental points of just and honorable peace," Pius XII maintained the need to "ensure the right to life and the independence of all nations, large and small, powerful and weak" and to conduct a "benevolent examination" of the "real needs and the just requests of nations and peoples, as well as of ethnic minorities." However, the conflict could not find a solution if, in reconstruction, man did not let himself be guided by the rules of divine law.[40]

On December 21, 1939, Cardinal Hlond sent Pius XII a detailed report on the brutal persecution against the Church in German-occupied Poland. Two days later, the pope ordered the preparation of a dossier to be discussed at a special meeting of the Congregation of Extraordinary Ecclesiastical Affairs to decide on the measures to be adopted.[41] In a second report, sent by the primate of Poland on January 6, 1940, the intentions of the extermination of the Polish population were clearly outlined.[42] After reading these reports, and the discussion in the plenary session of the congregation, the Pope ordered "giving some information to Vatican Radio for the German program on the conditions of the Church in Poland."[43]

During the following days, there were programs in which the violence perpetrated on the Polish population in the region governed by the Germans were amply described. The French ambassador, Charles-Roux, had also noted this in his diary and on January 23, he wrote to the Quai d'Orsay:

> They had often repeated to me at the Secretariat of State that the Holy Father had restrained himself from expressing his thought on the German cruelty

for lack of proof. This point has therefore been exceeded. The accounts of German cruelty are so abundant that Pius XII, after having examined them, with all the impartiality and prudence that are appropriate to his teaching, no longer feels he has the right to doubt them.[44]

In the weekly review of Catholic news on January 22, 1940, Fr. Pellegrino described the situation in Poland in a fairly detailed way. The comparison he made between the persecution of the Polish Catholics by the Germans and that of the Spaniards by the "communists" during the first months of the Spanish Civil War is significant, finally defining the methods used by the Nazis as even worse than those of the Soviets:

> The conditions of religious, political, and economic life have thrown that noble people, even in the regions occupied by Germany, into a state of terror, of dehumanization and we would be about to say barbarian behavior very similar to that imposed on Spain in 1936 by the communists. One of the inhuman aspects of this terror is made up of the exodus of whole populations from their villages, destined to other distant regions. The exodus mainly takes place with brusque and immediate orders. In a few hours, the village or the part of the city must be cleared, the people leaving are only allowed to take with them minimum amounts of money, clothes, and objects; then they are pushed on to goods trains and guarded by soldiers. When they reach their destination, always unknown to the refugees, after a terrible journey and often in the open air and in the snow, they are left to their fate. Hunger and diseases are therefore their inheritance. These cases take place every day. The Poles have the sensation that someone wants to destroy them this way. As for the religious situation, from the reports received here so far, we see that the Germans are using the same means, and perhaps even worse than the Soviets. [. . .] These notes only give a pale idea of what Poland is like under the German regime.[45]

In the program in German, as well, the one that Pius XII explicitly wanted, the announcer dwelled at length on denouncing, not only the deportation of the priests, the closure of the churches, and the impossibility of doing even the most elementary functions of worship, but also the inhuman treatment to which the Poles were subjected:

> Many Polish families in various towns are completely broken up. The father is in prison, the son and daughter have been sent to hard labor in Germany and the mother has been driven from her home and deported to central Poland. Since last November, the Poles have been systematically driven out

of Posen, Pomerania, and Silesia, and sent to the so-called Protectorate. We have no words for the method employed. Poles have to leave their house within a few minutes and are brought, without any belongings, into the concentration camps, whence they are transported in closed trains to Central Poland. They are then "freed," which means that these poor people are left to their fate, without homes, clothes, and money. They are turned into beggars and left to their misery. Some of these journeys have been made in open trains in spite of the cold, others in closed goods trains—as for instance in the transport of Poles from Bromberg to Radow, when, for three days no one was allowed to leave the goods wagons.[46]

This was followed by a list of "inhuman deportations" with the precise indication of the date and of the towns where they took place and the number of people deported.

On January 23, the nunciature of France at the Holy See sent the Secretariat of State a copy of the issue of the Catholic newspaper *Aube*, which, on the front page, summarized the contents of the Vatican Radio program of January 22.[47] On January 24 and 25 a program in French, and one in Spanish for Latin America, went on the air with the same content. The program for Spain, however, was completely disrupted, to the extent that the monitor for the BBC noted that it had not been possible to hear anything and that, as far as he believed, it was the first time that Vatican Radio had been disturbed.[48]

In the program in English for North America, however, the announcer added new details on the persecutions. It went on the air at 3:30 a.m. (Italian time) on January 23, so it was received on the East Coast of the United States at 9:30 p.m. on January 22, so that some passages could be published the next day, both in the *New York Times* and the *Times* of London.[49]

The English-speaking announcer, like the others, insisted on underlining that the violence by the Germans against the most elementary principles of justice was, at times, worse than the atrocities perpetrated by the Soviets:

> Inexcusable excesses committed upon a helpless and homeless people, (as peaceful and unpretentious as any in Europe) are not confined to the sections of the country under Russian occupation [...]. Even more violent and persistent is the assault upon elementary justice and decency in that part of prostrate Poland which has fallen to German administration.

This is a significant statement in light of the fact that the media close to the Holy See, *L'Osservatore Romano* and Vatican Radio, had until then preferably given space to the news from the territories occupied by the Russians. There are two interesting aspects of the program for America compared to the others. First, the announcer included, in the barbarian acts committed by the Germans against the Poles, the persecutions against the Jews, denouncing the establishment of the ghettos and the abject conditions of life to which they were forced:

> A system of interior deportations and zonings is being organized in the depths of one of Europe's severest winters, on principles and by methods that can be described only as brutal. And stark hunger stares seventy percent of Poland's population in the face, as its reserves in foodstuffs and tools are shipped to Germany to replenish the granaries of the metropole. Jews and Poles are being herded into separate "ghettos," hermetically sealed and pitifully inadequate for the economic subsistence of the millions destined to live there.

Second, the news and the facts recounted were accompanied by adjectives and comments which contributed to describing the terrible situation of the Polish population. In addition to the previous quotations, it is worth mentioning other sentences: from Warsaw and Krakow, from Pomerania, Poznan, and Silesia come "daily tales of destitution and destruction and infamy of all description"; "the crowing iniquity in an administration that has never ceased to claim it had no claims against religion lies in the cynical suppression of all but the merest suggestion of religious worship"; the closure of the churches and the impossibility for Polish Catholics to go to pray in them was "one more grievous affront to the moral conscience of mankind, one more contemptuous insult to the law of nations."

The text of the program in English for North America was relaunched by Radio London in the service of programs for Italy by Harold Stevens,[50] by the BBC in Polish,[51] and by the British press. The article in the London *Times* was quoted in the editorial by Fr. John Murray in the February issue of *The Month*, the monthly magazine of the English province of the Society of Jesus, in which large extracts of the program were quoted, including the reference to the Jews.[52] The *English Catholic Newsletter*, a periodical that summarized the opinions of the English Catholic press on topics concerning the war, published by the Tablet Publishing Company in agreement with the Ministry of Information and also distributed in the United States and in Canada, did the same.[53] The denunciation by Vatican Radio was echoed by an article in the Catholic weekly *The Tablet*, which, after having recalled the condemnation of German policy in Poland by the Holy See's radio station, said that in those territories, "Those who are not dangerous and not useful to the Nazis, the aged, the very young, the Jewish elements, are transported into the reserves created for them."[54] One year later, the text of the program was republished in the book edited by the London group The Sword of the Spirit created by Cardinal Arthur Hinsley, archbishop of Westminster, which collected documents that illustrated the persecutions inflicted by the German authorities against the Catholic Church, its clergy and the Polish population.[55]

In another program in English, broadcast on the same day, the sentence with the reference to the Jews was not reported.[56] *The Tablet* quoted its content with an ample comment.[57] Unlike the program for the United States, it said that it limited itself to news from the dioceses of Gniezno and Poznan, which we know came from Hlond's report, which, in fact, was not explicitly mentioned.

Fr. Soccorsi, on the request of the Congregation for Extraordinary Ecclesiastical Affairs, provided Vatican Radio's scripts of the broadcasts which had aired over the past few days, specifying that:

> The English broadcast quoted and reported them [the texts] several times, but also adding on its account things that we had not said. In particular, it said that the news came from a report by His Eminence Cardinal Hlond; I can, in this regard, assure you that none of those assigned to the Radio mentioned the origin of the news [. . .]. On the other hand, it appears to me that the journalists here in Rome are informed of His Eminence's report; none of the Radio operators has had any contact with these journalists.[58]

The announcers effectively did not make any explicit reference to Hlond's report, which had been distributed to the journalists without the authorization of the Holy See.[59] It is also true that the BBC, in its programs in different languages, had rebroadcast, several times, the news given by Vatican Radio on the situation in Poland. This is shown by the bulletins of the *Giornale Radio* (radio news bulletins), which were compiled twice a day in the Vatican, summarizing the most important contents of the broadcasts of foreign radios.[60]

After descriptions of the situation in Poland had gone on the air and been widely circulated through the English-speaking world, the advisor of the German Embassy in the Holy See, Fritz Menshausen, was instructed by his government to protest the programs of Vatican Radio with the Secretariat of State.[61] In his meeting with Montini, the diplomat asked Vatican Radio to avoid, in future programs, anything that could have negative repercussions for Germany. The substitute of the Secretariat of Pius XII however, answered that "Vatican Radio, although at times it draws some news from the Secretariat of State, does not depend on and is not controlled by it, which learned of the text of the radio program after the event."[62] The Secretariat was not aware of the script read on the radio, but on the other hand, we know that it was Pius XII himself who gave the order to speak, and in which terms, about Poland.

The bulletins of the *Giornale Radio* from London said that "Vatican broadcasts were much disturbed this week when the news on Poland began"[63] and that "after the announcer had stopped giving the news on the state of the church in Poland, the disturbance ended."[64] It also appears that in a speech given on January 27, on the conditions of Poland invaded by the Germans, Churchill quoted the program of Vatican Radio of January 23. The *Catholic Times* wrote: "If the radio station of the Vatican denounces the treatment inflicted on Poland, everyone knew that the news of the horrors which appeared in the press was, at least in essence, true."[65]

After the protests by the German Embassy, the general of the Jesuits, Ledóchowski, wrote to Montini to give explanations on what had happened.[66] He said that he had learned of Pius XII's wishes that they speak about Poland on Vatican Radio and, for this purpose, he had written to Fr. Leiber so that he could thoroughly prepare the news on the subject, that was as important as it was delicate. Ledóchowski wanted them to work together with Cardinal Hlond on a text that briefly set forth the most certain facts; then, on the basis of that outline, the Jesuits in charge of the programs could adapt it to the needs of the individual countries. The general, however, did not have the time to follow up on his intention because the fathers (believing that they had to obey Pius XII's orders as soon as possible) had already done the programs. The reassurances of Ledóchowski that he told the censors to be stricter in the future came to nothing: first Secretary of State Maglione, and then immediately afterward Pius XII himself gave orders to the editors of Vatican Radio to suspend programs on the conditions in Poland.[67]

It is, perhaps, precisely after these new orders that Fr. Coffey, the speaker in charge of the broadcasts in English for America, tried to rebalance the denunciation made in his program of January 23 with another which emphasized the extraneousness of the Holy See to politics and its impartiality toward the contenders: "The Holy See condemns the injustices committed by either side in wartime and it would be neither just nor fitting to attribute political leanings to the Vatican, which must remain impartial."[68]

Afterward, the broadcasts in German and in Italian drew a parallel between the two occupiers of Poland. The fathers, commenting on an article in the newspaper of the Russian communist youth, compared the Soviet policy with that of the National Socialists. The aim of the Russian-German alliance, they said, was to "fight every Christian ideology": "the Soviet opposition against religion will be inspired by Marxist theory; while the German opposition is based on the racist theory." In addition, "Germany and Russia equally," the Soviet journal informed, "have reached agreement on the coordination of their action in the Jewish question."[69]

Browsing through the content of the broadcasts in the other languages, though, it is worth noting that the subsequent news on Poland focused mainly on the Russian zone. A broadcast in Dutch and another in English for Great Britain, talked about the trains in which the population was deported;[70] a news item in English for India and in Spanish for Spain described the execution of two Poles accused of listening to Vatican Radio;[71] in Polish and in German, the abuse inflicted on the population was denounced;[72] and many other news items of the same level were given in the following months. All this information referred only to the Poland governed by the Soviets. Yet, the measures of persecution implemented by the Germans were not of any minor intensity. Also concerning the denunciation of the creation of the ghettos and the deportation of the Jews, the extension of the laws of Nuremberg to all the new conquests of the Reich was not mentioned, nor were other reports, later on, about the restrictive measures of the *Generalegouvernment*. At the same time, however, the broadcasts, especially in German and Polish, which denounced the persecution of the Catholic Church in Germany, were not stopped. In a broadcast in German, Spanish, and Portuguese, information on the abuse and violations against the Church and the ecclesiastical organizations in Germany since 1938 was listed.[73]

Furthermore, it must be reported that the German and the Italian press tried, in every way possible, to deny the news circulated by Vatican Radio. *L'Osservatore Romano* had published the declarations of Minister Franck about the benevolent treatment of the Poles under the Germans, and the Secretariat of State did not uphold the request of the Polish ambassador to make a denial.[74]

So, why did Pius XII give Vatican Radio the task of denouncing the situation of the Church in German occupied Poland and why did he order suspension of these broadcasts immediately after the protests by the representative of the Reich, while they could continue those about the Church in Germany? Pius XII had refused, until then, to speak clearly and officially about the Polish occupation by Germany, the abuse inflicted on the population, and the difficulties encountered by the bishops and the clergy in exercising their pastoral functions. Pius XII could not hope that the Polish bishops, while bravely remaining in place, would be able to criticize the Nazi regime. He had left the German episcopate free to decide whether or not it was expedient to openly criticize the regime, but he could not expect the Poles to dare so much. Therefore, he decided to address the medium that, in his mind, was perhaps the safest for several reasons. *L'Osservatore Romano* was too exposed to the reprisals of the Italian fascists and, in any case, was too recognizable as the official organ of the Holy See. In actual fact, from the start of the war, the daily Catholic newspaper had, on several occasions, published news on the "separation of the Jewish elements from the rest of the population," their "transfer" to the reserve of Lublin, and their "migration," but without ever using the word "deportation," and often without making any explicit reference to the Nazis.[75]

Vatican Radio was chosen because it was the most fluid medium. Due to its natural constitution, there was both an extended capacity for penetration as well as the possibility of lasting only for the time of being on air. It is probable that Pius XII did not expect that the program, which according to his order was to be aired only in German, would be picked up by the press, in its many translations, even on the other side of the ocean, and would provoke the harsh protests of the German government, brought personally by the diplomat to the Secretariat of State. By giving orders to broadcast the news only in German, did Pius XII want to give some sort of warning to the Reich? In this case, Vatican Radio would not have been used so much as a means of propaganda, but rather of diplomacy, to show that the Holy See did not remain defenseless in the face of German violence in Poland. The controversy caused by the speakers who did not wait for Leiber's text, the unexpected international spread and rebound of the broadcasts, and the Menshausen protests convinced Pius XII to back down.

A further reason for Pius XII's decision could be the difficulty that the Holy See was having in sending someone to Poland, i.e., Msgr. Carlo Colli of the nunciature in Berlin, to study the religious situation closely and be able to take action accordingly. In the aforementioned conversation with the French ambassador, Tardini concluded: "Now we hope to get Msgr. Colli in there. So, we wait and refrain from aggravating the situation."[76]

It can also be maintained that Pacelli and his entourage began to realize the level of incisiveness of Vatican Radio only during these months of the war, i.e., they began, only then, to realize the effect that the programs could have. During 1940, they had to have become aware that Vatican Radio was not only listened to, but monitored by, the governments of the opposing sides and used as propaganda. Knowledge of this practice was clearly not predictable in the Curia. The case that had arisen around the broadcasts of January 1940 suggests the hypothesis that from that moment onward, including at the Ministry of Foreign Affairs of the Third Reich, the potential of Vatican Radio, and the importance of monitoring it, started to be recognized. The British, too, understood this, and gathered news from Vatican Radio that they would have been unlikely to acquire otherwise.[77] The *Sonderdienst Seehaus* started to systematically monitor Vatican Radio only at the end of 1940, after the *Reichssender Stuttgart Sonderdienst Landhaus*—the monitoring service based in Stuttgart, more modest than the one later established in Wannsee—intercepted the BBC's programs for abroad and realized that many of the programs from Vatican Radio were repeated by the BBC. An early example of this is the circulation of the message by the BBC on the situation in a Poland occupied by the Germans, which retransmitted thirteen times in two days, from January 22 to 24, in English, German, Czech, and Polish.[78] On the basis of these interceptions, the German Ministry for Foreign Affairs ordered Ambassador von Bergen to ask Pius XII's Secretariat of State for explanations.

The reconstructed story also helps to shed light on the issue of Pius XII's "silences." Italian historian Andrea Riccardi notes that the silence concerned the suffering of the Polish people before the one of the Jewish people, and that it was a matter of concern for Pius XII himself, who wondered how his political line was perceived.[79] The pope knew that his silence was criticized: he knew that the Poles were displeased and that they felt abandoned by the Holy See. He knew that the opinion that he should expose himself more on conditions in Poland was widespread, in both ecclesial and diplomatic circles. He justified his silence by resorting to the impartiality that the pope had to maintain in the face of a conflict involving Catholics on both sides. He had the problem, however, of showing that his demeanor toward Nazism would not be read as indifference to the suffering of the populations victimized by German violence. For this, he commissioned the article published in *L'Osservatore Romano* on October 15, 1939, and he gave orders to broadcast some news about the situation in Poland through Vatican Radio. In the following years, Pius XII, realized the dissatisfaction and disappointment of the Poles with the Vatican's position. He asked Jesuit general Ledóchowski to document the activity of the Society of Jesus on "relief and assistance to the victims of the war particularly of Poland." The general replied on December 11, that he had had the Polish substitute, Felix Lasoń, collect such documentation as would prove "the sovereign benevolence which the Holy Father has shown during these years toward tribulated Poland and the effective aid which His paternal goodness has been able to convey to her, even in the midst of so many difficulties and impediments that were fragmenting

Him."⁸⁰ The lengthy report contained a chapter on "Indirect Action and Manifestations of the Vatican in Favor of Poland" in which all Vatican Radio broadcasts, in the different languages, on the persecution of the Church in Poland from January 1940 to April 1941, were cited.

Vatican Radio's was an "indirect action," but still of the Vatican, as Ledóchowski wrote, and Pius XII played on this ambiguity: the texts of the broadcasts were used to deny the pope's silence, but in fact, we know that he was not the one speaking publicly.

A just war, but for whom?

The various reasons for the neutrality of the Holy See in the face of the war can include, as well as those already listed, the wish to avoid exploitation by the opposing propagandas and the fear of worsening the persecution of the Church in Germany.⁸¹ Vatican Radio seemed, from the outbreak of the hostilities, to reflect Pius XII's position on the conflict, invoking the return to Christian principles for the restoration of peace. Although the abuse and violence had not stopped in Germany, and indeed had been extended to all territories occupied by the Germans, the impartiality toward the opposing sides was praised again in a program in Italian by Fr. Pellegrino in February 1940. Referencing various articles in European newspapers to support his words, he spoke first about the "political impartiality" of the Holy See because as "Christian", i.e., "not Italian, German or French," it could guarantee the "protection of peace and the collaboration of peoples."⁸² This impartiality, however, was not to be understood as a "moral neutrality between good and evil, law and injustice."⁸³ Nevertheless, Pellegrino never ventured beyond this to clarify what this entailed in practical terms with respect to the decisions of the Holy See.

Politically speaking, the Holy See was considered neutral and inviolable territory by virtue of Article 24 of the Lateran Treaty: "In regard to the sovereignty appertaining to it also in the international realm, the Holy See declares that it desires to remain and will remain outside of any temporal rivalries between other States and the international congresses called to settle such matters, unless the contending parties make a mutual appeal to its mission of peace; it reserves to itself in any case the right to exercise its moral and spiritual power. Consequently, Vatican City will always and in every case be considered neutral and inviolable territory." Vatican City would always, and in every case, be considered neutral and inviolable territory. Nonetheless, as in the case of the two World Wars, the papacy and the Church were involved in the conflict—therefore, in this case, the Holy See's neutrality could not be compared to that of neutral countries—and this prompted the pope, a reference for Catholics all over the world, to assume a position of impartiality.[84]

However, there is one case in which the position of Vatican Radio regarding the war did not coincide with the pope's. Following the German invasion of Belgium, the Netherlands, and Luxembourg, Pius XII sent three telegrams of solidarity to the respective sovereigns, which were published on May 12 in *L'Osservatore Romano*. The fascist government, in retaliation, forced the newspaper to reduce its circulation and suspend the publication of the communiqués of war of the belligerents.[85] On May 13, 1940, during an audience between Pius XII and Italian Ambassador Dino Alfieri, where Alfieri relayed Mussolini's protests concerning the initiative that had seemed to him a "move against his policy,"[86] Pius XII stressed that the messages did not contain any offensive words against Germany and, on the contrary, asked the ambassador to act as an intermediary and send to Hitler and von Ribbentrop a message with his willingness for agreement on the German religious situation.[87]

On May 11, the French ambassador to the Holy See wrote to Myron Taylor who, the day before, had had a conversation with Pius XII. He "did not notice any emotion in him, I should say not enough, on account of the enormity of what had happened the night before. [. . .] He was anxious to know whether the German offensive would have success or not. I replied that it would not be successful and added that in any case the success of a criminal enterprise does not cancel the crime."[88] Charles-Roux tried to convince Pius XII to condemn "Herr Hitler" and his actions, but the pope laconically answered that "he would take into serious consideration the request of my government." Pius XII wanted to avoid an open rift with the Reich at all costs.

On the same day, a broadcast by Vatican Radio, in English for North America, condemned the policy of German aggression in a much clearer way compared to Pius XII. The pretext was the news, which had arrived from New York and retransmitted by Vatican Radio, of an appeal signed by Protestant pastors in which the war was condemned as "futile and destructive of all human values."[89] Many of these ministers, noted the speaker, had also protested because a personal envoy of the president of the United States to Pope Pius XII, Myron Taylor, was sent to Rome.[90]

The statement to which Vatican Radio referred was approved at the Methodists' General Conference held in Atlantic City, New Jersey, from April 24 to May 6, 1940: "The Methodist Church, although making no attempt to bind the conscience of its individual members, will not officially endorse, support, or participate in war."⁹¹ At the conference, the request for American support by the British Methodists was not accepted: "Peace right now will be best served by American neutrality . . . We must not yield to the fallacy that the United States must get into the war if it is to establish a new peace basis. We can serve best by staying out."⁹²

The Vatican Radio announcer commented on the decision of the American Methodists as follows:

> We consider this peace plea as most untimely and irrelevant at the present hour: only aggressive warfare can be condemned out of hand: surely for the Norwegians, the Poles, the Belgians and the Dutch this war is not futile. These countries only defend themselves and their rights against a country with whom war is a fundamental principle of policy. Their war is against a country which has made a fetish of State worship. No nation which fights for its fundamental rights should be condemned. The Pope has blessed the cause of Holland and Belgium just as he did that of Poland and Finland. To curse and condemn all war is to deny justice its sword. The present is no time for the Levite to leave the bleeding Samaritan to die by the roadside.

Only the war of aggression could be condemned without delay, maintained the speaker, and for the peoples that had undergone occupation by Germany, this was a war of defense, therefore legitimate. The right of nations to neutrality was, and would also have been subsequently, one of the claims most often maintained by the pope, which was effectively quoted in the program and also for his spiritual closeness to Poland and Finland, previously occupied by the Red Army. However, there is a difference between Pius XII's speeches and the broadcast in English on Vatican Radio: in the latter, the countries attacked by the Nazis were named, without leaving any doubt as to the identification of the invaders, whose warmongering and statolatric nature were denounced and of whom the responsibility for the events was recognized. The clear judgment passed upon the Third Reich was far from the general reference to the "territory exposed to the cruelties of war" contained in the telegrams from Pacelli who, as is known, had wanted to avoid explicitly condemning Germany.

The conclusion of the broadcast, however, says something more: it was not fair to curse and condemn all wars. For the announcer, the conditions existed to be able to apply the concept of "just war" to the present war. Traditionally, the teaching on war had been based on St. Augustine and his definition of *ius ad bellum*, namely, the right to go to war when legitimate authority undertakes it or when it is necessary to punish a fault, restoring justice with the intention of reestablishing peace. This type of right legitimizes, but at the same time, places limits on authority. For St. Augustine, the attitude of the spirit of those who fight is also important: fighting must not be out of hatred but pure intention, in obedience to legitimate powers. Underlying this reasoning is the "principle of presumption": it is presumed that the authorities declare war after having gained all the information that confirms taking such a step. The faithful are obliged to exercise the Christian virtue of obedience, in submission to political power. And so, the good Christian must also be a good soldier. For the Vatican Radio announcer, the invaded nations had the right to defend themselves and therefore their war against the aggressor could not be condemned. On the contrary, it could be deemed just.

The final metaphor gave a very precise clue as to what was to be done: "The present is no time for the Levite to leave the bleeding Samaritan to die by the roadside." Three explanations can be given for the slightly modified evangelical reference. First, an oversight can be thought of: in the well-known parable in Luke 10, 25–37, it is not the Samaritan who is attacked by the bandits but, on the contrary, it is the Samaritan who comes to the aid of an unidentified man left dying in the road, to the indifference of a priest and a Levite who pass him by without stopping. Second, the announcer, aware that the parable was better known as that of the "Good Samaritan," uses the image of the Samaritan to catch the audience's attention, not worrying about faithfully retelling the Biblical story because the message that he wants to get across is more important than philological accuracy. The third possibility is that the exchange between the Samaritan and the man that he helped was deliberate: by superimposing the Samaritan onto the neutral nations that had been attacked, the announcer may have wanted to suggest the goodness of that neutrality, which, if it had been respected, would not have sparked off a war. Having become necessary, it was not possible to leave those "bleeding" nations "to die by the roadside."

However that may be, the message was clear. The Levite, who represents religious law, had to be identified with anyone who, at that time, found reasons, including religious ones, not to fight alongside the nations that had been aggressed. I do not think that we can attribute the accusation of the American Methodists to act like the Levite, indifferent to suffering, to traditional Catholic anti-Protestant hostility. Rather, I believe that as the program was for North America, the announcer wanted to convince those listening (the Catholic hierarchy and the faithful) that the possible entry of the United States into war was, not only plausible, but justified.

We do not know who wrote this program, but it could have been the Jesuit from New York, Vincent A. McCormick, rector of the Gregorian University from 1933 to 1941. There are two reasons that lead to attributing McCormick with the authorship of the program: his nationality (while the announcer of the programs in English was an Irishman, Coffey), and a letter which he had sent two months earlier to Myron Taylor. In this letter of March 18, 1940, McCormick answered a question that the diplomat had asked, "What can the President do to help the present situation, especially to prevent the war from spreading?" McCormick answered:

> Let the President make it clear to the world, that America will not look with indifference on a victory of Germany and Russia. If all the Americas joined in such a declaration, so much the better. I see no more efficacious means for attaining the end you so nobly desire. Every understanding Christian would applaud such a declaration.[93]

These words could explain the great reluctance of McCormick toward the pacifist and anti-interventionist attitude of the American Methodists.

At the end of June, however, Vatican Radio aired a program, again for North America, in which it maintained that pacificism in this war was wrong and that American isolationism was no longer possible.[94] The program had been written by the American priest Joseph Hurley, a *minutante*[95] of the Secretariat of State since 1936, English translator and mediator with the United States during the papacy of Pius XI. In this case too, as had been the case for the program on Poland on June 22, 1940, the British press did not hesitate to publish its script.[96] Some passages seem to be in line with what the announcer maintained on May 13, who could therefore also be identified as Hurley:

> It is clear that we have been allowing our unreasoned fear of what we call entangling alliances to obscure an obvious duty of charity towards the defenders of our own cause, which the Pope has called the cause of universal morality. The conscience of the isolationist is today ill at ease. He is faced with the inevitable consequences of his selfishness and is visibly afraid that his eleventh-hour offer of help to the afflicted branch of his family has come too late even to save himself. It has taken the agony of small nations to remind him of his Christian duty to mankind. [. . .] The problem of international solidarity or international charity calls for immediate and vigorous action. Its evasion or solution will write the history of America and Europe for the next generation. [. . .] We have sympathy for the pacifists. They mean well,

but they are wrong. [. . .] The Church is no conscientious objector. Theodore Roosevelt was near the truth when he wrote: "Aggressive fighting for right is the noblest sport the world affords."

Hurley, despite the favor granted to him by Pius XI, never came into the good graces of Pius XII, who appointed him bishop of the diocese of St. Augustine in Florida about one month after the program went on the air; between 1940 and 1945, he became increasingly and openly critical of the non-interventionism of the American Catholics and a great supporter of President Roosevelt's politics.[97]

However, other programs went on the air, again in English for America, which tried to show the perfect correspondence of views between Vatican Radio and the pope to whom, it is worth recalling, the Jesuits made a special vow of obedience. For the entire duration of the war, Vatican Radio, in any language in which it aired, always tried to defend the impartial position of Pius XII. Nevertheless, some programs broke the silence of the Holy See. This was due to the peculiar sensitivity of some announcers, as in the case of the programs for America: despite the pope's reticence to openly indicate the nation responsible for the war, there were those who, resuming the theory of the "just war" from an anti-German point of view, identified, in a few phrases, the victims and the guilty.

The capitulation of France, the Vichy regime, and Vatican Radio

The entrance of German troops into Paris on June 14, 1940, followed the final capitulation of France. After the resignation of President Paul Reynaud, the assignment of asking for an armistice was given to Marshal Philippe Pétain, who, on June 25, announced that the armistices with Germany and Italy had been signed. At the end of his speech, he said:

> We must restore France. [. . .] Our defeat derives from our slackened position. The spirit of enjoyment has destroyed what the spirit of sacrifice built up. I invite you, first of all, to an intellectual and moral renewal.[98]

Drawing upon arguments from traditionalist and Maurrassian thought, Pétain maintained that, for the restoration of France, an action (first of all in the moral sense) against the slackening of customs, was necessary.[99] On July 9, during the assembly that decided the end of the Third Republic and conferred full powers on Pétain, even Pierre Laval declared that the defeat of France was a condemnation "not only of the parliamentary regime but of a world that has been and can no longer be."[100]

Pétain gave voice to the idea, widespread in many sectors of public opinion, according to which France was guilty.[101] The faults and the errors blamed, concerned both political and cultural aspects: the failure of the regime of parties and the democratic system, the showing of improper films and indecorous customs, and the observation that the debacle had been caused essentially by the absence of religion. This was the reason France had been abandoned by Providence and this was why they deserved defeat.[102]

The traditionalist right wing, the managerial classes, the rural world, the middle-classes working in industry, and, above all, Catholic France took the side of the Vichy regime. The condemnation of habits during the Third Republic, caused by people moving away from religion, had been one of the arguments most used by the French Catholic Church to contest the limits that were imposed on it by the 1905 law of separation. The Church had not stopped warning of the serious consequences that would come from this. In June 1940, then, it was not difficult to join the chorus of accusations that blamed the moral decadence of France for being responsible for the military defeat. The rhetoric that characterized the messages by the episcopal hierarchy aimed to prove to the faithful that the defeat of France was the consequence of the apostasy of the nation in the previous decades, during which the moral decadence of French society had come from the spoliation of the Church and its rights. This deterioration, taken as the main cause of the ruinous fall against the Germans, was therefore to act as a warning for the future.[103]

The shock of June 1940 led the population to accept that the political and trade union forces should be eliminated and to confer full trust on Marshal Pétain, to the extent where he became mythic.[104] *Maréchalisme* and the Catholic world agreed on the causes of the defeat and on the foundations on which the reconstruction of the country should have rested. The model of the organic and hierarchized society proposed by the *révolution nationale* was not disagreeable to the French Catholic Church, which had many enemies in common with the *État français*: laicism, Freemasons, and communism.[105] The regime was also guaranteed the support of the Catholic Church thanks to a series of measures favorable to it. The law of September 3, 1940 revoked the legislative measures which prevented teaching to the Catholic congregations; the law of February 15, 1941 restored the property of the Church that had been confiscated after 1905 to the diocesan associations; and the law of July 2, 1941, part of a policy to restore the family as the fundamental nucleus of society, made it more difficult to divorce. At a local level, the Catholics found satisfaction with two circulars from the Ministry of

Internal Affairs dated April 15 and July 18, 1941, which restored the crucifix in schools and town halls. Lastly, the Holy See also formally legitimized Vichy. The Vatican was one of the States that accredited a diplomat to the regime: Nuncio Valerio Valeri was appointed representative of the pope in the French Free Zone, while the conservative Léon Bérard became the French ambassador to the Holy See.

The first program of Vatican Radio on France's situation that we have information on was aired on June 19, 1940, in Spanish. The announcer maintained that, in France, there remained the presuppositions for the construction of a new Catholic nation.[106] Supporting his declaration, Fr. Ignazio Ortiz de Urbina, head of the programs in Spanish, recalled the speech given by Eugenio Pacelli at Notre-Dame Cathedral during his trip to France as pontifical legate from July 9 to 13 in 1937. The then secretary of state of Pius XI had said that the history of France was a testimony for the need to put the temporal aims of the country in harmony with the supernatural ones of religion.[107] In the program, Pacelli remarked as to how much the greatness of France depended on its capacity for being faithful to its mission as a Catholic nation. He also added that the French State had responsibilities for the deviations of the past from the loyalty to this mission, as the "shameful legislation which had banned religious orders from teaching in schools" showed. The words of Pacelli in 1937 were used by Urbina to underline the correlation between the national duties of a State and its supernatural mission, and therefore to warn France about "returning to paganism, which was greatly responsible for the catastrophes of the present."

On June 20, French radio broadcast the speech of the archbishop of Bordeaux, Monsignor Maurice Feltin, and the second address to the French by Pétain, in which he informed the population that he had asked the "adversaries to put an end to hostilities." In his speech, Feltin said:

> Catholics of France,
> At the time when the enemy armies are threatening the hill of Fourvière, H.E. Cardinal Gerlier, archbishop of Lyon, formerly bishop of Lourdes, asks me to be his mouthpiece to invite you all to look towards Our Lady of Lourdes, in an ardent intercession, so that the Virgin Mary, infinitely maternal, infuses in our nation the moral energy that will make her able to courageously support her harsh ordeal and face adversities. Whatever happens, the civilizing and traditional work of France is not destroyed. The French soul is injured, it is not dead, even if under the blows of the invader. A triduum of masses will be immediately celebrated in the Grotto of Lourdes so that, through the intercession of Our Lady, the redeeming blood of the heart of Jesus, mixed with

that of our sons so abundantly shed on our soil, allows us to obtain strength and recovery.

The speech was published in France by several newspapers.[108] The invocation of Our Lady of Lourdes, aimed at rallying the whole country, sought to mobilize the Catholics around a shrine which, already in other circumstances, had been indicated as a destination for pilgrimages.[109]

On June 21, *L'Osservatore Romano*, in the section on foreign news, wrote of the French situation: "In a new speech on the radio, the President Marshal Pétain, invited all the French people to ask Our Lady of Lourdes for her help to face, with dignity, the present painful situation."[110] In actual fact, Pétain had not made any reference at all to Lourdes.[111] The wrong information, according to which it was the newly-elected Pétain who made an appeal to the French so that they asked for the intercession of Our Lady of Lourdes to save France, was repeated by the English announcer of Vatican Radio programs for North America and the Philippines. In particular, he said:

> The noble appeal of Marshal Pétain for the help of Our Lady of Lourdes for strength in the hour of military disaster measured up to the best traditions of Catholic France, who is never more typically herself than when she is called upon to defend the last bases of the civilization that gave her life. Through centuries of joy and sorrow since the accession of Clovis, France has won. There is however a difference between military failure and spiritual defeat. To quote Pope Benedict XV, "Nations, Christian Nations above all, do not die." The Christian destiny of France is intact. France has never shrunk from calvary. In the critical period of the last war, the Catholic marshal, Fock [sic], called upon St. Joan of Arc to come to the aid of France. The heroine of Orleans came down from Heaven: but real victory is not to be won in arms, but is won in the heart, through prayer and faith in the Cross of Christ.[112]

The English-speaking announcer, like the Spanish-speaking one, recalled the "best traditions of Catholic France," going back to the late Middle Ages, to maintain that, even though she had been defeated militarily, she was now called on to defend the bases of civilization from which she was born and on which she had been built. Moreover, the evocation of Clovis and of Joan of Arc was anything but unusual in the Catholic press: the conversion of the former "saved nascent France" and the latter, "supernaturally [. . .] gave us victory," Abbé Bertoye had written in 1914 in the columns of *La Croix*, to show that if the then Republican government had entrusted itself to God, France would have won.[113] The explicit reference to World War I in the

Vatican Radio program referred to the definitive establishment, after her beatification in 1909, of the cult of Joan of Arc, who had called the French nation to unity against the enemy.[114] At the time, postcards showing the *pucelle d'Orléans* holding a flag with the fleur-de-lis, dressed as a knight amidst soldiers in the trench, or in the form of an immaterial being hovering over them as in a dream with the caption "May God protect France," were common.

If the reference to Marshal Foch, the captain who led the French army during the Great War, was likely—on August 23, 1920, after having visited the house of Joan of Arc in Domrémy, her birthplace, he had gone to receive communion at the shrine erected as a sign of recognition for the victory in the war[115]—there is however the problem of the attribution to Pétain of the incitement to the return to Christian values through the invitation to prayer at Lourdes. The English-speaking announcer probably took the news from *L'Osservatore Romano*—a habitual practice of Vatican Radio— while there does not seem to be any trace of it in any French newspaper. It may have been an accidental exchange of names by the journalist in charge of the section: the article mainly focused on the activities of those hours undertaken by the ministers in Bordeaux and, according to Wladimir d'Ormesson's diary, the speeches by Feltin and Pétain were broadcast at the same time.[116] From research, there do not appear to be any public speeches in which Pétain had turned to Lourdes to ask for intercession for France and the French.[117] In any case, even if this happened, the French Catholic press did not give any importance to it.

The replacement of the bishop's name for that of Pétain by the Vatican paper, subsequently reiterated by Vatican Radio, could be read as a sort of unconscious superimposition in days when a political and ideological upheaval was looming which, from the first remarks of Pétain, seemed to turn in favor of the French Catholic Church. The legend of the *vainqueur de Verdun* was about to be dusted off and corroborated by the relief of leaving the war: the detail of the prayer to the Virgin Mary was likely—Pétain could have said it, it would have been completely in line with his political project— and it would have been functional to the construction of the consensus around his figure outside of France, as well. The parallelism between Pétain/Lourdes and Foch/Joan of Arc had the clear objective of recalling, and therefore recovering, the Christian roots of France which, at that time in history, needed to be reestablished. Pétain was to acquire, soon after that, the epithet of *homme providential* (the man of Providence), capable of reuniting the nation on the basis of the Catholic principles that France had distanced herself from during the Third Republic.

There is another detail which must be emphasized regarding the program in English on Vatican Radio of June 25, 1940. In it, mention was made of the exhortation to the people at war on July 28, 1914, by Benedict XV. In that circumstance, the pope had said: "Lay aside your mutual purpose of destruction; remember that Nations do not die."[118] The nationalist Catholics, to whatever country they belonged, read in these words a blessing of their ideas. It was, however, with those same words that the pope admitted the impossibility of governing the opposition that divided the national churches in the circumstances of a world conflict.[119] In the economy of the words of the Vatican Radio announcer, on the other hand, the phrase "Nations, Christian Nations above all, do not die," was used to relaunch the idea of a French Catholic nation which, despite the recent defeat, could find again, precisely in Catholicism, the motor for her reconstruction.[120] It was repeated again a few days later in another program for the Philippines: "Unchristian France shall indeed pass away [. . .] But the true France—the France of the great saints [. . .] shall never die."[121] On July 16, this time in a program for India and Ceylon, the English announcer validated the motto "Christian France will never die, and Christian France alone," applauding the efforts of Pétain's government to rebuild the country based on Christian ideals and principles.[122]

If the information in English regarding France delivered the message that only with the return to the directions given by the Catholic Church could peace be reached, the programs in French on the Vichy regime that went on the air in the summer of 1940, curated by the Belgian Jesuit Emmanuel Mistiaen, lend themselves to another interpretation.

Emmanuel Mistiaen: Infusing courage in the French people

Born in Leuven in 1893, Emmanuel Mistiaen entered the Society of Jesus in 1911, and was ordained in 1925. He did not make the fourth vow, and in the 1930s, as spiritual coadjutor, he taught in the Jesuit colleges in Brussels, gave lectures, and wrote books on spirituality.

In the summer of 1939, the vicar of the Society of Jesus, Maurice Schurmans, wrote a letter on behalf of the general to the vice-provincial of the northern Belgian province, Ferdinand Willaert, informing him that the Holy See was committed to boosting the Vatican Radio broadcasting service to be ready in autumn, and that the Jesuits were looking for collaborators. In particular, the general asked for a non-Flemish-speaking Jesuit, coming from the northern Belgian province, which had remained unoccupied since the division of the country, who would be in charge of the French broadcasts for France.

At the end of September 1939, Mistiaen arrived in Rome.[123] Father Mistiaen entered the *Domus Scriptorum* of the Society of Jesus and resided in Borgo Santo Spirito, which was, from the end of 1927, the seat of the General Curia of the Society. But on June 14, 1940, after Italy had entered the war alongside Germany, Ledóchowski asked Maglione if Mistiaen could be transferred within the Vatican walls in order to protect him, not only because of his nationality, but also because of the content of the scripts he wrote for the programs in French. According to a report written by a fascist spy in the Vatican, in August Mistiaen moved to *La Specola*.[125] Living in the Vatican, Mistiaen was able to get to know the diplomatic agents of France, Great Britain, and Poland, who lived in Santa Marta.[126]

The French ambassador, Wladimir d'Ormesson, wrote in his diary that Mistiaen was his only real point of reference in the Vatican, and that his twice-weekly lectures on the radio were "always excellent," because "he always finds the way of including [in them] the most courageous and direct allusions." He was the only one "to relieve the conscience. It is to be feared that for this they may quieten him one of these days, so great is the cowardice..."[127] Mistiaen's courage had greatly impressed the French ambassador, so much so that he wrote profusely about him in his final report to Minister of Foreign Affairs Paul Baudoin, whom he assured that "even though he is Belgian and a Jesuit, Fr. Mistiaen is deeply and ardently a Francophile [...] He does not hesitate to condemn the adverse methods. I will never be able to show well enough how much we owe in this regard to the Jesuit priest."[128]

D'Ormesson was not the only one to consider Mistiaen's radio talks exceptional. In the South of France, a group of Catholic resistance fighters began to print a clandestine newssheet entitled *La Voix du Vatican*, which reproduced the scripts of his programs. The creation of the newssheet was due to the canon Louis Ruy of the Jesuit College (now Lycée) Saint-Joseph in Avignon who, on the evening of June 30, 1940, received Vatican Radio in French for the first time in the room of the surveillant, a certain Cavatorta. According to the account of the Jesuit Jean Roche, the two were convinced to take down the programs in shorthand by the announcer's promise to speak three times a week and give words of comfort and affection to the French.[129] A former pupil of the Jesuit College, an activist of the Sillon, and a member of the local section of the Parti Démocrate Populaire, Henri Barral, had the programs taken down in shorthand by Cavatorta, typed, and reproduced at his own expense. Their production soon went from Avignon to Marseille, under the Catholic Action activist Jules Xavier Perrin.[130] Between the beginning of July 1940 and the end of October 1942, thirty issues of *La Voix du Vatican* appeared, consisting of between three and six pages each, which reproduced a selection of the texts by Fr. Mistiaen. An average of 1,500 copies were printed, and their circulation ended up covering the whole of the Mediterranean region.

La Voix du Vatican can be deemed the first clandestine Catholic periodical of the French Resistance,[131] the "forefather" of the *Cahiers du Témoignage chrétien*, as Henri de Lubac defined it in his *Souvenirs*.[132] In actual fact, there is not only a "spiritual filiation" between the two, as de Lubac also recognized, but it was on the basis of *La Voix du Vatican* that the decision to start *Témoignage chrétien* was made. After the censorship of the weekly *Temps nouveau*, of which he was the propagandist, Louis Cruvillier decided, together with a group of friends, to develop *La Voix du Vatican* and make it into a real periodical of the French Resistance. The *Cahiers* came into being from the meeting with Fr. Pierre Chaillet.[133] The presentation of the first issue of the paper clearly admitted the source of inspiration, quoting some of Mistiaen's words:

> There can be no doubt that our present-day world is a prison of the mind, before being a prison of the body, which it is as well. Honesty demands that we refuse to see what is true: it is no small affair for us. As our conscience is torn by two powers, the one which gives us the lie and the one which refuses us the truth. It is our right and our duty to be twice as prudent and watchful, when those who speak put us in the impossible position of receiving any other than what they say, nothing outside of them. [. . .] Who alerts our vigilance? It is the *Voix du Vatican*, which you have to listen to every evening (except Sundays) at 7 p.m. on 48.47. Vatican Radio has good reasons to speak. It knows that censorship, in all countries under the control of the Germans, refuses us the truth and that propaganda gives us the lie. Children of the light, Christians must know and must bear witness. On their level, which is that of the Kingdom of God and his Justice, no opportunism, no carnal fear can dispense them from this testimony which they must oppose to the caricature of justice, the caricature of truth and the caricature, alas, of honor.[134]

From the end of 1941, the people who produced and circulated *La Voix du Vatican* were also involved in the clandestine propaganda of *Témoignage chrétien*. From the region of Lyon, the two papers were circulated in the Marseille area by Jules Xavier Perrin, in Avignon by Robert Maddalena,[135] and in Toulon by André Mandouze.[136]

As recalled by Roche, in the first programs of Vatican Radio after the armistice, Mistiaen endeavored to give strength and hope to the tormented French nation, inviting listeners to not despair and patiently begin the work of reconstruction. With an attitude of empathy, Mistiaen encouraged the French to not lose confidence.[137] The words he repeated were "trust, courage, strength"; "preserve" was the task that he gave the French, "to preserve the character and the race" because "nothing is lost, everything is safe if you are faithful and preserve."[138] A summary of the programs of those days, with the quotation of some passages, was published by *Le Figaro* and then by *The Tablet*, which thus ensured the circulation of his words in English-speaking contexts as well.[139] The article by Paul Lesourd for the French daily newspaper highlighted what Mistiaen maintained about the sentiment of patriotism, that it had to overcome political and racial conflicts, be founded on the love of the past and the land, and not on the defeat of one race by another. He returned later to the topic of patriotism, without specific allusions to the new regime, while the first and only reference to Pétain was in the program of July 6. On that occasion, he said:

> Marshal Pétain attended the funeral for the French who had died for France in the Cathedral of Bordeaux. This man who has lived history, this man, this soldier who had made history, was in the cathedral of Bordeaux before the dead of this war. What did he think in front of them, he who took on his old shoulders, with unsurpassed heroism, the responsibilities for a terrible armistice and the occupation of the richest and most populated parts of France? What did he think before these young men who died between the border of Belgium and the center of France? Didn't their sad and distant voices perhaps ask him: what is the reason for this sacrifice?[140]

Mistiaen highlighted the difficult task that weighed on the "old shoulders" of the marshal, who with the "heroism" that distinguished him, had taken on the responsibility for a "terrible armistice" and the German occupation of the richest part of France. He did not go as far as to give explicit support to Pétain or his governance, but in attempting to infuse courage to the French, he exhorted them to have confidence in the impenetrable designs of God, whose hand would certainly have led the country out of the ruins of defeat.

The French announcer later returned to the figure of the "chief" but without naming Pétain. In a program on "authority and conscience," he maintained that the man with a formed conscience also had to have, at the same time, the "sense of community" and that of "personal dignity," a delicate game of which the "real leader" had to take account.[141] The "real authority" had respect for man, it was never brutal, and it was first of a moral order. Count Godfrey of Bouillon, who led the First Crusade, was taken as an example of the good leader:

Godfrey of Bouillon, refusing the insignia of sovereignty in Jerusalem, reigns better than the happiest of tyrants and earns a moral authority that allows him to speak truly as a master, to settle the most difficult questions without making enemies and without sacrificing the principles of the great Christian freedom.

This reference to the historical character acted as an example which should have inspired the leaders of the French State. Mistiaen thus avoided a political judgment on the current situation in France but gave, at the same time, guidelines that the rulers should have followed.

The ideas that the French programs, in the first months of the regime, seem to have in common is the bond between patriotism and Christianity. If it is true, as ascertained earlier, that the return to "France the Catholic Nation" had been the hope of other announcers of Vatican Radio, the style adopted by Mistiaen seems much less triumphant and more pastoral than propagandistic.

In an attempt to exhort the French to "start over again," Mistiaen recalled that "in a country that is well made, Christianity will live forever." After having "restored in us the Christian man," Providence would have conducted "without violence, to the use of our freedom in our country which takes part in the invincibility of Christ, because it has the Christian meaning."[142] Christian freedom, already evoked in an earlier program,[143] and picked up again later, was the haven to which God would have led the country. Mistiaen explained the road that had to be taken to reconstruct faith and France: "The problem of the country is a problem of faith [...] and it is not a problem of the nation [...] love for the country, its interest must naturally regulate all men's actions." In other words, Christianity provided a style of real patriotism, and to rise up again France had to look to her Christian past and continue with a consideration respectful of Christian precepts.[144]

In August and September, Mistiaen alternated two types of programs: one which was more exhortative in nature, characterized by more speculative content, to infuse strength into French listeners,[145] and the other with more concrete references, even though only in some specific cases, to the present situation.

One of the most explicit in this regard was that of August 21, which opened with a quotation from the French newspaper which invited learning "the virtue of silence."[146] The quotation is attributed, as it has been possible to ascertain, to the Catholic newspaper *La Croix*: "[The virtue of silence] is current, vis-à-vis the occupant, vis-à-vis the foreigner. In front of our brothers in pain, in our surroundings, let us have the modesty and the courage not to complain. Let us remember the phrase taught us by our fathers: 'Let us always think about it, let us never speak of it.'"[147]

The article in *La Croix*, quoted by Mistiaen, first named "the occupant," "the foreigner," and through the words of Léon Gambetta (pronounced after the defeat against Prussia at the Battle of Sedan) tried to offer a solution to the immense difficulty of the occupation and to suppress the impractical desire for revenge. But the silence evoked by the Vatican Radio announcer was also encouraged in order to fight insinuating propaganda made up of "repeated and worrying slogans which disturb the spirits and penetrate our matters." The "inner silence," on the other hand, was taught to be prudent in the face of the "dictators of the spirit," from whom it was necessary to take care. These concepts had been covered by Mistiaen in a book published in 1936 precisely entitled *Le Silence*, a sort of guidebook for spiritual exercises,[148] from which he took some sentences (without naming it):

> Dear listeners, we must enter the domain of silence, we have to run away from this din, from this noise that has been created around us to upset us and to destroy us. [. . .] Instead of the radio that screeches, grunts and mechanically reproduces these deformed noises of the world, all the souls can be the soil of the morning that received dew [. . .]; we can choose, instead of being in a public square full of foreigners and merchants, to be in a secret garden, in peace in a cloister [. . .].

In the current context, the words of Mistiaen took on a completely different meaning compared to 1936. It is probable that the reference was also to the German occupier. The armistice had imposed the end of the radio programs and, although Vichy had quickly obtained the use of the stations in the Southern Zone, the reorganization of State broadcasting in an anti-liberal sense took place slowly and did not undergo an acceleration until between 1941 and 1942.[149] The *Propaganda Abteilung*, on the other hand, created on July 18, 1940, and the headquarters of which had moved in December to the Hotel Majestic in Paris, had at its service, three State radios and two private ones, known as Radio Paris, which in the four years of occupation became the main instrument of German propaganda.[150] The reference by Mistiaen to the radio which "screeches and grunts" was perhaps to be attributed to Radio Paris.

From the month of September, the accusations made toward National Socialist propaganda regarding attacks on the Catholic Church became increasingly frequent. Radio Paris had aired a program in which they energetically hurled against the revocation of the law of separation of 1905 and against the Vichy regime growing close to the Catholic Church.[151] Apparently, the Radio Paris journalist was being ironic about the expressions of religious ferment in France to the extent of asking whether Vichy was aspiring to become a theocratic government. According to a Mistiaen report, the speaker from the Occupied Zone suggested that the Church did not get mixed up in political affairs. Mistiaen did not openly take the defense of the government of Free France but dwelled on the examination at length of what was a good judgment on matters, without being conditioned by interests on one side or the other. His style was characteristic and easy to identify by listeners: allusions, references taken from history and literature, and the use of rhetoric artifices, were part of a strategy to avoid censorship, since complaints from the German Embassy at the Holy See had become more frequent. Although Menshausen's reporting of calumnious sentences toward Germany was denied by giving him the original scripts of the programs by the Secretariat of State, it was necessary to be increasingly careful, because it was clear by then that Vatican Radio was under the surveillance of the Reich.[152]

3

Vatican Radio, National Socialism, and Communism

Vatican Radio under German attack

Between April and June 1940, exchanges took place between Undersecretary of State of the Third Reich Ernst von Weizsäcker, the apostolic nuncio in Berlin Cesare Orsenigo, the German ambassador to the Holy See Diego von Bergen, his *chargé d'affaires* Fritz Menshauen, and the Vatican Secretariat of State. They reveal that the information collected on Vatican Radio programs by the German Ministry of Foreign Affairs was used in front of the nuncio, and therefore the Holy See, to justify the persecution of the clergy and Catholics in the territories as they were gradually occupied, and as a weapon of blackmail: if Vatican Radio stopped condemning the anti-Catholic measures taken in the territories of the Reich, the persecutions would come to an end.[1] Assuming that the concern and irritation that Vatican Radio caused to several German ministries were real, the cause and effect between the anti-Nazi content of the programs and the reprisals on the Catholics, in particular the Polish clergy, is to doubt. In fact, it is possible that on the part of the German diplomacy an instrumental use was made of these programs to justify, *ex post*, the violence that would have occurred in any case.

In April 1940, concerned about this situation, Pius XII tackled the matter in a letter to Bishop of Berlin Konrad von Preysing, explaining the reason why he had deemed it necessary to broadcast those programs:

> The news was given because we considered that complete silence by the Holy See in relation to the public, could have made the German Catholics lose courage and, outside Germany, leave room for misunderstandings, suggesting that the situation of the Church in Germany was normal or had improved. It is this camouflage, skillfully orchestrated and still successfully, that the broadcasters wanted to unmask.[2]

But continued the pope, complaints and genuine requests for help had arrived from the bishops due to the reprisals caused by the news broadcast by Vatican Radio. This was why he had given the order to suspend these programs "until we could safely assess the pros and cons." He asked the German prelate for his opinion on this delicate matter. Von Preysing answered on May 1:

> The Holy See cannot stop bringing religious news, including what happens in Germany, to the knowledge of the global public. I would abstain from making public the documents of internal relations, petitions, and protests as such. But the communications on the measures against the Church above all if known, expropriations, disbanding of circles, confiscation of funds of the Catholic institutions following the law against the communists etc., in my opinion can without a doubt be aired.[3]

Following the advice of the bishop of Berlin, the programs continued. Pius XII, via steps taken through the media of communication and diplomatic channels, was trying to understand how the Holy See could maintain its impartiality without sacrificing the defense of the rights of Catholics.

In September, General Ledóchowski wrote to Montini who, aware that Vatican Radio programs could have been the "occasion for some recriminations," ordered the storage of the programs in different languages in a special archive to be at the disposal of the Secretariat of State.[4] The transcription of the scripts was entrusted to a Polish coadjutor "so that a good and faithful copy is always at the disposal of Your Excellence: I say faithful because I have given the order to all the Fathers who speak on the Radio that first they write down everything that they have to say and do not believe they can add anything more than they have written." As already mentioned,[5] on October 1, Montini wrote to Ledóchowski, saying that Pius XII deemed it opportune for the scripts of the programs to be sent to the Secretariat of State the day after they had been on the air.[6] General Ledóchowski answered that it seemed a necessary solution both because the Secretariat would always be precisely informed of what was said on Vatican Radio and because this way he could give instructions to the fathers.[7] It is effectively confirmed that from October 8, 1940 the Secretariat of State received the scripts of the programs.[8] Monsignor Pietro Sigismondi was responsible for the revision of the programs, and any observations were to be approved by Tardini and then sent to the general.[9] Despite the fact that, apart from some exceptions, the Archive of the Secretariat of State has not kept the scripts, a digest of the broadcasts, starting from November 15, 1940, was drafted by Rev. Jacques Martin.[10]

The incidents foreseen by Ledóchowski became more frequent precisely from October 1940 onward due to some programs about the Catholic Church in Alsace and Lorraine. These two regions, which for centuries had been contended between France and Germany, had passed under German control after the occupation. Despite the wars over the frontiers, which saw these lands alternately belonging to one State and then to the other, the Concordat signed by Pius VII and Napoleon in 1801 had always remained valid. The Alsatian Church had been able to keep some privileges even when, after having returned to French administration after World War I, the laws of separation were in force in the rest of France. The occupation of France in World War II caused the extension, to Alsace and Lorraine, of the limitations in the exercises of the cult and teachings already enforced in the other territories occupied by the Germans.[11]

A program in German included the speech by Joseph Bürckel, in which he announced to the population of Metz the abolition of the Catholic confessional and private schools.[12] On October 9, the programs in Italian, Spanish, and English gave the following news, which was also repeated on October 15, in English:

> The National Socialist party is actively trying to make its ideas penetrate in Alsace-Lothringen. [...] All the Catholic schools have been closed. Some hundreds of religious, priests, brothers and nuns have so been barred from the work of education. Hitler Youth groups have been set up everywhere. Children are being taken to the Reich and there educated in the Nazi ideology. The diocesan seminaries and missionary schools no longer exist. [...] The present Bishop of Metz, Mgr. Heintz, has been forbidden by the German authorities to exercise his office. The cathedral of Strasbourg has been closed for all religious functions. By arrangement telegrams were sent to the Führer asking for the closing of the cathedral to forestall the activities of political Catholicism.[13]

Vatican Radio had denounced what was happening in the dioceses of Strasbourg and Metz: the former was without a bishop because it was impossible for him to return, and in the latter, the ordinary had been prevented from exercising the ministry.

On October 19, the chargé d'affaires of the German Embassy at the Holy See went to the Secretariat of State to request the script of the program of October 15, asserting that Vatican Radio "speaking of the situation in Alsace

Lorraine and of the policy established there by the German authorities, had defined the first tragic and the second inhumane, barbarian or something similar."[14] As can be noted from the quote, these incriminating phrases do not seem to appear. On October 23, during an audience with Pius XII, it was decided that it was better not to hand over the script and to tell Menshausen that Vatican Radio had learned the news from the newspapers and other foreign broadcasts.[15]

On October 25, the German diplomat was received by Tardini, according to whom, Maglione had not had the exact script from the broadcaster, but only the list of news items broadcast regarding the closure of the Catholic schools and seminaries and the priests being prevented from teaching religion in schools, about which the German government could not complain, as it was the truth.[16] The impatient reaction of Menshausen was recorded by Tardini in his note:

> The chargé d'affaires . . . is getting angry. He complains that, as it is a public fact, as is a radio broadcast, he cannot have the script. He says that his government is bombarding him with telegrams to have it. [. . .] The chargé d'affaires, getting more and more heated, observes: 1. That the German radio and press have abstained for a long time from attacking the Vatican and the Holy See, 2. That Radio Vatican has a hostile attitude towards Germany, 3. That the asserted autonomy of Vatican Radio is not admissible, as the Holy See is more totalitarian than all regimes and as the Secretariat of State has many ways of curbing the radio, 4. That if things continue this way, there will no doubt be some very strong replies.

The Secretariat of State did not know the content of the programs before they went on the air, as we have seen. In a later conversation between Tardini and Soccorsi, in the presence of Cardinal Maglione, it was explained what had happened. The incriminating phrases reported by the German chargé d'affaires were authentic, but did not belong to the program of October 15 in English for Europe, but to that of October 17 for the United States.[17] Father Soccorsi had given the unabridged script of the program to the director of Associated Press, who had asked him for it, stating that in America reception was not good. In actual fact, the agency had acted on behalf of the German Embassy, which came into possession of a script for which it asked the Secretariat of State for explanations. When Menshausen wrongly asked the Secretariat of State for the script of the program broadcast on October 15, he was answered correctly (without giving it to him) that the script did not include incriminating phrases. At that point, the diplomat grew angry, not understanding why the Secretariat denied the existence of those phrases which Fr. Soccorsi had given to the journalists. In the face of such insistence, on October 27, Tardini gave Menshausen the script of the program broadcast on October 15. The secretary of Extraordinary Ecclesiastical Affairs explained that the accused program was actually that of October 17 for the United States, in which the announcer had made additions without the consent of Vatican Radio's editorial staff. On the contrary, they had given orders to avoid words that were too strong and restrict announcers to ascertained facts. At first, Menshausen was satisfied, but after returning to the German Embassy he telephoned Tardini to ask him again for the script of October 17 "as a great favor."[18] "To get rid of him once and for all, I immediately sent it to him with a gendarme." In the program of October 17, the announcer had effectively added the following:

> Today the Catholics of Alsace and Lorraine are being tried in the fire of cruel persecution. [...] Today they are under the heavy rule of the Nazis, who are using every means to indoctrinate them with the pernicious aberrations of their party philosophy of life. State schools have been reorganized along the lines of these false, immoral principles.[19]

From the report written by Menshausen for the Ministry of Foreign Affairs in Berlin, it can be deduced that he was aware that the Jesuit in charge of the programs in English for America was Vincent McCormick. An American and rector of the Gregorian University, he had replaced Fr. Coffey, who had had to leave Rome. Ledóchowski was aware that McCormick was "much less experienced than him" and that he had already made mistakes.[20]

For the time being, the affair ended with the recommendation made to Fr. Soccorsi, first by Maglione and then by Pius XII himself "to restrict the radio programs to the facts that were truly ascertained without comments or strong words. Facta loquuntur [Facts speak for themselves]."[21] But now, each time that Vatican Radio broadcast news on the religious situation in Germany, or in the territories occupied by the Germans, some reaction from the German Embassy was expected.

At the same time as clarity was being sought on the programs concerning Alsace and Lorraine, Ledóchowski told Tardini that Vatican Radio, in a program in Spanish, had denied a number of news items published by the Catholic newspaper *Ya*, and specifically: that after the annual Conference of Fulda, the Catholic hierarchy had ordered prayers for the Führer; the Catholic papers had reappeared in Germany and that they could speak freely of religion, politics, and the economy; the German bishops had protested about the destruction of churches by the RAF; that they were organizing a trip to Rome in the hope of a rapprochement between the papacy and the Nazi regime; and that Catholicism was also flourishing again in occupied Poland.[22] However, what is most interesting here is what Ledóchowski told Tardini about Vatican Radio and the German reaction:

> He [Ledóchowski] expects an outcry but adds: 1. That there is no other means of defense than the Radio. 2. That the Nazis are more afraid of the truth than of the cannon. 3. That, even if the program is jammed in one nation, it can be heard in others. Moreover, it is enough for it to reach one place to then be known everywhere.[23]

Menshausen also asked for clarifications on another program in English which included the news of the congratulations by Pius XII to the British royal family for having escaped danger during the repeated bombings of Buckingham Palace.[24] Tardini asked Ledóchowski if this was true, and he answered that it was again the program for America of September 22 which was repeated for England on September 24. The general once again assured Menshausen that McCormick had been warned "not to speak of things that are in relation to Germany."[25]

In a later conversation, in person, between Tardini and Ledóchowski about Vatican Radio, they tried to establish new rules and have them already in force respected more closely by the broadcasters. Under the close control of the general, they wanted to exploit the programs in Spanish and Portuguese for the news concerning the religious situation in Germany and in the territories that they occupied, because through reception in Latin America it would be circulated "in one way or another (by the radio, the press etc.)" in the United States and other countries. On the other hand, he would ask the fathers in charge of the programs in English to be more cautious, as "those are the ones that have created problems."[26] According to Ledóchowski, from the comparison of the script in Spanish in response to *Ya*, and that of the program in English "referring to a very delicate subject, i.e. the situation of the Church in Germany," it could be seen immediately "that the [Spanish] one is much more ... skillful": he admitted that, although having been scrupulous for the programs in English, he had given the priests greater freedom. For the future he proposed to "order those who prepare the programs in other languages to strictly follow the Spanish wording (keeping the words and the tone!)" and to "limit programs in English [...] to other subjects—without going into the more ... controversial ones."

Moreover, Orsenigo sent the following message on October 19:

> Unfortunately, these programs, which the Government believes it can deem unfair and not in line with the neutrality of the Holy See, have great repercussions on the government spheres, because they are collected, reproduced in numerous copies which are then distributed to all the government offices, in such a way that the atmosphere then remains poisoned for a few days.[27]

This statement confirmed that Vatican Radio was regularly monitored by the Nazi government. Maybe it was precisely the complaints of the German Embassy, together with the alert given by the nuncio, which made Pius XII more inclined to a drastic solution: to reduce the number of programs. This was the order given to Soccorsi, according to what Ledóchowski wrote to Maglione.[28] However, as Tardini had told him to wait until the next day "to know the wishes of the Holy Father more exactly," the general took advantage of this to explain his point of view in greater detail, defending, in part, the work of Vatican Radio, and try to reassure that greater attention would be paid in the future. Ledóchowski wrote:

> Vatican Radio is becoming better known every day and listened to in many parts of the world, as also shown by some extracts of letters which I have given to His Excellence Mons. Tardini.[29] The largest Agencies in Spain and in North and South America and other countries are interested in it and therefore know very well the schedule for the quarter November-January [...]. Such a sudden change in the schedule would probably have a great effect and could perhaps also be interpreted in a way that is not desired by the Holy See.

Ledóchowski was convincing to the extent that, at the audience between Pius XII and his secretary of state, it was decided to continue with all the programs "on condition that they are well revised."[30]

Shortly afterward, the German chargé d'affaires returned with a new complaint by his government concerning another Vatican Radio program that was considered "against Hitler and Nazism."[31] Menshausen had brought along a script, which according to him had been read on October 6, 1940, containing harsh criticism of a pastoral letter by Monsignor Rarkowski, in which the German military bishop had defended the Nazi government from the accusation of being the sole party responsible for the war. The pope also took an interest in the question, because it seems that the words were extremely critical of the Third Reich.[32] Tardini asked Ledóchowski for information and he replied: "Vatican Radio had no German program on October 6, 1940 at 8 p.m. and did not cover the pastoral letter by His Excellence the

Military Bishop of Germany."³³ It seems that there was a clandestine radio station, a "pseudo–Vatican Radio," Tardini said to Menshausen, which had the clear intention of wanting to "perturb the relations—already very delicate—between the Holy See and the German government."³⁴ In any case, as Tardini wrote to Ledóchowski, the important thing was that Vatican Radio "continued its programs calmly. It is necessary to be limited to the facts ascertained, avoid comments, leave aside phrases that are too strong or words that do not seem to be very respectful: nonetheless, speak. Not saying anything would fail a duty towards truth and honesty."³⁵ And he added: "For this reason I take the liberty to make Your Very Reverend Paternity consider whether it would not be better that the programs for the United States also gave—about Germany—the same news with the same methods." Ledóchowski, saying he was "very pleased," added that he would restart broadcasts about the situation of the Church in Poland.³⁶

In the end, despite the German complaints, Vatican Radio continued its activity. The fear of the German authorities monitoring for the anti-Nazi propaganda, shows the leading role taken on by Vatican Radio in those first years of the conflict, not only for its influence at the level of public opinion, but also because it became an instrument of political pressure.

The management of Vatican Radio reveals slightly different positions among the ecclesiastical concerned. On the one hand, the Jesuits, Ledóchowski and Soccorsi, defended the work of the fathers in charge of the broadcasts and underlined the importance for the programs to continue, given the capacity of the radio to spread news everywhere; on the other hand, the curial Maglione and Montini had more neutral attitudes. Tardini, although tending to be less confident, had acknowledged the usefulness of Vatican Radio, since the Holy See should not remain silent. Pius XII hesitated but was increasingly conscious of the importance of this instrument.

Vatican Radio between neutrality and pro-Americanism

Sending Myron Taylor to Rome as the "personal representative of the President of the United States with His Holiness Pius XII" had the purpose of sounding out the possibility of finding support in the Vatican for the objectives of American policy in relation to the war, and to ensure that Pius XII did not turn toward an accommodating solution with the Nazi regime.

Although it had been President Roosevelt's goal at least until spring 1940, a compromise peace was no longer deemed possible.³⁷ Having abandoned the idea of negotiations with Hitler, Washington and the Holy See tried to join forces to prevent Italy from entering the war. In general, the United States' government attributed considerable importance to the Vatican, both for the role of mediation it could play and, later, for the political support it could give to any future, post-war arrangement. Formally, at the start of the war, as he wrote in a letter to Pius XII on February 14, 1940, Roosevelt wanted to give support to their parallel efforts for peace and to relieve the suffering of the populations. On February 27, Myron Taylor was received in the Vatican and accredited with honors usually granted to ambassadors, although he was not actually one. The instructions received for his humanitarian and political mission were to encourage the freedom of religion, freedom of communication, and the reduction of weapons and free trade between nations.[38]

On January 9, 1941, the apostolic delegate in Washington, Amleto Cicognani, sent the speech opening the 77th Congress of the United States by President Roosevelt to the Holy See. It now appeared clear, according to Cicognani, that the neutrality of the United States government was reduced to simple non-belligerence.[39] As the war had become a fight between democratic and totalitarian principles, the United States, announced President Roosevelt, could not fail to engage itself and give as much help as possible to the UK, to provide full support to the peoples who were determined to resist aggression, and keep war out of their hemisphere. Victory over the dictators would redraw a "world founded on four essential human freedoms": freedom of speech, freedom of worship, freedom from poverty, and freedom from fear.[40]

The following week, Cicognani wrote to Maglione that Roosevelt had told him to consider his "four points [. . .] in harmony with [the] five points of the Christmas address of His Holiness."[41] On December 24, 1940, Pius XII dictated to the Sacred College the conditions necessary for the "new order": "the condemnation of systems and practices" that divided peoples; the "observance of the pacts" for the coexistence of the "powerful peoples and of weak peoples"; "the return to a serious and profound morality in the rules of the consortium between Nations," which denied the principle according to which "force creates right" but did not exclude "an opportune and legitimate use of force to protect impugned pacific rights with violence or to repair its wounds"; a fairer distribution of wealth; and a more "sincere juridical and economic solidarity [. . .] according to the precepts of divine law, amongst the peoples ensured of their autonomy and independence."[42]

Pius XII's speech did not only seem to correspond with the words of President Roosevelt, but it also had an equal and contrary effect in Italy as well. In transmitting it to Minister of Foreign Affairs Galeazzo Ciano, Ambassador to the Holy See Bernardo Attolico described it as a speech "of a pope—naturally not always completely coinciding with the ideas of others—and kept up on a very high religious and philosophical level." The recognition of the need for a new world order by Pius XII had surprised Attolico because he had read it "in undeniable harmony with the main directions of Italian foreign policy."[43] According to Attolico, the press should have emphasized even "one of the central points of the thought and ideology of Pius XII," already mentioned in the homily of November 24, namely the need for all States to be given the means to be able to guarantee sustenance for their citizens. The homily of November 24, in which the pope had hoped for a "fairer and more equal order, [...] which tends to attribute to all peoples [...] the share due to each one of them on this earth, of the sources of prosperity and power,"[44] had pleasantly surprised Attolico because he deemed the concept expressed in it "perfectly in tune not only with the spirit of the times, but the very reasons for our war."[45] In addition, in the November homily, Pius XII stressed what he had already said in September, on the occasion of the Italian Catholic Action meeting. Namely:

> Grant the fighters, with the heroism in fulfilling their duty, even up to the supreme sacrifice, for the defense of the land, that noble sense of humanity, which in every event does not do to others what you would not like done to oneself or to one's own people.[46]

Attolico's comment was: "The Holy Father has therefore spoken as a Pope like a Pope, but without His words being able in the slightest to harm the legitimate interests of Caesar."[47]

The Christmas speech of Pius XII, on the other hand, had not convinced the British at all. The Foreign Office wrote to the British minister at the Holy See, Francis d'Arcy Osborne, that the pope's words, although containing some points that could be shared and praised, did not deserve a personal message of appreciation by the government. In an internal note, it was underlined that the central point, the emphasis on the "new order" would certainly be exploited by the propaganda of the Axis—and indeed this occurred. It was therefore decided that a word of approval would be given only if it was certain that this would stimulate Pius XII to make further efforts useful to the British.[48]

A program in English by Vatican Radio for Catholics in the United States echoed the words of the pope on the legitimate use of force, explaining that, although war was a curse, at times it could also be a duty. Aired shortly after the two speeches by Roosevelt, which suggested that the United States would not stay neutral in the face of the conflict but, if necessary, would play an active role in the war, seemed to give support to the latter possibility.

The script, which we have in the summary made by the BBC Monitoring Service, said:

> War is a curse, but it may sometimes be a duty to resist forcefully the invasion of an unjust aggressor and wage war to vindicate a vital right violated by an enemy nation. Any contrary principle would guarantee impunity to tyrants, robbers, those for whom might makes right, and condemn mankind to intolerable slavery. 'Nothing is more unfortunate than the good fortune of sinners.' The spirit of Christianity has always been the first to defend the order of justice and morality. The agonies of war are far less painful than Christian civilization's collapse and, if they powerfully preach the unity of the human race, they will have been a grace rather than a curse.[49]

The author, probably Fr. McCormick, set forth without ambiguity the opinion that in the face of the invasion by an aggressor, it was a duty to denounce the violation of a right by the enemy nation, because not doing so would guarantee impunity for tyrants and condemn humanity to slavery; this defense of justice and morality was not only in line with Christian principles, it was a duty imposed by the Christian spirit itself. These words echoed those said previously in May, again in a program for America.[50]

The programs in English for North America continued to condemn National Socialism until April 1941. In the program of February 7, for example, some passages from a pastoral letter of the Dutch episcopate were read, which prohibited Catholics from belonging to the NSB, the Dutch National Socialist party:

> This letter reaffirms the ecclesiastical censures previously published against Liberalism, Socialism, Communism, and National Socialism. [. . .] Regarding the National Socialist Party in Holland, the letter adds to the previous censures that, in view of changed circumstances, it is now gravely sinful even to be a member of that party.[51]

It was rebroadcast on March 26 in Spanish, on April 25 in German, and picked up by *The Tablet* on May 3:

> We continue to refuse the Holy Sacraments and Ecclesiastical Funeral to the following: [. . .] Catholics known to be real adherents to the National-Socialist Movement. In view of changed conditions, we add the following. [. . .] With reference to the National-Socialist Movement, we emphasize what we said before, because one realizes with increasing clarity that this movement not

only threatens the Church in the free exercise of its mission, but also constitutes a danger to all who belong to this movement as far as concerns the fulfilment of their Christian duties. It must be stated that even mere adherence to the Party with one's conscience cannot be conceded. We wish those concerned to abandon the erring path and conciliate themselves with God and the Church.[52]

A few days later, the encyclicals of Pius XI were recalled, which condemned the "insidious atheistic and de-Christianising influences" in Mexico, Russia, and Germany.[53]

More politically exposed texts were alternated with readings closer to those suggested in the speeches of the Vatican hierarchy. From the middle of February, while continuing to denounce the abuse by the Germans, a series of programs confronted, with a certain frequency, the topic of the neutrality of the Holy See, giving support to Pius XII's position:

The Church of Christ, to quote Leo XIII, superior as she is to every other society, resolutely refuses to subject herself to the fleeting exigencies of politics. Guardian always of her own rights, and most observant of the rights of others, she holds that it is not her province to decide which is the best among the diverse forms of Government and the civil institutions of Christian states. She does not disapprove of any provided the respect due to religion and the observance of good morals be attained. [. . .] It is clear that all attempts to involve the Church in party strife are worthy only of condemnation. The Holy Father considers himself the pastor of all men. It is wrong therefore, to interpret his solicitude for the men of all camps at the present moment as something political.[54]

The Church could not choose which type of political system was the best and the pope could not take the side of any contender, because he was the common father of all men. Supporting this theory, the article of the bishop of Lausanne-Geneva-Fribourg, Marius Besson, published in the *Schweizerische Katholische Wochenzeitung* was read in another program. He maintained that the Church could not let itself be involved in the political problems of the various countries, it could not be bound by any special form of government but left peoples free to choose the one that best respected the law of God. In politics, the Church had the duty to obey moral law, respect the traditions and institutions of the country, respect the civil authorities, and cooperate with the military.[55] However, in the same program, there was also a news item from *L'Osservatore Romano*, according to which, ten

Benedictine abbeys had been closed and six others had been evacuated due to the measures taken in Germany and in the occupied territories, including recently, against the various religious orders and institutions.

The same happened in another program for North America. First, statements by the ministers of Labour and Worship of the Reich were listed: it was not desirable that those fit to work entered religious orders or convents; it was no longer possible to leave work to join religious congregations; the German authorities had the power to assign anyone to any type of work, agricultural or industrial.[56]

Immediately afterward, however, the same program broadcast the homily pronounced by Archbishop of Munich Cardinal Faulhaber, on the anniversary of the coronation of Pius XII. This homily centered on the neutrality of the Holy See: in it, Faulhaber maintained that the pope was in the difficult position of a father who is in the middle of his sons who are quarreling and therefore had to remain neutral.[57] On the basis of the five points listed by Pius XII in his 1940 Christmas speech, and the concern he expressed on several occasions for the German prisoners of war, it was impossible to state that "the Holy Father is for the enemies of the German people and has abandoned in our regard his benevolent neutrality." The homily was deemed of such great importance that in the program of April 11[58] the article commenting on it, published a few days earlier by *L'Osservatore Romano*, was broadcast:

> The Pope is impartial, nor can it be otherwise because a father, master, and judge, he treats everyone according to justice. But he cannot be neutral in the sense of being indifferent, to whom discerning just from unjust does not matter or is not his duty and worry whether one or the other prevail while the destiny of Christian civilization and the moral prosperity of the world is linked to it.[59]

The sequence of these program snapshots capture, very clearly, the position of the Holy See. In the programs for North America, the Jesuit in charge took more liberties compared to the others. Concern for the persecution of the Church in the territories occupied by the Germans stood out, and some programs seemed to voice the hope that the United States would take on a more active role in the conflict. It nevertheless remained clear that Pius XII would never compromise himself to support any particular contender, according to the distinction between impartiality in the face of the involvement of the Catholics on both sides of the front, and the impossibility of remaining neutral (namely indifferent) in the face of the destiny of humanity.

There were, therefore, various elements which contributed to outlining the choice of scripts to be aired for North America. The first can be identified in the figure of the Jesuit in charge of the programs in English, Vincent McCormick. Thanks to his role at Vatican Radio, his position and nationality allowed him to be in contact with both the milieux of Rome and the Curia and with the US diplomatic corps. As he was the rector of the Gregorian University and assistant of the province of North America of the Society of Jesus, he was in close contact with all the leading Jesuits. As an English speaker and an American citizen, he translated the speeches of Pius XII and had close relations both with Myron Taylor and Harold Tittmann, *chargé d'affaires* during the absence from Rome of Roosevelt's representative. During the war, McCormick worked hard to collect and circulate documentation that showed the opposition of the Church to National Socialism: from his diary, it emerges, however, that from 1942, it was increasingly difficult for him to justify the neutrality of the Holy See.[60] The decision to broadcast scripts that, in a certain sense, seemed to approve of the United States' possible entrance into the war and, at the same time, denounced the abuses of Catholics by the Germans, probably went through him.

But if the supervision of the scripts read on the radio, at this time not yet pre-selected by the Secretariat of State, was the job, in the final analysis of the general of the Jesuits it is probable that the line adopted for the programs for North America was, in part, laid down or at least agreed with, by Ledóchowski as well. There are multiple clues that suggest such a hypothesis.

Włodzimierz Dionizy Ledóchowski (Loosdorf 1866–Rome 1942) was born in lower Austria to a family of Polish descent, studied at the Theresianum in Vienna, and graduated with a law degree from the Jegellonian University in Kraków. After entering the Gregorian University, he decided to join the Society of Jesus. In 1901 he became vice-provincial and, a year later, provincial of the province of Galicia. From 1906 to February 1915, he was assistant to the general of German Assistance. In 1915 he was elected superior general of the Society.[61] Advisor to the Holy See on affairs involving Russia, he directed the Vatican anti-communism campaign in the 1920s and 1930s and was a staunch proponent of linking communism and Judaism to the destruction of Christian society.[62] His antisemitism was the reason he delayed the delivery of the draft of the encyclical *Humani generis unitas* to Pius XI. He also sympathized with the fascist regime of Mussolini. His attitude toward Nazism was less clear-cut: in the middle of the 1930s, Ledóchowski was favorable to a condemnation of Nazi theories in contradiction to Christian doctrine but, at the same time, when he read the draft of the encyclical *Mit brennender Sorge* he advised greater caution, suggesting that the excessively harsh expressions contained in the document be toned down.[63] Nonetheless, he was well aware of the harassment that the Nazi authorities had always perpetrated against the German Jesuits.[64] Ledóchowski's opposition to National Socialism was reported to the fascist government as early as the summer of 1939 by Italian Ambassador to the Holy See Count Pignatti, according to whom, during his generalate, the religious order had become decidedly anti-Nazi.[65] A witness of this was Tittmann who, on May 2, 1941, sent a telegram to US Secretary of State Cordell Hull, in which he said that he had had a long conversation with Ledóchowski, summarized as follows:

> Polish blood ... naturally enhances his own bitterness toward Nazis but courageous and fighting attitude of Jesuits in general seems in striking contrast with almost pusillanimous atmosphere encountered at present within Vatican.[66]

Ledóchowski stated that he was ready to face martyrdom for his opposition to the Axis, but Tittmann assured him that the United States was determined to conclude the battle successfully. Despite the reassurances, Ledóchowski was worried for the existence of a "fifth column everywhere but more especially in United States and Latin America." For him, the American hierarchy "was not free from guilt in this respect" and Cardinal William O'Connell, archbishop of Boston, and John Timothy McNicholas, archbishop of Cincinnati, in particular, did not seem to realize that Hitler was destroying the Church. The German and American clergy "were likewise lukewarm."

Tittmann's telegram confirms Ledóchowski's aversion for Nazism, at least in relation to the persecution policy to the detriment of the Church in Poland and clarifies the strenuous defense of Vatican Radio by the general of the Jesuits before the Secretariat of State and Pius XII from fall 1940 until April 1941. In the conversation with Tardini on October 28, 1940, and in his letters to Maglione, Ledóchowski admitted that the programs in English risked more open condemnations, that the fathers responsible for those programs had been given greater freedom, but also that he would check them more closely. To still find, in 1941, scripts regarding the war that were very similar to those of the previous year suggests that Ledóchowski, while he was not enthusiastic about it, did not hinder the broadcasts.

The reference to the two American prelates, O'Connell and McNicholas, leaders of the American clergy who were isolationists compared to the policy that the United States had in relation to the European war, suggests that the Vatican Radio programs for North America had a propagandistic purpose for the faithful and, above all, for the episcopate: to show the terrible situation of the Catholics in Germany and stress the need for the neutrality of the Holy See but, at the same time, encourage the United States to not remain defenseless. The American Catholics were effectively not unanimous in their attitude toward the war. The majority were against a possible intervention by the United States, especially the Irish, German, and Italian components who sympathized with the fascist regimes.[67] The fact that between April and May 1941, O'Connell, McNicholas, and Monsignor Michael Curley, archbishop of Baltimore, had openly declared their disapproval of intervening in the war, and the ambiguous position held by the NCWC, induced Tittmann to write to US Secretary of State Cordell Hull, that "There is current feeling in certain non-Vatican ecclesiastical circles in Rome which are vigorously opposing Hitler that a strong group in the Catholic hierarchy in the United States is not sufficiently convinced that a Nazi victory means the destruction of religion, at least in those territories which are under Nazi control."[68] It is probable that Ledóchowski was one of those ecclesiastics.

The fear of the presence of a "fifth column" in Latin America, expressed by the general in his conversation with Tittmann, explains the importance given by Ledóchowski, and apparently also by Pius XII, to the programs in Spanish and Portuguese for the South American countries. He had written that it seemed to him "that according to the mind of the Holy Father it is of supreme importance that Spain and South America are well informed otherwise public opinion, due to the skillful propaganda of the adversaries, will be increasingly induced to make very serious and dangerous errors."[69]

More openly, anti-Nazi programs were followed by others with more lukewarm opinions, tending to stress the neutrality to which the Holy See was obliged. This can be explained by the pressure that the Secretariat of State put on Vatican Radio, ensuring that tones remained calm, considering the continuous complaints by the German government.

But political neutrality, and the insistence on the universal fatherhood of the pope, were at times accompanied (as in the case when the words of the bishop of Lausanne were read out on the radio) by the exhortation to obey the civil authorities and cooperate with military authorities. These were indications, valid for all the faithful, to whichever country they belonged, and which at a national level legitimized the patriotic participation of Catholics in war. When in doubt, the subject could not escape obedience because the principle of presumption applied. In the case of the programs for North America as well, they could be read as instructions on the support that the clergy and the faithful should give to the Roosevelt government. Two interventions by the secretary of state himself sealed the position of the Holy See before the United States' diplomats. In a letter to Cicognani, Maglione maintained that the "Holy See, while leaving a just freedom to the Bishops, cannot want the member of this Episcopate to pronounce themselves in public either collectively or individually for or against the war."[70]

Following that, however, he expressed the wish that the bishops could find a way to make the difficult conditions of the Catholics in Germany and in the occupied countries known to the faithful, specifying:

> By doing so they must act on their own initiative and not in the name of the Holy See. Indeed, in this regard, I must add that any Very Excellent Prelate who intends to speak about the sad religious situation in Germany and the occupied countries, must be deemed obliged in conscience not to allow it to be supposed and let alone mention that the news given comes from the Holy See. Your Excellency will, naturally, be very reserved and will not speak of the aforementioned situation except to people of whom you can be sure that they will not reveal the source of the information they receive.

In September, replying to Taylor who asked him how the episcopate should position itself in the face of war and the attitude of the United States, Maglione wrote: "The priests and especially the prelates would do very well to inculcate the duties of good citizens to everyone, and to leave the responsibility for the decisions about the preparation for war, the conflict etc. to the competent government authorities."[71]

The Holy See and international politics in the programs in Spanish

In the program for North America of May 2, 1941, the English-speaking announcer paid a real tribute to Salazar and Pétain. Regarding the Portuguese president, he said, "Salazar is a realist. His loyalties are his religion and his country. He can rule his people because he reflects all that is best in their national traditions and character."[72] This was followed by praise for the public statute published by the Portuguese government on the ecclesiastical rights in the lands of its empire, which guaranteed the free exercise of its authority by the Church. The signing of the Concordat and the missionary agreement on May 7, 1940, was a particularly significant moment for both the history of relations between the Holy See and Portugal and the consequences of Catholicism in Portuguese society.[73]

In the second part of the same program, the announcer celebrated the Pétain's visit to the shrine of Lourdes, made on April 20, 1941, quoting the exchange of telegrams between the French head of State and Pius XII, and highlighting that "greater demonstration of reverence and love awaited him. The streets were thronged with people, almost frantic with joy." The content of this program recalls those programs which went on the air in 1940, again in English, but for the Philippines or India,[74] to the extent that they could be presumed to be the work of the same author. Denouncing the anti-religious policy of the Third Reich and supporting a possible entrance into the war by the United States did not automatically mean condemning one political regime and approving another. The Catholic authoritarian regimes still appeared to be the best solution possible: this is what clearly emerges, especially in the programs in Spanish for Spain and Latin America.

In these years, before the arrival of Enrique Pérez García in 1943, the priests in charge of the Spanish programs were Ignacio Ortiz de Urbina and Mateo Domingo Mayor. Two patterns of programs in Spanish alternated: one had the list of the daily audiences of the pope, a commentary on his speeches, and the announcement of practical information on the Vatican Radio programs; the other, news from the world, the commented reading of pastoral letters, speeches by politicians, newspaper articles, and conversations on important topics, often curated by Fr. Veneziano Lopez.

On February 3, 1941, Vatican Radio for Spain aired a program regarding the closure of a monastery in Austria, which was mainly inhabited by Swiss fathers who were paid off with five francs and expelled across the Swiss border, said the announcer. The Jesuit in charge, after having said that the Gestapo had broken into the convent at 9:30 a.m. and ordered the priests to leave by 6:00 p.m. on the same day, commented the event as follows:

> Thus, in a few hours, one more candle on the altar of the Faith was extinguished. Remember that the Spanish Republic, when it expelled a certain religious order, allowed it 10 days in which to go. These fathers were allowed eight hours. We wish Spaniards to ponder this example in order to get an exact idea of the situation of the Catholic Church in Germany.[75]

The comparison with the behavior of the Republicans in Spain in relation to the Austrian religious orders, and the invitation extended explicitly to Spanish listeners to understand how much worse the treatment for religious by the Gestapo was, respected, only in part, the order given by Pius XII to use the programs in Spanish to give news about the situation of the Church in

Germany, without further comments, because the announcer did not decline from commenting on the event, juxtaposing the "reds" and the "blacks."

The topic was also widely tackled in the following month, always through quoting events that featured the Catholic hierarchy or faithful, forced to face the difficulties imposed by the German occupation. This was the case, for example, of a program on the state of the Church in Poland, in which—in a tone that "let a definite hostility transpire," as the BBC monitor commented—the restrictions imposed on the exercise of worship were listed.[76] A few days later, other news was given on Poland, specifically on the expulsion of bishops from their dioceses.[77]

In another program, "again with the firm intention of giving our listeners an idea as complete as possible of the religious situation in Germany," an article from the *Völkischer Beobachter* was summarized concerning the condition of the Church in Slovakia which would "act to perfectly show what National Socialism thought of the profession of the Roman Catholic apostolic religion."[78] The article identified the connection with the Holy See as the cause of the Slovak Catholic Church's misfortune, since, unlike the national Orthodox churches in other Slavic countries, which identified the national question with the religious question, the Catholic Church failed to support Slovak nationalism. In showing how the Germans incited the distancing from communion with Rome, Vatican Radio in Spanish tried to denounce the persecutory policy of Nazism on the Catholic Church in all the occupied territories.

Another intervention of note was that of March 26, in which a summary was given in Spanish of the collective pastoral letter of the Dutch episcopate of January 13, 1941—also read in English for North America, in German, and published by *The Tablet*.[79] The most significant parts of the summary, broadcast for Spanish listeners, were those regarding the denunciation of the fight against Christ, which burned "more violently than ever all over the world."[80] It was the foundations of the faith: "We are asking you, our dear faithful, not to let yourself be dragged along by false or strange teachings, because nobody can lay down other foundations except in Christ."[81] The letter, explained the announcer without dwelling too long on the subject, exposed the first attacks against the faith at that time; he amply mentioned the words of the Dutch bishops, aimed at showing how God was the common father and how only Jesus Christ could save everyone, "without distinction whether or Jews or Greeks, lord of all and rich for all those who invoke him."[82] The Church, through which Christ continued to live, was not interested in political questions, "but nobody can accuse the Church of doing politics when it uses legal means to extend on earth the kingdom of God, let alone when it opposes the current falsehoods that threaten its existence. Defending itself against this is a duty that God has imposed on it."

Between the end of March and the beginning of April a summary of the pastoral letter from Archbishop of Freiburg (Baden-Württenberg) Monsignor Conrad Gröber, was read in various languages.[83] From Gröber's letter, the passage in which the bishop stated that only those who were Christian were really German, was broadcast in Spanish, while the part in which he repeated the traditional accusation against the Jews of being responsible for the death of Jesus and the reference to the curse that fell on them, was completely omitted.[84] Reporting its content, Vatican Radio aimed to disprove those who maintained that the Catholic religion in Germany was respected:

> Monsignor Gröber states that in Germany, as far as Catholic Action is concerned, there have been great changes, unprecedented restrictions and ruin; he maintains that the state of affairs is all the more sorrowful due to the affluence of principles opposed to Catholicism, as opposed as fire and water are.

The Jesuit in charge of the programs in Spanish said at the end:

> Repeating this information, we want to repeat all the many pieces of news on the situation of the Catholic Church in Germany. Be they what they are. . . or journalism, the truth is this, nothing more than this, and by stating this we are fully aware that our words are in contradiction with others that the good Spanish Catholics had certainly heard for not very long.

The announcer intended to refer to the propagandistic campaign in favor of the National Socialist policy which was carried out in Spain by the press of the Francoist regime.

But, as anticipated, the programs in Spanish were not limited to criticizing the religious policy of the Nazi regime: they were also used to repropose the most suitable models for the needs of a Christian society, which, in the chaos of a Europe at war, was well represented by Francoist Spain.

It was on Vatican Radio that Pius XII sent, in a radio message on April 16, 1939, his congratulations for the victory of "Christian heroism," of the "nation elected by God as the main instrument of evangelization of the New World and as the unassailable stronghold of the Catholic faith" against "materialist atheism"; he praised the "Head of State and many of his faithful collaborators" because they had shown "very noble Christian feelings" and had protected the "supreme religious and social interests, in conformity with the teachings of the Apostolic See"; he expressed gratitude for all those who had sacrificed themselves "in defense of the inalienable rights of God and of religion."[85] During the Spanish Civil War, the evident contrast between the impossibility of practicing Catholic worship in government-controlled Spain, when it was not translated into real persecution, and the favor granted to the Church in nationalist Spain, attracted the support of the Holy See to the latter, and in May 1938 it sent an apostolic nuncio for the *de facto* recognition of the government of Salamanca.[86] At the end of the Spanish Civil War, the role that the Church had been summoned to play in the regime established by Franco in institutions, education, the daily activities of the Spanish people, and in the influence of the customs as a sign of traditionalism, could not fail to be praised by the Holy See, which was to seal Christian presence in Spanish society with the Concordat of 1953.[87]

During World War II, the programs in Spanish exalted the idea of the Catholic nation, hoping it would be implemented in unoccupied France and pointing out its positive aspects in Portugal and Spain. On March 29, 1941 *The Tablet* published what Vatican Radio reported about the "two great works of Christian zeal and charity, which are particularly appropriate to present-day needs and circumstances," developed in Portugal, and progressing there in a most satisfactory manner: the Portuguese League of Catholic Workers, inaugurated by the primate Archbishop of Lisbon Card. Emmanuel Cerejeira, and the movement born to help children affected by the war "without distinction of creed or nationality."[88] On June 18, the Convention signed between the Holy See and the Spanish government, which regulated the appointment of bishops and contemplated the signature of a Concordat for all matters concerning the relations between Church and State, was read out.[89] In another program, the Convention was praised, together with the speech by the Spanish minister at the Vatican, summarized as follows by the BBC monitor:

> Spain, guided by General Franco, had not only got back to her former paths, but had travelled much further along them than in the past. He joined the names of His Holiness and General Franco in a common act of homage. Spain's position was clearly seen in her national crusade, and in her attitude to present events.[90]

The praise for the Spanish situation was alternated with news on Portugal, France, or other countries, with the intention of showing that peace reigned where the rights of the Church were respected. Salazar's speech to the nation, celebrating his fifty-second birthday, was therefore read out and commented on in full: in it, he maintained that the Catholic Church was the greatest and most combative organization in the world;[91] he put into relief everything the Vichy government was doing against the Freemasons and in favor of the Catholic institutions;[92] he instated on the Catholic character of France, guided by Our Lady of Lourdes;[93] he praised Chile, "a great Catholic nation";[94] and he exalted the attempt by the Portuguese government to "re-Christianize Christmas" by replacing the fir tree, "a Christmas decoration imported from Germany," with the nativity scene.[95]

One of the reasons for such emphasis on the programs in Spanish is, without doubt, the attempt to fight National Socialist propaganda, which was very widespread in Spain and Latin America, tending to encourage them to enter the war alongside the powers of the Axis[96] and to maintain that there was full religious freedom in the territories of the Third Reich. On November 29, 1940, Maglione wrote to the nuncio in Madrid, Gaetano Cicognani, to inform him that the newspapers *Ya* and *Arriba* had used benevolent expressions for Hitler and his policy.[97] Cicognani answered:

> The German government carries out an intense campaign here to spread amongst the Spanish people the idea that its form of regime meets a modern and more efficient conception of the State [. . .]; that it does not hinder religion in any way and gives Catholics complete freedom, although it demands certain rules to be observed, laid down solely for reasons of good order and discipline.[98]

A few days later, in a report to the Secretariat of State, the nuncio wrote:

> As for the claimed respect by Hitler and his Government for religion and Catholicism, the truth is making its way thanks to the news coming from Germany, the circulation of books and magazines, even though sporadically, and also due to the programs of Vatican Radio, which has a very large audience here.[99]

The propaganda that tried to instill in Francoist Spain the values of National Socialism had continued, without interruption, from the years of the Spanish Civil War. Vatican Radio was one of the means used by the Holy See to avert this danger, alongside the circulation of works that attempted to inform the population of the real attitude of the Third Reich toward the Church. Among these, *El cristianismo en el Tercer Reich*, a translation from English of the book *The Persecution of the Catholic Church in the Third Reich*, published in England in 1940, and also containing some programs of Vatican Radio, must be recalled.[100]

"La Collaboration" between Vichy France and Occupied France

The situation in France was peculiar with respect to that of other countries. Vichy was looked on with favor by the Holy See, at least until 1942.[101] It is sufficient to remember the support that the Vatican is alleged to have granted to the possible creation of a "Latin bloc" including France, Italy, Spain, and Portugal,[102] or the affair linked to the writing of the *Principes de la Communauté*, for which Pétain had asked the opinion of the Holy See. The *Principes* consisted of a list of sixteen theories that were to form the ideological base of the "new order," inaugurated by the National Revolution. Pétain gave the first draft, signed on January 14, 1941, to Archbishop of Lyon Pierre-Marie Gerlier, and in turn he gave it to Monsignor Jean-Arthur Chollet, secretary of the Permanent Commission of the Assembly of Cardinals and Archbishops (ACA), so that he could check its adherence with Christian teachings. Chollet wrote two reports, a longer one for the ACA and a shorter one for Pius XII, in which he highlighted some doctrinal errors.[103] The draft of the *Principes* and Chollet's report were carefully examined by Pius XII, who, through Maglione, ordered the correction of the points in question and that the Holy See was to be kept updated on the details of the preparation and the publication of the document.[104]

News about Free France also came through Nuncio Valerio Valeri who, in his reports to the Secretariat of State, did not hide the confidence that he placed in the Vichy regime. He felt a certain relief for the averted danger of the British attack and the Gaullist troops in Dakar. He threw himself into making lists and descriptions of the good social reforms of Pétain's government, expressed his agreement for the introduction of the moderate anti-Jewish statute, and was satisfied by the reforms concerning religion.[105]

Valeri's confidence remained unchanged, even after the Montoire agreements. The meetings were held in the small village on the Loire between Laval and Hitler first (on October 22, 1940), and then between Hitler and Pétain (on October 24), after months of pressing requests by the French to the Germans, and officially sanctioned the collaboration between the Vichy regime and the National Socialists.[106] Although no document was signed by the parties, Laval could publicly announce that first contacts had been made with the German authorities and Pétain could confirm: "J'entre dans la voie de la collaboration [I am taking the path of collaboration]."[107] Pétain was seeking a way to meet the exorbitant war indemnities, bolster supplies, and encourage the return of the populations and family reunions, which had been hindered by the division of the French territory.

After the Montoire meeting, Nuncio Valeri told Secretary of State Maglione of the content of the conversation between Laval and Hitler.[108] The foreign minister of Vichy had had a positive impression of the Führer, that of a man "with a calm and almost gentle character." As for the content of the conversations, the nuncio assured, "Mr. Laval gave me to understand that it was above all about the general lines of a collaboration between France and Germany." He also spoke of some "rumors artfully spread amongst the public or in good faith" that had appeared, in the light of the words of Laval, "exaggerated." In a meeting with Deputy Prime Minister François Darlan in June the following year, Valeri learned that Pétain considered the collaboration the only "way out" for France and, to use Hitler's words, it could be defined "a marriage of intelligence and not of love."[109] While, in general, the French episcopate preferred to keep silent on the new collaborationist politics of Vichy, some personalities, including the bishop of Arras, Monsignor Henri-Edouard Dutoit, Abbé Daniel Bergey in Bordeaux, and other representatives of the local clergy openly declared their favorable position.[110]

Father Mistiaen spoke explicitly about the collaboration in a program on February 24, 1941, which was jammed and, at a certain point, completely covered by other radios.[111] The term "collaboration" actually recurred on few occasions, while "integration" or "to be integrated" were mainly used, which were more incisive in the economy of Mistiaen's discourse and less compromising. For the whole of the script, Mistiaen expressed his fear regarding the evil consequences that, in the name of collaboration and integration with values that were not theirs, would bring: "depersonalization," "sacrifice," "slavery," and "privatization":

> It is extremely worrying to repeatedly and insistently hear at the moment these words which can cover everything, without taking the trouble to establish their meaning, or to remove the veil from the future which they are preparing, whilst those to whom they are addressed have no other guarantee than vague words and eloquent promises, [...] if, however, we see implemented the contrary of what they had boasted about.

Pierre Limagne, a journalist with *La Croix*, wrote in his *Ephémérides*[112] that the regional censorship had made a "scene" on the telephone because an extract from this Vatican Radio program had been submitted for publication. The gesture had been interpreted as a personal insult to Pétain and the case would be taken to the central censorship.[113]

Although the two regimes, Vichy and Hitlerian, were not explicitly named, the latter had already been criticized for some months by Mistiaen. On November 13, 1940, just after Pétain revealed the result of the Montoire meeting, Mistiaen inaugurated a new series of Sunday conferences entitled *Catholicity*, in which he often approached the topic of persecutions.[114] The first addressed the persecution of the Christians during the Roman Empire, preceded by a preamble on the universalism of the Church: in it he predicted the self-destruction of all systems that claimed to contradict the universal law of "full equality between men":

> This is how we learn and it is a little necessary today, you will admit—we learn not to be worried by the theories of those who want to replace human nature and the body of man in a closed system where a knowledgeable hierarchy distinguishes the noble natures and the vile natures, as in the times of Sparta and of all paganism.[115]

One of the ways used by Mistiaen to approach the problems of the present, without falling afoul of Vichy censorship or the remonstrances of the German government, was to take examples from history so that the references were not explicit. In this case, from the very first lines, the allusion to the racism and neo-paganism of National Socialism could be seen, a reference that could also be found later in the program when Mistiaen defined Emperor Decius as "a restorer of the pagan institutions" who had as his program "the extermination of Christianity." Mistiaen, however, was quick to clarify that the Church was not against the Roman Empire, because "Christians, as St. Paul asks, are submitted to their earthly sovereigns." This statement was inserted in the wake of what, in those months, both the press and Vatican Radio had continually stated about the obedience due one's government. But, Mistiaen added, if there was a contradiction between the orders of the rulers and those of God, those of God had to be obeyed. After giving other examples of persecutions, the program ended by noting that Christianity always emerged the winner from the events, a warning against all those who hoped "today" to convince Christians to put their religion solely at the service of the State.

Limagne also detected a reference to the present in the program of December 8, in which Mistiaen tackled the question of Aryanism. "Today's program," he wrote, "consecrated to the Aryans of the 4th century who recognized a certain spiritual sovereignty in their temporal leader, makes us think twice as much about the Aryans of the 20th century."[116] He was aware that Aryanism, although it had been condemned as heresy, had circulated among the Germanic peoples, so that Limagne, in his consideration, had played on the double meaning of Germanic Aryans of the 4th century and German Aryans of the 20th century (understood as the racist theory). It is highly likely that this was precisely Mistiaen's objective.

A reflection on the importance of historical memory was the object of a whole program in which Mistiaen tried to focus on the importance of reflection and meditation in learning lessons from the past in order to face the difficulties of the present. If we do not bear in mind the history of our country, "what can I know and how can I judge today?" and "how will I ever be able to get out of the clutches of my present history?"[117]

There were also, however, more open condemnations of National Socialism. This was the case, for example, with a program regarding the situation of the Church in Poland, aired in English and, in a shorter but no less effective form, in French.[118] The Spanish press spread the (fake) news reported by a religious of Breslau that "harmonious cooperation" existed between the Catholic associations and the German government. The Secretariat of State, concerned about the spread of fake news about the situation of the Catholic Church in Germany, was in contact with the nuncio in Madrid, Gaetano Cicognani, to try to counter this propaganda. In fact, in their programs, the English and French announcers explained that in a Poland controlled by the Germans, the Polish religious and lay associations had been closed down, the Faculty of Theology was closed, and the teachers had been reduced to poverty, sent to concentration camps with the clergy, deported, or killed. "These are ascertained facts; there are others," concluded Mistiaen. His description clashed with the image of a Germany that respected the freedom of worship given by the Spanish press, to the extent that a summary of the program that was sent to the censorship of Vichy for publication in the newspaper *La Croix*, was obviously not authorized.[119]

The contrast between the principles of National Socialism and Christianity were highlighted by Mistiaen in another program, in which he said that in the face of the violence perpetrated, it was not possible to maintain, as certain newspapers did, that National Socialism was based on Christian principles.[120]

From January, however, the jamming of Vatican Radio became more intense. It was Mistiaen himself who reported this, repeating on several occasions in his programs:

> We apologize once again for speaking more slowly and repeating ourselves sometimes. For some weeks now, Vatican Radio has been disturbed by a cause of which we do not know the source. Nevertheless, we have not entrusted to

the waves other than the essential principles of natural law, of divine law and rigorously ascertained facts of which we hold irrefutable proof. We must conclude that these maneuvers are proof of the fear that there is on the earth of hearing what is true and just. Let this be a warning, a pressing invitation to keep prudent confidentiality towards everything that flees light, as Our Lord said, of everything that it needs for its success in multiplying the efforts of a propaganda that has been refused a hundred times and is untruthful.[121]

In a later program Mistiaen, about to give news about a visit by the apostolic delegate to internees in camps in England, ironically commented: "I don't think that this part of our program will be disturbed..."[122] In this way, between the lines, he made it clear that he knew perfectly well that it was the Germans who were responsible for the jamming.[123]

Nevertheless, between March and April 1941, there were more and more denunciations in French regarding the situation of the Church in Germany. In addition to the already recalled letter by the bishop of Freiburg, in two programs on March 28 and 30, 1941, news was collected on religious life in the Reich, which until then, said Mistiaen, had been fragmentary.[124] He denounced the closure of the convents, "the uniquely pagan atmosphere" created by publications (such as Rosenberg's *Mythus des 20. Jahrhunderts*), the education given to the young, the threat of the creation of a national religion, the racist spiritual conception of the regime, and a series of impediments imposed on the Catholic faithful. "Here are the facts," he concluded, "meditate on them. Pray with us so that the Church in Germany, which is going through some very serious hours, emerges strengthened and alive from this ordeal." On April 3, 1941, Menshausen went to Tardini with a report from his government about the reply in German by the BBC, to this program in French.[125]

Mistiaen succeeded in broadcasting another whole program on the situation in Alsace,[126] and another one in which he dwelled on making some considerations about the occupied countries. He said that in the German occupied or annexed countries the attacks on the Church were the most violent and described, in detail, the situation of the clergy and the religious there. He concluded: "the only divinity is race, blood and we can add, propaganda [...] this religion must be the only religion of the Reich."[127] This program became an object of attention by the Secretariat of State. A note dated April 22, 1941, says that it was taken up by several radio news bulletins and by Reuters. The author of the note (it could have been Tardini) wrote that this program "cannot be qualified as strong, at least as far as the form is concerned. It is, on the other hand, strong in its substance. Moreover, it must be noted that these are facts (definite, of course) of which the various programs have been talking for some time now."[128] However, a note by Sigismondi, added by hand on the document, tells us that Pius XII had listened to the program and found it "strong in the tone and that Father Ledóchowski had to be warned." The next day, on April 25, Pius XII gave the order "not to speak any longer about the persecution of the Church in Germany."

The censorship by Pius XII and the reaction of the European countries

On April 30, 1941, Jacques Martin, who had been compiling the digest of the broadcasts since November 1940, was ordered to "see diligently if and how much Vatican Radio says these days about Germany."[129]

Pius XII instructed his private secretary, Fr. Robert Leiber[130] to inform Ledóchowski of his decision to suspend the programs focusing on the religious situation in the Third Reich.[131] The general informed Vicar Father Maurits Schurmans, censor of Mistiaen's programs, and asked Soccorsi to do the same with the other Jesuits.[132] Leiber then wrote to Ledóchowski, telling him that the pope had also asked "to reduce to a minimum the number and the time of the Vatican programs."[133] On April 29, 1941, Maglione had the general contacted to confirm the prohibition of speaking about Germany "under the precept of obedience," but as for the reduction of the programs, he told him that the pope considered it of secondary importance.[134]

Subsequently, Ledóchowski informed the secretary of state that Vatican Radio was abiding by the order of Pius XII, and that the news of the changes underway had already reached the press agencies.[135] As far as reduction of the programs was concerned, he repeated what he had already maintained the previous fall, i.e., that the schedule had already been published by the newspapers and that a sudden change would make a great impression, especially because the radio was gaining increasing prestige, as shown by the listener letters received by Vatican Radio.[136]

Maglione's note on Ledóchowski's letter was blunt: "Germany—absolutely no news until new order." The same thing was repeated by Fr. Leiber: "The Holy Father has declared that the reduction or shortening are a subordinate question and once again he has underlined with great urgency that it is imperative to be quiet about Germany." However, he also added a new and interesting detail: the pope had made an observation from which, Leiber confided, it could be deduced that he did not give much importance to Vatican Radio. He most likely wanted only to refer to the news about the Church in the German area: Leiber noted that the effect of the programs was small and disproportionate to the danger that the Holy See was facing at that time. "The Holy Father had said that the people of Berlin were very bitter about Vatican Radio," but this, Leiber added, "proves that it works. Otherwise at the most they would make fun of it. But I thought that it was better not to answer."[137]

However, Pius XII was very irritated when he found out that, in the May 2 issue of *L'Osservatore Romano*, the schedule of Vatican Radio programs had been published, without any changes.[138] The order to limit the programs was sent to Ledóchowski, but something went wrong and *L'Osservatore Romano* published the old schedule. Ledóchowski wrote immediately, apologizing for what had happened and asking that Fr. Leiber, who knew the pope's mind, take "senior management of the radio."[139] Two days later, Tacchi Venturi visited the general to tell him that Pius XII had called him the evening before "after a year and a half," expressing to him "very excitedly" "his great displeasure on the unobedience [inubbidienza] of the Father General in running the Radio."[140] It appears that Ledóchowski was in the dark about the initiative of *L'Osservatore Romano* and that Pius XII was further irritated following an incident with the Italian government: at an audience with the students of the Italian Catholic University Federation (Fuci) on Whit Sunday, 1,500 copies of an anti-fascist flyer had been distributed. When Mussolini learned of this, he threatened to break off relations with the Holy See. This was why Pius XII said that the greatest moderation had to be exercised. Pius XII had been very distressed as to what to do, as shown by a letter from Leiber to Ledóchowski,[141] even wondering whether it was not better to silence Vatican Radio once and for all. His private secretary advised him against acting this way, Vatican Radio had to be kept active to be at the disposal of Pius XII himself. The pope then thought that it was opportune to reduce the programs to a minimum. On this Leiber agreed, observing that if the programs were rare and shorter, "the silence of the Vatican would have been understood."

Mistiaen did not conceal from his listeners his regret for the impossibility of continuing to freely broadcast his scripts. On May 4, 1941, the BBC monitor collected Mistiaen's words with which he announced that from then onward some programs would no longer be aired:

> We must inform you with great regret that our Sunday broadcasts will no longer take place. In the broadcasts of the last year and a half we have tried to spread confidence, serenity, and hope. All this remains between us. The voice must cease to speak. We shall meet again for some short communications in the evenings at the usual hours. We are deeply grieved, dear listeners, to have to say these words. Goodbye dear listeners, God bless you! *Laudetur*.[142]

The BBC monitor added in brackets: "Note: This announcement, which was given in a halting, sad tone was not jammed. Nor was the German Service which preceded it." *La Croix* dedicated a short column to the communication in which the original sentence in French spoken by Mistiaen was published: "La voix doit se taire. [The voice must be silent]."[143]

The programs that followed had "silence" as their main subject. A topic that was not new, given that the previous year, in the first months after the armistice, it had been praised by Mistiaen with regard to the nebulous proclamations of the Vichy and National Socialist propaganda.[144] Now, in an even tenser climate, Mistiaen returned with insistence to the topic, highlighting the positive aspects of "what is not said." From this moment onward, Mistiaen ended all of his programs with the expression, "Courage, confiance, Dieu vous garde [Courage, trust, God protect you]." Suddenly, the internal censorship wanted to impose the suppression of those words, considered "a seditious encouragement to resistance."[145]

The interventions of Cardinal Maglione, Ledóchowski, and Leiber meant that Mistiaen could continue to say the final exhortation, until the new censor, Monsignor Gustavo Testa, succeeded in imposing his will. This is what can be inferred from a letter, dated July 18, 1966, from Mistiaen to Harold Tittmann, Jr., President Roosevelt's representative at the Vatican.[146] They were linked by a deep friendship which began when the diplomat's family had moved to Vatican City after the United States entered the war. Mistiaen revealed to Tittmann that, at the time of the events, "they have told me that we had to make programs that were 'without color, flavor or smell' to prove that the Pope was not free!" After the war, Mistiaen also talked about this with Paul Duclos, who wrote that the Secretariat of State had informed the French-speaking announcer of: "the clear will of the Holy Father to give the world the impression [...] that the Vatican organ did not have the freedom necessary."[147]

Silence was necessary to "put man back into order," "For the honor and the salvation of men and peoples, we have to find again at any cost the lost harmony, the dignity, the basis of our values, the key to our forgotten greatness."[148] The effect of these programs was apophatic: the insistence on silence, although understood in its positive aspects, only underlined the lack of freedom of expression of the Vatican Radio speakers. In later programs, Mistiaen continued to speak of the effects of silence on spiritual life, drawing inspiration from *Le Silence*, the book that he had written in the 1930s.[149] It is significant that in the programs of those months, the endings were accompanied by pieces of music, the notes of which, according to Mistiaen, could be a source of inspiration for meditation.[150] His aim was to infuse courage and strength into the faithful: "Have faith, dear listeners, [...] despite all the appearances, continue to think following the principles of God and you will be safe."[151]

During May 1941, the ambassadors to the Holy See from Poland, Germany, and Great Britain, and their respective governments, learned that "the higher authorities had ordered Vatican Radio not to speak about Germany." The secretary of state denied this and Tardini wondered whether the circulation of the news would have been beneficial to the Holy See.[152]

This time, complaints came from the British government. A coded message from the apostolic delegate in London, William Godfrey, was received by Secretary of State Maglione: "Foreign Ministry informs me: that telegram from His Majesty is serious, regardless of the recent change of tone in the Vatican Radio programs which would allegedly be due to an agreement (?) under pressure of the Axis. This sympathy (?) he told me would be an important victory for the propaganda of the Axis and consequently for aggression and paganism."[153] Maglione answered Godfrey immediately, asking him to reassure the minister that "no agreement has been made in this regard with the Power of the Axis and that the Holy See intends to maintain its independence and acolyte [faithful?] impartiality."[154]

Godfrey made a further mention of this in another letter to Cardinal Maglione.[155] The Foreign Office, Godfrey explained, was complaining that "after April 26, Vatican Radio remained silent regarding the persecution of religion in Germany and in some areas occupied by the Germans." Until then, the BBC had regularly retransmitted the radio programs of Vatican Radio, which also enjoyed the praise of Minister of Information Alfred Duff Cooper. A few days later, the plenipotentiary minister of the British legation at the Holy See, Francis d'Arcy Osborne, gave Pius XII a memorandum from his government protesting the suspension of Vatican Radio's transmissions on Germany:

> His Majesty's Government have learned with astonishment, concern, and deep distress that, towards the end of April, the Vatican Radio abruptly suspended all references to Germany, and all mention of German measures against the Church and the lying claims of German propaganda. This sudden silence on a subject of imperative concern to Catholics can only be attributed to successful pressure on the Vatican by the German authorities, and His Majesty's Government cannot but regard the decision of the Vatican to yield to this pressure as highly regrettable and inconsistent with the best interests of the Holy See and the Catholic Church.[156]

As it was known that the principles of Christianity were incompatible with National Socialist ideology, the document continued, it was difficult to understand how the Vatican could have taken a step which would inevitably encourage the ambitions of Hitler, and at a time when, as President Roosevelt said, "the whole world is divided between human slavery and human freedom, between pagan brutality and the Christian ideal." He concluded:

> There can be no doubt that, with the help of the United States, the Allied cause will prevail, and the Christian ideal triumph over pagan brutality. The day of the vindication of justice, fair dealing and human liberty may come sooner than might now be expected. What then will be the feeling of the Catholics of the world if it may be said of their Church that, after at first standing courageously against Nazi paganism, it subsequently consented, by surrender and silence, to discredit the principles on which it is based and by which it lives?

The pope replied to the English protests once again that there was no agreement or undertaking with the powers of the Axis but that the reprisals against the Catholics and the religious by the German government, caused by the programs on Vatican Radio, could not be ignored by the Holy See.[157]

Pius XII's decision led to chaos and concern in other ministries of the British government. From the start of 1941, the head of the Intelligence Unit of the Press Censorship Bureau, John de la Vallette, in contact with the BBC, made agreements so that the news obtained from monitoring Vatican Radio was sent as quickly as possible, because, he wrote, "Our Roman Catholic Section is anxious to give the greatest possible publicity to Vatican broadcasts which either deny specific German allegations or attack Nazi theory and practice."[158] In turn, the BBC had been appointed by the Ministry of Information to pay particular attention to the broadcasts from the Vatican and to give them due publicity in questions of foreign policy, both on their Overseas Service and on the Home Service.[159]

The disappointment regarding the suspension of the news on Germany was recorded in a letter from Richard Hope to A.W.G. Randall of the Foreign Office: in it Hope said that it was now clear that the prohibition by Pius XII had already come into force. As seen in the scripts broadcast by Vatican Radio and transmitted to Randall, there was nothing that could minimally offend Germany.[160] At that point at the Foreign Office they thought of asking the BBC and the press to denounce the silence of Vatican Radio.[161] To this end, a draft was drawn up which stated that Mussolini had been persuaded by Hitler to force Vatican Radio to close or at least to avoid being critical toward the German anti-Christian measures in favor of Nazi paganism. And, it added, that millions of listeners of the Vatican programs all over the world, who had found inspiration in the courageous words of the station, could not wait for it to begin again. These were, in essence, also the guidelines followed when drawing up the report given to the Secretariat of State by Osborne on June 10.

Actually, intervention by the Italian diplomacy had not been necessary to induce the suspension of the programs regarding the situation of the Church in Germany because the repeated visits by the German chargé d'affaires had been persuasive. However, the fascist regime had also continued to monitor Vatican Radio. The Ministry for Internal Affairs and the political police, with its network of informers in Vatican circles,[162] had always carefully followed the organization and the activities of Vatican Radio, sending, if necessary, radio bulletins, detailed reports, news, or indiscretions to the Ministry of Foreign Affairs.[163]

On June 13, Ambassador Bernardo Attolico went to the Secretariat of State to ask for explanations about the script of a Vatican Radio program in Polish, which contained words that Pius XII was alleged to have said when receiving Laureta Lubowidzka, the Polish mother superior of the Sisters of the Congregation of Jesus of Nazareth, in an audience.[164] The script said that the pope told Mother Lubowidzka that he always had Poland in his heart. Having learned that enemy propaganda tried to make the Poles believe that the Holy Father was not interested in them, Pius XII asked whether the Polish people believe these statements. Mother Lubowidzka answered that there was a minority that let itself be deceived. Pius XII then exclaimed: "Write to them, tell them that they must not believe the enemy propaganda. Let them know that the Pope loves Poland very much." Pius XII repeated the phrase "This is the truth" three times. During the audience, the pope exclaimed on several occasions: "Poor Poland!" "We do not doubt that God, with his beneficial hand, will do what you invoke." The announcer commented:

> Dear listeners, the Holy Father is the defender of our cause before the world and before God. He painfully feels all the suffering of Poland and of the Poles. We therefore do not believe the false propaganda of the enemy, which wants to arouse in us mistrust of the Pope and the Holy See. This propaganda wants to transform us into a herd of men without intelligence and without ideals, submitted to an enemy, that now is stronger.[165]

As a result of Attolico's intervention, Pius XII ordered Maglione to appoint someone from the Secretariat of State "for the prior revision of the programs of Vatican Radio." This solution had become an "absolute necessity" following the program on the audience with Mother Lubowidzka, because the pope "knew nothing about this program."[166] Ledóchowski wrote to Maglione to explain what had happened: the announcer, Młodochowski, admitted that he had uttered the incriminating sentences while being carried away by emotion. Ledóchowski assured Maglione that in the future he himself would censor the (already reduced) Polish broadcasts. He added, "It is a wonder that even these small broadcasts prohibited under very severe penalties in the occupied territories and nevertheless heard, are followed with such attention."[167] Afterward, Ledóchowski called the fathers to an extraordinary meeting in the Sala delle Consulte and informed them that Monsignor Młodochowski had communicated things said by Pius XII to some Polish nuns that should not have been reported over the radio, and that the announcer had added some words which were not in the script. Pius XII, continued the general, had decided that from then on, the censorship of scripts would be carried out by Monsignor Saverio Ritter, the former nuncio in Prague: every day at 11:00 a.m. a priest would take the Italian, French, Spanish, and English scripts to the Secretariat of State while the German ones remained in the hands of Leiber. Ritter was to prepare his observations for 3:00 p.m. and would reach an agreement *sub secreto* with Ledóchowski, who observed: "these difficulties [. . .] are a sign of the importance given to the radio by those who monitor it so meticulously."[168] From then onward, the sources show a change in procedure between the management of Vatican Radio and the Secretariat of State: what was broadcast by the radio station had to be checked beforehand by the Secretariat of State.[169] The procedure remained the same until the occupation of Rome by the German in September, 1943.[170]

During World War II, the problems arising out of the connection between Vatican Radio and the Holy See became a reason for considerable conflict with the governments of the countries in the opposite factions, and can, today, be considered a deciding factor in the historic opinion on the legacy of Pius XII. The pope and his Curia effectively realized the power of Vatican Radio, but the uncertainties, doubts, and indecisions regarding the most opportune moves led Pius XII and his entourage to, once again, choose prudence, to the extent of imposing censorship of scripts by the Secretariat of State.[171] At this point, however, they began to understand that a profitable way existed in turning the more delicate situations to their own advantage. Tardini and Montini were skillful in repeating to the representatives of the accredited embassies that Vatican Radio was not an official organ of the Holy See and that the Secretariat of State was not aware of or responsible for what was broadcast. At first, the reactions of the embassy representatives clearly suggested that it was not credible that the Holy See did not officially oversee Vatican Radio or that it was not informed as to what was broadcast. But, in the end, they gave in to the Vatican's reassurances. Ambassador Bernardo Attolico, in a letter to Minister of Popular Culture Alessandro Pavolini, wrote that on several occasions he had observed that Vatican Radio was effectively not under the control of the Secretariat of State, and Menshausen wrote the same to von Bergen.[172] This was not enough to make the foreign ministers desist (first those powers of the Axis and then the Foreign Office), or from protesting, but the Holy See benefited from continuing to maintain this theory of the absolute freedom of Vatican Radio.

However, the case of the June 10 program in Polish proves that this theory, supported officially, could be opportunely denied in specific circumstances, i.e., when, in internal circles of the Catholic Church, it was advantageous to pass Vatican Radio off as the unofficial voice of Pius XII. In fact, a translation of the program in Polish, about the audience with Lubowidzka, was attached to a letter from Maglione to Nuncio Valerio Valeri in which Maglione tried to prove that Pius XII wanted to help the Poles, that he had not abandoned them as certain propaganda led people to believe—to prove the "paternal feelings" of Pius XII toward the Polish people.[173] The program that had been the object of Italian protests, and the reason for the intensification of checks on the scripts, turned out to be useful to show what the Holy See was doing for Poland.

There was a fine line between propaganda and diplomacy, perhaps not yet fully defined but which was beginning to appear during the course of a new war, one with new methods, to which the Vatican chancellery was trying to adapt. The decisions concerning Vatican Radio were not made around a table—like during the 1930s when radio was something brand new—but they attempted to exploit all the advantages of the new medium, as they gradually understood its potential.

Which enemy is more dangerous: National Socialism or Communism?

The Catholic hierarchy increasingly compared National Socialism and communism because of their anti-religious policies. Communism had been condemned from the doctrinal point of view in various nineteenth century pontifical documents such as Pius IX's *Syllabus* (1864) and Leo XIII's encyclical *Quod apostolici muneris* (1878). It was stigmatized by the Catholic press as the worst evil that could befall modern society, often tracing its origins back to the participants in the anti-Catholic conspiracy (the Jews, the Protestants, and the Freemasons).[174] It was considered to inspire a dangerous system of government that, from the Soviet Union, was trying to expand to the West and which, after not wanting to reach an agreement with the Holy See in the 1920s, had to be contained by any means available.[175]

The attitude toward National Socialism had been almost the complete opposite. Until Hitler's rise to power in 1933, the German bishops had opposed its ideology, prohibiting the faithful from joining the party, but after the declaration by the new chancellor of the Reich and his ministers that they wanted to defend Christian values and fight Bolshevism, the German Catholic Church and the Holy See changed their minds.[176] Pius XI pronounced himself in favor of Hitler's fight against communism. The difficulty in recognizing the dangerousness of National Socialism, and therefore of condemning it, lay in the conviction that opposition to the liberal and democratic tradition was a point that National Socialism shared with the Church and offered the possibility of collaboration.[177]

In the 1930s, the Catholic organs of the press closest to the Holy See, *L'Osservatore Romano* and *La Civiltà Cattolica*, emphasized the fear of the international spread of communism, but often put Bolshevism and National Socialism on the same level. It was after the outbreak of the Spanish Civil War that, on the scales of dangerousness, communism began to weigh heavier, with National Socialism considered a lesser evil.[178] The different attitude of the teachings of the Church to National Socialist and communist ideologies, both the objects of papal condemnation, emerges from the two Pius XI's encyclicals of March 1937, *Mit brennender Sorge* and *Divini Redemptoris*. While the first encyclical, written by Pacelli, condemned the doctrinal errors of Nazism, without ever naming it explicitly, and leaving open the possibility of a change of heart, the second, which was drawn up with the participation of a group of Jesuits together with Fr. Ledóchowski (but which also enjoyed the personal contribution of Pius XI) identified atheist communism as the main danger for the Catholic Church. It defined communism as "intrinsically perverse," excluding the possibility of any collaboration whatsoever.[179] With the publication of the two encyclicals, the Church distanced itself from both National Socialism and communism. As Tardini had hoped in his *votum* to the Holy Office in April 1936, the condemnation of the errors of one (racist nationalism) was not to be interpreted in favor of the other (communism).[180]

From the second half of the 1930s, Pius XI began to despair at renewing a compromise with the Nazi regime and he compared it, in public and in private, to communism on an increasingly frequent basis.[181] Although many of his close entourage and the German bishops did not support this view, some members of the Italian episcopate reached the same conclusions.[182]

Part of the diocesan press, in its comments on *Mit brennender Sorge*, also compared the Nazi heresy to the communist one.[183] Vatican Radio did the same (as discussed earlier), perhaps more than any other organ of the press.[184]

In the last year of his pontificate, Pius XI took firmer positions with regard to fascism and, at times, less intransigent positions toward the communists who "held out their hand" in France.[185] His successor, on the other hand, as early as the day after his investiture, sought an arrangement with the authoritarian regimes, including Hitler's.[186]

The outbreak of World War II, which proceeded in ways that the Church found hard to completely understand, induced the Holy See to remain impartial. It was again Vatican Radio, in early 1940, that reproposed the comparison between the violence of the Nazis and the communists, denouncing the situation of occupied Poland. But after the protests of the German chargé d'affaires, Pius XII gave orders to suspend those programs. Nevertheless, until April 1941, when Pius XII prohibited giving news about the Church in the territories of the Reich, Vatican Radio continued to denounce the persecution of the Catholics by the Germans. On the one hand, the age-old fear of an expansion of Russian influence over the West survived and therefore the spread of communism, which without a doubt had to be stopped. On the other hand, with the acknowledgment of the destructive policy of National Socialism, the awareness rose that, in the event of a victory by the Germans, the return of respect for the freedom and the rights of the Church was unlikely. If the theory of choosing the lesser evil had often come to the rescue in the decisions to be taken, this time the Holy See tried to pick its way carefully, while not having a clear perspective as to which was the more dangerous.

The invasion of the Soviet Union by Germany (June 22, 1941) did not have the effect in the Vatican that the Germans and Italians expected: the two governments hoped that the Holy See "would say some words in favor of the anti-Bolshevik crusade." But, as Maglione said in a conversation with the Italian ambassador to the Holy See, Attolico, summarized by Tardini in his notes: "Nazism, the persecutor of the Church, really cannot speak of 'crusade', because due to its initial alliance with Russia, the Italian newspapers could no longer criticize communism." The Holy See, instead, "has nothing to add and nothing to take away from what it has repeatedly said and therefore it cannot uphold certain wishes, that would succeed only in giving the word of the Holy See a political nature, with severe harm for the superior religious and moral interests."[187] Tardini emphasized the same concepts in a personal conversation with Attolico: "The Holy See has already reproached, condemned, and anathematized Bolshevism with all its mistakes. There is nothing to add and nothing to take away from what has been said. Speaking, now, could easily have a political nature, while the Holy See has spoken clearly, *tempore non suspecto*."[188] He then continued, making a stab at Germany for the Molotov-Ribbentrop Pact:

> It is clear that those who, in the past have made agreements of friendship with Russia now have to explain their attitude: those who until yesterday declared that the alliance with Russia was a guarantee of peace in the East and today goes ... on a crusade, it is clear that they have to explain their change of attitude. But not the Holy See. Nothing has changed. Speaking now could also be interpreted as obedience to the advice of Farinacci!

The theme of the "crusade" had particularly touched Tardini, who effectively insisted on this point:

> In tribute to the declarations, condemnations etc., made by the Holy See, I will be delighted if I see communism put out of action. It is the worst enemy of the Church, but it is not the only one, Nazism has carried out and is carrying out a full-fledged persecution of the Church. Therefore, the swastika is not precisely the cross of the crusades. Yet the Germans (not Mussolini) were the first to speak of a crusade! [...] If the Holy See were to recall publicly the errors and the horrors of communism, it could not forget the aberrations and the persecutions of Nazism.

In the face of insistence by Attolico, who presented a situation of a Church that was worse under Soviet dominion than under German control, Tardini concluded: "Moreover, it is exactly for this reason that I, at the present time, instead of applying the doctrine of the crusades, apply the proverb 'one devil drives out another,' all the better if this other is the worse." Although Tardini meant for "the worse" to refer to communism, nonetheless he spoke about two devils. Besides, a footnote clarified that Pius XII, returning the document after having read it, observed that the religious situation in Germany had worsened, effectively neutralizing what Tardini had said without great conviction about the "worst devil." If, from the theoretical point of view, there still existed qualitative differences between the two ideologies, from the practical point of view, these tended to cancel themselves out, as the refusal to join the National Socialist crusade confirms. In a later audience with Attolico, who had returned to the question, Tardini repeated:

> As for communism, it is truly atheist and to be condemned. But Nazism is also to be very greatly condemned. [...] If a Bishop were to say to the Italian people the wrongs communism has done and is doing, justice and truth would want him to also say the wrongs that Nazism has done and is doing. It is the duty of the bishops to let Catholics know the real situation of Catholicism in Germany as well.[189]

Tardini, in the new context of World War II, put the dangerousness of communism and of Nazism on the same level. This opinion was dictated by the sensation, now fully agreed to within the Vatican, that it would be unlikely to obtain any reassuring guarantee from the Reich. Shortly after Germany sent the first troops into Soviet territory, Tardini himself noted the urgency to send military chaplains to Russia, the Baltic countries, and Ukraine, because "when the Germans have entered there definitively, it will be impossible for anyone sent by the Holy See to go to those places."[190] His hope, in the final analysis, was that "Providence wants, in its goodness and mercy, to draw from this tragedy the destruction of the two great evils that threaten humanity, civilization and religion: communism and Nazism!"[191]

The first radio message by Pius XII after the attack on the Soviet Union was read in English and was directed at the faithful who had gathered for the Eucharistic Congress of the United States. The pope said that while they were living in a country where religious practice was allowed, in other parts of the world the Church was persecuted with such skill that it was impossible to measure its effects.[192] Pius XII's words read on June 26, 1941, repeated those said in the Easter message, quoted explicitly, in which Pius XII had said that he wanted to take a word of comfort "where the Church, the Bride of Christ, is suffering in particular."[193] Religious freedom in the United States, which guaranteed the exercise of the Catholic cult, was contrasted with the persecution of the Church, but without specifying who was responsible for it.

On April 6, 1941, the Polish president in exile Władysław Raczkiewicz wrote to the pope to ask him for a word of hope and encouragement for his people.[194] The letter most likely did not arrive in the Vatican until the end of May, as suggested by a note of the Secretariat of State.[195] Pius XII answered on June 25, assuring Raczkiewicz that he was aware of the situation in Poland and, repeating his Easter message, pointed out that he had contacted the rulers of the occupying countries, asking them to act humanely toward the prisoners and populace. The letter was sent to Raczkiewicz via the apostolic delegate in London to give it to the president, but also asking that it not be circulated.[196]

Vatican Radio, which from the second half of June onward was closely monitored by the Secretariat of State, was a specular reflection of the attitude of the Holy See: no tipping the balance to one side or the other, in the sense that there was no clear position taken against or in favor of either side of the Russian campaign. Fr. Mistiaen had no doubts about communism and National Socialism: "both deserve the same shame."[197] In his programs from fall 1940 to spring 1941, Mistiaen did not spare either regime from open criticism. Regarding National Socialism, he condemned, above all, the wish to carry out a revolution without God: "This is where there is the essential contradiction of which the regime will die, sooner or later. They wanted to create a man without God, and man needs God."[198]

In general, the fathers appointed for the Vatican Radio programs were probably aware that in the war between the Soviet Union and Germany the victory of one or the other would, by no means, guarantee the protection of Catholic rights, and so denouncing abuse of one side would have given the impression that Vatican Radio supported the other. But we cannot also fail to note that condemnations of communism were pronounced in a much clearer way than condemnations of the Nazis. This reveals the blind spot in which the Vatican Radio announcers found themselves: between obeying the orders of Pius XII and the need to not make the Nazis appear as paladins of anti-Bolshevism and religious freedom. Some examples will clarify the situation.

In August, a program in German and one in Spanish spoke of the threat of communism. In the former, it was recalled that Pius XII invited the faithful to pray "for the conversion of atheists and believers in laicism," because many students who had come from the East to study at European universities were convinced that Christianity was obsolete, and once they returned home, they became the "champions of communism without God."[199] The latter, on the other hand, with reference to the conflict in the Soviet Union, maintained that Catholic priests, speaking to the peoples of the countries at war, were overjoyed to know that everyone (as good Catholics) was convinced that the "Reds" had to be punished by God.[200]

In October, in a program for Germany, there was a long discussion on the survival of the religious spirit in the Russian population which, despite the attempts by the government to eradicate it, in actual fact, had never happened.[201] The conversation opened with a quotation by a Georgian writer who described the irreligious attitude of peoples in Europe and America, asserting that they were letting God die, while in the Soviet Union, a real battle was being conducted against Him. According to the doctrine promoted by the Bolsheviks, a new man was being born in Russia, with the sole duty of serving the country: all his feelings would have been subordinate to this purpose. After having described how there had been an attempt to eliminate the survival of religious worship, the announcer wondered whether, in the end, a society with God had been created, observing that the answer was negative. The occupation of the Axis powers had shown how secretly religious the Russian people were: "Even within the ranks of the Bolshevik Army, Christianity had not completely died." Examples followed that addressed the liturgical services of the Russian Orthodox Church for prisoners and other Orthodox Masses attended by hundreds of people, who not only remembered the words of the hymns, but also took communion. The program closed by recognizing that Nietzsche did not win theorizing a dying God, but Dostoevskij, who recognized that religion could not be completely eliminated from the human soul, did.

On November 5, an article from *L'Osservatore Romano* was read on Vatican Radio in French, Italian, German, English, Spanish, and Dutch. It had in turn been taken from two articles by Fr. Pellegrino on anti-religious propaganda in the Soviet Union published in *La Civiltà Cattolica*.[202] The summary published in the Vatican newspaper, and its subsequent repetition on the radio, emphasized, through the quotation of articles from *Pravda* and other Russian periodicals such as *Antireligioshnik* and *Bezboshnik*, that the religious freedom proclaimed by the Soviet Constitution in 1936 was continuously denounced by new proclamations praising atheism. However, other articles from *L'Osservatore Romano*, collected under the title *Documentation*, were read. The first, entitled *The Reich as a mission*, based on a brochure which invited the German population to persevere toward liberation from the outdated values of Christianity, and the second, taken from the weekly *Nordland*, the organ of the *Gottgläubige Deutsche*, which summarized a sort of National Socialist catechism of the members of the *Deutsche Glaubensbewegung*, an association which repudiated the Jewish-Christian concept of God based on prophecies, replacing it with a naturalist concept.[203] In the case of these articles concerning the Third Reich, no comment followed by the journalists of *L'Osservatore Romano* or the announcers of Vatican Radio, who clearly tried to mitigate the denunciation of religious persecution and avoid exposing themselves to the remonstrances of the German government.

The references to Germany, therefore, were not lacking, but they were characterized by greater caution. In a program in Polish, for example, the anniversary of the Battle of Chocim was celebrated. It was fought in 1621 by the Polish Confederation against the Turks, after which Gregory XV sent King Sigismund III a message of congratulations containing the following passage: "Poland calls you her savior and Germany the champion of her safety."[204] In the present situation in which Germany was a threat for Polish Catholics, recalling the phrase by Gregory XV which had celebrated the Polish protection of the Germans could be read as a sort of paradox.

Another conversation that alluded to the National Socialist anti-religious policy, broadcast, unsurprisingly, in German and Spanish, compared the Catholic dogma and a *Weltanschauung* that wanted to replace Christ as the foundation of civilization:

> No one else can lay a foundation once laid by Jesus Christ. Those who attempt to do so are imposters. Is there a new dogma? No! There is only one dogma, that revealed by the Holy Ghost and formulated by the Church. A group that may today hold power will by tomorrow have disappeared. The Christian dogma will be the same tomorrow as today.[205]

Lastly, on December 30, a program in Spanish by Fr. Jesus Iturrio denounced the pervasive spread, in Spain, of the German nihilist philosophies of Nietzsche and Heidegger, while the Spanish ought to have instead been inspired by Christian philosophers.[206]

The guard against communism had not been lowered, but Nazism was now perceived as a similar, if not equivalent, danger.

4   Vatican Radio, Racism, Antisemitism, and the Shoah

Racism, eugenics, and euthanasia condemned by Vatican Radio
The spread of racial theories at the end of the nineteenth century linked to the rise of new nationalisms, prompted the Catholic Church confront racism, which became a cogent concern after the adoption of racial policies by the fascist regimes during the 1930s. The Holy See tried to fight the anti-Christian content of the theory[1] but also to reach compromises in practice, if deemed opportune.[2]

The debate on racial theories had, until then, focused mainly on discussions surrounding eugenics and birth control in the United States and Europe.[3] The doctrinal response was first directed to the studies of the natural sciences which investigated the correspondence between the somatic features of human groups and spiritual ones, then to eugenics, and lastly to the racist theories of National Socialism and the claim of "monogenism," i.e., the single common origin of man in God, and as a consequence the essential unity of the human race.[4]

The Catholic Church's opposition to racism appealed to the unity of humankind, its common origin in God, insisting on the accidental and non-essential character of differences between "races." A theorist of the monogenesis, but also of the differences between races, was the Viennese Catholic anthropologist Wilhelm Schmidt, director of the Pontifical Lateran Ethnological Missionary Museum, who, in 1935, published the book *Rasse und Volk*, which became a reference text for Pius XI and for Catholics on these issues. Schmidt's position was somewhat contradictory when he tried to remain loyal to the universality of the value of the human person and his racial science.[5]

Pius XI officially condemned the voluntary limitation of births and sterilization in the encyclical *Casti Connubii* (1930),[6] and eugenics with the decree of the Holy Office of March 21, 1931.[7] However, these documents "left plenty of room for Catholics in France, Germany, or in the United States to reach differing conclusions on bettering the race."⁸

An official stance of the Holy See on racism was missing. Only after the Nazi Party came to power did the need become more urgent to clarify which doctrinal basis the Church's attitude toward racism rested upon, as highlighted by a memo drafted in September 1933 in the Secretariat of State by an anonymous author, which pointed out the contradictions between Christian and racist doctrine. This document was then used to draft another memo that Pacelli sent to the German government on May 14, 1934, which said that "the absolutization of racial thought, and especially its proclamation as a substitute for religion" was an erroneous position "whose pernicious fruits will not be long in coming."⁹

In 1937, in the encyclical *Mit brennender Sorge*, Pius XI blamed the exaltation of race as a fundamental value of the human community and its divinization as an idolatrous cult. In April 1938, the secretary of the Congregation of Seminars and Universities, Ernesto Ruffini, on the order of the pope, signed an anti-racist syllabus made up of eight erroneous theories to refute.[10] In 1938, in several speeches Pius XI clarified the irreconcilable nature of the Catholic doctrine's idea of universal fraternity with racism and nationalism.[11]

The draft of the encyclical on racism and antisemitism, which remained on the desk of Pius XI, together with the speech written for the anniversary of the Lateran Pacts, disappeared a few hours after his death.[12] *Humani generis unitas* was not published by his successor, who used some of the passages in his first encyclical, *Summi pontificatus*, without explicitly mentioning racism.[13]

The gradual awareness that Pius XI had come to in the last year of his pontificate about the irreconcilability between Christian doctrine and the racist (and antisemitic) policies of the Italian and German governments, and which was to reach its acme with the issuance of the encyclical on the unity of the human race, was not shared by his successor who silenced the issue.[14] Nonetheless, as outgoing secretary of state (upon the death of Pius XI), Pacelli wrote the "Relazione sugli Stati" (Report on States), the practice of reporting to the new pontiff on the main issues concerning the diplomatic relations between the Holy See and the States. But, as Giovanni Coco has observed, the outgoing secretary was also the newly elected pope, so the report reveals Pius XII's view on the matters. The entry on Italy focused on "Italian Racism" and "Italian Catholic Action," a sign that Pius XII felt that these were the two most important affairs concerning relations between Italy and the Holy See.[15]

The racial question was not tackled by Pius XII, who only approved a decree of the Holy Office on February 22, 1940, which condemned sterilization and euthanasia.[16] Meanwhile, the Italian Jesuits bi-weekly *La Civiltà Cattolica*, edited by Fathers Mario Barbera and Antonio Messineo, continued to publish (and did so until 1943) articles that showed the possibility of a compromise on the racial laws between the Italian government and the Holy See.[17] Again, though, it was Vatican Radio that broke the silence.

Vatican Radio dedicated a considerable number of programs in the different languages to the topic of eugenics and racism, apparently without causing any protests. Broadly speaking, their aim seems to have been proving that racism was an error from a doctrinal point of view.

In a program in Spanish, the announcer tried to explain how it was not possible to fight the false political theories excluding Christianity, because the errors could be defeated only with the truth: "The Catholic truth excludes all errors, whether they are racism or Communism, liberalism or statolatry."[18] The condemnation of racism was combined with that of other ideologies which were the result of anti-Christian modernity. In a program in French for France before the German invasion, the description of the blessing of the candles on February 2, 1940, which included the papal blessing of the representatives of the Church in the world, emphasized the universality of the Church "against the apostles of the inequality of the races, who should have seen their theories be jeopardized."[19]

The subject of race was also often discussed in the programs in German. In a talk on Epiphany (1941) the speaker said that the Magi are the representatives "of the three races descendant from Noah" which means the "equality of all nations before Christ."[20] On May 1941, in a series called *Church and society*, it was stated that there could not be any real right in a community that denied, a priori, the equality of the human race by introducing unequal laws, distinctions between races, and civilizations that were superior to others.[21] One year later, it was explained that all men were children of the Church, without distinction, in the name of the solemn law of unity and human solidarity. God had approved the division of humanity into different groups but had united them in faithfulness to Him: all men, of whatever background or origin, had the same rights as children of the Church, which did not make any distinction between "pagans" and Jews, slaves and free men. This was not in contradiction with the love each person owed to their country: "The warmest love for one's nearest is only natural, as long as it is not to the detriment of Christian love."[22]

The German announcer, who from this time onward can be identified as Fr. Ambord, read the translation of an article written by the Dominican

Mariano Cordovani and published by *L'Osservatore Romano*, commenting on the recent condemnation of the Protestant theologian Wolfgang Stroothencke's book, *Erbplege und Christentum*, which justified eugenics to save racial characteristics, from a Christian perspective.[23] The volume brought together the lectures given to young Germans, tending to show that Christian ethics did not condemn but, on the contrary, at times required "voluntary sterilization or sterilization imposed by the State, free euthanasia or prescribed by the authority for reasons of race." These statements, explained the Dominican theologian, were in open contrast with the anti-eugenic teachings set forth by Pius XI in the encyclical *Casti connubii*. Despite the intense disturbance of the French radio programs, the article was also read by Fr. Mistiaen who, quoting Cordovani, concluded that those who denied the "inviolable dignity of whoever possesses human nature," those who did not admit "the inviolable right to life or to the integrity of the body of each innocent man" should be considered the expression of "brutal materialism and paganism."[24]

In another program, Fr. Ambord clarified that there was no link between "race and religion," as the Berlin and Rome "race departments" maintained. The content of his broadcast was the reading of a telegram from NCWC for the Catholic Section to the British Minister of Information:

> In a badly jammed broadcast in German for Germany Vatican Radio March eleventh declared publications of Aryan Godbelievers, although they may be couched in scientific language, are not imbued with spirit of scientific research but by desire to fight Christianity and Church stop said quote It is to be emphasized that whole complex of racial theories is by no means based on that scientific clarity which would be necessary to establish any hypotheses about connection between race and religion stop Neither the so-called race office in Berlin nor similar institution in Rome which was founded later are basing their conceptions of the Nordic or the Italic man which are referred to in scientific publications and periodicals on truly scientific foundations stop Their theories are dictated by practical considerations and political utility.[25]

On November 20, 1941, the BBC monitor noted that the German announcer quoted some passages from Pius XI's speeches that praised the Catholic Church which united "all nations and all races. All men have a single origin."[26] Only a few days later, the same announcer proposed a summary of Pius XI's speech of July 28, 1938, censored at the time by the fascist regime, in which the pope established the incompatibility of racism with Catholicism.[27] To find the endorsement of the Holy See, the speakers had to rely on the words of the predecessor to the reigning pontiff.

It was again Mistiaen who denounced several times, and without mincing his words, the evil consequences of racist ideology, becoming a spokesman for the concern of the Church regarding the racial divisions that dominated society:

> Since the last century, the Church has been disturbed by the theories of those who want to establish a chosen race, theirs, and an inferior mass subject to a tyrant-God [. . .]. In reality, we find ourselves facing a separate and divided world and it is not necessary to have great comprehension of the times in which we are living to realize that men are irremediably classified in élite races and inferior races.[28]

The answer that the Catholic faithful were called to give to those who wanted to divide the world was clearly stated by Mistiaen: since it had been religious indifference that fostered the spread of these divisions, it was necessary to go back to the only principle that could put things right in the world.

In another program, he tackled the question of the equality of men according to the principle of human dignity:

> The human community exists not due to a juxtaposition of a certain number of individuals in which we can, to favor some and destroy others, ignoring the rights and the nature of the latter. The human community exists due to the union, the intimate union of the natures that have their expression, their sole expression in people. He who has made it a principle to violate the nature of people, with the pretext of saving, of creating a superior humanity, introduces into his system an internal contradiction, a seed of death. He sacrifices the rights of what he is, breaks away from reality, succeeds in destroying the only thing necessary to his people, the human nature that lives in the person. [. . .] [The Church] says that everyone has the same rights, all without any exception, they have to be respected, when it is about the essential prerogatives of their nature. [. . .] There is nothing to be done against the truth. This truth is that men are equal and that they have an identical nature.[29]

On April 16, 1942, Mistiaen read some passages from a speech that was given by Cardinal Archbishop of Malines Jozef Ernest Van Roey, to the women of the Catholic Action meeting in Brussels on March 4.[30] The Belgian primate said that blood, the material element, could not be the source of intelligence, but it was the soul and the body together that formed the human person. It had a value, permanent and immortal, and although it had necessary relations with "race" it could not be subordinate: "All the races can be perfected! [...] If all the races can be perfected, they are essentially the same, because they have the same origin and the same purpose and are all redeemed by Christ the Redeemer."[31]

The opposition to Nazism by the Vatican Radio announcers, through their own scripts or, as in the case of Van Roey, through the reading of the ecclesiastical hierarchy's speeches, was based essentially on the defense of the right of the person as a creature of God. Equality derived from all mankind being the children of God and therefore of the Church, as well as the identical human nature that lives in all people and represents a higher value compared to the diversity deriving from race or blood. In this, the crux of the opposition of the Catholic Church to racism was the transcendent foundation of the person, derived from being a divine creature.[32] In his radio message of June 1, 1941, delivered on the fiftieth anniversary of the *Rerum novarum*, Pius XII recalled the natural imprescriptible rights belonging to the human person as the image of God.[33]

What is striking is that in all of these objections to racism, the identification of the victims, e.g. the Jews, was lacking. Therefore, we must wonder if the general statements of principle had the purpose of extending, as far as possible, the denunciation of racism, or on the contrary, if they hid the intention of the Church in not taking the sides of the persecuted groups in order to not be too exposed, which would have been the case if they had been explicitly named. There is no evidence as to whether the order to limit the complaint to a condemnation of principle had come directly from Vatican Radio's director or the Secretariat of State. However, it is certain that the silence concerning the Jews as victims of the racial theories had been a widespread attitude in the ecclesiastical hierarchy in the previous decade.

But that had not always been the case. It must be observed that there is a clear distinction between the defense of the Jews from physical violence and the discriminating legislation. In the twentieth century history of the papacy, on two occasions Pius X and Benedict XV officially condemned the violence against Jews on the basis of the law of the Gospel and natural law. In the 1905 letter *Poloniae populum*, Pius X had denounced "the public massacres of Jews that the law of Gospels—which requests that we love all without distinction—detests and condemns."[34] In the 1916 letter to the American Jewish Committee, which had begged the Holy See to intervene in defense of persecuted Jews in the Russian Empire, Benedict XV's secretary of state wrote that the Church "considers all men to be brethren" and will not cease "to inculcate the observance among individuals of the principles of natural law and to reprove every violation of it. This law should be observed and respected in relation to the Children of Israel as it should be to all men, for it would not conform to justice and religion itself to derogate therefrom solely because of a difference of religious faith."[35] This document recalled the natural law regulating relations between Christians and Jews. In the Thomistic doctrine, natural law is the foundation of any other law (civil or religious), since it reflects the eternal divine law impressed by God in creation. In this sense the Jews' rights were guaranteed, and they should not be victimized by violence. In 1928, eventually, the Congregation of the Holy Office condemned the "hatred against the chosen people."

Nonetheless, none of the cited documents dealt with the Jews' civil and political rights, which the Church had always opposed. Then in the 1930s, with the National Socialist and Italian fascists' racial laws, the Jews' discrimination made their civil and political rights part of the agenda. The Catholic Church considered the Jews a matter of concern insofar as they were the depositary people of Old Testament revelations, into which Christ was born, and as such they were part of the economy of Christian salvation. On the racial connotation conferred on Jews, the Church could forcefully intervene, since it collided with Christian principles when the fascist laws claimed to erase the value of baptism or marriage, affecting converted Jews and the possibility of further conversions. The Church could not accept that civil laws presumed to replace divine law, penalizing those who had joined the Christian community to all intents and purposes or would have wanted to.

On the basis of natural law and, paradoxically, on the role given to the Jewish people in the economy of salvation, the Church would have had sufficient theological reasons to firmly oppose the persecution of Jews during the war—as Benedict XV made clear through Gasparri's letter to the American Jewish Committee. Despite Vatican Radio speakers' efforts, who embraced personalism as the foundation of their human person rights defense,[36] their disapproval was not explicitly directed to the Jews' persecution because of two hindrances. One being strategic and the other ideological. First, the fear of reprisals on Catholics seems to have been ever-present, even with Vatican Radio, as Pius XII's order to stop anti-German broadcasts has demonstrated. Second, as we will explore in the next chapter, the Church's recent turn to personalism, as a guardian of the rights of the person, did not coincide with the defense of human rights, understood as the inalienable rights of man defined by the Declaration of 1789, and therefore with the complete rejection of antisemitism. The gap between the two—human personal rights and human civil rights—was bridged by the Church's jurisdiction over the definition of rights and their beneficiaries. In the case of the Jews, it still weighed an anti-Jewish legacy, which recognized the Jews' right to existence and to bodily integrity but did not allow a defense that would have made the individuals the bearers of civil rights like all other people. And that was true, also, for the Vatican Radio speakers, with very few exceptions, as we will address.

Anti-Judaism and antisemitism in Vatican Radio programs

The studies on the relationship between the Catholic Church, the Jews, and antisemitism in the first half of the twentieth century have revealed the persistence of a theological anti-Judaism which, when it did not contribute to fueling modern antisemitism, prevented its total and incontrovertible condemnation.[37] The Catholic press, circulated nationally or in dioceses, and run by ecclesiastics, presumed to explain the Catholic position on the subject, based, however, on the political opportunities of the time. The promotion of old (and new) anti-Jewish stereotypes conveyed an interpretation of the political or social facts through the shared language of antisemitism to which the faithful were accustomed. In many cases, these kinds of antisemitic articles were also a means for criticizing modern society.[38]

The comparison with the press helps to define the position of Vatican Radio. In general, it could be observed that the antisemitic rage that had characterized, for example, several articles of *La Civiltà Cattolica*, was softened in the radio talks. The traditional antisemitic stereotypes were occasionally reproposed, together with the condemnation of the racist neo-paganism, proclamations of kindness, and the sense of protection that the Church had for the Jews (as according to the tradition of double protection—of the Catholics from the Jews and the Jews from their persecutors).

From the available sources, it seems that Vatican Radio did not deal with the question of antisemitism in the 1930s, but it is possible that some news was given without any accounts remaining. So far, it has only been possible to trace a broadcast written in Dutch by the delegate general director of the Apostolate of Prayer,[39] the Jesuit Jacob Zeij, aired on November 28, 1938.[40] The text, which explained the prayer intention for the month of December 1938, was dedicated to the conversion of Jews. Although it did not contain aggressive accusations against Jews, it repeated ideas prevalent among Catholics in those years, such as that of the Jews' historical aversion to Christians, their obstinacy, and the consequent difficulty of converting them.

As far as World War II is concerned, on the one hand we have already mentioned the diffusion of broadcasts on the deportation and ghettos given by British radio and press in January 1940. On the other hand, from the

German invasion of Poland until the beginning of 1940, *L'Osservatore Romano* gave information on the deportation of the Polish Jews, avoiding using the term "deportation" or mentioning the violence used by the Nazis against the Jews.[41]

The first time that the deportation of the Jews was mentioned by Vatican Radio was in the Italian program of May 13, 1940, which explicitly denounced that "five thousand Poles, Ukrainians and Jews had been deported."[42]

Although Vatican Radio, unlike *L'Osservatore Romano*, used terms like "inhumane deportations," this kind of information was not frequent and, in the broadcasts, antisemitism was presented with, at times, contradictory news and comments. It seems that the announcers gave the news according to their personal sensitivities, not following any given editorial line, expressing the common concern for the Catholic population, the traditional theology on Judaism, traditional stereotypes, and also, in some cases, the condemnation of antisemitism. Some examples will help clarify this picture.

It is known that once the racial laws were issued in several European countries, the ecclesiastical complaints had, as their primary objective, attenuating the effects of these racial legislations on the Jews who had converted to Catholicism. The ecclesiology of those years had, as its main objective, safeguarding the Catholic Church in all its components and expressions, and only, secondarily, what lay outside of it. In January 1940, Fathers Francesco Pellegrino and Francis Joy, respectively in charge of the programs in Italian and English, gave the news on the creation of a committee of assistance by the Hungarian episcopate.[43] On Christmas Day 1939, Archbishop of Kalocsa Monsignor Gyula Zichy issued a pastoral letter to his diocese in which he asked that the Catholic brothers affected by the Second Law on Jews not be abandoned. Father Pellegrino noted that the archbishop's letter concerned the converted Jews because the Church could not forget the divine precept of Christ who commanded charity toward all. For this purpose, the Hungarian episcopate had formed a committee to give material and moral help to all of those who had been affected by the anti-Jewish legislation. Pellegrino explained on Radio Vatican: "This is to avoid that these poor creatures are also threatened in their faith. It took courage and charity to form this committee which by its very physiognomy seems to be a severe criticism of unjust laws." The initiative was "peremptory evidence of the holy freedom of the Church and is not concerned so much about knowing whether its measures will be popular or not as to staying faithful to the teachings of its Divine Teacher."[44]

This committee of Catholics was the Holy Cross Society, an organization founded in 1939 by Mons. Zichy on the wishes of the ordinaries of Hungary and made up of laymen and clergy, with the purpose of helping Catholics of Jewish origin.[45] The Second Law on the Jews, passed by the Hungarian parliament on May 15, 1939, limited the percentage of Jews who could hold government positions and practice certain professions and commercial activities to 5% (compared to the 20% of the First Law of 1938). Cardinal Jusztinián György Serédi, archbishop of Esztergom and primate of Hungary, along with the archbishop of Szeged, Gyula Glatterfelder (members of the Senate in representation of the Catholic episcopate), had supported the antisemitic laws, except to complain that they defined as Jews even those who had been baptized after August 1, 1919, who were *de facto* Catholics.[46] The position of Hungarian Jews progressively worsened. In 1941,[47] Hungary, following their entrance into the war against Russia on the side of Germany, passed another series of anti-Jewish measures. Again, the Church engaged in strong defense only of those Catholics touched by the laws.[48]

A communiqué from a Hungarian agency arrived at the Secretariat of State with a plea in favor of Hungarian Catholic Jews pronounced by Mons. Zichy on Christmas 1939, so that it could be published in *L'Osservatore Romano*. An internal note reveals that "L'Osservatore does not feel it can take the responsibility for the publication" of Zichy's communiqué.[49] The newspaper of the Holy See had published briefly, and without any comment, the news of the approval of the Second Law on the Jews by the Hungarian Chamber of Deputies, before it was ultimately passed by the High Chamber in March 1939.[50] It must be noted that on the same day that Vatican Radio broadcast the news of the creation of the committee in defense of Catholic Jews—perhaps precisely instructed to do so by the Secretariat of State—*L'Osservatore Romano* underlined the successful result of the Italian-Hungarian talks in Venice that sanctioned the "perfect identity of views" between the two governments and the confirmation of the proposition of "friendship and close collaboration."[51]

The topic of relations between Jews and Catholics was brought to the attention of listeners in other programs, especially concerning the difficulties that the arrival of the Jewish refugees in other countries would have created for Catholic populations. The Italian Jesuit Pellegrino, speaking of the situation in Leopoli occupied by the Soviets, was concerned because "in addition to the persecutions of the Bolsheviks against the Catholics there are the reprisals of the Jews, more and more numerous, as 200,000 coming from the territories occupied by the Germans have sought refuge there."[52]

The English Jesuit, Francis Joy, describing the situation of Ukrainian Catholics, foresaw their difficulties increasing, caused by the considerable number of Jews arriving from Poland, "who have always been strongly hostile to Catholics."[53] He repeated this sentiment a few months later, quoting an article in a Catholic newspaper in which Jews and Catholics were invited to collaborate for peaceful coexistence.[54] At the same time though, he reproposed some stereotypes that had been at the basis of the racial legislation that had affected the Jews in the 1930s. For peaceful coexistence among Catholics, non-Catholics, and Jews, they had to give up antisemitism and anti-Catholicism respectively: "There cannot be peace between Catholics and Jews if the formers see a Jewish origin behind every moral or economic evil of our time." It was possible, however, Father Joy continued, that due to the high number of Jewish refugees, Jewish influence would increase in the Catholic countries:

> The growing Jewish control of the film industry is an evil as also is the buying-up of those property. While good Catholics are especially willing to show Christian charity towards Jewish fugitives in these trying times, we have a right to expect not only public utterances of gratitude, but a decrease in the desire for economic control.

The Jewish control over the economy was one of the classic antisemitic accusations, in this case inserted in a context in which Father Joy wanted to paradoxically stimulate Catholics to give up antisemitism. With the same intention, a few hours earlier, Joy read an article from the *Rabbinical Assembly Bulletin* which praised Christian resistance to the neo-paganism of the Third Reich.[55] According to the provost of the Jewish Theological Seminary of America, the severest criticisms of the Nazi regime were made by Pius XI and Pius XII, and the Jews would have remembered this. Quoting the words of the rector of the rabbinical seminary, Joy highlighted the inclination of the medieval popes toward the Jews as an example of the behavior that Catholics ought to have.

However, the desire to reach peaceful coexistence and satisfaction for the help provided to the Jews by the Catholics were accompanied by the fear aroused by convictions rooted in the collective imagination and by the new situation of emergency that the Church and the governments would have had to face, i.e., the forced transfer of whole populations.

A program in Spanish commented on the influence of the Jewish refugees, prompted by an article in an Irish newspaper. The article stated that the Irish were not antisemites and the Jews who had lived in Ireland for a long time had the best qualities: however, the domination of the Jews in industry and trade, in particular textiles, was a different matter, "all the more so because the tastes that the Jews developed in this sector are extraneous to Irish ideas."[56] These were the same limits of the British Jesuit observed above. The antisemitic stereotype conveyed by the Vatican Radio announcer was not only linked to forms of religious anti-Judaism, but also concerned the social threat of the Jews, understood as a people, who could have demonstrated harmful behavior in a society which should have been based on Christian principles.[57]

The Italian and Spanish fathers also analyzed the Jewish immigration to Palestine, against which, according to the Jesuits, Christians, and Muslims ought to have joined forces:

> The Christians are a small minority in Palestine. [...] What are the relations between the different religious groups? The Mahometans are, as is known, the ones who dominate; while the Christians for 1300 years have been considered citizens who are more tolerated than recognized. But they both use the same language. Since the majority of the Muslims descend from apostate Christians, both Muslims and Christians feel compact against Jewish immigration: and this is the first case in history in which converging national interests bring together individuals of such a different religion. It is therefore not lawful to conclude that the two elements will succeed in forming a unique and merged nation. The great difficulty that opposes the merger is the oriental conception of the nation, according to which nationalism is based on the identity of religion.[58]

The interweaving between theological and political reasons for Catholic anti-Zionism is known. The Church awaited the fulfillment of the Pauline prophecy: "a hardening has come upon Israel in part, until the full number of the Gentiles comes in and thus all Israel will be saved" (Rom. 11, 25–26), and as St. Augustine wrote in *De civitate Dei*: "they are found scattered among all nations, in whatever direction the Church of Christ expands" until their definitive conversion to Christianity. Over the centuries, the Holy See's concern was to protect the holy sites under Ottoman rule from Muslims but, especially, from the activities of the Russians on behalf of the Greek Orthodox Church, and also from the increase in Jewish emigration to Palestine.[59] But in the Vatican Radio broadcast, the two announcers highlight, above all else, the convergence of the geopolitical interests of Christians and Muslims which had led to an (albeit precarious) anti-Jewish alliance.

The German announcer, particularly gifted at dealing with theological questions, tried in one of his programs to give a positive interpretation of the ancient bond between God and his people, underlining the role played by the Jews in laying the foundations of the teachings of Christ.[60] In another program on Adam's sin, he recalled that the Catholic truths did not include any racial theory.[61]

However, the announcer who stood out the most was, without a doubt, Father Emmanuel Mistiaen. Only twelve days after his investiture as head of the *État français*, Marshal Pétain and his government, with the law of July 22, 1940, established a commission to review all of the naturalizations granted since 1927 and to withdraw French nationality from those who were judged undesirable. In this way, 6,000 Jews lost French nationality.[62] On August 27, the Marchandeau law decree was revoked. Issued on April 21, 1939, it had punished the press attacks against groups of people belonging to a specific "race" or religion. On October 3, 1940, the Statute of Jews, which defined who was Jewish in the eyes of the French State (according to even stricter rules than those of the laws of Nuremberg), was approved, excluding Jews from any employment that could influence public opinion (teaching, the press, radio, cinema, and theater), and limiting the number of Jews who could practice liberal professions. The following day, another law authorized the prefects to intern the Jews in "special camps" or to assign them a compulsory residence under the close surveillance of the police. On October 7, Algerian Jews were deprived of French nationality. The first ordinance of the government of occupation in northern France was on September 27. In actual fact, the German authorities had already ordered the expulsion of three thousand Alsatian Jews from the region incorporated into the Third Reich, with the intention, at least until 1941, of chasing the Jews out of the territories as they were gradually occupied.

The Catholic hierarchy did not protest, and public opinion was indifferent.[63] Vatican Radio did not broadcast any information on the antisemitic measures taken in France, but Mistiaen found ways to allude to them through the condemnation of the ancient heresy of Marcionism. In the program of November 17, 1940, published by *La Croix* a few weeks later, the Jesuit tackled the subject in these terms:

> In the face of the most unbridled Marcionism, the Church defends the sole truth than can satisfy all men, save them from separations and from fratricide struggles, give them a common purpose and claim the essential equality of human nature: a single God. [. . .] This is our first answer to those who want to divide men.[64]

The Church's condemnation of Marcionist anti-Judaism, characterized by the rejection of the Old Testament and by the distinction between a severe God of the Jews and a merciful one of the Christians, was evoked by Mistiaen with the clear intention of condemning modern antisemitism. Pierre Limagne, in a note to his *Ephémérides,* wrote that Vichy censorship had not understood "the relationship between Marcion and ... Hitler" and had therefore allowed the publication of this script by *La Croix.*[65]

The last news broadcast of the year, addressing antisemitism, was given in French on November 30 in a bulletin which announced, quoting the leading Italian press agency, Agenzia Stefani, that the measures taken against the Jews in the Netherlands had caused a strike of forty-eight hours by lecturers and students at the Universities of Delft and Leiden. The first anti-Jewish decree in the Netherlands had been issued on October 22, 1940: as well as defining who was to be considered Jewish, it ordered the census of Jewish companies and their "Aryanization." The Germans imposed the closure of the universities until there was a new order.[66]

In 1941, the mass deportations of Jews from the territories of the Reich took place, which were to be ultimately concluded by their murder in the extermination camps; in the same year the construction of the ghettos of Krakow and Lublin was completed (the Warsaw ghetto had already been finished in Fall 1940). After the invasion of the Soviet Union, the SS and the political police units received the order to kill the Jewish populations on the spot during their advance, while the Reichssicherheitshauptamt-RSHA (the Central Office of the Security of the Reich) had been appointed to organize their massacre.[67] As historiography has demonstrated, the Holy See was not yet aware of Hitler's program of annihilation, but certainly knew about the deportations and the very real condemnation to death to which the deported Jews were destined.[68]

Very little, or nothing at all, of this was leaked by the Catholic press or Vatican Radio. If we exclude the programs on racism, in 1941 those broadcasts concerning the Jews were few and insisted on the Catholic teachings on Judaism, without providing any information on the terrifying condition of the Jews in Europe. In some programs in German, Judaism was mentioned in regard to its relationship with Christianity, for example, to defend it from the blaming of the *Gottgläubingen,* who scorned "the Jewish race" for having created a "so-called prophetic religion" from which Christianity descended.[69] Other times, through one of the most common stereotypes, the "influential" Jews were accused of launching anti-Catholic campaigns together with the Protestants.[70]

What seems significant to highlight, and which the scripts read on Vatican Radio and the articles in the Catholic press have in common (with exceptions that have and will be commented on), is the persistence of the coexistence of the condemnation of racist theories alongside the stereotypes of religious anti-Judaism. The Italian announcer, for example, read an article by Aristide Brunello on the Octave of Prayer for Christian Unity on the same day as its publication in *L'Osservatore Romano*.[71] The Jesuit invited his audience to pray "for the amendment and the conversion" of the Jewish people. They were called the "prodigious people" and "fortunate people" for having enjoyed the light of the Revelation, but also recalled that on Good Friday each year, the Church "remembering the tremendous deicide committed by this people," prayed in its favor, "asking God for the veil that prevented Jews from seeing the truth to be removed, that their hearts convert, that their blindness stops and that at last they recognize Jesus." The Octave, which was held every year from January 18 to 25, included the recital of prayers for the restoration of the unity of the Church, i.e., the return of the "infidels, schismatics and heretics" to Catholicism. The Jews were part of the first group and, in his exhortation, Brunello repeated what Catholic tradition taught about them and how it could be remedied: their blindness and obstinacy in the face of the divinity of Jesus, the accusation of deicide, and the prayer for their change of mind recited on Good Friday.[72] The decision of the Italian announcer to read this article on Vatican Radio, and to give it further resonance, cannot be overlooked. It is not only a question of acknowledging what is obvious, i.e., that the interpretation of the role of Judaism in the economy of the salvation had not been questioned, but of taking note of the detachment in the mindset of the majority of the clergy and the Catholic hierarchy between the level of religious belief and the level of reality, and how the former systematically prevailed over the other.

Two years later, Vatican Radio dedicated a daily lecture to each Christian denomination, but also included one regarding the conversion of Jews and Muslims.[73] On January 23, 1943, the one on the Israelites, given by Monsignor Ferrero di Cavallerleone, went on the air.[74] Despite the recognition of the bond between Judaism and Christianity, the Jews were accused of deicide and invited to convert. The divine punishment for having despised Christ, which is why the Jewish nation had not known joy or peace, was recalled. It was necessary to pray for its conversion while making it understood that, in this attitude, there was no intention of destroying its individuality as a people. The existence of different "groups of Jews" could be recognized, but "only after having rejected, according to the law of reason and the teachings of Christ, the theory of the racial division of human beings." It was the usual distinction between an anti-Judaism that could be overcome through conversion, and racial antisemitism which was not acceptable because it denied the work of God as the creator of man.

During 1942, the programs that condemned racism and quoted pastoral letters by bishops who called for the unity of the human race were fairly frequent. Nevertheless, the attention on Jews as a people, as the victims of persecution, seems to remain scarce.

One example of this is the choice made by the editors of Vatican Radio in the face of two texts from the Dutch episcopate. A program broadcast between July 20 and 29 in Italian, and then in English and Polish, included the message by Archbishop of Utrecht Johannes de Jong on sterilization. He reminded Catholic doctors that, as the Dutch authorities had lost control over medical questions, they had to be aware of attempts to force them to carry out practices contrary to Catholic ethics, and to oppose these with all the means at their disposal. The archbishop, continued the announcer, had been attacked because he had repeatedly declared that he was against sterilization because of its negative consequences.[75] However, Vatican Radio did not broadcast the pastoral letter of public protest against the deportation of the Jews, prepared in collaboration by the Catholic bishops and representatives of the Dutch Reformed Churches on July 20, and read from the pulpits on July 26, 1942. We know that the text was not sent to Pius XII until October 9 by the internuncio of the Hague, Monsignor Giobbe, together with another letter from the archbishop of Utrecht and the Dutch bishops against the deportation of Christian Jews.[76] On July 28, the pope was briefly informed, by the nuncio in Berlin, that in the Netherlands, the deportations of "non-Aryans" had begun, but that a joint complaint by the Protestants and the Catholic bishops had prevented there also being "Catholic non-Aryans" among them. The information turned out to be false.[77]

Perhaps Vatican Radio did not have more detailed information on the pastoral letter of July 26, when the news of Cardinal de Jong's position on sterilization was broadcast. However, it cannot be ruled out that the text had reached Vatican Radio in those days, or even later, and that it was a deliberate decision not to broadcast the pastoral letter in defense of the Jews. Its reading during public religious functions in the Netherlands had caused reprisals by the German authorities, which ordered the deportation of all the Jews, including those who had converted who were, until then, excluded thanks to an agreement between the Christian Churches and the Reichskommissar.[78]

The most interesting program is the one broadcast in French on the evening of September 14, 1942. The BBC monitor tried to transcribe the script, but the reception was very disturbed.[79] The first concepts summarized by the monitor recalled "the symbolism of the Cross," "Mankind's most precious possession. The world would pass judgement under it, on those disloyal to Christianity. Each individual was entitled to the same rights and privileges as his fellows." The jamming of Vatican Radio became even greater later but, perhaps to make up for the loss of the content, the monitor described the tone of voice of the Vatican announcer:

> His voice rising to tones of anger and indignation, the commentator is then heard mentioning the words "Jews" and "treason", adding: 'What right has one section of humanity—after 20 centuries of Christianity to ... with the freedom of the children of God?'

Fortunately, we have the entire script that was broadcast by the French Resistance.[80] The program was dedicated to the Exaltation of the Cross, celebrated on September 14: a cross, Mistiaen said, that was often attacked. In the part that the BBC had not been able to transcribe, Mistiaen referred to the Jews as the "chosen people" who gave birth to Jesus:

> He [Our Lord Jesus Christ] bent down first over the sheep that belonged to his beloved people, to the Jewish people, to all those of his race from whom the salvation of the world came, to which his mother, his friends and his apostles belonged. He bent known with infinite love over this Jewish people.

The words and tone used by Mistiaen about the Jewish people conveyed a positive message which, although it had been present at other times in Vatican Radio programs, had been frequently accompanied by reservations. It was followed by a reminder of the love of God for all men, and there was recognition of their equal dignity, Mistiaen asked:

> With what right, yes, with what right, after 20 centuries of Christianity can a man still make differences between men; with what right does he declare himself a judge of men, with what right does he treat them as if they did not enjoy the freedom of the children of God? How to hope, therefore, after so many historical events, to be able to separate men, and degrade a considerable part of them and how to hope to succeed?

He concluded by inviting the faithful to do what true Christians were summoned to do, namely:

> We must have profound respect for human nature, and it is a duty to proclaim more respect, more solidarity and love even for those who are more unfortunate, more abandoned, and more persecuted. It is here that the mark of the

real Christian lies. We must do everything to support these unfortunate and persecuted people, because we do not have the right, without committing a major sin, of participating in the tragedies and in the degradation of men for whom Our Lord died.

Mistiaen was speaking to a France which, in the immediately preceding months had undergone important changes at political level, with tragic consequences for the destiny of the French Jews. In the French Free Zone in 1941, new antisemitic measures had been taken: on June 2, the second Statute on the Jews had been passed, which further extended the number of those who were subject to discrimination; and from July, Jews had been excluded from any State employment, with the institution of the *numerus clausus* in schools and liberal professions. From the Drancy internment camp in the Occupied Zone, and Compiègne, the first convoy left for Auschwitz on March 27, 1942, transporting the Jews who had been arrested in Paris between the previous August and December.[81] On July 16 and 17, there was the "great round-up of the Winter Velodrome (Vél d'hiv)," that is the arrest and internment in the velodrome of the 15th arrondissement of Paris of an (estimated) 28,000 Jews, stateless or foreigners.[82] In April, Laval had returned to power as the head of the government of Vichy and had reinforced his alliance with Germany. In early July, together with Pétain, he gave his assent for the deportation of foreign Jews from Vichy. The great operation of the search for and deportation of Jews to Drancy, and from there toward the east, took place.[83]

The operations of the summer of 1942 caused a decisive change in French public opinion, which until that time, had generally not been very concerned by the French-German management of the "Jewish question." The tone of anger and indignation with which Mistiaen read his script on the radio clearly reflects the state of mind of a religious who, aware of what was happening in France and elsewhere, tried to make his listeners understand the tragic nature of the event, although through carefully measured words. The care taken in describing the relationship between God and the Jewish people seems an attempt at recalling particular attention to the subject. However, between this speech and the one in which he asked how it was possible to degrade a part of humanity, warning the Catholics to avoid taking part in humanity's debasement, Mistiaen included a passage which opened up the message of Christian salvation in a universalistic sense:

> He [the Lord] bent over all the sheep in the world and St John tells us, before his passion, he went amongst the Gentiles. He greeted in them the promises of the Christian world. The first effort of his disciples when they entered the

pagan mass of the universe was to give men the feeling of human dignity. Those who refused in their heart to recognize the dignity of all the children of God commit a sacrilege; [...] Jesus died for all men.

Mistiaen's words clashed with the mandate of caution adopted by the Holy See as well as by the Catholic hierarchy in France.[84] Nuncio Valeri informed Cardinal Maglione of the internment at the Vél' d'hiv' and of the decision, made at a meeting of cardinals and archbishops, not to make their protest public but to have Cardinal Suhard write a confidential letter to Pétain.[85] The same nuncio, however, reassured the Holy See that it was a "fairly platonic protest."[86]

In early August, Valeri had to inform Rome that deportations had also begun in the French Free Zone.[87] Some French bishops condemned what had happened: the most accurate words came from Monsignor Jules-Géraud Saliège and were circulated in the parishes of the diocese of Toulon.[88] Bishop of Montauban Pierre-Marie Théas, on August 30, also had a letter of vigorous protest for the deportations read out.[89] The words, the concepts, and the style of Mistiaen were very close to those of the two French bishops, but it is not possible to clarify whether Mistiaen knew of their letters or not.[90] The essential difference, however, remains: the program of Vatican Radio made no precise reference to the deportations that had taken place. The decision, clearly made at higher levels, had to do with the relations of the Holy See with Vichy. There was no wish to break away from Vichy and the loyalty to Pétain was not in question, being fully reasserted by the ecclesiastical hierarchies between September and October.[91]

The denunciation of the racial laws in Croatia

When the Independent State of Croatia (NDH) was proclaimed on April 10, 1941, it had approximately 6.5 million inhabitants, the majority of whom were Catholics: of the remainder, 30% were Orthodox Serbs (1,845,000 people) and 0.6% were Jews (39,000).[92] The fundamental ideological principle of the Ustaša was "the reference to the Catholic-Islamic Croatian ethnic unity against the Balkan-Asian Serbs," a racial nationalism corroborated by antisemitism.[93] Only twenty days after the birth of the new State, led by Ante Pavelić with the title of Poglavnik (the guide), two racist decrees were passed: one on racial affinity and the other on the protection of the blood and the Aryan honor of the Croatian people. If, for the Orthodox-Serbian minority, it was difficult to talk in terms of racial identity, for the Jews and the Roma the task was easier because it was sufficient to be inspired by the laws of Nuremberg. The first law decreed that an individual was to be considered "Aryan" if he could prove having an "Aryan" forefather through a certificate of birth, baptism, or marriage of his parents and grandparents.[94] The same decree established that those who had at least three Jewish grandparents were to be considered of the "Jewish race."[95] A second measure prohibited marriage between "Aryans" and "non-Aryans."

The capture and deportation of Jews to the Jasenovac concentration camp, organized directly by the Ustaša, began in May 1941. Archbishop of Zagreb Aloysius Stepinac intervened immediately by sending various letters to the minister of Internal Affairs, Andrija Artuković, in defense of the Jews who had converted to Catholicism who were being affected by the racial laws, and to ask for the suppression of the obligation by the Israelites to wear the star of David.[96] The Croatian Episcopal Conference, meeting from November 17 to 20, 1941, addressed a petition to Pavelić which was sent to the Holy See by Stepinac, together with a brief account of the assembly. In the appeal, the Croatian bishops asked that the personal and civil liberties of the Jews who had converted to Catholicism, who for this reason could no longer be considered Jews, were protected, together with their property.[97]

Before thousands of Croatian Jews were deported to Auschwitz in August 1942, Stepinac again tried to make the government desist from proceeding with the massacre of "innocent people," "citizens who individually cannot be accused of any crime."[98] In addition to the persecution of the Jews, the region was the scene of mass deportations and massacres of Serbs and Roma. The Serbs who lived in Croatia were forced to move to Serbia, occupied by the Germans: those who remained were forced to convert to Catholicism or interned in the concentrations camps where many were killed.[99]

The Holy See sent an apostolic visitor, Benedictine Abbot Giuseppe Ramiro Marcone, to the new Croatia, which presented itself as a Catholic State, to encourage relations with the Ustaša government.[100] Secretary of State Maglione entrusted him with the answer to the letter from Stepinac, which informed the Holy See of what the Bishops' Conference had decided, praising the attention of the Croatian bishops to the Jews and, above all, the claim of the right to deal with the conversions to Catholicism, which had to be sincere and not forced.[101] A few months later, Maglione, in a letter to the archbishop of Belgrade, renewed the importance of the free and intimate "return of the dissidents to the Catholic Church" against any external pressure, where "dissidents" meant the Orthodox.[102] The international press had spoken of "forced conversions" which took place in Croatia, so Vatican Radio was instructed to dissociate the Catholic Church from this accusation. In a program in English, it was assured that no type of pressure had been exercised by the civil and ecclesiastical authorities on the conversions to

Catholicism.[103] Vatican Radio, used to answering anti-Catholic propaganda on the religious situation, maintained that in the ancient conflict between Catholic and Orthodox, the part of the victims and of the torturers was played alternately by both, therefore it was important to be cautious in accusing the Church.

As far as the "Jewish question" is concerned, on March 30, 1943, Maglione asked Marcone to speak to the government so that the deportation of baptized Jews who remained in Croatia could be avoided.[104] The request had been solicited by a telegram from the apostolic delegate in Washington, Amleto Cicognani, who had sent the plea of some rabbis to Pius XII so that he might intervene to stop the deportation of the Jews.[105] On April 2, Maglione wrote again to Marcone to inform him that Orthodox Serbian propaganda was accusing the Catholics, and in particular the Croatian episcopate, of not having protested against the mistreatment inflicted by the Croatian government on the Serb population, but on the contrary, of even having collaborated.[106] Maglione warned Marcone about these accusations which could "cause significant damage to the prestige of the Catholic name," and asked him to speak to the archbishop of Zagreb to highlight the inaccuracy of these statements, inviting him to collect and send to him "all those elements that could be of use, if the circumstances required it, to opportunely enlighten public opinion." The documents at our disposal do not specify who was responsible for the anti-Catholic propaganda, if it was the Yugoslavian government in exile, the Chetniks (the pan-Serbian resistance movement), or the communist partisans of Tito.

On May 8, 1943, Marcone sent a memorandum on the attitude of the Catholic clergy toward the Orthodox Serbs to the Maglione, stating that the episcopate had protested against the "interferences by the government on the conversion of the schismatics," claiming jurisdiction over the evangelization of the peoples with respect to "freedom of conscience."[107] Stepinac, visiting Rome from May 28 to June 4, brought with him the evidence of what the Croatian Church had done in favor of the Serbian and Jewish minorities.[108] The Secretariat of State was thus able to prepare a list of the thirty-four documents presented by Stepinac.[109]

In the meantime, Vatican Radio began to be increasingly involved in Croatian affairs. On March 6, 1943, Stepinac protested the racial discriminations by the government: he had contacted Pavelić to prevent the annulment of mixed marriages; to ask him to guarantee "the most elementary right, the right to life" of all of the converts to Catholicism, whether from Judaism or Orthodox Christianity; and to not allow other deportations of innocent people.[110] On March 14, the archbishop pronounced a sermon in which he stated that "every man, of whatever race or nation, [. . .] carries within himself the imprint of God the Creator and has inalienable rights of which he cannot be deprived arbitrarily or limited by any human power."[111] He was able to ensure that Jewish wives, with their children, were not arrested and sent to the concentration camps.[112] On May 12, Vatican Radio broadcast in German a summary of Stepinac's interventions:

> In Croatia, early in March this year, all Jews, including those who had become Catholics but who, according to the Nurnberg Laws, are still regarded as Jews, were requested to register with the police. As it was feared that they would be taken to concentration camps, the Archbishop of Zagreb lodged an energic protest with Dr. Pavelitch as soon as the order was published. On the following Sunday the Archbishop defined his attitude to this order in a sermon. He said, 'No worldly power, no political organization, has the right to persecute a man on account of the race to which he belongs. Christian bishops oppose this and will fight against such persecutions.' A few days later the orders were withdrawn by the State authorities.[113]

The declarations of the archbishop referred to the attempt to deport the Croatian Jews who had remained in the zone occupied by the Germans.[114] Unlike other broadcasts we have previously seen, this one explicitly referred to the Jews as victims of discrimination, saying that they were in danger of being taken to concentration camps, and explicitly spoke of the persecution against them.

On July 6, 1943, Vatican Radio (again in German) returned to the question of racism, presenting the zeal of Stepinac as a model for the fight of the Catholic Church against the violation of human rights. The program opened as follows:

> At the present time it is more necessary than ever to point out the inviolability of human rights granted by God. In this we follow the words of the Supreme Shepherd of the Church and other priests of the Catholic world, and a special importance must be given to utterances of the bishops. It was possible to read in the press, even in the neutral press, that the bishops of the territory of Croatia had not done their duty to explain and defend human and Christian rights; this is wrong. Both jointly and individually they have made their position clear on this question. One of the best-known fighters for the rights of man and moral freedom is the Archbishop of Zagreb, Mgr. Dr. Alois Stepinac. In many sermons he has branded the violation of morals and of the doctrines of the church. In innumerable written memoranda and verbal

interventions, he fought the cause of all those who are unjustly persecuted, be they Jews, Serbians, Gypsies or Catholic Croats. He was, and it [sic] is, the only refuge for these people. A special chapter is his charitable action for all without distinction of religion or nationality.[115]

The announcer continued by reading some extracts of Stepinac's sermon for the Feast of Christ the King on October 25, 1942, the text of which was part of the set of documents taken to Rome and presented to Pius XII on May 30, 1943, proving the activities of the Croatian Catholic Church in favor of Jews and Serbs.[116]

Jews were also explicitly mentioned in this broadcast. It must be specified that the Vatican Radio announcer explained that Stepinac had given that sermon when a decree of the Ustaša government had ordered the registration of all Jews, imposing upon them the obligation of wearing a distinctive sign, proceeding with the confiscation of their property and, lastly, their internment.

As a matter of fact, the decree mentioned dated back to April 1941, while the first phase of deportations to Auschwitz began in July 1942. In August 1941, Maglione, having learned of the first deportations to Jasenovac concentration camp, which had begun a few weeks earlier, had written to Marcone: "If Your Eminence can find a suitable occasion, you should recommend, in a very discreet way, that is not interpreted as official, the use of moderation in relation to the Jews in Croatian territory. Your Eminence should act in such a way that . . . the impression of local cooperation with the civil authorities is preserved."[117]

The ambiguity of the Holy See's position with regard to the Croatian regime, which proclaimed itself to be manifestly Catholic, was clear from the outset so that it prompted Maglione to ask about the Jews, but without giving the impression that the Holy See wanted to break with the civil authorities on this issue. In any case, the chronology of the events does not correspond with the one given by Vatican Radio: the programs of 1943 were the only ones that denounced the racial laws in Croatia,[118] but Maglione's letter proves that the Vatican was well informed on the destiny of the Croatian Jews from the beginning, so why wait two years before broadcasting the news? The fact that the original text of the July broadcast is preserved, unlike the others, among the papers of the *Commissione Soccorsi*, suggests that there is a connection between this broadcast and the documents taken to Rome by Stepinac. Vatican Radio could have been ordered to make broadcasts that highlighted what the Croatian episcopate had done in defense of the minorities under the Ustaša regime, aiming to prove the groundlessness of the anti-Catholic propaganda. If, in the summer 1941, Pius XII wanted to avoid compromising the relationship with Pavelić's regime, and in the following year had left Stepinac to deal with the Ustaša's crimes, in 1943 he must have considered it advantageous to raise a protest through the radio in defense of the Croatian episcopate and the Holy See from anti-Catholic charges.

After the telegram from Cicognani at the end of March 1943, in which the apostolic delegate asked what the Holy See could do to prevent the deportation of the Jews,[119] Cardinal Maglione wrote down a list of the nunciatures to ask for information.[120] In this note, the secretary of state wondered whether it was opportune to explicitly mention the interest of the Holy See in the telegram reply to Cicognani. He decided that "An open mention would not seem convenient, not only because we never know what may happen from one moment to the next . . . but also to prevent Germany learning of the declarations of the Holy See, making the anti-Jewish measures in the territories they occupy even more severe and make new and stronger insistences on the Governments of the Axis." Three months later, Vatican Radio announced in German what the Catholic Church was doing in favor of the Jews. Since Vatican Radio was not considered an official organ by the Holy See, the programs in German could have been a way to break the silence. This tactic had already been tested between 1940 and 1941: every time a representative of the German Embassy or a diplomat from other countries complained about Vatican Radio programs, the Secretariat of State answered that the Curia was not informed of their contents because it was not the official radio of the Holy See. In this case as well, Vatican Radio helped the Vatican keep its difficult diplomatic balance.

To conclude, assumptions can be made as to the reasons why Vatican Radio decided to broadcast this news in German. If these programs were directed to the Balkans, it must be considered that Vatican Radio did not broadcast in Serb-Croatian; the most popular foreign language in those territories was still German, considering the long domination of the Habsburg Empire. This is confirmed by the letters in German from listeners who wrote to Vatican Radio in 1941.[121] Alternatively, if the intention of the programs was to affect the propaganda of the Serbian Resistance, in which the British government could have been involved,[122] German was still the best language to use for two reasons. If, on the one hand, answering in English would have been too direct, on the other hand, the Vatican knew perfectly well that its radio station was monitored by the British who could easily receive and translate the German programs. The BBC, like Radio New York, rebroadcast, in Serbo-Croatian, the July 6 Vatican Radio program in

German on July 7 and 8.¹²³ In addition, showing the action of Archbishop Stepinac, challenging the disturbance by the Nazis or their complaints, reinforced the counterpropaganda of the Catholic Church in the eyes of the world.

The Slovakian episcopate and the Jews

Monsignor Jozef Tiso became president of Slovakia after the declaration of independence on March 14, 1939, under German protection. The anti-Jewish measures of the Slovakian State, collected in the Law of September 9, 1941, were passed in a climate of widespread antisemitism, corroborated by the equally widespread traditional Catholic anti-Judaism, which is why they found no resistance in the population or in the episcopate, whose actions were limited to the defense of the Catholic Jews.¹²⁴

The fact that Slovakia had proclaimed itself a Catholic State, with a priest at its head, pushed the Secretariat of State of Pius XII to intervene with greater decision, both through the chargé d'affaires in Bratislava, Giuseppe Burzio, and with letters from Maglione to the Slovakian prime minister.¹²⁵ As Tardini had noted in his answer to British Minister Osborne, who urged the Vatican to complain about the deportations of the Slovakian Jews, "the Holy See cannot make Hitler stay in his place, everyone understands that. But that it cannot curb a priest, who can understand it?"¹²⁶ In March 1942, the deportation of all Jews, except for those baptized before March 14, 1939, was ordered. In a telegram, Burzio informed Rome of the imminent deportation, specifying that it was an initiative taken by Prime Minister Tuka, without any pressure by Germany.¹²⁷ President Tiso had "vehemently defended the legitimacy of the measure and dared to say (he who so greatly displays his Catholicism) that he sees nothing inhuman or anti-Christian in it." The note closed with the clarification that the "deportation 80,000 people to Poland at the mercy of the Germans is equivalent to condemning the majority to certain death." Maglione tried to intervene again through Minister Karol Sidor, while the Slovakian episcopate, which until then, also according to Burzio, had not been too energetic, published a collective letter to deplore the measures against the Jews.¹²⁸

In early 1943, the rumors of an imminent "displacement" of Slovakian Jews caused the episcopate to intervene again. This time, Vatican Radio, which until then had been silent on the Slovakian case, broadcast in French, English, and German the collective pastoral letter of March 8, which was read in the churches on March 21.¹²⁹ In the letter, the bishops proclaimed the principles of natural law according to which "nobody must be persecuted or punished without sufficient reasons [. . .]. If one or more members of a nation a group or a national minority are guilty this does not mean that a whole nation, a group or a national minority are." The State had to defend natural law because it was at the basis of the Constitution, which stated that nobody could be punished for an action that was not criminal. Therefore, the episcopate felt that it was their duty to raise their voice "against the measures that affect masses not only of people of our religion but also other compatriots of ours, without a careful preliminary examination of the responsibilities of each one of them." In the second part of the pastoral letter, another document was referred to, signed by the episcopate the year before, on the baptism of the Jews.[130] It was the collective letter, published on April 26, 1942, addressed to those who had protested against administering forced baptism of the Jews and to ask that they be treated humanely. The letter recalled that the Church could not refuse to baptize those who had given proof of their sincerity in their desire to convert and promised to respect the religious and moral precepts of Catholicism. It was a necessary clarification after a certain discontent had been recorded among the Catholic faithful for the neophytes, due to the life they led before becoming Christians. This is what Vatican Radio said:

> We address ourselves to those who say they would not go to Church if this or that person were there, and who repulse the converted instead of helping them by word and example in faith and in Christian life. If we demand that civic rights and the protection of the State should be granted to every citizen without distinction of origin and nationality, we demand all the more emphatically the acknowledgment of all Christian rights for everyone who has received the Holy Sacrament of Baptism.

The pastoral letter, translated from Slovakian, was sent by Burzio to the Secretariat of State on April 10, and they clearly gave a copy of it to Vatican Radio.[131]

The events linked to the document were reported by the Vatican chargé d'affaires to Maglione. Slovakian Minister of Internal Affairs Alexander Mach, having learned of the contents of the collective letter four days before it was read out from the pulpits, called the bishop of Nitra to ask him to desist from the intention of making it known. In his turn, the bishop asked the auxiliary bishop of Trnovo to tell Mach that it was impossible to withdraw the document and, regarding the minimization of its effect, "the best thing will be to leave the affair to run its course [. . .]. In a week, nobody will be talking about it anymore. [. . .] The text of the common declaration is such that it cannot offend anyone."[132] Satisfied, the minister did not raise any further objections. According to a report by German Ambassador Hans Ludin, however, the letter encountered the resistance of some bishops when it was being drawn up and some priests refused to read it out.[133] After Burzio's intervention to avert the deportation of the Jews who were left in Slovakia, the secretary of state had also protested with a note to the Slovakian legation.[134] It is probable that the broadcasting of the letter of the Slovakian episcopate by Vatican Radio was part of the strategy to show that the Catholic Church had not been silent in the face of the discriminations against the Jews. Looking closely, however, it was about making known a general ill-treatment, to denounce once again, above all, the extension of the racial laws to converted Jews and to warn of other general "measures" against them.[135]

The last hope for the Hungarian Jews:
Requests for the intervention of the Holy See through Vatican Radio

As will be seen in the next chapter, after the occupation of Rome by the Germans, Vatican Radio decreased the number, the duration, and the content of its programs. Until Rome's liberation in June 1944, the little news on the Italian situation was accompanied by absolute silence on other fronts.

Perhaps the most deafening silence was that concerning the political upheavals in Hungary and the fate of the Hungarian Jews from March 1944. The establishment of a government controlled by the Germans meant the application of the "final solution" on the only Jewish community that had been able to escape extermination among the States controlled by the Nazis.[136] The Hungarian Catholic Church was not able to oppose it in any way.[137] Although Pius XII had written to the regent of Hungary, Miklós Horthy and the Hungarian government had been "submerged by a flood of telegrams" from the Holy See, the primate of Hungary, Cardinal Serédi, answered the representative of the Christian Jews at the Jewish Council of Budapest, Sándor Török, who had suggested excommunicating those who were compromised in the antisemitic operations, in these terms: "If His Holiness the Pope does nothing against Hitler, what can I do in my narrower jurisdiction?"[138] On September 6, the Apostolic Nuncio Angelo Rotta sent a telegram to the Holy See stating that the Red Army was about to cross the Hungarian frontier and that the Holy See's intercession with the British and the Americans would be of help.[139] On the Jews, however, he reported: "The question of the Jews has lost its severity; elements responsible for the enormities committed have been eliminated." In actual fact, there had been the mere replacement of the prime minister: following the pro-German Sztojay, the reticent collaborator Lakatos became the head of the government.[140] On September 23, Tardini wrote to the delegate in

Washington, sending him Rotta's message both on the danger of the Soviet invasion and the apparent normalization of the Jewish question.¹⁴¹ On September 27, the same reassurance was sent by Cicognani to Leon Kubowitzki of the World Jewish Congress, who had asked Pius XII to intervene in favor of the Hungarian Jews: "The situation in Hungary is much less severe, since the people responsible for the persecutions have been removed."¹⁴²

At the same time, Horthy had written to Pius XII, telling him of the tragic situation in his country and of the Jews in particular.¹⁴³ The pope answered him one month later that, as in the past, even now he would not have left anything untried to avoid the horrors of the war.¹⁴⁴

The little news on Hungary was given by Vatican Radio in Spanish on August 24 and mainly concerned the arrival of refugees in Rome, where, it was said, they could have found free medical consultation.¹⁴⁵ A few days later, again in Spanish, a speech by Cardinal Serédi for the Feast of the Assumption, was broadcast. In it he said that society had to be based on the family, the nation, and the Church.¹⁴⁶

The Soviet invasion of Hungary started in October. The head of the Arrow Cross Party, Szalasi, became the new prime minister and ordered the deportation of the Jews who were left, and they were evacuated in forced marches in the absence of an adequate system of transport. The delegate in Washington, Cicognani, sent a telegram to the Secretariat of State with the following message:

> Rabbis and Representatives of Jewish Committees continue to come to the Apostolic Delegation to beg the Holy Father, as situation desperate for the Jews in Hungary, make an appeal over Vatican Radio to the Hungarian people so that every citizen who can take in and protect the Jews. The Apostolic Nunciature can perhaps do nothing at this time while Vatican Radio appeal (?), including through the secret organization that is very active, it would be immediately known and well received and would be very useful, especially in the provincial cities and in the countryside where it seems that the German army and police are not yet sufficiently organized.¹⁴⁷

Tardini immediately sent the following telegram to Budapest:

> According to news received Jews Hungary are again threatened by deportation and persecution. I beg Your Excellency the Most Rev. to send me some information on this. Holy See relies on constant action Your Excellency and Episcopate for all possible protection of the persecuted.¹⁴⁸

Monsignor Angelo Dell'Acqua, then *minutante* of the Secretariat of State, wrote a note in which he asked whether the Holy See should not make a more general appeal, not only in favor of the Hungarian Jews, but also of the Catholics who, in different countries, were persecuted. It is worth quoting the full text:

> The rabbis in Washington—as noted by the coded message sent by His Excellence the Apostolic Delegate—insist on a public appeal by the Holy See in favor of the Jews of Hungary. There can be no doubt that the situation of the Jews in Hungary is very serious and many of them may already have been killed. We therefore must come to their aid with every possible action. But we must not forget that the situation of many Catholics in various countries is no less serious, such as in Italy, in Hungary itself, and in Poland. As for Italy, from the recent reports sent by the Most Excellent ordinaries of Tuscany, the dead, the executed in the region of Tuscany are in their hundreds. Now, even before the Jews, the Catholic are entitled to a public intervention by the Holy See, because war, even in its already harsh necessities, must be conducted in a human and loyal way. The war has now reached a point that we can call tremendous, for the systems, truly inhuman, that have been adopted and tend to become even harsher [...] In the case of Italy, for example, as well as the action on Germany, an action on the allies and on the Italian government itself would be needed for them to desist from inciting the partisans from killing the Germans in any place and in any way [...] Concluding: Any public appeal should not, in my opinion, be limited to the Hungarian Jewish question, but have a much wider and more general character.[149]

Even more emblematic from Dell'Acqua's point of view is the note written on October 23:

> This Note was written on Saturday based on the coded message of Washington. Now I see the telegram to Baron Apor from which the situation of the Hungarian Jews is apparently immensely serious. If superior motives were to advise against a more general appeal, a new public action by the Holy See in favor of the Jews of Hungary would appear appropriate, *si vera sunt exposita*. The idea of an open telegram to Cardinal Seredy could be taken into consideration.[150]

Two *memoranda* reached the Holy See: one from the United States dated October 25, delivered to Pius XII by Taylor on October 28, the other on

November 1, sent by Osborne to support Cicognani's suggestion. Despite the insistent requests, Vatican Radio did not broadcast any public message.[151]

As has been observed, the decision of Pius XII to remain silent on the Shoah was not due to a lack of information on the fate of the deportees, or to pro-Nazism, but was a tragic and aware choice,[152] closely connected with the decision to keep the Holy See's line of impartiality right until the end.[153] Perhaps the authority of a word proffered by the Holy See would have awoken the consciences of the Catholics and would have spurred them to a bolder resistance, or at least alert the Jews who could have tried to seek safety. Moreover, requests for appeals of this type had already arrived at the Secretariat of State the previous year, but even then, they had remained unanswered.

On January 22, 1943, Angelo Giuseppe Roncalli, apostolic delegate in Istanbul, sent Maglione the proposals put forward by Rabbi Chaim Barlas of the Jewish Agency for Palestine to the regent of the nunciature in Cairo, White Father Arthur Hughes, to ask the Holy See to try and help the Jews flee from the Reich and intercede for them to arrive in Palestine.[154] In addition, the Holy See was also asked to "declare in a possible appeal on the radio [...] that helping the persecuted Jews is considered a good action by the Church. This would reinforce the feelings of those Catholics who, as we know and appreciate, help the Jews who are condemned to die of starvation in the occupied territories in Europe." In his answer, Maglione assured that the Holy See "has not failed to do what was in its power to make the severe conditions of the Jewish populations in some countries less difficult," but declared it was impossible to intercede for the transfer of the Jews to neutral countries, or at least to Palestine, "in the freedom of which the Holy See is so very interested. This observation is, naturally, of a confidential nature for Your Paternity."[155] The third point indicated by Barlas, the one concerning the appeal to be broadcast by Vatican Radio, was completely avoided by the secretary of state, yet the representative of the Jewish Agency was only asking the Holy See for a simple declaration, moreover, easily justifiable as an act of charity and assistance which was fully part of the Catholic Church's ideology.

Since the 1960s, historians have never ceased to question the motives that led Pius XII to choose absolute public reserve on the fate of the European Jews.[156] The *lectio facilior* of a pro-Nazi and antisemitic pope has had a certain following, but it has also been finely confuted.[157] Extending, however, the question to the rest of the Catholic hierarchy, the reasons for the actions or inertia are perhaps to be sought in the way and extent to which they were capable, or incapable, of reading the historical change that they were living through in the light of their own biography, which was part of a history of the Catholic Church of which these reasons were a constituent part. What happened in the final moments of the five years of war reinforces this hypothesis. Pius XII's speech to the Sacred College on June 2, 1945 is well known: he spoke of the Nazi crimes, of the persecution of the Church in Germany, and of the Polish clergy, but he did not mention the extermination of the Jews.[158] The fact that Pius XII, not even when the war was over, spoke an explicit word on the drama of the Jewish people, clearly reflects a mindset that has to be explained, as has been attempted with reference to the early years of the war.

The attitude of Vatican Radio on the Jewish persecution discussed so far, may help to understand Pius XII's public silence or at least add a piece to the complex reconstruction. A broadcast in Italian aired on January 24, 1945, recorded by the BBC, is worth quoting it in full:

> After reviewing the Jews' history and sufferings, the speaker stresses that when a Jew becomes a Christian, he has not to abandon his own people or even his religion or the Law of Moses, for Jesus represents the fulfilment of the Old Testament. The real Jews are actually those who become Christians. The others, even if of a praiseworthy life, are deprived of divine enlightenment. We non-Jewish Christians acknowledge our debt to the Jews, the Old Testament and the liturgy common to both. We pray not only for the Jews who lived before Christ but also for the living ones and wish Jews and non-Jews to unite. Then we, the non-Jews who through God's merit have believed in Jesus, should feel ourselves in a stronger position when appealing to those peoples still in religious darkness. We invite the Jews to draw closer to us and to discuss matters in a brotherly spirit. Antisemitic propaganda has often given rise to misunderstanding and discord, and we acknowledge that some Catholics have not always shown the desirable objectivity, thus aggravating the evil. By entering the Catholic Church, the Jews will find themselves among their Fathers, and their own Sister, the Virgin Mother, will welcome them. (Reference to St. Paul, and further appeal to Jews to enter) 'the Catholic Church to achieve the desired unity of all men.'[159]

The script was part of the series of speeches which were habitually broadcast during the week of prayer for Christian unity. These words were pronounced a few days before the liberation of the extermination camp at Auschwitz. In an unchanged, general picture on the relations between Jews and Christians, the broadcast repeated the traditional Catholic doctrine toward Judaism, although with slightly different tones and assertions. It is precisely this nuance that contains the step ahead and, at the same time, the limit of the understanding of the historical tragedy that took place with the Shoah, and which only decades later would lead to a deep change in the relationship between Judaism and Christianity. Reading the New Testament, in the light of the coming of Christ, had not changed: it seems to echo in that "the real Jews are in reality those who become Christians," the conversion of Nathanael, the "true Israelite. There is no duplicity in him" (John 1, 45–51). The only way to salvation was shown in the invitation to conversion, although free of the usual anti-Jewish invective. And yet, in the second part of the program, two new elements were introduced: the invitation to the discussion with "fraternal spirit" and the reference to "misunderstandings" and "discord" which, as outcomes of antisemitism, led to the admission that some Catholics had not acted correctly, aggravating the situation. Moreover, the lexicon betrays the inability to understand the dramatic nature of the events which had taken place in very recent years and in part were not yet over. It is precisely this snapshot that captures the climate and opinions that had been produced in the Curia during the second half of World War II. The author of the script is unknown; probably it was a Jesuit at the service of Vatican Radio, but in any case, he seems to embody some of the essential characteristics which cannot be overlooked to understand the Church of Pius XII at that precise time in history. The relationship between Judaism and Christianity had been one of the leading axes of Catholic theology and teaching for centuries. It produced a profound conditioning that was interwoven with the racist theories of the second half of the nineteenth century, leading to an antisemitism of Catholic origin which continued in the subsequent decades, and which became one of the most widespread elements of antisemitism in Europe. The small changes, the attempts at dialogue that were established even during the war,[160] had not fractured the fundamental structures of the persuasions and beliefs deposited in the mindsets of these men of the Church, who had been trained in the light of that theology.[161] And it is exactly its repetition in a January 1945 broadcast that shows the extent to which these theological structures were not only present, but represented a certainty, a guarantee of the continuity of the Catholic Church in a panorama of rubble. An anchor which these ecclesiastics clutched on to. Pius XII, in his message on June 2, 1945, absolved the Church and the German people of any responsibility whatsoever for the crimes committed by the Nazis. Once again, it was faith in something that could not collapse that was in action: indeed, it could not collapse because now was the time for reconstruction and not affliction.

5 Toward the Axis Defeat: Vatican Radio, the Occupation of Rome, and the End of the War

The programs in German from 1942 to 1943: The megaphone of the bishops

Beginning on September 1, 1939, German Minister for Propaganda Joseph Goebbels issued the regulation on exceptional broadcasting measures (*Verordnung über außerordentliche Rundfunkmaßnahmen*) which prohibited listening to foreign radios: the transgression was punishable by arrest and even, in some cases, by the death penalty.[1] From then on, in order to listen to Vatican Radio, German Catholics had to infringe upon this rule.[2] Following the German occupation, this prohibition was extended to Poland in addition to the forbiddance of owning a radio; nonetheless, recalled by the BBC's Polish section, the scripts of Vatican Radio programs circulated, thanks also to the clandestine press.[3]

Religious and priests often ignored these prohibitions because they were sure to be protected by the Concordat.[4] Goebbels worked tenaciously to eliminate these privileges and the SS *Sicherheitsdienst* subjected the clergy to systematic control. The German clergy listened to Vatican Radio, as inferred by the sermons of the parish priests: the religious were determined "to use the messages of foreign broadcasters in a cautious way for propaganda purposes."[5] In spring of 1939, Hitler prohibited religious functions from being broadcast on German radios, but Goebbels disagreed with this measure and tried, unsuccessfully, to make the Führer change his mind. On September 18, 1939, he proposed reintroducing religious programs to discourage people listening to them on foreign radio stations. The Auswärtiges Amt (Foreign Office) agreed, but Hitler did not change his mind.[6]

Reading prohibited newspapers and books and listening to radios was considered anti-State behavior (*Staatsfeindliches Verhalten*).[7] To date, it has not been possible to make an estimate of the total number of religious who were put on trial or were sentenced for having listened to Vatican Radio. The station belonged to a foreign State and therefore listening to it came under the ordinance of Goebbels. This ordinance, together with the jamming of foreign radio stations by the Nazi government, influenced the number of Vatican Radio listeners in Germany, which decreased during the war. Between 1938 and 1939, thousands of letters were received at Vatican Radio from German listeners, up to two hundred per week.[8] The letters show that listeners would often sit in groups of as many as twenty people around a single radio, including many Protestants and their pastors. The comments were favorable and enthusiastic: "As for the news, you are the only reliable source"; "We follow your programs with consolation and avidity: they are a true grace; our spiritual food; a real necessity for us!"; "We would like more frequent programs." In the following years, fewer and fewer letters from Germany arrived in Rome. Nonetheless, the station decided to continue its programs because it knew that someone would be able to listen and spread its news.

Between 1942 and 1943 the programs in German included readings of pastoral letters and the homilies of the German episcopate, as well as those of the diocesan ordinaries of other countries, deemed significant for listeners in the Third Reich. In general, it can be observed that while in 1941, several broadcasts were devoted to the equality of human rights with respect to human dignity and especially to natural law, the speeches of the German episcopate that were chosen for broadcast during 1942 rebalanced the broadcasts directed to Germany by showing the patriotism of the German Church.

The outbreak of the war had induced the German episcopate to take a stance that was in line with the Catholic tradition of loyalty to civil authorities, encouraging the faithful to do their duty for their country and pray for victory.[9] However, as the conflict made its exceptionality with regard to methods of war clear (massacres and deportations), uncertainties and tensions lacerated the episcopate. To simplify, two lines of conduct can be identified: the majority, headed by Cardinal Adolf Bertram, bishop of Breslau and president of the Bishops' Conference of Fulda, was more inclined to a compromise with National Socialism and contrary to public interventions of dissent, and the minority, inspired by the archbishop of Berlin, Konrad von Preysing, was more willing to run the risk of openly criticizing the regime. Nuncio Cesare Orsenigo deemed it necessary to abstain from public declarations against Hitler and his government because they would have been read as hostile to the State: it was not possible to criticize National Socialism without being considered traitors of the fatherland.[10] The German episcopate continued to act according to a criterion of distinction between fatherland, State, and party (obedience to authority and solidarity with the nation at war, but without supporting the National Socialist party in full).

This was not accepted by the regime because of its characteristic superimposition of the party with the State.[11] Caution and reticence, adopted by the episcopate, were felt necessary to save what could be saved. The attitude of the bishops was also weighed by the "stab in the back" myth, according to which domestic anti-national defeatism was the cause of Germany's defeat in the First World War, a legend often used by Nazi propaganda. The archbishop of Munich, Michael von Faulhaber, said this clearly in his speech at the conference of Bavarian bishops on March 30 and 31, 1943:

> Tension and dissent are also spread in Catholic milieus by dramatic questions such as these: why don't the bishops take the field? Why don't the bishops speak out? The answer is: We could never do a greater favor to the adversaries of the Church if we now put the large calibers into the battery. Now that it is in difficulty, it would immediately bring back to life the story of the stab in the back. My impression is that this is exactly what they are waiting for.[12]

Pius XII, fearing that any pronouncement he made would have repercussions on the German Catholics, let the bishops speak if they considered it opportune, supporting them in their public stances.[13]

An analysis of the programs in German shows that during 1942, Vatican Radio broadcast pastoral letters of the German episcopate conveying a double message: the Church had not abandoned the German people although it could not avoid criticizing racist and liberticide theories, a criticism which was presented in perfect harmony with the loyalty due the fatherland.

1942 began, for German listeners, with two programs on courage.[14] In the second one, in particular, the New Year message from the archbishop of Freiburg, Monsignor Conrad Gröber, was read out, in which he hoped that it was not "the night for our nation and fatherland, but a night during which the eternal stars continue to shine and after which the bright dawn of a happier day can return."[15] In the invocation in favor of the "nation and fatherland," the archbishop prudently did not speak explicitly of a victory or of peace but employed the metaphor of light and darkness to express the hope for happier days.

Gröber's pastoral letter of January 27 was also read out. The BBC monitor reported the following passage:

> At no time we injure the interests of the Fatherland or impair them. We recognize in the State only the tool of Him who creates eternal order. The Church did not fail when asked to do its duty for King and Country. There came the war of 1914. The whole of Germany at that time was full of religious fervor.

When the collapse came, the Church did everything in its power to inspire the people for the last effort. The archbishop says the German defeat made him weep. After the war, the fight against Rome flared up again and some people ascribed the guilt for the war and the Treaty of Versailles to the Church.[16]

The essence of Gröber's letter was to defend the Church from accusations of not supporting the German people during the war, namely from that defeatism that was at the base of the "stab in the back" myth. Gröber, one of the bishops most often quoted by Vatican Radio, had gone from initially supporting National Socialism to being one of the most avid supporters of the need for public condemnation of religious persecution in Germany. But, as observed in the interventions of the German announcer, and confirmed by historiography, he was also a patriot, and as such, tried to support the morale of the soldiers and their families.[17] A few months after the tribute of his pastoral letter to the pope and its reading by Vatican Radio, Gröber wrote again to Pius XII. This time it was a lengthy account on the state of his diocese in which he reported that the Nazis had gone from theory to practice in their aim of annihilating Judaism, adding that by then, at least 220,000 Israelites had been killed.[18] This news was not relayed by Vatican Radio.

Other pastoral letters were read to consolidate the bond between Christianity and Germanism. This is the case, for example, of the address by the bishop of Münster, August von Galen, to Catholic parents regarding religious education, so that they would remember their sacred duty to give their children a Christian education, especially today "that school no longer takes on this duty, as it once did."[19] To celebrate the fiftieth anniversary of his ordainment as a priest and his silver jubilee as archbishop of Munich, Cardinal Faulhaber wrote a pastoral letter, repeated by Vatican Radio and by *The Tablet*, in which he stressed the commitment of seminarians in his diocese in serving the fatherland.[20]

The episcopal jubilee of Pius XII was the occasion for the German bishops, gathered at a conference in Bonn, to address a letter to their faithful so that they would make a pilgrimage "in spirit" to Rome to reinforce their faith and their obedience to the pope.[21] The text, also broadcast by Vatican Radio, contained praise for the nunciature of Pacelli in Germany:

> Pius XII spent more than half his years as a Bishop in our Fatherland, not grudgingly like many, a foreigner who considers his stay beyond the Alps as a sort of exile, not as a cold observer who notices, registers, and draws conclusions; no, he looked about him with his eyes of love, being greatly interested in the heartbeats of this Nation, which is alien in blood but near in faith [. . .].

Archbishop Pacelli's mission in Germany was a mission of peace and of spiritual reconstruction.[22]

Pacelli was exalted, not only as a promoter of peace, but above all for his attachment to Germany, with the intention of showing that Pius XII, precisely because of his love for the German people, could not desire Germany's defeat.

On September 18, another document from the German bishops, meeting at a plenary conference in Fulda between August 18 and 20, 1942, was read.[23] This time, again thanks to Vatican Radio, the English Catholic weekly *The Tablet* was able to give it wide resonance.[24] As they had already done individually in their pastoral letters, the bishops stressed their closeness to the heroic soldiers who were fighting and dying for their country. They recalled that obeying the orders of the authorities was a religious duty linked to eternal salvation, according to a topic that had now become a classic of Catholic teaching and was reproposed in several speeches, including by Pius XII himself. They then addressed the priests who had remained at home, who prayed and courageously continued to look after those who were under their protection. They continued, addressing the nuns, the mothers and the brothers and sisters who had lost sons, fathers, and husbands, asking that the merciful Father let peace fall on the country and on the Earth. Then they added:

> During these days, we have been occupied with serious questions and immediate anxieties, and we considered it our sacred duty to turn to the competent authorities. However, in this time of difficulties of war (kriegsschweren), we do not think it appropriate to give further details in this episcopal letter.

It is not exactly clear what the bishops were referring to. However, the Church, the letter continued, had the courage to fight against all falsehoods and errors, including: "liberalism, excessive emphasis on the individual personality and the reduction of community rights" and "anti-Christian collectivism in all its forms"; it fought for "freedom of conscience, for human dignity and for the freedom of rights conferred on man directly by God."

The Tablet, noting that the radio was the only means of communication that had given news of this collective letter, hypothesized that the German bishops had drawn up a document that was actually far longer than the one read out by Vatican Radio, which, with its summary, had given the impression of a reconciling attitude of the German episcopate toward the government.[25]

The Tablet, however, did not think it possible that Vatican Radio had manipulated the wording of the pastoral letter on its own initiative to make it more indulgent with respect to the Reich. Rather, it suggested that the Nazis had prevented the unabridged broadcasting of the text. In actual fact, from the comparison of the script transcribed by the BBC monitor and the original one from the Bishops' conference published in the *Akten deutscher Bischöfe*, there did not seem to be any substantial differences, therefore Vatican Radio had not made any strategic cuts to the collective pastoral letter, nor had the bishops gone any further in their condemnation.

The last sermon, by a German bishop, broadcast by Vatican Radio on December 21, 1942, was that of the bishop of Fulda, Johannes Schmidt, which was pronounced on October 25 for the Feast of Christ the King.[26] According to the announcer, it was a magnificent speech. Monsignor Schmidt regretted that, in Germany, there was still so much propaganda against the Christian faith:

> A good many in our Fatherland reject Christ as the universal King, and nothing is so antagonistic to them as the unity of all men in His Kingdom. They want to split up mankind and hold that varying national and racial characteristics preclude spiritual unity and community.

The bishop emphasized the absolute nature of Christian Truth against the danger of racism; it was not possible that each nation embodied a truth of their own in contrast with it.

1943 brought several upheavals on the battlefields and at the political level, starting with the decisive turning point represented by the surrender of the Germans in Stalingrad. In the middle of a series of programs of a religious nature, explicit reference was made to current affairs in a speech by the archbishop of Cologne, Josef Frings, in which he attempted to explain the surrender in Stalingrad to the faithful:

> We are deeply moved and humbled before the heroism of the fighters of Stalingrad. [. . .] We have understood God's call. The time has come to turn to Him in a "storm of prayer". May He protect our soldiers and our Fatherland.[27]

The archbishop asked for special prayers and services for the German nation and ordered the celebration of the *Requiem* in all churches for the men who had fallen at Stalingrad. The pastoral letter from the bishop of Regensburg,

Monsignor Michael Buchberger, broadcast the following week, invoked a crusade of prayer for peace, the fatherland, and the soldiers in combat.[28]

In the program of March 22, 1943, some points of a collective pastoral letter from the German episcopate written the previous year, which had not yet been broadcast by Vatican Radio unlike the others already mentioned, were read out.[29] On December 10, 1941, the German episcopate had given the government a report providing documentary evidence of the persecution of German Catholics and asking for the respect of the natural rights of each human being.[30] The National Socialist government did not answer, but the expectation of the Catholic faithful of a clear and public stance by the episcopate, and the pressure in this direction by Pius XII himself,[31] induced the German bishops to draw up a collective pastoral letter, dated March 22, 1942 and summarized by Vatican Radio exactly one year later, on March 22, 1943.[32] Although we do not know why Vatican Radio decided not to broadcast the text immediately following its publication, we can hypothesize that they wanted to be prudent considering that a few days earlier the German ambassador to the Holy See had requested the script of a program that had been broadcast on March 12, 1942, which said:

> In the meantime, the face of the times has changed thoroughly. The extreme liberalism of that time has been followed by modern totalitarianism; the belief in the worth and value of the individual has been replaced by the belief in the absolute value of the national community, the collective, the race. [. . .] The Christian meaning of life is thereby denied and the supremacy of a personal God over the personal life and the fate of the peoples is questioned. Thus, our time with its collectivization drives even more strongly to the fight against the church, against its teachings and institutions than the time of liberalism.[33]

There was some turmoil at the Secretariat of State since the revisor of the texts, Monsignor Pietro Sigismondi, had not censored this passage.

Returning to the program with the pastoral letter of 1942, contrary to what the announcer maintained at the beginning, the document had not been read out in all of the German churches when it was drawn up. The original text encountered the opposition of, above all, Cardinal Bertram, who did not deem it opportune to expose the Church to further reprisals by the Reich, and so it was decided to draw up a summarized version.[34] The part quoted in the German program concerned the respect of the "universal rights of men conferred by God," without which Western culture would have collapsed, i.e., the natural right to freedom, with the limits imposed by God and by the duty of obedience to authority, the natural right to life and to sustenance, the natural right to private property, and the natural right to the defense of one's honor.[35] The letter continued, proving the engagement of Christians in the defense of the fatherland: in the battlefields and at home, they had "heroically" and with "steadfast loyalty" carried out their duty. But the Catholics could not be asked to prove their loyalty for the fatherland to the detriment of their faith: "We remain steadfastly loyal to our fatherland, precisely because we keep our faith in our Savior and in our Church at any cost." In conclusion, the blessing for the Church and for the fatherland and an "honorable, successful and lasting peace" was invoked.

Some points of this collective pastoral letter appeared in the 1942 Christmas radio message by Pius XII. He said:

> Those who want the star of peace to appear and stay over society [. . .] must support the respect and the practical implementation of the following fundamental rights of the person: the right to keep and develop bodily, intellectual and moral life, and particularly the right to religious education and training; the right to private and public worship of God, including religious charitable action; the right, in general, to marriage and the achievement of its purpose, the right to conjugal and domestic society; the right to work as an indispensable means to maintain family life; the right to the free choice of status, therefore also of the priestly and religious status; the right to the use of material goods, aware of one's duties and of social limitations.[36]

The Christmas radio message had been aired, as was usual, in all Vatican Radio languages.[37] The wide resonance of the pope's speech could have encouraged Vatican Radio to read the collective letter of the German episcopate (one year after its issue but just three months after the papal Christmas message), because of the similarity of the topics the two texts dealt with.

Pius XII's December 24, 1942 speech is historically recognized because it contains a passage in which the pope alluded to the extermination of the Jews, but without explicitly naming them,[38] and because, from that moment onward, various Italian Catholic intellectuals began to project an alternative to Mussolini's regime in the afterwar reconstruction, convinced that Pius XII advocated democracy.[39] "Not lamentation, but action is the precept of the hour; not lamentation about what is or what was, but reconstruction of what will and must arise for the good of society" was the phrase in the radio message that rekindled the hopes and the reorganization of the Italian Catholic movement. The pope claimed that "the origin and essential purpose of social life" should be "the preservation, development, and perfecting of the human person," and therefore condemned those doctrines or social constructions that misconceived this respect due to the person, even in the differences between men. The Franciscan Agostino Gemelli organized internal study seminars at the Catholic University with the help of professors such as Amintore Fanfani, Antonio Amorth, Giuseppe Dossetti, and Giuseppe Lazzati. The Milan group wondered whether Pius XII had intended to condemn dictatorships and promote democratic forms of political life. To clarify this and other points of the radio message, Fr. Gemelli wrote a letter to the Secretariat of State on April 29, 1943, to which Montini responded with a document, personally reviewed by Pius XII. The question of whether the people should "participate in legislative and executive activity through freely elected representatives" was answered: "Explicitly nothing of this is contained either here or in the chapter *Dignity and Rights of the Human Person*. Implicitly it is said: that the State Constitution and legislation must have regard to the rights of the lower social entities and individuals. Nothing is said around the technical question, how this is to be done (e.g., through Parliament or in some other form)."[40]

The clarification interpreted, in a reductive sense, the openness that the radio message had hinted at. It would be two more years before Pius XII would openly give his consent to the democratic legal system.

In a report by the *Sicherheitsdienst*, the radio message was judged as an attack on Germany, to the extent that von Ribbentrop immediately instructed Ambassador von Bergen to seek an audience with Pius XII, as it seemed that there was now proof that the Vatican was about to give up its traditional neutrality.[41] However, the Allies did not receive the radio message warmly either, as it was considered too weak in view of the circumstances.[42]

The German announcer of Vatican Radio tried to remove every doubt regarding the pope's speech. According to the announcer, nobody moved by good intentions could say that Pius XII had remained silent, even though he had not sided with either of the belligerent factions.[43] But he could not be said to be neutral when it concerned the laws of God, the Church, or human dignity, because he condemned all the false systems that contradicted them.[44] In the generality of the condemnation ("the Pope condemns false systems wherever they are if they contradict the law of God"), it seemed that he wanted to deny that the Holy See had sided openly against the Axis.

The effort to defend the decisions of Pius XII by the Vatican broadcaster seemed to be an answer to the continuous pressure from the Allied diplomacy. In the September talks between Myron Taylor, Roosevelt's representative in the Vatican, first with Pius XII and then with Maglione, Taylor tried to convince the Holy See of the need for strong words by the pope condemning the atrocities committed by Germany.[45] Numerous allies wrote to the Holy See to condemn the Nazi barbarities. A note by Tardini explained that the Holy See was proceeding secretly to help those who had been affected and that speaking would have endangered the rescue operations.[46] Despite the pressure, Pius XII did not want to sign the Joint Declaration by Members of the United Nations of December 17, 1942, which condemned the persecution of the Jews by the Nazis.[47]

The decision of the father responsible for the programs in German may have corresponded to Pius XII's desire during this phase of the conflict, to have the bishops speak up and have their pastoral letters obtain the maximum circulation possible through Vatican Radio. Nonetheless, this excessive publicity in Germany created alarmism in the episcopate. The monitoring of Vatican Radio by the Sonderdienst Seehaus had continued. On August 3, 1942, an article from the *Schweizer Rundschau* was read, which said: "the prayer for final victory is no prayer at all. There is but one prayer today—for peace. [. . .] Be less attached to final victory, and more to peace. [. . .] Working in the armament industry is worse than unemployment."[48] These words were reported by the German Embassy to the Secretariat of State, which replied that "the incriminated phrases were not addressed to Germany alone, but to the whole of humanity."[49]

In defense of Pius XII: The programs in Polish

In 1941, some voices were raised in protest against the excessive reserve of Pius XII toward the situation of the Church in Poland. On August 2, Cardinal Hlond sent Maglione a memo informing him that the Polish government in exile in London was receiving information about the alarming religious conditions in Poland and the mistrust that the population had in the Holy See, who they felt was guilty of not having taken a stance against the Axis.[50] Maglione answered the memo through Nuncio Valeri, giving him the script of the Vatican Radio program about the audience granted to the Polish nun Laureta Lubowidzka, which had created quite a turmoil for Vatican Radio in 1941.[51] A few months later, another letter arrived at the Vatican, this time from the archbishop of Krakow, Adam Stefan Sapieha, who after having listed the persecutory actions of the Germans against the Polish religious, begged Pius XII to raise "a voice of protest and blame" because "the Catholic world is expecting this defense of justice, even if it were not to change the way the German government acted."[52] Maglione answered Sapieha, sending him the same script of the Vatican Radio program questioned a few months earlier by the Italian ambassador, together with other speeches by Pius XII. These records should have been used to counterattack the propaganda against the Holy See.[53]

In 1942, some Vatican Radio programs in Polish tried to defend Pius XII from these attacks. For example, taking up an article from the *L'Osservatore Romano* on the celebration of the third year of Pius XII's papacy, the announcer claimed that it was the pope's prerogative to decide whether, when, and how to speak. When Pius XII chose silence, the criticisms decreased as well, proving that he was right.[54]

In another program, the Polish announcer tried to take an example from history to explain the current situation, as the Jesuits of Vatican Radio often did. It was recalled that in the summer of 1797 Napoleon had invaded the papal States, defeating the papal army at Ancona, extorting money, and looting the riches of the Holy See. In response to protests by Pius VI, Bonaparte, who had proclaimed himself the protector of the Church, put forward the right to occupy the city of Ancona. Years later, when Pius VII refused to form an alliance with him against the British, Napoleon stated on February 13, 1806, that he was the emperor and therefore his enemies also had to be the enemies of the pope, even though the pope was the sovereign of Rome. The "ill" pope answered that, as the "vice regent of the Eternal Word," he had the obligation of answering exclusively to the will of God to maintain peace with anyone "without distinction between Catholics and heretics, far or near," and was willing to undergo the consequences with "apostolic resignment, because every ordeal to which he was subjected came from God." With the Russian Campaign, however, the announcer reminded the audience, the decline of Napoleon had begun. Pius VII had foreseen this, the Church had remained intact, and he could return to Rome amid the enthusiasm and the joy of the people.[55] This history lesson, given in Polish by Vatican Radio, suggested analogies with the present situation of the Church, the position of Pius XII, and the trend of the war on the battlefields. The announcer showed that the aggression toward the Catholic Church could not last and that the attitude of Pius VII, entrusting himself to God's will and under his protection trying to keep peace, in the end had been repaid by his triumphant return to Rome. But the reference to the Russian campaign could also not be a coincidence: in the winter of 1941, the Soviet counteroffensive had begun, and in January 1942, only two months before the program aired, succeeded in making the Germans retreat hundreds of miles from the Moscow front.

The programs that followed had the purpose of comforting the Polish population, whether in their home country or in exile. We do not know to what extent the Vatican Radio programs could be received in Poland, but as for the other programs for the territories of the Reich, they hoped that the messages arrived in some way or another. In any case, they could have formed evidence of the Holy See's interest in relation to the complaints of the bishops. In May, the announcer tried to infuse courage, assuring that the suffering and the tears shed by the Poles would not have been in vain.[56] In July it was announced that the mission of love of Pius XII, especially for the Polish people, was well known: the pope had intervened successfully in the exchange of seriously wounded prisoners, had relieved the anxiety of finding the missing, and had always indicated in his speeches and encyclicals the foundations of the new order, i.e., justice and Christian love.[57]

In April 1943, the seven sorrows of Our Lady of Sorrows were individually equivalent to what is called the seven stations of the calvary of the Polish nation today. The message in this case again was one of hope:

> If the Polish nation which, as is generally known, today perhaps suffers most, though for no fault of its own, wishes to endure and to live, it must learn to suffer like the Mother under the cross. [. . .] Dear listeners! Who of us can doubt that Mary will remember us in Her joy, and will hasten the hour of our joy and resurrection by Her intercession? Let us pray to Her.[58]

In May, a letter from the pope was prepared to be sent to the Polish bishops on the occasion of the *ad limina* visit that they should have made, to exhort them to persevere in the faith. It was decided not to send it, as the speech of June 2, 1943, by Pius XII to the Holy College already contained a passage dedicated to Poland[59] and was also the subject of a Vatican Radio program on June 4.[60]

However, Pius XII still did not succeed in being persuasive in his politics concerning Poland, not even in the inner Vatican circles.[61] The diary of Fr. McCormick provides some clues as to the different positions held among the ecclesiastics. Referring to the speech of June 2, 1943, he rejoiced that the pope had spoken on behalf of Poland but "it was so phrased that it could also be taken as directed at the Soviet Union."[62] In fact, McCormick wrote:

> Why not mention Holland, Slovenia, France? It would be too clearly unequivocally against Germany and Italy? And is it true that air war has brought destruction for 1st time to non-belligerents & non-military objectives? Has no one ever heard of heavy, long-range artillery? Rheims Cathedral and all eastern France 27 years ago? If Eng[land] and USA began deporting Italian manpower & youth & girls forcibly to work for them, then we should hear

protests of the inhuman, illegal methods of war. Poor Holland, Belgium and Norway![63]

Pius XII's decision to leave the responsibility for what they considered opportune to say publicly, to the episcopates, had the effect of weakening the pronouncements both by the bishops and the pope. However, this allowed Pius XII to remain impartial before the two belligerent sides, a purpose that had guided his policy from the outbreak of the conflict. The aim of remaining neutral, extending beyond the clear loss of ground by Germany, was to be used by the Holy See in acting as a mediator in the peace process to avert the danger that an "unconditioned surrender" imposed by the Allies would open the doors to the spread of communism in Europe.[64] The reserve and the weakness of the public speeches were counterbalanced by private talks in which the cautious and allusive collaborators of Pius XII, tried to suggest to the British, American, and German diplomats the moves that might bring each one to yield to compromise.[65]

In this dual strategy, the role of Vatican Radio seems to have been that of supporting both what needed to be known and what diplomacy required.[66] The public aspect, it has been seen, was backed up by the reproduction of as many episcopal interventions as possible. The diplomatic aspect was supported by the decision to show, through more or less allusive broadcasts, not only to the public, but also to the governments involved, that the Holy See did not remain inactive.

"V for Vatican": Mistiaen between Resistance and censorship

The clandestine journal *La Voix du Vatican*, which reproduced Vatican Radio's programs in French, had suspended publication in May 1941 after Mistiaen's announcement that "the voice had to be quiet." It reappeared in September with bulletin number 15, which opened with the following announcement:

> It is with joy that we resume the circulation of these pages that the Radio of the Vatican, which was dead or almost, had forced us to suspend. We consider this resumption as a duty. The Vatican makes every effort, despite all the obstacles, to cry out the Truth to the world. It is our duty to echo it. We count on you.[67]

Limagne wrote in his diary that Vatican Radio had restarted to tell "not a few truths."[68] The programs in the first few days of September tried to urge listeners to broaden their horizons, in order to better understand events,[69] without being duped by devious propaganda:

> We know that our conscience is ripped apart by increasingly enterprising propaganda: the type that plunges lies into the spirit and which denies us the truth. [. . .] We have to be doubly cautious and diffident when those who speak to us put us in the impossibility of receiving anything else but what they say and refuse to let us know what is said outside their circle and their milieu.[70]

Another piece of advice given by Mistiaen was that of weighing thoughts and actions, remembering that God was watching, so that men ceased to "act like animals."[71] But, if it were not possible to act honestly, thought should become an absolute force and reserve of energy: "Today, when our thought cannot yet turn into action, it has to be all the more solid."[72]

In the programs of these months, the topics were mainly of a religious and spiritual nature, such as the explanation of the Gospels or the lives of the saints. For example, on September 29, Mistiaen dedicated a program to the virtues of the Archangel Michael.[73] In the Book of the Apocalypse where Michael defeated the dragon representing the demon, the iconographic image of the archangel was that of a majestic being and a warrior who fought evil, with the power of weighing souls before the Last Judgment. Mistiaen exalted St. Michael mainly as a defender of the Church and protector of the Christian people against those who wanted to encourage a world without God.

In a program on St. Thérèse of the Child Jesus, Mistiaen repeated the concept that he had already expressed in the program on the Archangel Michael: God did not let himself be deceived by those who wanted to be his equal and claimed to replace Him.[74] Thérèse of Lisieux supported and consoled through spiritual virtues, led men toward peace and calm, and was an example of "resistance without heroism" in supporting suffering and pain.[75]

A particularity of this period is that almost all of Vatican Radio's programs were followed by musical intermezzos. Each program in mid-October, for example, was associated with a movement from Beethoven's Fifth Symphony. Composed between 1807 and 1808, the symphony was the symbol of the struggle of man against fate, and during World War II its first notes opened the programs of Radio Londra. The editor of *The Tablet* noticed the unusual association between the movements of the symphony and the French broadcasts, to the point of entitling his comment, *V for Vatican:*

> Rather surprisingly, the Vatican Wireless has lately been concluding some of its programs in French, by playing parts of Beethoven's Fifth Symphony. On Monday of last week, a talk on "Patience" was followed by the playing of the *second movement*; next day a homily in which the French were exhorted to maintain their serenity and to put their faith in God was followed by the *third movement*, which contains the Victory motif. On the Wednesday the *fourth movement* followed a talk on mysticism. The music was not announced as the Fifth Symphony.[76]

The Tablet journalist, with a *calembour*, associated the musical choice of Vatican Radio with the programs addressed to the European Resistance that were being aired on Radio Londra. The first four notes of the Fifth Symphony reproduce the sequence "short-short-short-long," which in Morse Code indicates the letter "v." This way, Radio Londra opened its programs recalling the idea of "victory." In actual fact, as can be noted from the quotation, Vatican Radio avoided broadcasting the first movement. However, doubt remains that we cannot solve for a lack of sources, as to the intentional nature of the choice made by the Jesuits of Vatican Radio to broadcast Beethoven's Fifth: had *The Tablet* journalist overinterpreted or was that exactly the effect that was desired?

Beethoven was one of the composers most heard on the airwaves in the following months, as well. On October 30, 1941, his Symphony No. 3 was played after a conversation on the importance of being able to smile in the face of adversity.[77] Beethoven had initially dedicated the *Eroica* to Napoleon, in whom he saw embodied the ideal of freedom. But once he had crowned himself emperor, the composer no longer wanted any connection with Bonaparte to be made. Perhaps this decision by Vatican Radio was not accidental either.

Taking into account the exclusively religious content of the programs during this period, it is surprising that the jamming of Vatican Radio continued—even to the point of making it necessary to change the station's wavelength, which went from 48.47 meters to 49.96.[78] Perhaps the jamming came, not only from the Germans, but from Vichy as well.[79] Limagne reports the case of a Catholic bookseller in Lyon, a certain Crozier, who was arrested because he was accused of circulating clandestine publications, in particular the lectures on Vatican Radio.[80] Clearly, it was *La Voix du Vatican*. The news that, in France, Mistiaen's programs were also circulated by the French

Resistance had reached the Holy See. Monsignor Valeri had sent Maglione copies of the newspaper, from the first to the seventeenth issue (so until the programs of October 1941), concerned by their circulation in the Occupied Zone, especially in Paris. The nuncio noted that the paper faithfully reproduced the Vatican Radio programs and he reported this to the Secretariat of State since "the authorities of the occupation would be displeased with that sort of propaganda and would have said that, if it were to continue, they would take measures."[81] Unfortunately, we do not have Maglione's answer, but in November of the same year, Valeri received a letter from a certain Doctor L. Frédénucci in Marseille who asked him if the pieces in *La Voix du Vatican* really corresponded to what was broadcast by Vatican Radio. The reason for the question concerned the program of September 15, in which Mistiaen rectified an article that had been published in *La Croix* referencing the renewed consecration of the city of Lyon to Notre-Dame de Fourvière.[82] The article, written by Antoine Lestra, a lawyer and journalist belonging to the monarchic and antidemocratic current of intransigent Catholicism,[83] attributed to Pétain, "the head of State that Providence gave us to bring France back to the sources of its life," the merit of having allowed the vows that the civic authorities of Lyon had offered to Our Lady of Fourvière to be renewed. Mistiaen had not appreciated the homage to Pétain and the consequent mix of religious and political matters, which had taken from "this fine spiritual assembly its foundation of serenity, honesty and freedom."[84] The nuncio answered Frédénucci, trying to diminish the official nature and therefore the reliability of the reproduction of the Vatican Radio programs, saying that he, too, received the publication, irregularly, and that he doubted that Vatican Radio would have expressed itself that way.[85]

If we exclude the program on Fourvière, the others continued to address neutral topics. However, they were interpreted as a way to oppose the "work of national restoration undertaken by the Marshal."[86] These were the words used by the bishop of Aix-en-Provence in the diocesan weekly *Semaine religieuse* of November 23, 1941 to warn the faithful of his diocese against the authors of the clandestine leaflet *La Voix du Vatican*, accused of giving directions to public opinion through the publication of "so-called Vatican programs" inspired by Gaullism and Anglophilia.[87] The comment of the bishop of Aix did not pass unobserved. The nuncio wrote to him to ask for the whole collection of the *La Voix du Vatican*.[88]

In the meantime, the fate of so-called Free France was about to be doubly bound to that of Germany. Laval, at the head of the Vichy government since April 18, 1942, accentuated collaboration with the occupier in the Northern Zone. The French historian Jacques Sémelin portrayed the situation under

Vichy with the excellent expression: the regime "has legitimized the occupation of the country and made resistance to the occupier illegitimate."[89] Mistiaen's religious programs, offering listeners alternatives such as honesty, respect, calm, and gentleness to those values that the totalitarian ideologies wanted to impose on them, represented a sort of non-violent resistance. While the Holy See avoided officially taking a position other than supporting Vichy, Mistiaen offered the faithful suggestions, including practical ones, on how to survive that regime recognized by the Church.[90] As the French academic Renée Bédarida has highlighted, the very vocabulary used by Mistiaen (struggle, fighting, battle, force of resistance) was that of the first French Resistance fighters, but vested with a spiritual dimension.[91]

In April 1942, the Secretariat of State received news of an article published in the *Union Française* of Lyon, by a priest called C. Bouvier, that attacked *La Voix du Vatican* as a journal contrary to the collaboration, which circulated in ecclesiastical circles.[92] A note written at the Secretariat of State commented that the clandestine paper, "both for the title it boasts and the absolutely political inclination," was "far more compromising than the Cahiers [du Témoignage Chrétien]."[93] Perhaps the editor of this note was unaware that the person responsible for the content of *La Voix du Vatican* was a Jesuit who lived right in the Vatican (Mistiaen). Maglione asked Valeri to ascertain whether what had been stated corresponded to the truth.[94] The nuncio wrote to the bishop of Lyon, Mons. Gerlier, who assured him that Bouvier did not belong to the clergy of his diocese and that *Union Française* was a "paper more or less unknown to the public and that is published apparently on behalf of or on the inspiration of the occupying power."[95]

If, on the one hand, concern was growing in Rome about the spread and the politicization of Mistiaen's programs, on the other hand, the letters from listeners who confirmed the attachment of the faithful to the French program of Vatican Radio continued to reach the Vatican from different parts of the world.[96] Those who wrote to Vatican Radio were convinced that they were listening to a spokesman of Pius XII. In actual truth, the position of Mistiaen in the Vatican became increasingly difficult in those years. He could count on the support of General Ledóchowski and Fr. Leiber, but censorship in 1942 had become even more strict. In his correspondence with Tittmann in the 1960s, Mistiaen wrote: "It is difficult to realize the atmosphere of the radio during the war"; his Spanish and Italian colleagues, "all more or less sympathetic to the Nazis," made life impossible for those who thought differently to the point that, Mistiaen concluded, "if Father Ledóchowski and Father Leiber had not defended me, I would have had to take the road for Lisbon."⁹⁷ Toward the end of 1942, "exhausted by the ridiculous intromissions" which had become stronger since the death of Ledóchowski on December 13, Mistiaen asked to leave Vatican Radio and be sent to England.[98] But Pius XII did not accept sending Mistiaen away.[99] The French Jesuit Albert Dauchy, called back to Vatican Radio in November 1941 (perhaps following the discovery of the existence of *La Voix du Vatican* by the Secretariat of State),[100] said that the censorship wanted to forbid examples taken from Church history in which allusions to the present situation could be found, as well as prohibit the final motto of Mistiaen's programs, "Courage, trust, God is guarding you!"[101] The proposal to omit those words was initially suggested by Monsignor Antonio Riberi to Fr. Urbina in November 1941. When he learned of this, Ledóchowski wrote to Maglione to advise him against giving such an order, considering the success of Mistiaen's programs.[102] Two years later, the regent of the Apostolic Delegation in Egypt, Arthur Hughes M.Afr., complained, in his turn, about the final expression with which Mistiaen ended the programs in French because he found it "unbecoming for the decorum of the Holy See" and "taunting."[103] From January 1944, Mistiaen was forced to no longer use his motto of encouragement.

Apparently, Pius XII had taken contradictory measures. How can this be explained? From an analysis of the programs and the sources available, it emerges that Mistiaen was not favorable to the Vichy regime, he was totally against collaborationism, and clearly anti-Nazi. Pius XII, in spite of doubts, had left the control of Vatican Radio to Ledóchowski, but had imposed the prior revision of scripts under the auspices of the Secretariat of State. Censorship had also hit the French programs, to the extent that Mistiaen, like the others, had to produce more sober and cautious scripts. Of course, Pius XII could only approve the censorship, and did not intervene until the end of 1942, when he opposed moving Mistiaen, who was not greatly loved by his colleagues and was irritated because he could not speak freely on Vatican Radio. It could be hypothesized that Pius XII's decision was an attempt at restoring a certain balance among the positions in the Vatican: avoiding excessive exposure, but at the same time avoiding giving a sign of subjugation, as the suspension of Mistiaen could have been interpreted, as his absence as a Vatican Radio announcer would not have gone unobserved. Stopping French programs completely and eliminating the leading speaker would have meant, in some way, making the scales lean toward the pro-Germans, precisely when, toward the end of 1942, the war was starting to turn against the Axis. Allowing Mistiaen's programs on the air, without their original edge, was a stratagem for launching a twofold message to the outside world: that Pius XII was unable to speak freely, and that his positions were absolutely not leveled on those of the Axis.

The condemnation of the "*Service obligatoire du travail*"

In November 1942, the German troops invaded the South of France, submitting the whole of the French territory to the control of the Reich and reducing the Vichy government to a formal institution without real powers. An extraordinary meeting of the Assembly of Cardinals and Archbishops, which could be attended only by seven prelates, deliberated that it was necessary to remain faithful to the government of Laval and Marshal Pétain, who still represented legitimate authority.[104] In early January 1943, Cardinal Emmanuel Suhard, archbishop of Paris, for the first time since the start of the war, went to Pius XII, who received him twice in audiences lasting ninety minutes each. Confirming his esteem for Pétain, Pius XII advised him not to ask the government for the impossible and to make do with the reasonable.

Two days after the start of Operation Anton (the operation of the invasion of the rest of France by the Germans), a Vatican Radio announcer, presumably Fr. Dauchy, having concluded a report on the state of the missions in Africa, added: "Events are also precipitating in our midst of Europeans and the difficulties of the war are growing more and more intensely from one day to the next."[105] In this situation, the Church represented the force necessary to restore order to the world and the place where men could find peace again. The next day, this time through the voice of Mistiaen, listeners were encouraged to adapt to the circumstances and to have hope.[106] Subsequent programs were dedicated to gentleness, which required great force in the face of the persecutors in power,[107] and to silence as a haven from the problems of the present.[108]

While Mistiaen never stopped infusing hope in his listeners, the clandestine paper *La Voix du Vatican* suspended its publications because the excessive jamming made it impossible to transcribe the broadcasts.[109]

In the face of the invasion of French territory, Fr. Mistiaen continued to encourage the people not to surrender:

> Courage, trust and resistance. Let's recover, let's develop in ourselves the deep feeling of our country, of our land, home... not a feeling that is brutally asserted against other races, but the deep feeling that preserves others... Keep the Christian message of the country intact, it will be your strength and you will see with Christ, who has never been defeated, and who never will be.

The country will be Christian, a civilization to last will be Christian. If it is not, it will be pointed at by the finger of death.[110]

Mistiaen, with his usual allusive style, condemned those coercive laws that prevented men from expressing their freedom. The script, obtained by the shorthand takers of Toulon, has parts missing, but from the sentences transcribed it seems that Mistiaen was defending the perfectioning of every human person as the primary purpose of "community life, in society and in the nation," with laws that allowed men to think autonomously. On the contrary, "when coercion is a universal means of government and administration, we can imagine that people do not feel well."[111]

In browsing through the scripts of the programs of these months, there is the perception of an escalation leading to the more explicit condemnation of "the compulsory work service." On February 16, 1943, the Vichy government established the *Service obligatoire du travail* (STO), which forced between 650,000 and 700,000 young people, between the ages of twenty-one and twenty-three, into forced labor in Germany or on the Atlantic coast of France, to assist in preparing the defenses for the Allied invasions.[112] The first to make a declaration, to be read without comment in all the churches of the diocese, was the archbishop of Lyon on February 21: it concerned the rights of the families affected by the painful consequences of the war, with the plea to the members of Catholic Action to support those who had been called up for obligatory work and their families.[113] The archbishop of Paris stated that he shared the "general emotion"; and the bishop of Besançon requested that the "indefeasible rights of Christian morals concerning the human person and the family" be guaranteed.[114] The *Jeunesse Etudiante Chrétienne* (JEC) protested with a communiqué that created internal division.[115] The speech of the archbishop of Lille, on the other hand, was used by pro-German propaganda to prove that the Church was encouraging youngsters to leave for Germany. On March 15, he spoke to young people in Roubaix, where it seems that he said to them that, being forced, they would have to leave with a spirit of sacrifice together with non-Christians and take advantage of the opportunity to convert them.[116] *La Croix* also interpreted the speech by Cardinal Liénart as an invitation to Catholics to do their duty for the country, but the archbishop gave another long speech, this time broadcast on Vatican Radio, contradicting the distortion made by propaganda.[117]

At the plenary meeting of April 7 and 8, the French cardinals drew up a fairly ambiguous text on the law of February 16: it defended the government, but at the same time, admitted (for the first time) to an objection of conscience in the face of the law of the *État français*.[118] This document was also read by Vatican Radio some time afterward, but only in English and in German.[119] The problem of the French episcopate, as *mutatis mutandis* for the German one, was how to respect the prescriptive value of obedience to authority in a situation in which the attainment of the common good did not seem to be among its objectives.

But from the Holy See, no precise directives came on the position. If the episcopate did not seem united in condemning the law on the STO (Cardinal Suhard, for example, was reluctant to adopt the declaration of the Assembly), Vatican Radio in French was more decisive. The first comment appeared on February 19 and as always, started with a reference to the past:

> The Church is indefatigable through the history of men in the defense of its rights to bodily life and to free balanced life, it is for this reason that the Church, until now, has done all it could to suppress slavery and corporal violence that it condemns; it is the Church that attacks, emerging from paganism, slavery and cannot wait to free the slaves, that it treats all men like creatures of God, who have the same right to dispose of their body.[120]

This allowed subsequent clarification that:

> The Church did not believe that a social life was possible if it were based on a system that increased the mass of slaves grouped together for the well-being and the pleasure of a small number. The Church knew well that the heart of each of these persons was a considerable power of rancor, of hatred and of revolt, that it would have circumvented and helped the foundations of this false peace, even kept with force.

The announcer spoke of "masses of slaves" used for the good of a few, an allusion that let him go as far as the explicit condemnation of slavery to which a group of people had been reduced in that period:

> The Church no longer accepts the regime based on forced labor, or on collective or individual deportations, on the expropriations of peoples, on the dispersion of families. No! The Church has always protested against expropriation, deportation, uprooting families and men and will always protest, it has supported all the force of private individuals and States... [...] Yes, my friends, yes, corporal life is sacred and nobody on earth has the right to act against it [...].

What the French episcopate had not been able to say clearly was expressed unambiguously by Vatican Radio, which not only used a lexicon which left no doubt as to what was being contested, but made the position of the Church on the government's decision very clear: "The Church does not accept ... The Church has always protested."

On the morning of February 20, Radio Londra retransmitted Vatican Radio's program, as can be seen from a letter from French Ambassador Léon Bérard to Monsignor Montini. Bérard commented:

> This morning, Radio Londra... quoted a passage from yesterday Friday evening program on Vatican Radio. Alluding to the law through which the French government ordered the conscription of some categories of young people for the compulsory work service, Vatican Radio declared that these measures were contrary to the dignity and to the freedom of the human person according to natural law. I am convinced, in the first place, that if the Vatican radio station has made itself understood on the prerogatives of being reasonable and free, which are so fought over and threatened today in many ways, by the teachings which each of us applauds, it has abstained from taking the French government into question. I would like it to show me a country where work is truly free at the moment...[121]

To reassure the ambassador, Montini gave him the script of the program, which did not name the French government explicitly as Bérard imagined, despite the precise allusions, which were picked up by Radio Londra and made explicit.[122]

The condemnation of deportations and the need for respect of individual rights were the subjects of other programs between February and March, which referred back to the points in Pius XII's Christmas speech on dignity and the rights of the human person, which were also the subject of the programs in English:

> We have already said it: the Church has never accepted the regime of collective or individual deportation, the dispersion of families..... Corporal freedom of man... has supported the efforts to save humanity from these barbarian practices.[123]

For Mistiaen it was no longer possible to think of reconstructing the world from the rubble of war without respecting "the corporal, intellectual, social, moral and religious freedom of man."[124]

Rome: An open city

In Spring 1943, through an exchange of letters between Pius XII and President Roosevelt, the Holy See acknowledged that an Allied air operation on Rome could not be avoided.[125] The commitment to respect places of worship and to aim exclusively at military objectives, confirmed by Roosevelt on July 10 while the landing in Sicily was taking place, did not reassure Pius XII and his entourage.[126] On July 19, the American Air Force, in the attempt to blow up the railway junction north of Rome, bombed and destroyed the Basilica di San Lorenzo Fuori le Mura. On that occasion, Pius XII left the Vatican to go to the San Lorenzo neighborhood to contemplate the ruins and bring comfort to the population affected. The episode is remembered, above all, for the people's reaction at the sight of the pope, proof of the affection and trust that the Romans had for the only authority of a supranational stature on whom they could rely.[127]

The chronicle of the visit to the bomb site was given by *L'Osservatore Romano*[128] in an article broadcast on Vatican Radio in Italian and in English on the evening of July 20.[129] The journalist of the Vatican newspaper and the radio announcers highlighted the private character and initiative of Pius XII who was accompanied only by Monsignor Montini. The pope had not left Vatican City since May 1940.

The following day, the letter from the pope to Cardinal Vicar Francesco Marchetti Selvaggiani, in which he recalled that Rome was the "holy city of Catholicism," full of monuments, art, and the guardian of documents and relics, was also read on Vatican Radio.[130] Despite the pleas, the hope of seeing Rome preserved had not been realized.

Vatican Radio continued to speak about what had happened. Details of the help that the Church was giving to the reconstruction were aired in a program in Italian, discussing the priests who were hosting the evictees, and the Vatican State's distribution of water, milk, and food. An appeal was also launched to car owners to lend their vehicles to help in the evacuation of people and to make monetary donations. In this emergency, the station had become key to circulating requests for help.

The answer to the letter of July 10 from President Roosevelt by Pius XII had a gestation of about ten days, with Rome being bombed in the meantime. The letter, in which the neutrality of the Vatican and the impossibility of attacking Rome without inflicting an incommensurable loss to the heritage of religion and civilization, was given to Tittmann on July 27 to be delivered to the United States, even though it actually bore the date of July 20.[131] Vatican Radio in German had to promptly deny the news that Pius XII had sent a personal letter of protest to President Roosevelt and that the Vatican's secretary of state had received his personal representative in an audience on the same evening as the air raids.[132] Both of the insinuations, said the announcer, were without any grounds, and regarding the damage to San Lorenzo, he specified that in Pius XII's evaluation, the damage was not intentional."[133] This way, they probably wanted to avoid easy exploitation of the pope's two gestures (the letter to Roosevelt and the visit to San Lorenzo) by National Socialist propaganda.

The political upheavals that took place in Italy in 1943 did not make news in the Vatican Radio programs. From that time onward, the Holy See oriented its means of communication toward the strictest neutrality. The Secretariat of State had, moreover, been called on several times to intercede with Great Britain and the United States so that Italy would sign a separate peace, which did not include the departure of Mussolini. On July 25, however, Montini was informed that the Grand Council of Fascism had removed Mussolini from the position of head of the Italian government.[134] The Duce was arrested, and a new government was established with Marshal Pietro Badoglio at its head. Acknowledging the growing tensions between Italy and Germany, on July 31, Cardinal Maglione decided to call the ambassadors of Portugal, Spain, Argentina, and Hungary to ask them to express to Ernst von Weizsäcker, the new German ambassador to the Holy See, the confidence that, in the case of a rift with the Italian ally, Vatican City, insofar as being a neutral State, would be respected.[135] On August 4, in the face of uncertainty, the secretary of state also united the cardinals, resident in Rome, to give them information.[136]

German divisions had crossed the Alps and occupied the Brenner Pass, Bolzano, and South Tyrol. As Maglione explained, "the Holy See continues to act with the usual prudence, avoiding everything that can offer an excuse to the Germans to attack it." The account by Tardini concluded with his manifesting the traditional fear: "A very dangerous state of mind will follow, because it could give rise to communism." In the forty days between the fall of fascism and the signature of the armistice (September 3, 1943), the Holy See tried to limit the damage of the war in Italian territory, in particular to Rome and its population, as much as possible, and to fight the void of power to avoid civil disorder and the dreaded hypothesis of a massive adhesion to communism.[137] Overall, the reaction of the Vatican to the fall of fascism was "perplexed, prudent, fearful and, above all, extremely cautious on the diplomatic level."[138]

Vatican Radio, this time, completely reflected the prudence of Vatican diplomacy. In the news bulletins in Italian, they tried to highlight, above all, the welfare work of the clergy. In Sicily, where the battle for the liberation of the island was taking place, the archbishop of Palermo decided to remain in order to support the priests who were helping the population, and the clergy were collaborating with the civil authorities to help the victims of the air raids.[139] Vatican Radio tried to contact a correspondent in Barcellona Pozzo di Gotto to obtain news on the area of Messina.[140] New experimental programs were launched with the purpose of reaching Italian listeners in the most efficient way.[141] On August 31, 1943, Fr. Soccorsi received the news from the general director of the EIAR that at an interministerial meeting, the Vatican's request to use the medium wavelength at 531 meters had been accepted. To this purpose, the rental of a 50 kw transmitter was also offered.[142] On October 14, Vatican Radio announced that it was testing the medium wavelength at 531 meters, which in Italy had been used for many years by the EIAR, and for a short period by Radio Palermo after the occupation of Sicily by the Allies.[143]

From August 1943, the role of Vatican Radio became very important. The contribution of Vatican Radio to the Vatican Information Department (UI—*Ufficio Informazioni Vaticano*) cannot be forgotten.[144] The UI office had been created at the beginning of the war to receive and sort through requests for information on missing military and civil personnel, using the international network of connections made up (mainly) of apostolic delegations and nunciatures.[145] The "Radio Section," which was established in the second half of 1940, broadcast lists of the names of prisoners and missing on set days and at set times. The news from the broadcasts, received by the nunciatures, the delegations, or the diocesan curias, was then forwarded to the families.[146] After the landing of the Allies in Sicily, thousands of requests arrived daily at the UI from Italians in search of news on the fate of their loved ones in the areas, as they were gradually liberated by the British and Americans.[147] The British government, however, opposed the work of the Holy See in relation to both the civilians in the south of Italy, as well as the imprisoned soldiers. This is the reason why the reception of Vatican Radio in those areas, although hindered, became fundamental in those months.[148]

In December, Cardinal Maglione wrote to the director of the UI, Russian Monsignor Alexander Evreinov, that the messages read on Vatican Radio, for the provinces of Italy occupied by the British and American troops, should be subjected to "strict vigilance," "revised each time by responsible people: one can be the head of the department that does this work, the other will be Your Excellence yourself [Evreinov], or one of your trusted collaborators. The announcer must also be strictly obliged to adhere faithfully to what he has been given to read, without making any additions or modifications."[149] Evreinov reassured Maglione that it had been decided to adopt a single model for the messages for southern Italy. To be certain that the order would be put into practice, Montini repeated it on January 10.[150] The reason for so much attention could be looked for in that hostility that had been hinted at by the British government toward the work of the UI in southern Italy, to which must be added the aversion also shown by the United States.[151] Behind the refusal to provide the lists of prisoners, there was the fear that the Vatican Radio service could involuntarily help the activity of enemy espionage.[152]

The programs in Italian also broadcast the Italian bishops' invitation to the faithful to remain united in prayer and in the respect of authority. The Italian announcer summarized the meaning of the interventions of the bishops: the order was "obedience to the constituted authority"; "to disobey the powers that be was to oppose divine order and to court disaster."[153] The new Italian government, he continued, had had the war in legacy and although everyone hoped for peace, nobody could desire it without honor and justice. It was therefore necessary to wait patiently, with rigid discipline, in austerity, in sacrifice, and in collaboration to prepare a better future.

Meanwhile, on August 6, Pius XII addressed a letter, published in *L'Osservatore Romano* and read in Italian on Vatican Radio, to the secretary of state.[154] The pope, it said, had left nothing untried to lead nations to peace and the bishops had the task of calling public prayers, "united in a holy crusade." From the diplomatic point of view, Pius XII tried, in every way, to push the Italian government to declare Rome an open city, which happened on August 14 with a unilateral declaration, considered "grotesque" and non-binding by the British.[155] The news was given with joy and relief by Vatican Radio in all languages, highlighting, in particular, the role that Pius XII had played.[156] In all of the programs, the demonstrations of joy shown by the population, who had rushed to acclaim the pope, were described. The previous day, however, the capital had again been bombed by the Allies and, for the second time, Pius XII visited the bombed neighborhoods with Montini. The news was given in German and in Dutch, while the BBC Monitoring Service did not record a program in English about the event.[157]

"Vatican Radio is very limited in its comments and silent"

The announcement of the unconditional surrender of Italy to the Allies (September 8, 1943), the occupation of Rome by the Nazis, the escape of Pietro Badoglio and King Vittorio Emanuele III from the capital, and the liberation of Mussolini, were not commented on in the Vatican Radio programs. The station was busy reassuring listeners that, despite everything, the activities of the Holy See continued regularly. Actually, a significant change had come about.

In a memo of the Secretariat of State, some doubts about the continuation of Vatican Radio's activities were set forth. Since the entrances to the Vatican could be controlled by German military, the question arose as to whether the fathers who did not live in Vatican City should continue their broadcasts, at the risk of being stopped, questioned, and searched by German guards. If they had to continue, they wondered if it would not be better for the fathers, instead of traveling in the dark of the night (until 10:15 p.m.), to go in the daytime in order to have their emissions recorded on tape.[158] Fr. Soccorsi noted that there were many difficulties with recordings, the registration did not eliminate the problem of the smooth traffic between the General Curia of the Society of Jesus at Borgo Santo Spirito and the Secretariat of State (for censorship) or between the General Curia and Vatican Radio (for registration). He believed that the problems would be solved if the fathers resided at the Vatican (as the Belgian and the German already did).[159] When asked if the Jesuits employed at Vatican Radio could find lodgings inside the Vatican, at first it was replied that it was possible under a guarantee by Vicar General Fr. Ambrogio Magni of their irreproachable conduct.[160] Nonetheless, after an audience with the Holy Father it was replied: "non expedire" (not appropriate).

According to the directives given by the pope, broadcasts had to be reduced "to pure chronicle of news that cannot stir up difficulties."[161] Vatican Radio programs were reduced to a simple information service of the Vatican and the only texts read were articles taken from *L'Osservatore Romano*, which, in turn, had reduced the number of its pages. It was diminished to "only giving religious news, abiding by the pure facts; no reflections inspired by Catholic thought must be expressed; the prior censorship no longer has any place." The aim was to "empty the programs, to give only 'some meager news.'"[162]

During the month of September, exchanges between Fr. Soccorsi and the Secretariat of State intensified: the director of Vatican Radio was concerned about scrupulously following the new directives.[163]

But before these instructions arrived, the collective pastoral letter from the German bishops, signed on August 18 and read from the pulpits on August 29, had been broadcast in German on September 7 and 8. Introducing it, the announcer said that it was "a noble testimony of our time, of what afflicts us but also of its greatness." According to the BBC Digest, no further comments appear to have been made.[164] The *Sicherheitsdienst* had not been completely negative about the episcopal document, either.[165] However, in early

October, Cardinal Bertram, through Nuncio Orsenigo, asked the Secretariat of State to keep an eye on Vatican Radio for any use that the enemies of Germany made of the letter of the Bishops' Conference of Fulda.[166] At an audience with Montini, Pius XII was surprised by Bertram's recommendation since, as he said, "Vatican Radio is very limited in its comments and silent." The fear of the German Bishops' Conference president, who was actually not present at the last meeting because he was ill and was replaced by Cardinal Faulhaber, was possibly addressed to the use that the English or American press and radio might have made, and had effectively already made, of the words of the German hierarchy, repeated by Vatican Radio. However, after it was published in *The Tablet*, no exploitations of it are found if we exclude the clarification that the letter had been broadcast by Vatican Radio before the Germans took control of Rome.[167]

On September 11, the day after the Germans occupied Rome, some programs, "for purely technical reasons"[168] did not go on the air. However, the one in German did, and according to *The Tablet* contained some passages that could refer to the situation at the time:[169]

> All history is a struggle in this world [. . .] In certain periods the struggle rises to heights which seem to surpass all limits of human endurance. That is the hour for pessimists. Those of little faith cry out, 'Lord, save us or we perish'. Those who are lacking in faith lament; but we hope. Are we not living through such a phase once more in these days? The waves are high; they threaten to swallow us. The struggle moves up to a crisis. In the struggle for the secular world, the hour of world imperialism has struck. In the struggle for the religious world the hour of materialism is about to end. In the struggle for the moral world the last hour of naturalism has arrived.

The analysis made by the United States Foreign Broadcast Information Service on Vatican Radio and press during that period confirms that there was no normal activity of radio broadcasting alongside the use of the radio for diplomatic purposes and for postal communications.[170] The German occupation of Rome, as confirmed by the report to the FBIS of October 1, was followed by a definitive reduction in the length of the programs and a change with regard to the content.[171] Apart from the announcements taken from the *L'Osservatore Romano*, the clerk wrote, "Vatican Radio has not broadcast anything socially or politically relevant." The author of the report for the FBIS explored the explanation of the new attitude of Vatican Radio, given by the BBC in a program directed to the German Catholics on September 26:

> The Vatican radio which was highly respected, even in non-Catholic circles, for its views on principles and vital questions of the present, has stopped these broadcasts following the taking over of protection of Vatican City by the German Wehrmacht. The Vatican broadcasts are now limited to the transmission of purely Church news.[172]

In France, on the other hand, Pierre Limagne wrote that, as Vatican Radio "is hardly giving any signs of life," there had been rumors that the station was being controlled by the Germans[173] and that the Nazis had "got their hands on the station."[174] Soccorsi informed Montini that Radio Londra had noticed the change of programs and stated that Vatican Radio was "occupied, controlled and watched over in all its accesses by the Germans," and that Pius XII was a prisoner in the Vatican.[175] On the same day, Vatican Radio in English assured that no German soldier had crossed the border of the State of the Vatican. Toward the end of October, with a statement published by the *L'Osservatore Romano*, and broadcast by Vatican Radio in Italian, attempts were made to deny these rumors and ensure that the German troops were respecting the activities of the Holy See and the rights and integrity of Vatican City.[176]

The attitude of the Holy See toward the German occupation of Rome has to be read in the light of its two greatest concerns in those months: seeing Rome, the symbol of Christianity, transformed into a battlefield, and the fear that the National Socialist rule would be replaced by communist rule.[177] The Allies were afraid that the Germans appeared as "protector(s) against communism and revolution" and used the idea of anticommunism to gain the support of the Vatican. There were, however, also rumors of the possibility that the Nazis had occupied the Vatican and kidnapped the Pope.[178] There had effectively been some signs pointing in this direction. A piece of paper was delivered anonymously, which said:

> German planes fly over the Vatican whenever the Holy Father is in the gardens. It is not improbable that a possible landing is being studied, near where His Holiness usually stops, in the intention of making a sudden attack in a broader style than that of the Gran Sasso and Sorrento. "Percutiam pastorem et dispergentur ove gregis." The Holy Father is begged to stay alert. It would be opportune to give instructions to Vatican Radio that, if necessary, before being occupied, it launches repeatedly, for as long as possible, an SOS to all the faithful in the world.[179]

Afterward, a confidential report was also sent by the Ministry of Internal Affairs:

A plan of invasion of the Vatican City by German troops is attributed to General Stahl. This invasion would take place if the German military command were to decide to resist indefinitely in Rome, transforming the city into a real battlefield. The aim of the invasion would be the kidnapping of the Pope, with his consequent transfer to a place yet to be decided.[180]

The apostolic delegate in London, Monsignor Godfrey, sent a confidential memo to the Secretariat of State, written by a member of the Department of Intelligence, published by the Research Department of the Foreign Office, and circulated among diplomats and journalists, which was very critical of the Holy See.[181] The document highlighted the diligent study that the Foreign Office continued to make of Vatican Radio programs and *L'Osservatore Romano*. The opinion on the change of programs was ruthless: "It would have played a more dignified part if it had been less obsequious in the matter of wireless programmes." Nothing similar to what Vatican Radio did before the occupation of Rome. "Vatican wireless propaganda on the world situation, though adapted to conditions of different countries, had been following definite lines. Take for instance its treatment of the war, of racialism and of the rights of individuals and groups." It continued that, prior to German occupation, Vatican Radio "frequently condemned (though not by name) these unpeaceful, largely Nazi and Fascist, doctrines," and concluded, "this propaganda has seemed designed to allay warring passions, correct wrong doctrines [. . .] and finally to attract the minds of its hearers to a basic Christian society which will make the disintegration of present régimes of small account. But this task has been suspended because the Germans are in Rome." The memorandum made "a particularly pitiful impression" on Maglione and he asked Godfrey to "put the attitude of the Holy See, which was not understood and badly set forth, into the correct light."[182]

Nonetheless, the silence of Vatican Radio continued. No mention was made of the roundup of Roman Jews on October 16, 1943.[183] No comment was made on the establishment of the Repubblica Sociale Italiana (RSI) in the north of the Italian Peninsula. The new State was not officially recognized by the Holy See[184] and the clergy were ordered to remain prudent and not to compromise themselves. Vatican Radio did not even read an article from the *L'Osservatore Romano* which condemned the order of internment of all of the Jews resident in the territory of the RSI and the confiscation of their property.[185] Probably, to the contrary of what happened, Vatican Radio did not want to circulate the comment outside national, or even Roman, borders.[186]

The war is over

From the second half of 1943, the foreign monitoring services of Vatican Radio attested to the predominant attention that the station reserved for the situation in Italy, particularly in Rome.[187] The very fact that most of the programs were based on reading articles from *L'Osservatore Romano* could only give the programs an essentially Italy-centric perspective. Italy had, of course, become a new theater of conflict between armies, but the Holy See's interest in Rome and Italy was, and remained, special. Vatican Radio, despite its natural international vocation, acted as a megaphone for Pius XII's concern for the center of Christianity.

Vatican media aimed at protecting the neutrality of the Holy See until the very end, now defending its extra-territoriality. The case of the violation of the extra-territoriality of the Benedictine abbey of San Paolo Fuori le Mura by the police of the RSI in the night between February 3 and 4, 1944, which led to the arrest of dozens of refugees and the consequent order to no longer give asylum to the persecuted, had a far-reaching echo in the foreign press, thanks to it being broadcast by Vatican Radio.[188] The Lateran Pacts were still valid, so the territory within the Leonine walls and all of the basilicas and seminaries spread throughout Rome, which enjoyed Vatican territoriality, could not be violated. Tardini's notes reveal the doubts and hesitations on broadcasting any radio programs about this and other events. On February 4, he noted: "It would seem opportune for Vatican Radio announced in a sober and dignified way the violation of the extra-territoriality and the protest made by the Holy See." But, he added immediately, if what happened in the Basilica of San Paolo had only been a rehearsal for something bigger that might happen, perhaps it was better not to publicize the event too much to avoid reactions of greater violence, but restricting news only to diplomatic activity.[189] In the following days, Cardinal Maglione, with the approval of Pius XII, appointed Tardini to draw up a draft note for the diplomatic corps accredited to the Holy See, and a protest to include in *L'Osservatore Romano* to be read on Vatican Radio.[190] This was done on February 7:

> In the night between February 3 and 4, armed guards, presenting themselves as divisions of the Republican police, under the command of Dr. Pietro Caruso—whose appointment as Head of the Police of Rome had been published by Italian newspapers a few days ago—forcefully entered the Patriarchal Basilica of San Paolo, violating the rights of extra-territoriality guaranteed by the solemn Treaty. Vatican officials, warned of what was happening, immediately went to San Paolo and found Mr. Caruso and his armed guards

there and lodged a formal protest. The Holy See publicly repeats its immense disapproval.[191]

The devastating effects of the violation of extra-territoriality on the refugees were also condemned following the bombing of Castel Gandolfo (February 10, 1944).[192] The authorities appointed to guard the papal villa in Castelli Romani said that thousands of defenseless people, including women and children, had not been able to be evacuated.

In early March, more bombs fell near the Vatican territories.[193] Tardini recorded in his notes a certain impatience for the behavior of the Allies and, above all, of President Roosevelt, who "blames it all on the Germans," wondering "whether it would not be opportune for Vatican Radio to begin to say something as well..."[194] He therefore considered the idea of letting the world know, through Vatican Radio, the real situation in Rome and the responsibility of the Allies for the bombing of the city. He observed:

> The Allied bombs destroy the Ostiense station and a train of munitions has blown up. What's more, they destroy several houses and kill many people in the area. We give the "news" to Vatican Radio; but only about the killing of the civilians, without saying anything about the military objective that was hit. With this, does Vatican Radio remain really "impartial"? That's what I ask myself.[195]

Pius XII had effectively given orders to consider resuming Vatican Radio programming in a more regular way, but on April 1, 1944, another order was given for everything to remain the same, with the programs lasting only a few minutes and the broadcasting of recorded discs. In Pius XII's decision, letters from Fr. Mistiaen and from the English announcer had had "its weight." They pointed out that improving and enriching the programs to bring comfort could take on a political meaning: why speak of this only now that the Italians and the Germans were having the worst of it?[196]

On the days that preceded and followed the liberation of Rome, Vatican Radio announcers warned of the possibility of a suspension in programming due to continuous voltage drops.[197] The day after June 4, 1944, the population of Rome flocked to St. Peter's Square to acclaim Pius XII and express their gratitude to him. This gesture, together with the image of the people huddling around Pius XII when he left the Vatican twice after the bombings of Roman neighborhoods, has rightly been deemed significant by historiography.[198] The comparison that Italian historian Federico Chabod made with the assault and the pillage by the Visigoths in the year 410 remains effective to understand what happened in 1944, and the capacity of the Roman Church to stand up, in place of the imperial power, as the defender of the population against the "barbarians."[199] In the fifth century, as in 1944, the void of civilian power was filled by religious power, the authority of which exceeded any other form whatsoever of political organization in the capital.[200]

In the broadcast in Italian on June 7, the crowd that had poured into St. Peter's Square was described. The fact, underlined the announcer, was all the more meaningful as there had been no announcement that Pius XII would be on the balcony and there were no means of transport or communication.[201]

Involved in the celebrations of the liberation of Rome, Vatican Radio did not give the news of the landing in Normandy. Although no documents are available that show if and how the news on the progress of the Allied advance in France was going—perhaps due to the failure of recording by the Monitoring Service more than the voluntary omission by the French-speaking announcer—the programs had gradually restarted in August. More concrete information on the liberation of Paris (August 25), according to the sources available, was broadcast in Spanish much later (October 17) through the broadcast of the words of archbishop Suhard.[202] In the meantime, Mistiaen had gone back to broadcasting his texts of a religious nature, but with implicit references to the contemporary period. He recalled the feats of the Church over the centuries to make the Kingdom of God on Earth, made up of free and brotherly nations. The constitutions of which should have been based on the equality between all men.[203]

As far as the programs for Germany were concerned, a series of eight episodes on the unity of Christians was put on air, with a focus on the Oriental Churches, given by lecturers at the Pontifical Oriental Institute. Of these, it is worth highlighting the last one, in which, for the first time, Vatican Radio mentioned the concessions made by Stalin to the Russian Orthodox Church in September 1943.[204] The author of the program was the Jesuit Wilhelm de Vries, who hoped that the situation in Russia would evolve in the direction of a peaceful separation between the State and the Church and complete religious freedom, "as in the United States."[205] It is difficult to decipher the decision to broadcast lessons on the Oriental Churches, moreover without the usual controversial tones. With the nearing of the end of the war and the well-known fear of the Catholic Church for the spread of communism in Europe, texts with more controversial tones could perhaps have been expected. From the sources available, we can only say that the decision to broadcast the series was almost compulsory, destined as it was to make up for the absence of material from the German Church. On January 26, 1945, the announcement was made that firsthand news on the religious activity of the Church in Germany could no longer be received and that, for eighteen months, no collective pastoral letter from the German episcopate had been published.[206] Vatican Radio seemed to have recovered from the silence of the months during the occupation of Rome, but it was still anxiously waiting for the end of the war.

At the same time, with the increasingly probable victory of the Allies, Pius XII spoke of democracy in his Christmas radio message of 1944.[207] In his speech, the pope explained what the conditions had to be for a "real and healthy democracy, befitting the circumstances of the present hour."[208] Vatican Radio commented on this in some programs. In German, for example, the announcer criticized those newspapers which had called Pius XII a "democratic Pope."[209] In the Spanish program, as well, the explanation of Pius XII's words aimed at underlining the limits within which democracy would be acceptable, i.e., citizens should be prepared about their rights and duties and to express their opinions; the "mass" should not take over from the "people"; citizens should be aware of their responsibilities; and, especially, that the governors of a democratic regime should interpret God's aims for human society.[210]

On May 7, the microphones of Vatican Radio could finally pronounce words of joy for the end of the war. In English, thanks were addressed to the "Immaculate Queen of peace" because peace had been signed during the month dedicated to her.[211] In Italian, attention was on the celebrations in the capital, where the sound of the sirens and bells spread and blessed the news.[212] The message from Fr. Mistiaen was more reflective, as he had always been:

> For six years we have been encircled in a ring of iron; nations have seen their roads trodden by refugees, deportees, prisoners, and requisitioned people. And yet hope prevailed. Today, at last, our hearts are filled with joy; but let this joy not be vulgar and superficial—let it be respectful and dignified, in memory of so much suffering. Let us remember that many of our dear ones are in Heaven and let their memory hover over our joy. They died, loyal to their duty, to preserve liberty. Let us cherish them in our hearts.[213]

The exultation for the end of the war could not erase the very high costs that the whole of humanity had had to pay.

Epilogue: The 1950s

Launched in the 1930s, the apostolate on air by Vatican Radio proved its extraordinary potential to disseminate Catholic thought and teachings, reaching the faithful throughout the world during World War II.

The research for this book, thanks in part to new documents made available through the Vatican on the pontificate of Pius XII, has brought to light several aspects concerning the Holy See's relationship with the media and, through the prism of this relationship, the attitude maintained during World War II. With regard to the first aspect, the traditional prudence toward new instruments of communication gradually gave way to a certain enthusiasm for the various potentialities of the radio. Vatican Radio was one of the first radio stations to broadcast in numerous languages and reach multiple locations: the universal Christian message could thus become global.

Research reveals that during World War II there were different positions within the Roman Curia and the Society of Jesus about the war itself, the behavior that the pope was to maintain, and the role that Vatican Radio was to play. Thus, figures of Jesuits such as Vincent McCormick, Robert Leiber, Emmanuel Mistiaen, Beat Ambord, and Ortiz de Urbina, to name a few, who made their contributions to orienting the faithful during the conflict, are highlighted. From their broadcasts emerge different positions, some quite critical, toward Pius XII's maintained neutrality/impartiality. But there also emerges, despite the recognized threat of the Third Reich's anti-Christian policy, a preference for authoritarian regimes such as Portugal and Spain in which the leading role of the Catholic Church in society and the ordering of the State is recognized. Vatican Radio broadcasts show how denouncing the persecution of Catholics by the Nazis and trying to counter Third Reich propaganda, did not automatically mean siding with the democracies.

We have explored whether (and how) Vatican Radio addressed the issues of racism, antisemitism, and the Shoah. Although there were some broadcasts in which the persecution of Jews was mentioned (e.g., the reference to Polish ghettos in January 1940, and to deportations in May of that year;

Mistiaen's broadcasts in 1942 with the allusion to the deportation of French Jews; the broadcasts on Croatian antisemitic laws in July 1943) they were evidently too few to be incisive. Moreover, condemnation of racism was almost never accompanied by the identification of Jews as victims. Through this, it is possible to contribute to the debate around Pius XII's silences: how much did the censorship of the Secretariat of State, imposed since 1941, influence the way in which Vatican Radio dealt with these issues? There is no firm evidence on specific orders given in this regard, but it is likely that in the same year that the speakers were ordered to stop talking about the situation of Catholics in Germany, they were, a fortiori, unable to talk about the situation of Jews. In this regard, the key role of Jesuit General Ledóchowski, known (through the research) for his fierce antisemitism, has emerged. It is likely that he himself censored any broadcasts about the Jews. However, this research has highlighted his importance in ensuring that Vatican Radio could continue its broadcasts, despite the protests of the German Embassy to the Holy See, and also the protection that he offered to his Belgian confrere, Mistiaen, so that he could continue his broadcasts and instill courage in the French people during the war.

At the end of World War II, the global success of Vatican Radio convinced the Holy See to plan its expansion, increasing, year by year, the number of programs, and guaranteeing coverage in new countries; attempting to meet the needs of its listeners in a rapidly changing society thanks, in part, to advancing technical improvements.

Pius XII praised the qualities of the radio in a speech to the personnel of RAI (the Italian Radio and television company) in December 1944, with words which would be repeated in the encyclical dedicated to the means of communication, *Miranda prorsus,* in 1957.[1] The radio, he explained, "has the privilege of being as though unattached and free from those conditions of space and time, which prevent or delay all the other means of communication among people. With an infinitely faster wing than the soundwaves, as fast as light, it brings, in an instant, overcoming every frontier, the messages that are given to it."[2] He also added that the radio had civilizing intentions, the capacity to adapt languages and contents and, consequently, to be for everyone (youngsters, women, office workers, businessmen, doctors, and farmers).

The project to promote Vatican Radio began to take shape after the Congress of the International Telecommunications Union held in Atlantic City in 1947, attended by Director Filippo Soccorsi. To organize global coverage of the radio service, in order to guarantee that the Holy See was listened to all over the world, two new centers were planned, one to transmit from

Santa Maria di Galeria, about eleven miles from Rome, and one to receive in Castel Romano.³ Talks with the newly born Republican Italian government led to the signature of an agreement on October 8, 1951, ratified on June 13, 1952, after which work on these new centers could start.

On August 15, 1951, General of the Society of Jesus Jean-Baptiste Janssens, announced the Statute of Vatican Radio, in which the organization and the purposes of the station were defined: to spread the voice of the pope and the pontifical ceremonies, to establish direct connections between the Holy See and different countries, and to be an instrument of apostolate.⁴ In a letter to the Jesuits working at Vatican Radio, the general explained that they were assigned with the organization of the content of the programs and the responsibility for them, and that the Holy See would fund and watch over the general orientations.⁵

From 1951 to 1954, improvements were attempted for the programs in different languages, including suggestions coming from the nunciatures or the ecclesiastical hierarchies of the countries they were for. For example, Monsignor Stefan Wyszynski from Poland, at the time archbishop of Gniezno and Warsaw, left a note in which he highlighted the need for Vatican Radio to consider the needs of people resident in countries under the sphere of Soviet influence.⁶ Unlike free nations, in these countries the lack of free press and the discontinuous contact with the Holy See could be compensated by the radio. Listeners wanted to hear the voice of the pope, and as his speeches and the encyclicals were not printed, they wanted Vatican Radio to broadcast them. Wyszynski also suggested providing programs of apostolate both for Catholics and for communists: "The Catholics have to feel that the Holy See is not abandoning them, and the communists have to know at least that they have not stopped being children of God." Vatican Radio had to show trust in the ecclesiastical hierarchy who were fighting next to their brethren behind the Iron Curtain, avoiding excessive criticism, "because the listeners would have had in their mind, 'You come, live with us and then teach us.'"

On July 12, 1954, Janssens sent suggestions for improvements in programming to the Secretariat of State, which alongside technical ones were necessary since listeners were complaining of the low standards of the programs. He recommended that a group of collaborators was formed who would be kept up to date on world events and could work on preparing the programs. At its meeting on September 25, the Pontifical Commission for the Vatican City State examined and approved the suggestions of the general⁷ and set up a commission to assist, from doctrinal, political, and artistic points of view, the management of writing Vatican Radio programs.⁸ For this purpose, the following people were appointed by the Secretariat of State:[9] Cardinal Nicola Canali, president of the Pontifical Commission for the Vatican City State, Monsignors Felice Pirozzi, Corrado Bafile, Angelo Pedroni, Albino Galletto, and Achille Glorieux, Fathers Fiorillo Cavalli, Antonio Stefanizzi, Francesco Pellegrino, Prince Carlo Pacelli, and Count Enrico Galeazzi.

Fr. Stefanizzi pointed out to Monsignor Angelo Dell'Acqua that Vatican Radio must often express opinions, provide information, and deal with delicate subjects. In such circumstances, the need was felt "to hear the advice of consultants who could indicate a definite direction, provide exact information on news and also the news itself." Therefore, he asked for a monsignor of the first and second section of the Secretariat of State to be named, and to whom he could turn in case of doubts.[10] Monsignor Tardini gave the task respectively to Monsignor Corrado Bafile and Monsignor Angelo Pedroni.

The first meeting of the Programs Commission—which became the *Commission for the Vatican Radio Station*—directed by Canali, was held on May 30, 1955. *L'Osservatore Romano*, as it was in the past, and the new *Irvat* (Vatican Radio news bulletin) would orient the content of the programs. Each section manager, one for each language, had the task of checking the translations from the Italian bulletin into their language, with the possibility of adapting it to his particular country by consent of the *Irvat*'s director.

In 1955, Vatican Radio broadcast in twenty-eight languages, for a total of 239 weekly programs of fifteen minutes; eighteen Jesuits held managerial positions, and there were sixteen external announcers and seven translators. The fundamental criteria that the formation of the programs had to follow were established: "to orient minds in a Catholic way on current facts and problems; to fuel religious culture and life; to interest as vast a public as possible in the extraordinary events that take place in Rome." The point of view that the announcers had to express, Stefanizzi recommended, was that of the Holy See, "which speaks in different languages and is above the particular interests of the individual countries."[11] The greatest concern that emerges from the documents about this period of planning and experimentation of Vatican Radio is that the announcers had to reflect "faithfully the thoughts of the Holy See and the safe Catholic teachings."

The *Irvat* radio news bulletin was therefore given particular importance. Every day at 2:30 p.m. the bulletin was transmitted in Italian, followed by translations in seven languages. News was provided by the "press department" of the Vatican which also used foreign Catholic agencies.

When the new facilities started in 1957, the management of Vatican Radio tried to further improve the content and the presentation of the programs.[12] They began daily broadcasts for South America, China, Japan, India, and Australia. For the communist countries in Eastern Europe, a conversation on apologetics was distributed each week.[13]

As far as the 1950s are concerned, the new archive sources do not tell us much more about the content of the programs, except for the Italian ones. It is worth dwelling on this briefly because, as Stefanizzi wrote in his 1955 report, "the Italians expect much more from Vatican Radio than the other faithful."[14] In the Italy of the 1950s, the radio was the most common household appliance.[15] The Italian programs of Vatican Radio started at 9:15 p.m. and lasted thirty minutes as opposed to the fifteen minutes for the programs in other languages. The main news of the day was read along with a short comment on current affairs, a talk, a sketch, a piece of music, and a religious thought. The topics of the talks included religion and science, moral theology, discussions of subjects such as culture and current affairs, bibliographic reviews, orientations for professions, documentaries, and saints' profiles. In addition, there were sections on liturgical subjects, medicine, programs for women and the ill, the history of the Church, religious geography, Mariology, communism (called "the heresy of the century"), Catholic Action, and book reviews. In 1953, a program called *Radio Lent* was also inaugurated, which was to accompany the period of Lent each year, with talks by well-known Roman religious figures.

In February 1952, the transmission of the Rosary began—the first was recited by Pius XII himself—"on the occasion of the crusade 'for a better world.'"[16] Radio preaching by the Jesuit Riccardo Lombardi started in 1948 when, with the help of two other priests, he inaugurated the "crusade of goodness" to promote the social doctrine of the Church against the errors of communism, socialism, and capitalism in Italy. The following year, considering the international interest in Lombardi's preaching, the "crusade for goodness" became the "crusade for a new world." Lombardi had the full support of Pius XII who saw in his preaching a form of apostolate suitable for the establishment of Christian society. Endorsement took place in public as well, when on December 8, 1950, after the radio preaching of the "crusade for a better world," the program was followed by midnight Mass celebrated by the pope himself.[17] In Pius XII's view, Catholicism had to be able to give answers to all the problems of modern society, and the Catholics engaged in politics had to obey the directives of the ecclesiastical hierarchy. The programs of Vatican Radio also had to pursue this objective.

However, after World War II, another piece of technology had begun to spread throughout homes in the industrialized world, which would steal the stage from the radio—television. The habits and needs of mass media users changed, and so in the evenings, families preferred to gather in front of the television, which, unlike the radio, combined sound and pictures. On March 27, 1949, the US had the privilege to be the country to have the first televised papal message recorded by Pius XII and addressed to the American television audience. This was the first involvement of a pope with the new medium of television.[18]

It was not until 1983 that the Vatican Television Center was created. Whereas, until then, the filming and broadcasting of images was entrusted to RAI under a convention, the CTV became the instrument by which footage of the pope and the activities of the Holy See were made available to all television stations around the world, in order to ensure the widest possible dissemination.[19]

Although radio had lost some of its importance, it did not disappear; thanks, in part, to the invention of the transistor radio, which enabled the device to downsize and become portable with the use of batteries. This, together with a cultural shift in the direction of increasing individualism, including in the enjoyment of media, meant that the radio became the first mobile, personal electronic medium, no longer aimed at the family but at the individual. The second half of the twentieth century would usher in a new dialectic in the relationship between radio and television.[20]

Radio days were over.

Acknowledgments

I sincerely thank all the scholars with whom, in different ways and to different degrees, I have had the good fortune of working with during the years that I have been engaged in this research. It would be too long a list to name them all, but to each one goes my heartfelt gratitude. Special thanks to the archivists of the many archives that I have consulted.

The realization of this book would not have been possible without the support of Fordham University Press, specifically in the persons of Fredric Nachbaur, who followed me from the beginning believing in this volume, Kurt Piehler, and Kem Crimmins. For the translation from Italian, I thank Joan Rundo, and for the copyediting work, Lis Pearson. It has been a privilege to work with such capable and knowledgeable people. Special thanks also to Msgr. Dario Edoardo Viganò, Vice Chancellor for Communications of the Pontifical Academy of Sciences, and Vatican Media for the cover photo.

Notes

Introduction

1. On October 28, 2019, with the motu proprio *Historical experience*, Pope Francis restored the original name "Vatican Apostolic Archive," previously known as the Vatican Secret Archive. https://www.archivioapostolicovaticano.va/content/aav/en/news/news/Motu-Proprio-AAV.html.

2. https://www.vatican.va/content/francesco/en/speeches/2019/march/documents/papa-francesco_20190304_archivio-segretovaticano.html.

3. At least since when, in the 1960s, the controversy exploded on the "silences of Pius XII" following the performance of the play by Rolf Hochhuth, *The Deputy* (1963). The Holy See responded with the publication of the eleven volumes of the *Actes et documents du Saint-Siège relatifs à la Seconde Guerre Mondiale,* eds. P. Blet et al. (Città del Vaticano: Libreria Editrice Vaticana, 1970–1981), which are a selection of the documents of the Holy See from during the period of the war.

4. "Pio XII, la guerra e il silenzio del papa. Intervista a David I. Kertzer," in *Giornale di storia* https://www.giornaledistoria.net/saggi/mestiere-di-storico/pio-xii-la-guerra-e-il-silenzio-del-papa-intervista-a-david-kertzer/.; "Archives de Pie XII: des historiens livrent leurs premières impressions," in *La Croix*, May 21, 2020.

5. In the 1970s, Robert A. Graham, "La Radio Vaticana tra Londra e Berlino. Un dossier della guerra delle onde: 1940–1941," in *La Civiltà Cattolica* 1976, volume I, 132–150; Alberto Monticone, "La radio vaticana tra fascismo e guerra (1931–1944)," in *Chiesa e società dal secolo IV ai nostri giorni. Studi storici in onore del P. Ilarino da Milano*, volume II (Roma: Herder, 1979), 681–727. More recently, Roger Voog, "La voix du Vatican, juillet 1940–octobre 1942" in *Églises et Chrétiens dans la II guerre mondiale: la France. Actes du Colloque, Lyon 27–30 janvier 1978*, eds. X. de Montclos et al. (Lyon: Presses Universitaires de Lyon, 1982), 137–149; Marilyn J. Matelski, *Vatican Radio. Propaganda by the airwaves* (Westport: Praeger, 1995); and Jacques Adler, "Radio Vatican's Opposition to Nazi Ideology," in *Revue d'histoire ecclésiastique* 99 (2004): 722–757: 9.

6. Raffaella Perin, *La radio del papa. Propaganda e diplomazia nella seconda guerra mondiale* (Bologna: il Mulino, 2017).

7. Andrew Walker, "British Broadcasting Corporation: BBC Monitoring Service," in *Encyclopedia of Radio*, volume 1, ed. C.H. Sterling (New York: Taylor

& Francis Group, 2004), 211–214; Olive Renier and Vladimir Rubinstein, *Assigned to Listen. The Evesham Experience 1939–43* (London: BBC, 1986); and Ramon Silva, *BBC Monitoring Service, August 1939–August 1979*, 5; in Warburg Institute Archive (London—UK), Archive of E.H. Gombrich, box 2, World Service BBC. The addressees, in addition to the Ministry of Information, included the Admiralty, the Foreign Office, the War Office, the Ministry of the Air, the Dominions Office, the Colonial Office, the India Office, and the Intelligence Division of the Ministry of Economic Warfare.

8. Citations from the *Digest* will be identified as follows: *Daily Digest of Foreign Broadcasts*, Vatican Radio, language, country, date, time.

9. For an analysis of how the news that was collected by the British Monitoring Service was used as propaganda see Gordon Johnston and Emma Robertson, *BBC World Service. Overseas Broadcasting, 1932–2018* (London: Palgrave Macmillan, 2019).

10. This is what can be concluded from a document of the Sonderdienst Seehaus dated March 28, 1941, on the "systematic observation" of Vatican Radio for its "defamatory propaganda." See PAAA, Akten. Kirchenfragen, bd. 2, 28. The register of the programs is kept in BA, R 74: *Sonderdienst Seehaus der Deutschen Auslands-Rundfunkgesellschaft Interradio AG*. An incomplete collection of this documentation is also kept in the Library of Congress (Washington, D.C.). It can be presumed from this collection that the Sonderdienst often transcribed the programs in their original language and probably, depending on their importance, subsequently translated the texts into German. LOC, *Funk-Abhör-Berichte. Sendungen fremder Rundfunksender*. For a history of the Sonderdienst see Willi A. Boelke, "Das 'Seehaus' in Berlin-Wannsee. Zur Geschichte des deutschen 'Monitoring service' während des Zweiten Weltkrieges," in *Jahrbuch für die Geschichte Mittel- und Ostdeutschlands* 23 (1974): 231–269.

11. On the Foreign Broadcast Monitoring Service see Joseph E. Roop, *Foreign Broadcast Information Service. History. Part I 1941–1947* (Central Intelligence Agency, 1969). https://apps.dtic.mil/sti/citations/ADA510770. NARA, R.G. 208, Records of the Office of War Information, entry 352, Foreign Information Digests, boxes 1–8.

12. ASDMAE, Ambasciata Santa Sede, b. 163, sottofascicolo 1 and b. 147, fasc. 1, sottofascicolo 3.

13. ASDMAE, Ambasciata Santa Sede, b. 116, sottofascicolo 5. Radio Vatican News Bulletin.

14. See Renée Bédarida, "La Voix du Vatican (1940–1942). Bataille des ondes et Résistance spirituelle," in *Revue d'histoire de l'Église de France* 173 (1978): 215–243. A copy of *La Voix du Vatican* is in the library of the Institut Catholique de Paris. André Mandouze, the well-known scholar of St. Augustine and member of the Christian French Resistance under the Vichy regime, in 1941 when he taught in a lycée in Bourg, moved to Toulon, where until 1942, the year in which he was appointed assistant professor at the University of Lyon, he was in charge of the

département for the circulation of the *Cahiers du Témoignage chrétien*. In his archive, now at the Centre d'histoire de la résistance et de la déportation in Lyon, there are complete transcriptions of the programs of Vatican Radio in French from July 6 to September 25, 1940, thanks to which it has been possible to date some of them. It is not possible to say with any certainty whether another important source, the book entitled *Radio Vatican. Années 1940-1941-1942-1943. Emissions prises en sténo à Toulon*, now in the library of the Institut Catholique de Paris, belonged to him.

15. For an overview of the attitude of the Holy See toward the new media, see Raffaella Perin, "Popes and the Media," in *The Cambridge History of the Papacy*, volume 3, *Civil Society*, eds. J. Rollo-Koster et al. (Cambridge: Cambridge University Press, forthcoming).

16. See for example, the encyclicals *Mirari vos* of Gregory XVI; and *Nostis et Nobiscum, Quanta cura* and the *Syllabus* of Pius IX.

17. Alessandra Marani, "Il progetto politico-religioso di Leone XIII in Italia: la costituzione delle conferenze episcopali regionali," in *Episcopato e società tra Leone XIII e Pio X. Direttive romane ed esperienze locali in Emilia Romagna e Veneto*, ed. D. Menozzi (Bologna: il Mulino, 2000), 117–205: 18–19.

18. Adriana Chirico, *Profili giuridici della comunicazione nella Chiesa* (Bari: Cacucci, 2014), 33.

19. See Giovanni Vian, *La riforma della Chiesa per la restaurazione cristiana della società. Le visite apostoliche delle diocesi e dei seminari d'Italia promosse durante il pontificato di Pio X (1903–1914)* (Roma: Herder, 1998), 492–493: footnote 575; Alejandro M. Dieguez, "Se fossi Papa proibirei tutti i giornali." La stampa di Pio X, in *La riforma della Chiesa nelle riviste religiose italiane di inizio Novecento*, eds. D. Saresella and M. Benedetti (Milano: EBF, 2009), 13–26. The pope's opinion does not differ greatly from that of English politicians in the early nineteenth century, such as Edmund Burke, of the Whig Party who described the press as "the grand instrument of the subversion of order, morals, religion and human society itself." Not to mention the strict laws which limited the freedom of the press after the start of the French Revolution, passed by the government of William Pitt, perfectly aware of its subversive power. See Arthur Aspinall, *Politics and the Press c. 1780–1850* (London: Home & Van Thal, 1949), 1, 38 f.

20. Heidi J. S. Tworek, "Wireless Telegraphy," in *1914–1918-online. International Encyclopedia of the First World War*, eds. U. Daniel et al. (Berlin: Freie Universität Berlin, 2014). http://encyclopedia.1914-1918-online.net/article/wireless_telegraphy DOI: 10.15463/ie1418.10347.; and Heidi J. S. Tworek, *News from Germany. The competition to control world communications, 1900–1945* (Cambridge: Harvard University Press, 2019), 45 f.

21. For an interesting comparison between British and American radio throughout the 1930s see Alice Goldfarb Marquis, "Written on the Wind: The Impact of Radio during the 1930s," in *Journal of Contemporary History* 3 (1984): 385–415.

Notes to pages 6–7

22. See Robert S. Fortner, "Propaganda by Radio," in *Encyclopedia of Radio*, volume 3, ed. C.H. Sterling (New York: Taylor & Francis Group, 2004), 1113–1117. In the United States, "the father of entertainment broadcasting is David Sarnoff," who began as an office boy at the American Marconi Company and eventually became the president of RCA. In 1916, Sarnoff submitted a business plan to his superior at the Marconi Company in which the radio receiver would be a music box in people's houses, broadcasting music or lectures. See James Wood, *History of International Broadcasting*, volume 1 (London: The Institution of Engineering and Technology, 2008), 12. Nonetheless, the first person in America to broadcast entertainment programs regularly was Frank Conrad.

23. On October 24, 1923, Germany invented State broadcasting, the Reichspostministerium issuing a decree which introduced an entertainment broadcasting service in Germany. See Wood, *History of International Broadcasting*, 16; Robert G. Finney, "Radio Corporation of America," in *Encyclopedia of Radio*, volume 3, ed. C.H. Sterling (New York: Taylor & Francis Group, 2004), 1163–1165; Asa Briggs, *The History of Broadcasting in the United Kingdom*, 5 volumes, (Oxford: Oxford University Press, 1995); Fabrice D'Almeida and Christian Delporte, *Histoire des médias en France de la Grande Guerre à nos jours* (Paris: Flammarion, 2003), 80; Franco Monteleone, *Storia della radio e della televisione in Italia: società, politica, strategie, programmi, 1922–1992* (Venezia: Marsilio, 1992), 19 and *passim*; and Heidi J. S. Evans, "'The Path to Freedom'? Transocean and German Wireless Telegraphy, 1914–1922," in *Historical social research* 35 (1) (2010): 209–233: 221.

24. Andreas Fickers, "Visibly audible. The radio dial as mediating interface," in *The Oxford Handbook of Sound Studies*, eds. T. Pinch and K. Bijsterveld (New York: Oxford University Press, 2012), 411–439: 417.

25. Enrico Baragli, *Comunicazione comunione e chiesa* (Roma: Studio Romano della comunicazione sociale, 1973), 451–452: doc. 356.

26. Baragli, *Comunicazione comunione e chiesa*, 459–460: doc. 362.

27. Cf. Sara Airoldi, "Gli esordi dell'apostolato via etere: le radioprediche di Vittorino Facchinetti (1926–1936)," in *Società e Storia* 132 (2011): 301–330; Gianni Isola, *Abbassa la tua radio, per favore . . . Storia dell'ascolto radiofonico nell'Italia fascista* (Firenze: La Nuova Italia, 1990), 143–168; Gianni Isola, *L'ha scritto la radio. Storia e testi della radio durante il fascismo (1924–1944)* (Milano: Mondadori, 1998), 109–155; and Paul B. Campbell, "Religion on Radio," in *Encyclopedia of Radio*, volume 3, ed. C.H. Sterling (New York: Taylor & Francis Group, 2004), 1211–1216.

28. Stefano Pivato, "L'organizzazione cattolica della cultura di massa durante in fascismo," in *Italia contemporanea* 132 (1978): 3–25: 4; and Michel Lagrée, *La bénédiction de Prométhée. Religion et technologie XIX–XX siècle* (Paris: Fayard, 1999), 326–340.

29. *Divini illius Magistri* on Christian Education (December 31, 1929), https://www.papalencyclicals.net/pius11/p11rappr.htm.

30. See John Pollard, "Electronic pastors: radio, cinema, and television, from Pius XI to John XXIII," in *The Papacy since 1500 From Italian Prince to Universal Pastor*, eds. J. Corkery and T. Worcester (Cambridge: Cambridge University Press, 2010), 182–203: 183, footnote 5; and John Pollard, *The Unknown Pope: Benedict XV (1914–1922) and the Pursuit of Peace* (London: Continuum, 2005), 77.

31. Degna Marconi Paresce, *Marconi, mio padre* (Milano: Mondadori, 1967), 237.

32. Letter of Gianfranceschi to the engineer Luigi Respighi, executive officer for communications, July 25, 1925, in Fernando Bea and Alessandro De Carolis, *Ottant'anni della radio del papa*, volume I [Fernando Bea, *Da Pio XI a Giovanni Paolo II (1931–1981)*] (Città del Vaticano: Libreria Editrice Vaticana, 2011), 19. Bea, however, does not specify where this letter is kept.

33. Marconi, *Marconi, mio padre*, 280–281.

34. Carlo Confalonieri, *Pio XI visto da vicino* (Torino: Saie, 1957), 147–148. See also Marc Raboy, *Marconi. The man who networked the world* (New York: Oxford University Press, 2016), 563–569.

35. See art. 6 of the "Trattato fra la Santa Sede e l'Italia," in *Acta Apostolicae Sedis*, June 7, 1929, 209–221: 212.

36. The text of the agreement is in ASRS, AA.EE.SS., Pio XI, Stati Ecclesiastici, Pos. 409 P.O., fasc. 309, ff. 57–63.

37. ASRS, *AA.EE.SS.*, Pio XI, Stati Ecclesiastici, Pos. 409 P.O., fasc. 309, f. 76.

38. *Radiocorriere*. August 16–23, 1930.

39. ASRS, *AA.EE.SS.*, Pio XI, Stati Ecclesiastici, Pos. 409 P.O., fasc. 310, ff. 11–12.

1. The Popes and the Media: The Origins of Vatican Radio (1931–1939)

1. "Il primo radiomessaggio a tutte le genti e ad ogni creatura," in *Discorsi di Pio XI*, volume II, 1929–1933, ed. D. Bertetto (Torino: Società editrice internazionale, 1960), 479–483.

2. For this quotation and for the chronicle of the day with analysis of the main Italian and foreign newspapers, see Fernando Bea, *Da Pio XI a Giovanni Paolo II (1931–1981)* (Città del Vaticano: Libreria Editrice Vaticana, 2011), 38–58: 44.

3. See Alberto Monticone, "La radio vaticana tra fascismo e guerra (1931–1944)," in *Chiesa e società dal secolo IV ai nostri giorni. Studi storici in onore del P. Ilarino da Milano*, volume II (Roma: Herder, 1979), 686; and "Le trasmissioni della Stazione Radio," in *L'Osservatore Romano*, July 25, 1931, 2.

4. Born in Arcevia in 1875. After graduating with a degree in philosophy from the Gregorian University in 1902, he received degrees in mathematics and physics from the University of Rome, subjects he later taught at the Jesuit Istituto Massimo in Rome and at the Gregorian University, of which he also became rector. He published more than 150 scientific articles on electrophysics, acoustics, optics, and astronomy. Benedict XV appointed him president of the Pontifical Academy of Sciences in 1921. See the entry "Gianfranceschi Giuseppe" in *Diccionario histórico de la Compañia de Jesús biográfico-temático*, volume II,

eds. C. E. O'Neill, J.M. Domínguez (Madrid: Universidad Pontificia Comillas, 2001), 1724.

5. Francesco Farusi and Gianni Bosca, "La radio vaticana. Note storiche," in *Radiotelevisione per Cristo* (Catania: Edizioni Paoline, 1961), 7–67: 38.

6. Monticone, *La radio vaticana tra fascismo e guerra (1931–1944)*, 684: footnote 7.

7. "Per la prima radiotrasmissione del "Giornale scientifico," in *Discorsi di Pio XI*, volume II, 530–531.

8. "Le nuove esperienze di Marconi alla presenza del S. Padre," in *L'Illustrazione Vaticana* 9 (1932): 429–431.

9. See Laura Pettinaroli, *La politique russe du Saint-Siège (1905–1939)* (Rome: École française de Rome, 2015), 744–745.

10. Born in Rome in 1900 to a family of papal tradition (whose members were professionals or technicians in the papal administration), he pursued classical studies at the Jesuit Collegio Romano. In 1922, after graduating with degrees in mathematics and physics from the University of Rome, he entered the Turin province of the Society of Jesus. Director of Vatican Radio from 1934 to 1953 and lecturer at the Pontifical Gregorian University, between 1950 and 1952 he planned a new and more powerful radio facility outside of the Vatican's borders, which then became the Santa Maria di Galeria radio plants.

11. ASRS, *AA.EE.SS.*, Pio XI, Stati Ecclesiastici, Pos. 483 P.O., fasc. 503, f. 14.

12. See Raffaella Perin, "Introduction" in *The Popes on Air: The History of Vatican Radio from Its Origins to World War II* (New York: Fordham University Press, 2024).

13. Enrico Baragli, *Comunicazione comunione e chiesa* (Roma: Studio Romano della comunicazione sociale, 1973), 510: doc. 420.

14. See Hubert Gruber, "Friedrich Muckermann," in *Neue Deutsche Biographie* 18 (1997): 258–260; http://www.deutsche-biographie.de/sfz65916.html.

15. The Secretariat against Atheism was established in April 1934 to coordinate the activity of the Catholic international press against communism. See Filippo Frangioni, "L'Urss e la propaganda contro la religione. Per una definizione dell'anticomunismo nella Santa Sede degli anni Trenta," in *Pius XI: Keywords. International conference Milan 2009*, eds. A. Guasco and R. Perin (Berlin: LIT Verlag, 2010), 299–311: 305–306. In a few years, the Secretariat was able to collect countless documents (magazines, booklets, brochures) on communist propaganda at an international level. Two exhibitions on the material collected were organized in 1936 and 1938 at the Russicum. In 1936, *Lettres de Rome* had more than one thousand subscribers. See Giorgio Petracchi, "I gesuiti e il comunismo tra le due guerre," in *La Chiesa cattolica e il totalitarismo. Atti del convegno Torino, 25–26 ottobre 2001*, ed. V. Ferrone (Firenze: Olschki, 2004), 123–152; Philippe Chenaux, *L'ultima eresia. La Chiesa Cattolica e il comunismo in Europa da Lenin a Giovanni Paolo II*, Italian translation (Roma: Carocci, 2009), 63–64; and Giuliana Chamedes, *A Twentieth Century Crusade. The Vatican's*

Battle to Remake Christian Europe (Cambridge: Harvard University Press, 2019), 121–166.

16. Ledóchowski to Muckermann, May 29, 1936, in ARSI, Regg. epp. Germ. Inf.

17. Friedrich Muckermann, *Im Kampf zwischen zwei Epochen. Lebenserinnerungen*, ed. N. Junk (Mainz: Matthias-Grünewald-Verlag, 1973), 296–302.

18. Unsigned and undated typescript. ASRS, *AA.EE.SS.*, Pio XI, Stati Ecclesiastici, Pos. 409 P.O., fasc. 309, ff. 66–70.

19. "All'Ufficio Cattolico di Radiodiffusione. L'apostolato delle radiodiffusioni," November 10, 1936, in *Discorsi di Pio XI*, volume III, 588–591: 590.

20. "All'Ufficio Cattolico di Radiodiffusione," 588.

21. ASRS, *AA.EE.SS.*, Pio XI, Stati Ecclesiastici, Pos. 533 P.O., fasc. 556, f. 7.

22. AAV, *Arch. Nunz. Italia*, b. 9, fasc. 3, ff. 8–9.

23. This is what Monsignor Domenico Tardini wrote to the nuncio in Berne, Filippo Bernardini. ASRS, *AA.EE.SS.*, Pio XI, Stati Ecclesiastici, Pos. 536 P.O., fasc. 559, ff. 13–14v.

24. ASRS, *AA.EE.SS.*, Pio XI, Stati Ecclesiastici, Pos. 536 P.O., fasc. 560, ff. 23–29: 25. For the official text and the signatory countries, see Société des Nations, *Convention Internationale concernant l'emploi de la radiodiffusion dans l'intérêt de la paix* (Genève, le 23 septembre 1936), Série de Publications de la Société des Nations, 1937.

25. Montini to Soccorsi, July 20, 1938, in AAV, Segr. di Stato, Solennità e Congressi, pos. 81, ff. 2–3.

26. AAV, Segr. di Stato, Solennità e Congressi, pos. 81, f. 29.

27. ASRS, *AA.EE.SS.*, Pio XI, Stati Ecclesiastici, Pos. 472 P.O., fasc. 473, ff. 15–16. *Rapport sur nos travaux par Mgr. Bernhard Marshall*, in ASRS, *AA.EE.SS.*, Pio XI, Stati Ecclesiastici, Pos. 472 P.O., fasc. 473, ff. 14–15. The bulletin is not dated but I can suppose it is from 1934. For some information, see also Federico Ruozzi, "Voci e immagini della fede: radio e tv," in *Cristiani d'Italia. Chiesa, società, stato, 1861–2011*, ed. A. Melloni (Roma: Istituto della Enciclopedia Italiana, 2011), 471–486: 473.

28. ASRS, *AA.EE.SS.*, Pio XI, Stati Ecclesiastici, Pos. 472 P.O., fasc. 473, f. 75.

29. "All'Ufficio Cattolico di Radiodiffusione," in *Discorsi di Pio XI*, vol. III, 588–591: 590; Ps 18, 5.

30. Maurice Hankart, "I rapporti fra la stampa e la radio," in *L'Osservatore Romano*, November 19, 1936, 3.

31. Filippo Soccorsi, "La radio e i cattolici," in *L'Osservatore Romano*, March 7, 1937, 2.

32. ASRV, Filippo Soccorsi, *Note sul primo decennio della Radio Vaticana 1931–1941*, 9.

33. Soccorsi, *Note sul primo decennio della Radio Vaticana 1931–1941*, 11.

34. Muckermann, *Im Kampf zwischen zwei Epochen*, 296.

35. ASRS, *AA.EE.SS.*, Pio XI, Stati Ecclesiastici, Pos. 536 P.O., fasc. 560, ff. 36–39. See also the presentation of the project to the general of the Jesuits in ARSI,

Provincia Romana, Epistolae, 1051-III, 1–9, and his answer in ARSI, Assistentia Italiae, Provincia Romana, vol. XVI (1932–1937).

36. Soccorsi, *Note sul primo decennio della Radio Vaticana*, 12. The information that follows is taken from here unless otherwise indicated.

37. Edward J. Coffey, (Springfield, MA 1897–Rome 1986) belonged to the province of New York of the Society of Jesus, was a professor of philosophy at the Gregorian University, and collaborated with Vatican Radio.

38. John Patrick Delaney (Liverpool 1906–Baguio City Philippines 1956) belonged to the province of New York of the Society of Jesus. He worked for Vatican Radio between 1938 and 1939. When Delaney returned to the US, he founded the Institute of Social Order, and in 1945 went to the Philippines where he reorganized the University of Manila. Cf. Oscar L. Evangelista, "Some Historical Notes of Father John P. Delaney, Sj and His Student Welfare Ideas," in *Icons and Institutions* (Quezon City: The University of the Philippines Press, 2008), 1–24.

39. Ignacio Ortiz de Urbina Aguirre (Azpeitia 1902–Loyola 1982) spent his life mainly in Rome where he arrived in 1925 to follow the four-year course of theology at the Gregorian University. After receiving his doctorate at Bonn in Oriental Patrology he taught at the Pontifical Oriental Institute from 1933 to 1982. He contributed to the semestral journal *Orientalia Christiana Periodica*. He was the director of Vatican Radio for some years. See the entry "Ignacio Ortiz de Urbina" in *Diccionario histórico de la Compañia de Jesús*, volume III, 2928, and in the *Diccionario biográfico español*, Real Academia de la Historia, 2009, vol. XXXIX, 151–152.

40. Alfred Lutterbeck (Münster 1902–Cologne 1966) belonged to the province of Lower Germany of the Society of Jesus. He was a contributor to the journal *Die Katholischen Missionen*.

41. ACS, Min. Int., Dir. Gen. di PS, Divisione Affari Generali e Riservati, 1938, b. 37 e b. 38/A. The original archive file, which contains the interceptions by the listening center of the Ministry of Internal Affairs of the programs of Vatican Radio, bears the heading *International anticommunist front*.

42. See Giorgio Petracchi, "Roma e/o Mosca? Il fascismo di fronte allo specchio," in *Nuova storia contemporanea* 1 (2002): 69–92; Roberto Pertici, "Il vario anticomunismo italiano (1936–1960): lineamenti di una storia," in *Due nazioni. Legittimazione e delegittimazione nella storia dell'Italia contemporanea*, eds. L. Di Nucci and E. Galli della Loggia (Bologna: il Mulino, 2003), 263–334; and Maria Teresa Giusti, *Relazioni pericolose. Italia fascista e Russia comunista* (Bologna: il Mulino, 2023).

43. ACS, Min. Int., PS, Divisione Affari Generali e Riservati, cat. R.G., pacco 429, anno 1936, fasc. 19, Lettres de Rome.

44. AAV, Arch. Nunz. Svizzera, b. 108, f. 197.

45. The expression was used by Pius XI in a conversation with Mussolini on the third anniversary of the Concordat. Quoted in Emilio Gentile, *Contro Cesare. Cristianesimo e totalitarismo nell'epoca dei fascismi* (Milano: Feltrinelli, 2010), 284.

46. ASRV, *Partecipazione della Radio Vaticana a conferenze internazionali (1933–1953). Attività dei membri dell'UIR volte a favorire la comprensione reciproca e la pace tra i popoli.*

47. See Fulvio De Giorgi, "La Spagna franchista vista dalla chiesa italiana," in *Fascismo e franchismo. Relazioni, immagini, rappresentazioni*, eds. G. Di Febo and R. Moro (Soveria Mannelli: Rubbettino, 2005), 417–439: 422–423.

48. News bulletin of February 17, 1937, 4:30 p.m. in Spanish, ACS, Min. Int., Dir. Gen. di PS, Divisione Affari Generali e Riservati, 1938, b. 38/A.

49. News bulletin of March 3, 1937, 8:00 p.m. in Spanish, ACS, Min. Int., Dir. Gen. di PS, Divisione Affari Generali e Riservati, 1938, b. 38/A.

50. News bulletin of April 7, 1937, 4:30 p.m. in Spanish, ACS, Min. Int., Dir. Gen. di PS, Divisione Affari Generali e Riservati, 1938, b. 37.

51. See Giovanni Miccoli, *I dilemmi e i silenzi di Pio XII. Vaticano, Seconda guerra mondiale e Shoah* (Milano: Bur, 2007), 215. For a different attitude on *L'Osservatore Romano*, see Alfonso Botti, "Dal 18 luglio al 14 settembre 1936: come la S. Sede cambiò rotta sul conflitto spagnolo," in *Spagna contemporanea* 40 (2011): 111–148.

52. Filippo Frangioni, "Unione Sovietica e guerra di Spagna: comunismo e Santa Sede," in *Diplomazia senza eserciti. Le relazioni internazionali della Chiesa di Pio XI*, ed. E. Fattorini (Roma: Carocci, 2013), 19–54: 23.

53. Étienne Fouilloux, "Pie XI et la 'Russie'. Bref état de la question," in *Pius XI: Keywords*, 271–277: 271.

54. News bulletin of July 27, 1937, 4:30 p.m. in English. ACS, Min. Int., Dir. Gen. di PS, Divisione Affari Generali e Riservati, 1938, b. 37.

55. Quoted by Frangioni, *L'Urss e la propaganda contro la religione*, 301.

56. See the quotations and observations in Gentile, *Contro Cesare*, 53, 265–266.

57. Renatro Moro, "Religione del trascendente e religioni politiche. Il cattolicesimo italiano di fronte alla sacralizzazione fascista della politica," in *Mondo Contemporaneo* 1 (2005): 9–67: 31.

58. On the events linked to the Cristero war, see Paolo Valvo, *Pio XI e la "Cristiada": Fede, guerra e diplomazia in Messico (1926–1929)* (Brescia: Morcelliana, 2016).

59. News bulletin of November 20, 1936, 8:00 p.m. in German. ACS, Min. Int., Dir. Gen. di PS, Divisione Affari Generali e Riservati, 1938, b. 38/A.

60. News bulletin of November 24, 1936, 4:30 p.m. in English. ACS, Min. Int., Dir. Gen. di PS, Divisione Affari Generali e Riservati, 1938, b. 38/A.

61. News bulletin of July 6, 1937, 8:00 p.m. in English. ACS, Min. Int., Dir. Gen. di PS, Divisione Affari Generali e Riservati, 1938, b. 37.

62. Rudolf Schlesinger, "Il Comintern e la questione coloniale," in *Annali dell'Istituto Giangiacomo Feltrinelli* (1967): 50–135.

63. Muckermann, *Im Kampf zwischen zwei Epochen*, 298. On the suppression of the Catholic press, see Guenter Lewy, *The Catholic Church and Nazi Germany* (New York: McGraw-Hill, 1964); and Alessandro Bellino, *Il Vaticano e Hitler*.

Santa Sede, Chiesa tedesca e nazismo (1922–1939) (Milano: Guerini e Associati, 2019), 169 f. On the position of the clergy toward National Socialism see Kevin Spicer, *Resisting the Third Reich. The Catholic Clergy in Hitler's Berlin* (DeKalb: Northern Illinois University Press, 2004).

64. Doc. 609, *Akten Kardinal Michael von Faulhabers 1917–1945*, volume II, *1935–1945*, ed. L. Volk (Mainz: Matthias-Grünewald-Verlag, 1978), 282–284: 283.

65. Doc. 398, in *Akten deutscher Bischöfe über die Lage der Kirche 1933–1945*, volume IV, *1936–1939*, 267–272: 270–271.

66. Doc. 1, in *Berichte des SD und der Gestapo über Kirchen und Kirchenvolk in Deutschland 1934–1944*, ed. H. Boberach (Mainz: Matthias-Grünewald-Verlag, 1971), 3–63: 38.

67. News bulletin of January 29, 1937, 8:30 p.m. in German. Religious persecution in Russia and in Spain was denounced in the same program. ACS, Min. Int., Dir. Gen. di PS, Divisione Affari Generali e Riservati, 1938, b. 37.

68. News bulletin of January 28, 1937, 8:00 p.m. in Italian. The critical situation of Catholics in Spain and Russia was also discussed earlier in this program. ACS, Min. Int., Dir. Gen. di PS, Divisione Affari Generali e Riservati, 1938, b. 38/A.

69. News bulletin of February 18, 1937, 8:00 p.m. in French. ACS, Min. Int., Dir. Gen. di PS, Divisione Affari Generali e Riservati, 1938, b. 38/A.

70. News bulletin of February 26, 1937, 8:00 p.m. in German. ACS, Min. Int., Dir. Gen. di PS, Divisione Affari Generali e Riservati, 1938, b. 37.

71. News bulletin of May 31, 1937, 4:30 p.m. in Italian, ACS, Min. Int., Dir. Gen. di PS, Divisione Affari Generali e Riservati, 1938, b. 37.

72. For example, in the article "Vatikan und Nationalsozialismus," in *Der deutsche Weg*, December 20, 1934.

73. T.E. Delaney to M.J. Ready, November 3, 1938, in ACUA, box 35, file Information Media. Radio. Broadcasts 1929–44.

74. Doc. 14, *Berichte des SD und der Gestapo*, 301–330: 303–304. For further discussion on the question of the German programs more extensively see Raffaella Perin, "Heiliger Stuhl, Drittes Reich und Radio Vaticana. Die Beziehungen zwischen dem Vatikan und dem nationalsozialistischem Deutschland im Spiegel des päpstlichen Rundfunksenders (1936–1943)," in *Quellen und Forschungen aus italienischen Archiven und Bibliotheken* 100 (2020): 471–494.

75. News bulletin of July 30, 1937, 8:00 p.m. in German, ACS, Min. Int., Dir. Gen. di PS, Divisione Affari Generali e Riservati, 1938, b. 37.

76. On the episode, see Georges Passelecq and Bernard Suchecky, *L'encyclique cachée de Pie XI. Une occasion manquée de l'Église face à l'antisémitisme* (Paris: La Découverte, 1995), 97–103; and Paolo Valvo, *Dio salvi l'Austria! 1938: il Vaticano e l'Anschluss* (Milano: Mursia, 2010), 181 f.

77. The note was written during the audience of Pius XI with Pacelli. ASRS, *AA.EE.SS.*, Pio XI, Stati Ecclesiastici, Pos. 430a P.O., fasc. 355.

78. ASRS, *AA.EE.SS.*, Pio XI, Austria, Pos. 912–914 P.O., fasc. 71, ff. 14–17.

79. See Bellino, *Il Vaticano e Hitler*, 114–115.

80. See Emma Fattorini, *Germania e Santa Sede. Le nunziature di Pacelli tra la Grande Guerra e la Repubblica di Weimar* (Bologna: il Mulino, 1992); Hubert Wolf, *The Pope and the Devil: The Vatican's Archives and the Third Reich* (Cambridge: Harvard University Press, 2008), 151–154; and Marie Levant, *Pacelli à Berlin. Le Vatican et l'Allemagne, de Weimar à Hitler (1919–1934)* (Rennes: Presse Universitaire de Rennes, 2019), 301 f.

81. A version in French of the script of the program was published by *La Documentation catholique* on April 20, 1938, reproduced by Passelecq and Suchecky, *L'encyclique cachée*, 99–102, but, contrary to what is said here, the text was not taken from *L'Osservatore Romano* which did not publish the program, but from the Dutch *Tijd* of April 1.

82. ASRS, *AA.EE.SS.*, Pio XI, Austria, Pos. 912–914 P.O., fasc. 71, ff. 14–17.

83. Johannes Schwarte, *Gustav Gundlach S.J. (1892–1963): Maßgeblicher Repräsentant des katholischen Soziallehrte während der Pontifikate Pius' XI. und Pius' XII.* (München-Padeborn-Wien: Schöningh, 1975), 66–71. The *Catholic Herald* wrote that the announcer was a certain Father Immer. See "Vatican and Austrian Bishops' Declaration," in *The Catholic Herald*, April 8, 1938, 1. In this regard, *L'Osservatore Romano* declared on April 8: "Research and the information [about the program] reached elsewhere, to the point of wanting to identify the author of the conversation in the Jesuit Father who usually reads the communications in German, as though all the announcers of the radios of each country were the authors of everything that they read." Gustav Gundlach, born in 1892, collaborated on the draft of the encyclicals *Quadragesimo anno*, *Divini Redemptoris*, and *Humani generis unitas*, and wrote the entry of *Antisemitismus* in the *Lexicon für Theologie und Kirche*. He died in 1963.

84. Note by Tardini of April 2, 1938, in ASRS, *AA.EE.SS.*, Pio XI, Austria, Pos. 912–914 P.O., fasc. 71, ff. 18–19.

85. ASRS, *AA.EE.SS.*, Pio XI, Austria, Pos. 912–914 P.O., fasc. 71, f. 24.

86. ASRS, *AA.EE.SS.*, Pio XI, Austria, Pos. 912–914 P.O., fasc. 71, f. 25. The *Catholic Herald* wrote: "Although this transmission has been disowned by the Vatican, it has been specified that this does not mean disagreement with what is stated in it as an important private opinion on the situation. In the future, the Vatican programs will be more strictly censored."

87. Tardini to Pignatti, April 3, 1938, in ASRS, *AA.EE.SS.*, Pio XI, Austria, Pos. 912–914 P.O., fasc. 71, ff. 37–38v.

88. Valvo, *Dio salvi l'Austria! 1938*, 197–199.

89. "Precisazione necessaria," in *L'Osservatore Romano*, April 4, 1938, 1.

90. Audience of April 3, 1938, in ASRS, *AA.EE.SS.*, Pio XI, Stati Ecclesiastici, Pos. 430a P.O., fasc. 355.

91. Schwarte, *Gustav Gundlach S.J.*, 71.

92. At the Cairo conference, Britain proposed a right of precedence in occupying the airwaves that were unused and assigned to a station by third

parties. *Promemoria 25 marzo 1939*, ARSI, Ex Ass. Italiae, VII Domus Scriptorum—Radio Vaticana, Epistolae, 1004, fasc. 4.

93. ASDMAE, Embassy of Italy to the Holy See, b. 118, fasc. 1, sf. 1.

94. Letter of Delaney to Fr. Provincial, August 3, 1938. Delaney, John P. New York Province Archive, Box 2.0015, in Jesuit Archives & Research Center, St. Louis, Missouri.

95. In the quoted letter of August 1938, Delaney explains the project in detail and the difficulties of fulfilling it. See also ARSI, Ex-Ass. Italiae, VII. Domus Scriptorum—Radio Vaticana, Epistolae, 1005, fasc. 4.

96. Letter of Delaney to Fr. Provincial, August 3, 1938.

97. AAV, Segr. di Stato, 1938, SCV 83, ff. 2–4.

98. Letter of Delaney to Rev. Joseph Murphy, October 20, 1938. Delaney, John P. New York Province Archive, Box 2.0015, in Jesuit Archives & Research Center, St. Louis, Missouri.

99. William Shirer, *Twentieth Century Journey*, volume 2, *The Nightmare Years 1930–1940* (New York: Bantam, 1984), 391–393.

100. Letter of Delaney to Murphy, April 13, 1939; Delaney, John P. New York Province Archive, Box 2.0015, in Jesuit Archives & Research Center, St. Louis, Missouri.

101. *Promemoria,* March 25, 1939.

102. In February 1935, Monsignor Neveu reported to Monsigneur Giobbe, a minutes-taker of the Congregation of the Extraordinary Ecclesiastical Affairs, the interference of the Vatican Radio programs in Russia. See Pettinaroli, *La politique russe du Saint-Siège*, 744. However, a regular broadcasting service in Russian did not start until spring 1943.

103. *Note sul primo decennio della Radio Vaticana*, 15.

104. Joseph Louis Vaughn (San Francisco 1890–Los Angeles 1961).

105. Luigi Ambruzzi (Vallenoncello 1881–Lonigo 1965).

106. Salvatore Gallo (Canicattini Bagni 1893–Acireale 1969). *Radio Vaticana 1931/1971* (Roma 1972), 18, in ASRV.

107. Joseph Boubée (Albi 1872–Rome 1940) was French general secretary of the International Eucharistic Congresses, and in 1940 a member of the private Secretariat of Pius XII but died on October 26. Some information on Boubée can be gathered from the report of a fascist spy in the Vatican. See ACS, Minculpop, Reports (1922–1945), b. 34, f. Radio Vaticana, sottofascicolo 2; ASDMAE, Embassy to the Holy See, b. 163, fasc. Radio Vaticana.

108. See Robert Graham, "La Radio Vaticana tra Londra e Berlino. Un dossier della guerra delle onde: 1940–1941," in *La Civiltà Cattolica* [1976], volume I: 134, footnote 3. Josef Młodochowski, born in Mielec in 1891, theologian and rector of the Polish College from 1938 until his death in Rome in 1943; Felix Lason (Krakov 1900–Kalisz in 1973); Ludwik Semkowski (Lwòw 1891–Grottaferrata 1977), for five years taught Holy Scriptures at the Pontifical Polish College in Rome, where he was rector from 1954 to 1959.

109. See Graham, *La Radio Vaticana*, 134, footnote 3. Beat Ambord (Grenjiols 1904–Bad Schönbrunn 1969) was chaplain in the parish of St. Mary in Basle from July 1938 to February 1941, and from February 20, 1941 was announcer on Vatican Radio; Francis Joy (Kerry 1903–Dublin 1977); Vincent McCormick (Brooklyn 1886–St. Andrew in Hudson 1963) entered the Society of Jesus in 1903. In 1927, he became rector of the College of the Jesuits in Woodstock and in 1933 was appointed rector of the Gregorian University in Rome. After the United States joined the war, he left his position as rector and in 1946 he became the American assistant to the new general of the Society, John Baptist Janssens. See James Hennessey, "American Jesuit in Wartime Rome: The Diary of Vincent A. McCormick, s.j., 1942–1945," in *Mid-America* 56 (1974): 32–55. George Delannoye (Antwerp 1893–Rome 1982) taught philosophy at the Gregorian University and at the Lateranense. Enrique Peréz Garcìa (Madrid 1904–Rome 1975) was an announcer on Vatican Radio from 1943 and director of programs from 1948 to 1953.

110. Francesco Pellegrino (Cosenza 1907–Rome 1976) was called to Rome by Ledóchowski and, in 1934, participated in the setting up of the Catholic press exposition at the Vatican. In 1937, he was assigned to the Russicum in Rome as editor of *Lettres de Rome*, the information and training organ of the Secretariat against Atheism. In 1939, he was attached to the group of fathers in charge of Vatican Radio and news broadcasting, and after a brief period at *La Civiltà Cattolica* until July 1943, he moved permanently to Rome to the residence of the *Domus Scriptores*. In 1953 he was appointed program director of Vatican Radio, and from 1956 until 1975 he was completely entrusted with all Italian programming.

111. Galileo Venturini s.j. (1850–1951) was a well-known preacher, animator of the Apostleship of Prayer. Carlo Miccinelli s.j. (Rome 1876–Rome 1969) was a historian, author of a book on Pope Innocent XI.

112. See *Catalogus Provinciae Romanae Societatis Iesu anni 1940*, Tip. Pont. Università Gregoriana, Roma 1940. Domus Scriptorum Societatis: Johannes Haarselhorst (Tilburg 1900–Nijmengen 1984). Mateo Domingo Mayor (Bemillo de Sayago 1897–Salamanca 1991).

113. Maurice Schurmans (Boom 1901–Drongen 1970), Belgian vicar general of the order of the Society of Jesus from 1938, according to Ledóchowski's wishes. After the latter's death in 1942, Schurmans asked to be sent as a missionary to Belgian Congo which, because of the war, could not receive aid directly from Belgium. He was appointed rector of the minor seminary of Lemfu in 1943, and two years later he became superior general of the mission. See the entry in *Diccionario histórico de la Compañia de Jesús*, vol. IV, 3536.

114. This was what French Ambassador to the Holy See Wladimir d'Ormesson maintained in his parting report of October 30, 1940, to Minister of Foreign Affairs Paul Baudouin. *Envoi d'un rapport d'ensemble de la mission de M. d'Ormesson au*

Vatican et d'une étude sur la composition de la Curie romaine, in CAD, Guerre 1939–1945, Vichy, Europe, Saint-Siège, 549–550, 16–19.

115. It was perhaps Ferdinand Baumann, of the province of Upper Germany.

116. It was perhaps Peter McKone of the province of New England.

117. ARSI, Ex-Ass. Italiae, VII. Domus Scriptorum—Radio Vaticana, Epistolae, 1005, fasc. 4.

118. *Progetto di norme circa la revisione delle Letture Radio*, ARSI, Ex-Ass. Italiae, VII. Domus Scriptorum—Radio Vaticana, Epistolae, 1005, fasc. 4.

119. *Promemoria 25 marzo 1939*.

120. ARSI, Ex-Ass. Italiae, VII. Domus Scriptorum—Radio Vaticana, Epistolae, 1005, fasc. 4.

121. Graham, *La Radio Vaticana*, 138.

122. Note by Tardini, October 28, 1940, in ADSS, vol. IV, doc. 132, 207–208: 207.

123. Letter of Delaney to Fr. Provincial, August 3, 1938.

124. Arturo Marzano, *Onde fasciste. La propaganda araba di Radio Bari (1934–43)* (Roma: Carocci, 2015), 13–14. For specific case studies see also Stephen Lovell, *Russia in the Microphone Age: A History of Soviet Radio, 1919–1970* (Oxford: Oxford University Press, 2015); Asa Briggs, *The History of Broadcasting in the United Kingdom*, 5 volumes, (Oxford: Oxford University Press, 1995), volume II, 369 f; and Esther Lo Biundo, *London calling Italy. BBC broadcasts during the Second World War* (Manchester: Manchester University Press, 2022).

125. Nelly Valsangiacomo, *Dietro al microfono. Intellettuali italiani alla Radio svizzera (1930–1980)* (Bellinzona: Edizioni Casagrande, 2015), 29. Valsangiacomo argues that since the conversation involves alternating roles between the speaker and the listener, the radio talk implies an interaction with the public, which is widely asymmetrical.

126. "Développement de la radiodiffusion," in *Radiodiffusion*, July 1937.

127. Ray Barfield, *Listening to Radio, 1920–1950* (Westport: Praeger, 1996), 25, 39.

128. IBU, *Rapport Général sur le développement et la situation actuelle de la Radiodiffusion internationale*, Genève, June 1943, 6.

129. Kenneth Wolfe, *The Churches and the British Broadcasting Corporation 1922–1956. The Politics of Broadcast Religion* (London: SCM Press, Ltd., 1984), 127–129.

2. Vatican Radio and the Outbreak of the War (1939–1940)

1. "Radiomessaggio di pace nell'imminente pericolo di guerra," in *Discorsi e radiomessaggi di Sua Santità Pio XII*, volume I (Città del Vaticano: Tipografia Poliglotta Vaticana, 1955), 303–307. The speech was written by Montini.

2. On the steps taken by Pius XII in the first months of his pontificate to prevent another conflict in Europe, see Andrea Riccardi, *La guerra del silenzio. Pio XII, il nazismo, gli ebrei* (Bari-Roma: Laterza, 2022), 65–75.

3. Pierre Blet, *Pie XII et la Seconde Guerre mondiale d'après les archives du Vatican* (Paris: Perrin, 2005), 29. On the steps taken by British and French diplomats with the Holy See, ibid. 13–35; Philippe Chenaux, *Pio XII. Diplomatico e pastore*, Italian trans. F. Cavarocchi (San Paolo: Cinisello Balsamo, 2004), 215–216; and David I. Kertzer, *The Pope at War. The Secret History of Pius XII, Mussolini, and Hitler* (New York: Random House, 2022), Chapters 4 and 7.

4. Note of Montini, August 28, 1939, in ADSS, vol. I, doc. 144, 256–257.

5. Note of Tardini, ibidem.

6. See Alessandro Duce, *Pio XII e la Polonia (1939–1945)* (Roma: Studium, 1997), 94 f; Michael Phayer, *The Catholic Church and the Holocaust, 1930–1965* (Bloomington: Indiana University Press, 2000), Chapter 2; and Riccardi, *La guerra del silenzio*, 88–95.

7. "Il radiomessaggio del Cardinale Hlond," in *L'Osservatore Romano*, October 2–3, 1939, 2. The speech, given on October 1 by Pius XII to the Poles at an audience; "La confortatrice parola del Vicario di Gesù Cristo alla nazione cattolica e fedele," in *L'Osservatore Romano*, October 1, 1939, 1.

8. Alberto Monticone, "L'offensiva radiofonica nazista contro il card. Hlond nel 1940," in *Revue d'Histoire Ecclésiastique* 3–4 (2015): 783–814. On Poland, the *Summi pontificatus* said: "The blood of countless human beings, even noncombatants, raises a piteous dirge over a nation such as Our dear Poland, which, for its fidelity to the Church, for its services in the defense of Christian civilization, written in indelible characters in the annals of history, has a right to the generous and brotherly sympathy of the whole world, while it awaits, relying on the powerful intercession of Mary, Help of Christians, the hour of a resurrection in harmony with the principles of justice and true peace."

9. "Santa Sede e Polonia," in *L'Osservatore Romano*, October 15, 1939, 1.

10. See Daniele Menozzi, *Chiesa, pace e guerra nel Novecento. Verso una delegittimazione religiosa dei conflitti* (Bologna: il Mulino, 2008), 30; Gabriele Rigano, "'La nostra neutralità ci rende tutti nemici!' La Santa Sede e i cattolici italiani: universalismo e nazionalismo durante la prima guerra mondiale," in *Storia e Politica. Annali della Fondazione Ugo La Malfa* (2018): 315–336; and Riccardi, *La guerra del silenzio*, 53–56. See also a summary of the positions of the popes in relation to the war from Benedict XV to Pius XII in Lucia Ceci, "La Chiesa cattolica e la politica armata," in *1914–1945. L'Italia nella guerra europea dei trent'anni*, ed. S. Neri Serneri (Roma: Viella, 2016), 223–236.

11. There is a vast amount of literature on the attitude of the Christian churches during World War I. See Annette Becker, *La guerre et la foi. De la mort à la mémoire (1914–1939)* (Paris: Armand Colin, 1994); John F. Pollard, *The Unknown Pope: Benedict 15. (1914–1922) and the Pursuit of Peace* (London: G. Chapman, 1999); Stéphane Audoin-Rouzeau and Annette Becker, *14–18, Retrouver la Guerre* (Paris: Gallimard, 2000); Xavier Boniface and François Cochet, eds., *Foi, religions et sacré dans la Grande Guerre* (Arras: Artois Presses Université, 2014);

Philip Jenkins, *The Great and Holy War. How World War I Became a Religious Crusade* (New York, HarperOne, 2014); and Alberto Melloni, dir., *Benedict XV. A Pope in the World of the 'Useless Slaughter,' (1914–1918)*, two volumes, eds. G. Cavagnini and G. Grossi (Turnhaut: Brepols, 2020).

12. Menozzi, *Chiesa, pace e guerra*, 149.

13. Francesco Pellegrino, *Discorsi alla Radio. Alla Radio Vaticana dal 1939 al 1949. All'EIAR dal 1942 al 1943* in ASRV. This is a book which collects the complete writings of the Jesuit priest Father Francesco Pellegrino read on Vatican Radio for the programs in Italian from October 1939 to April 1940. See Alberto Monticone, "Padre Francesco Pellegrino. Un gesuita ai microfoni della Radio vaticana e dell'EIAR," in *Quaderni di storia dell'Europa mediterranea* 2 (2020–2021): 97–134.

14. Raffaella Perin, *The Popes on Air: The History of Vatican Radio from Its Origins to World War II* (New York: Fordham University Press, 2024), Chapter 1. For a short Pellegrino biography see Chapter I, footnote 110.

15. "S. Francesco d'Assisi, patrono primario d'Italia," October 5, 1939, in Pellegrino, *Discorsi alla Radio*, 2.

16. Daniele Menozzi, "'Il più italiano dei santi, il più santo degli italiani': la nazionalizzazione di san Francesco tra le due guerre," in *Cattolicesimo, nazione e nazionalismo*, ed. D. Menozzi (Pisa: Edizioni della Normale, 2015), 87–109: 90–91; and Matteo Caponi, "Santi d'Italia dal Risorgimento alla Repubblica," in *L'Italia e i santi. Agiografie, riti e devozioni nella costruzione dell'identità nazionale*, eds. T. Caliò and D. Menozzi (Roma: Istituto della Enciclopedia Italiana, 2017), 577–601.

17. Daniele Menozzi, "Dalla nazionalizzazione alla fascistizzazione," in *Tra mito della nazionalità e mito della cristianità. Immagini di san Francesco dai "lumi" a Pio XII* (Spoleto: Cisam, 2022), 73–109.

18. "S. Francesco d'Assisi," 5.

19. Daniele Menozzi, "Il 'patrono d'Italia' nella seconda guerra mondiale," in *Tra mito della nazionalità*, 111–133.

20. ASRS, *AA.EE.SS.*, Pio XII, parte I, Italia, Pos. 1159, ff. 124–126. As the Italian historian Matteo Caponi underlined in the introduction to a monograph issue on patron saints, patron sainthood, by conveying an exemplary model, can define normative social criteria of belonging and exclusion. See Matteo Caponi, "Introduzione," in *Rivista di storia del cristianesimo* 2 (2017): 243–248.

21. "Rassegna settimanale di notizie religiose (2–8 ottobre 1939)," program of October 9, 1939, in Pellegrino, *Discorsi alla Radio*, 2.

22. The quotation is taken from Zechariah, 6, 12 "Ecce vir Oriens nomen eius," according to the Vulgate, but it was also used as the antiphon to Psalm 111 in the rite of the Tridentine Mass.

23. "Gesù Cristo Re della pace," program on October 26, 1939, in Pellegrino, *Discorsi alla Radio*. The quotations that follow are taken from here, unless otherwise indicated.

24. "Verso il conflitto europeo," in *La Civiltà Cattolica*, 1939, volume III, 547–565.

25. "Gesù Cristo Re della pace," 8.
26. "Gesù Cristo Re della pace," 7.
27. See for example, the article "Nazionalismo e amor di patria secondo la dottrina cattolica," in *La Civiltà Cattolica*, 1915, volume I, 129–144, 420–435.
28 *Ubi Arcano Dei Consilio*. On the Peace of Christ in His Kingdom. https://www.papalencyclicals.net/pius11/p11arcan.htm.
29. Georges Passelecq and Bernard Suchecky, *L'encyclique cachée de Pie XI. Une occasion manquée de l'Église face à l'antisémitisme* (Paris: La Découverte, 1995), 131–132.
30. Among the topics contained in *Humani generis unitas*, but not explicitly mentioned in *Summi pontificatus*, were racism and antisemitism.
31. *Summi pontificatus*. On the Unity of Human Society. https://www.papalencyclicals.net/pius12/p12summi.htm.
32. "Notiziario," Vatican City, in Pellegrino, *Discorsi alla Radio*, 1.
33. "Commenti all'enciclica Summi pontificatus. La Chiesa di fronte ad alcune concezioni moderne dello Stato," program of November 2, 1939, in Pellegrino, *Discorsi alla Radio*. The quotations that follow are all taken from here.
34. "Commenti all'enciclica Summi pontificatus. La consacrazione del genere umano al S. Cuore di Gesù," program of November 16, 1939, in Pellegrino, *Discorsi alla Radio*. The quotations that follow are taken from here.
35. "Commenti all'enciclica Summi pontificatus. Il passaggio del Signore," program of November 23, 1939, in Pellegrino, *Discorsi alla Radio*.
36. Two of the previous twentieth century magisterial documents on these questions were: the apostolic letter condemning the Sillon of 1910, *Notre charge apostolique*, in which Pius X called the faithful to build a "cité catholique" on the model of medieval Christianity; and the encyclical *Ubi arcano* by Pius XI, which banned "social modernism," or the implementation of a democratic secular society that excluded the fundamental principles established by the Church.
37. "L'enciclica 'Summi pontificatus' e le sue ripercussioni nella stampa mondiale," in *La Civiltà Cattolica*, 1940, volume II, 17–28. The quotations that follow are taken from here.
38. It was customary for *La Civiltà Cattolica* to publish papal documents followed by articles of explanation by eminent Jesuits.
39. Jonathan Huener, *The Polish Catholic Church under German Occupation: The Reichsgau Wartheland, 1939–1945* (Bloomington: Indiana University Press, 2021).
40. "Allocuzione natalizia del sommo pontefice al Sacro Collegio," in *La Civiltà Cattolica*, 1940, volume I, 5–13: 10–11.
41. Hlond to Maglione, December 21, 1939, in ADSS, volume IIIa, doc. 74, 162. Note by Tardini: 23.12.39. Ex audientia Em.mi (Ex audientia SS.mi).
42. The report was subsequently published in *The Persecution of the Catholic Church in German-occupied Poland* (London: Burns Oates, 1941), 3–24.

43. Note by Montini of January 19, 1940. Ex Audientia SS.mi., in ADSS, vol. IIIa, doc. 102, 204.

44. François Charles-Roux, *Huit ans au Vatican, 1932–1940* (Paris: Flammarion, 1947), 370.

45. "Rassegna settimanale di notizie cattoliche," program of January 22, 1940, in Pellegrino, *Discorsi alla radio*, 3. A brief comment also on eastern Poland followed on page 5. A copy of the script of the program is also in ASRS, *AA.EE. SS.*, Pio XII, parte I, Stati Ecclesiastici, Pos. 648, f. 4.

46. *Daily Digest of Foreign Broadcasts*, Vatican City, in German for Germany, January 23, 1940, 7:30 p.m. The original text in German was sent to the Secretariat of State and is in ASRS, *AA.EE.SS.*, Pio XII, parte I, Stati Ecclesiastici, Pos. 648, ff. 6–7.

47. "Radio-Vatican proteste contre les persécutions en Pologne," in *L'Aube*, January 23, 1940, in ASRS, *AA.EE.SS.*, Pio XII, parte I, Stati Ecclesiastici, Pos. 648, ff. 8–9.

48. *Daily Digest of Foreign Broadcasts*, Vatican City, in Spanish for Spain, January 24, 1940, 8:00 p.m.

49. The unabridged text of the program is in ASRS, *AA.EE.SS.*, Pio XII, parte I, Stati Ecclesiastici, Pos. 648, ff. 80–81. "Vatican Denounces Atrocities in Poland; Germans Called Even Worse Than Russians," in the *New York Times*, January 23, 1940, 1, 5; "'Martyr's fate' of Poland. Nazis denounced by Vatican. 'A Tale of Infamy,'" in *The Times*, January 23, 1940, 6.

50. BBC, Radio London, *Italian News Commentary*, 16, H. Stevens, February 9, 1940, 6:45 p.m.

51. BA, Sonderdienst Seehaus, R74/384, no. 459, Abendmeldung 22.1.1940, 82.

52. John Murray, "A papal pointer to peace," in *The Month* 175 (908) (1940): 129–138.

53. *English Catholic Newspaper*, January 27, 1940, 1.

54. "The World week by week. Mgr. Orsenigo for Poland," in *The Tablet*, March 2, 1940, 193.

55. "Vatican Broadcasts on Persecutions in German-occupied Poland," in *The Persecution of the Catholic Church*, 121–123.

56. ASRS, *AA.EE.SS.*, Pio XII, parte I, Stati Ecclesiastici, Pos. 648, ff. 82–83.

57. "The World week by week. The Vatican and Poland," in *The Tablet*, January 27, 1940, 1.

58. ASRS, *AA.EE.SS.*, Pio XII, parte I, Stati Ecclesiastici, Pos. 648, f. 5.

59. ASRS, *AA.EE.SS.*, Pio XII, parte I, Stati Ecclesiastici, Pos. 648, ff. 109–130.

60. ASRS, *AA.EE.SS.*, Pio XII, parte I, Stati Ecclesiastici, Pos. 648, ff. 13–29.

61. Note by Montini of January 27, 1940, in ASRS, *AA.EE.SS.*, Pio XII, parte I, Stati Ecclesiastici, Pos. 648, f. 11. Tardini reports in his diary a conversation he had with the French ambassador, who asked him why the Holy See was silent about the atrocities committed by the Germans in Poland. He replied that "the silence . . . was broken by Vatican Radio. These days the world is in turmoil precisely

because of a Vatican radio broadcast about this subject.... So that the silence is not ... absolute." But "every public manifestation is answered by a hardening of persecution. Therefore, it is necessary for the Holy See to be careful not to worsen the situation of the poor Poles, who are suffering enormously." Domenico Tardini, *Diario di un cardinale (1936–1944). La Chiesa negli anni delle ideologie nazifascista e comunista*, ed. S. Pagano (San Paolo: Cinisello Balsamo, 2020), entry of January 30, 1940, 181–182.

62. Robert A. Graham maintains that the program in English for North America quoted (literally) a report given personally to Pius XII by Thomas Reginek, vicar general of Katowice, who had fled from Poland. Robert Graham, "La Radio Vaticana tra Londra e Berlino. Un dossier della guerra delle onde: 1940–1941," in *La Civiltà Cattolica* 1976, volume I, 139–140: footnote 13.

63. Radio news bulletin, January 27, 1940, London in English, ASRS, *AA.EE. SS.*, Pio XII, parte I, Stati Ecclesiastici, Pos. 648, f. 23.

64. Radio news bulletin, January 28, 1940, London in Polish, ASRS, *AA.EE.SS.*, Pio XII, parte I, Stati Ecclesiastici, Pos. 648, f. 24.

65. Bulletin no. 33, January 31, 1940, evening, ASRS, *AA.EE.SS.*, Pio XII, parte I, Stati Ecclesiastici, Pos. 648, f. 39.

66. Ledóchowski to Montini, January 29, 1940, in ARSI, Epistolarum Registra, Epistolae ad Romam Curiam, IX.

67. Notes by Montini and Tardini of January 29 and 31, 1940, in ASRS, *AA.EE. SS.*, Pio XII, parte I, Stati Ecclesiastici, Pos. 648, f. 11.

68. *Daily Digest of Foreign Broadcasts*, Vatican Radio, in English for America, January 29, 1940, 2:30 a.m.

69. *Notiziario della Radio Vaticana*, program in German of February 27, 1940, 8:45 p.m. in ASDMAE, Embassy of the Holy See, b. 116, sottofascicolo 5. The article was published in *Komsomolskaja Pravda*, January 31, 1940.

70. *Daily Digest of Foreign Broadcasts*, Vatican Radio, in Dutch for Flanders and the Netherlands, March 18, 1940, 9:00 p.m.; in English for Great Britain, May 28, 1940, 8:00 p.m.

71. *Daily Digest of Foreign Broadcasts*, Vatican Radio, in English for India and Ceylon, April 9, 1940, 4:00 p.m.; in Spanish for Spain, May 4, 1940, 9:00 p.m.

72. *Daily Digest of Foreign Broadcasts*, Vatican Radio, in Polish for Poland, April 18, 1940, 8:00 p.m.; in German for Germany, May 28, 1940, 8:30 p.m.

73. This is what can be inferred from the notes of the monitoring center of the Ministry of Popular Culture (February-April 1940). *Notiziario della Radio Vaticana*, program in German on February 13, 1940; in Spanish on February 14; and in Portuguese on February 20, in ASDMAE, Embassy to the Holy See, b. 116, sottofascicolo 5.

74. "Dichiarazioni di Franck sulla Polonia," in *L'Osservatore Romano*, February 15, 1940, 6. ASRS, *AA.EE.SS.*, Pio XII, parte I, Stati Ecclesiastici, Pos. 648, ff. 163–173.

75. *L'Osservatore Romano* had published some articles on Poland in November 1939 and in February 1940, taking the news from the foreign press.

See the section "Notiziario polacco" of November 8, 9, 15, and 19, 1939 in which there appeared a few lines on the condition of the Jews in Poland; January 17, February 5–6, and 10, 1940. See the analysis by Susan Zuccotti, "*L'Osservatore Romano* and the Holocaust, 1939–1945," in *Holocaust and Genocide Studies* 2 (2003): 249–277: 253–255. The work of Andrea Grover is also useful, "*L'Osservatore Romano* and the Holocaust, 1933–45," in *Why Didn't the Press Shout? American and International Journalism During the Holocaust*, ed. R.M. Shapiro (Jersey City: Yeshiva University Press, 2003), 349–368.

76. Tardini, *Diario di un cardinale*, 182.

77. In response of Goebbels' Ministry of Propaganda, the Ministry of Information was created. Similarly, the decision to create a Religions Division was to counteract Hitler's use of religion in his plan to conquer Europe. During the war, the State required Christian endorsement of the British war. See Dianne Kirby, "The Church of England and "Religions Division" during the Second World War: Church-State Relations and the Anglo-Soviet Alliance," in *Electronic Journal of International History*: article 4. As far as the importance applied to Vatican Radio by the Roman Catholic section of the Religious Division for British propaganda see NA, INF, 1/405; INF 1/396 and INF, 1/781.

78. BA, Sonderdienst Seehaus, R 74/384; R 74/385.

79. Introduction and Chapter 3 in Riccardi, *La guerra del silenzio*.

80. ARSI, Epp. Regg. Ad Curiam Romanam, IX, 323 and Epp. Regg. Ad Cur. Rom., Allegata, VIII, all. 118.

81. See at least Giovanni Miccoli, "Pio XII e la guerra," in *Chiesa e guerra. Dalla "benedizione delle armi" alla "Pacem in terries*," eds. M. Franzinelli and R. Bottoni (Bologna: il Mulino, 2005), 393–416; and Menozzi, *Chiesa, pace e guerra*.

82. "L'alto prestigio del papato ai giorni nostri," program on February 15, 1940, in Pellegrino, *Discorsi alla Radio*, 4.

83. "L'alto prestigio del papato," 5.

84. Gabriele Rigano, *Benedetto XV tra nazionalismi e universalità della chiesa*, in *Benedetto XV e il suo tempo*, ed. D. Preda (Genova: Genova University Press, 2023), 356–378.

85. Chenaux, *Pio XII*, 229. Vatican Radio also broadcast the contents of the telegrams. One of the announcers who was to read was the French Jesuit Albert Dauchy who, in the 1970s, gave an interview on this experience. Dauchy recalls that Soccorsi "telephoned Monsignor Montini, who was then the deputy of the Secretary of State, to write a suitable diplomatic sentence to announce the telegram; the priest gave me the text in Italian, and I quickly translated it into French." ASRV, *Les temps héroïques de Radio Vatican*, interview with Fr. Albert Dauchy S.J., October 16, 1976.

86. Note by Montini, May 13, 1940, in ADSS, vol. I, doc. 313, 453–455: 454.

87. In the evening, the pope changed his mind and asked Montini to tell Alfieri not to give the message to Hitler and von Ribbentrop, but to await a more propitious moment. See also the observations by Giovanni Miccoli, *I dilemmi e i*

silenzi di Pio XII. Vaticano, Seconda guerra mondiale e Shoah (Milano: Bur, 2007), 56–58. Tardini had prepared a slightly harsher text for the telegrams which was not accepted. See Carlo F. Casula, *Domenico Tardini (1888–1961). L'azione della Santa Sede nella crisi fra le due guerre* (Roma: Studium, 1988), 163.

88. LOC, Myron Taylor's Papers, Box 1.

89. The unabridged text of the program was sent by the BBC to the Roman Catholic Section of the British Ministry of Information, which can be considered evidence of its importance. *News and views in English from Vatican City for North America,* May 13, 1940, in NA, INF 1/781.

90. The first address of the newly reunited Methodist Episcopal Church claimed that "we are ready to join with all other religious or secular organizations to promote world peace; but we deplore and must firmly resist any union of church and State and are and will be unalterably opposed to any establishment of diplomatic relations between the Vatican and the United States." Quoted in Robert W. Potter, "Methodists ready to aid peace move but bishops are "unalterably" opposed to U.S.-Vatican Diplomatic Link," in the *New York Times,* April 26, 1940, 10.

91. Quoted in Marilyn S. Ward, "Must the Christian Church condemn all use of military force?: The Methodist Episcopal Church and the endorsement of World War II," in *Methodist History* 35 (3) (April 1997): 157–168: 166.

92. Ward, "Must the Christian Church."

93. LOC, Myron Taylor's Papers, box 1.

94. The program has been highlighted by Charles R. Gallagher, *Vatican Secret Diplomacy. Joseph P. Hurley and Pope Pius XII* (New Haven: Yale University Press, 2008), 98–105. It was also received and summarized by the BBC Monitoring Service: *Daily Digest of Foreign Broadcasts,* Radio Vatican, in English for North America, June 28, 1940, 2:30 a.m.

95. The *minutante* prepares study materials for the definition or execution of matters within the competence of the Secretariat of State and drafts official acts and documents of the Apostolic See in Latin or a modern language (decrees, rescripts, apostolic letters, etc.).

96. "Voice of The Vatican. Duty to Fight for the Right," in *The Times,* July 5, 1940, 3a (first column); "The Church Abroad. Vatican City. The Vatican on Conscientious Objectors," in *The Tablet,* July 13, 1940, 30; "Editorial Comments," in *The Month* 176 (1940): 65–74.

97. Gallagher, *Vatican Secret Diplomacy,* 112.

98. "Appel du 25 juin 1940," in Phillipe Pétain, *Discours aux Français 17 juin 1940–20 juin 1944,* ed. J.C. Barbas (Paris: Éditions Albin Michel S.A., 1989), 63–66: 66.

99. François-Georges Dreyfus, *Histoire de Vichy* (Paris: Éditions de Fallois, 2004), 161. Charles Maurras was the leader of Action Française as well as editor of the anti-Republican, nationalist, and antisemitic newspaper of the same name. For Maurras, the defense of the Catholic religion was a political imperative as a

factor of stability and social order. Pétain and his government were also inspired by these Maurrassian principles.

100. Marc Ferro, *Pétain* (Paris: Fayard, 1987), 129.

101. Jacques Duquesne, *Les catholiques français sous l'Occupation* (Paris: Éditions Grasset et Fasquelle, 1996), 32.

102. On the real reasons for France's defeat, see Robert O. Paxton, *La France de Vichy 1940–1944* (Paris: Éditions du Seuil, 1973), 15–16; and Henry Rousso, *Le régime de Vichy* (Paris: Presses Universitaires de France, 2012), 9–10.

103. Renée Bédarida, *Les catholiques dans la guerre 1939–1945* (Paris: Hachette, 1998), 47. See also the many examples given by Duquesne, *Les catholiques français*, 51–54, and by Jean-Louis Clément, *Les évêques au temps de Vichy. Loyalisme sans inféodation* (Paris: Beauchesne, 1999), 21–25.

104. For a summary on the charismatic power exercised by Pétain, see Dreyfus, *Histoire de Vichy*, 207–209; there is also some information in the biography by Ferro, *Pétain*, 8–10, 58–59. On the shock of the defeat, see René Rémond, "L'opinion française des années 1930 aux années 1940. Poids de l'événement, permanence des mentalités," in *Le régime de Vichy et les français*, eds. J. P. Azéma and F. Bédarida (Paris: Fayard, 1992), 481–492.

105. Étienne Fouilloux, "L'Église catholique, le maréchal et Vichy," in *Les chrétiens français entre crise et libération 1937–1947* (Paris: Seuil, 1997), 115–131: 123–124.

106. *Daily Digest of Foreign Broadcasts*, Vatican Radio, in Spanish for Spain, June 19, 1940, 9:00 p.m. The program in Portuguese for Brazil of June 24 had the same contents.

107. "Discours de S. Em. le Card. Pacelli," in *La documentation catholique*, August 14, 1937, 253–265: 256.

108. "Communications officielles radiodiffusées de l'archevêque de Bordeaux," in *Le Temps*, June 19, 1940; "Une allocution de Mgr Feltin archevêque de Bordeaux," in *Le Petit Parisien*, June 20, 1940, 1; and "Appel aux catholiques de France de Mgr Feltin archevêque de Bordeaux," in *La Croix*, June 21, 1940, 1.

109. See Emma Fattorini, *Il culto mariano tra Ottocento e Novecento simboli e devozione. Ipotesi e prospettive di ricerca* (Milano: La Feltrinelli, 1999), 60.

110. "Notiziario internazionale. Consiglio dei ministri in Francia," in *L'Osservatore Romano*, June 21, 1940, 1.

111. *L'Osservatore Romano* mixes the various speeches of Pétain by referring to the appeal of June 17 only on June 22 and mixing it with that of June 20. See "Notiziario internazionale. Dichiarazioni del Maresciallo Pétain," in *L'Osservatore Romano*, June 22, 1940, 1.

112. *Daily Digest of Foreign Broadcasts*, Vatican Radio, in English for the Philippines, June 25, 1940, 2:30 p.m.

113. Franc [François d'Assise Bertoye], "A nos gouvernants," in *La Croix*, September 2, 1914, 1. Quoted in Sante Lesti, *Riti di guerra. Religione e politica nell'Europa della Grande Guerra* (Bologna: il Mulino, 2015), 16–17.

114. Gerd Krumeich, *Jeanne d'Arc à travers l'Histoire* (Paris: Albin Michel, 1993).

115. Michel Winock, "Jeanne d'Arc," in *Les lieux de mémoire*, volume III, *Les France. De l'archive à l'emblème*, ed. P. Nora (Paris: Gallimard, 1992), 685–733: 692. In 1929, the marshal, together with Maurice Barrès and others, wrote a book on Joan of Arc on the fifth centenary of the liberation of Orléans. See *L'hommage du Maréchal Foch. Sur Jeanne d'Arc*, in *Jeanne d'Arc* (Paris, Horizons de France, 1929).

116. *Journal Wladimir d'Ormesson*, AN, 156 Mi-116, note of June 20, 1940.

117. Pétain was not to go to Lourdes until April 1941.

118. *Apostolic Exhortation to the Peoples now at War and to their Rulers*, https://www.vatican.va/content/benedict-xv/en/apost_exhortations/documents/hf_ben-xv_exh_19150728_fummo-chiamati.html.

119. See Roberto Morozzo della Rocca, *Le nazioni non muoiono. Russia rivoluzionaria, Polonia indipendente e Santa Sede* (Bologna: il Mulino, 1992), 250; and Menozzi, *Chiesa, pace e guerra*, 27 f.

120. On the origin of the phrase "Catholic Nations will not die," see Ignazio Veca, "'Le nazioni cattoliche non muoiono.' Intorno alle origini del nazionalismo cattolico (1808–1849)," in *Cattolicesimo, Nazione e Nazionalismo*, 11–39: 30.

121. *Daily Digest of Foreign Broadcasts*, Vatican Radio, in English for the Philippines, July 2, 1940, 2:50 p.m.

122. *Daily Digest of Foreign Broadcasts*, Vatican Radio, in English for India and Ceylon, July 16, 1940, 4:00 p.m.

123. ARSI, Epistolarum Registra, Prov. Belgica Septentrionalis, I.

124. ARSI, Epistolarum Registra, Epistolae ad Romam Curiam, IX.

125. ACS, Minculpop, Reports, b. 34, fascicolo Radio Vaticana, sottofascicolo 2.

126. *Journal Wladimir d'Ormesson*, AN, 156 Mi-116.

127. *Journal Wladimir d'Ormesson*, AN, 156 Mi-116, note of September 20, 1940.

128. "Envoi d'un rapport d'ensemble de la mission de M. d'Ormesson au Vatican et d'une étude sur la composition de la Curie romaine," in CAD, *Guerre 1939–1945*, Vichy, Europe, Saint-Siège, 549–550, 17.

129. Renée Bédarida, "La Voix du Vatican (1940–1942). Bataille des ondes et Résistance spirituelle," in *Revue d'histoire de l'Église de France* 173 (1978): 215–243: 217. Jean Roche was prefect of studies and then rector, organizer of a center in the college active in the preparation of false documents for those wanted by the Vichy police, as well as the future deposit of arms of the Ajax network. Archives of the Lycée St. Joseph, Avignon, 0.10.3, La guerre de 40.

130. The distributor of *Sept* and *Temps present*, he could rely on this network to circulate *La Voix du Vatican* as well. Perrin was also the first to circulate the *Cahiers du Témoignage chrétien* in Marseille. See Bédarida, "La Voix du Vatican (1940–1942)": 217–219.

131. Renée Bédarida, "Voix chrétiennes dans la nuit," in *La presse clandestine, 1940–1944: colloque d'Avignon, les 20–21 juin 1985*, Association des médaillés de la Résistance de Vaucluse (Avignon: Conseil général de Vaucluse 1986), 57–66: 57.

132. Henri de Lubac, *Réstistance chrétienne à l'antisémitisme. Souvenirs 1940–1944* (Paris: Fayard, 1988), 128.

133. Jesuit Pierre Chaillet (1900–1972) taught in Austria in 1934, where he remained until the advent of Nazism. In 1940, from Budapest, where he was on a religious mission, he arrived in Marseille and from there in Vichy, where he joined the secret services under the false name of Prosper Charlier. He subsequently settled in the scholasticate of Fourvière and, in the summer of 1941, started *Témoignage chrétien*. In parallel with this clandestine activity, he joined the association Amitiés chrétiennes, which rescued Jewish children. After the German occupation of the Free Zone in 1943, Fr. Chaillet went to Paris where he started another organization of Resistance, the Cosor. *Témoignage du Père Chaillet racuelli par Mme Altman, le 5 février 1962*, AN, 72AJ/73, doc. n. 11. For a reconstruction of the events linked to the *Cahiers* see Renée Bédarida, *Les Armes de l'Esprit. Témoignage chrétien (1941–1944)* (Paris: Les éditions ouvrières, 1977), 47–62.

134. "France, prends garde de perdre ton âme," in *Cahiers du Témoignage chrétien* (November 1941), 1. The two quotations are taken from *La Voix du Vatican*, nos. 15 and 16, which are transcriptions of the programs from September 1–5, 1941.

135. Robert Maddalena (1906–1977) was a history teacher at the Collège Saint-Joseph in Avignon from 1940 to 1941; together with Fr. Roche he produced and circulated *La Voix du Vatican*. He was arrested on March 8, 1944, and deported to the Neuengamme concentration camp for his activities in the Resistance, especially for the circulation of *Témoignage chrétien*. The sector head for the Vaucluse of the Ajax-Micromegas network, he had turned the Collège Saint-Joseph into a center of the Resistance to provide false documents to Jews and members of the Resistance. *Témoignage de Maddalena Robert*, AN, 72AJ/73, doc. no. 5.

136. On the circulation of the two clandestine newssheets, see Bédarida, *Les Armes de l'Esprit*, 63–110.

137. *Daily Digest of Foreign Broadcasts*, Vatican Radio, in French for France, June 26 and 29, 1940, 8:00 p.m.

138. "La volonté de continuer," in *La Voix du Vatican*, no. 4. The program was of July 3, 1940.

139. "Les émissions françaises de Radio-Vatican. La maison et la patrie dans la renaissance française," in *Le Figaro*, July 8, 1940, 2; and "The Church Abroad. Vatican City. Consoling Words to France," in *The Tablet*, July 20, 1940, 50.

140. Vatican Radio, July 6, 1940, in *Fond André Mandouze*, Centre d'histoire de la Résistance et de la déportation de Lyon, Carton PV-Boîte 12/Chemise 5, Radio Vatican.

141. "Autorité et conscience," in *La Voix du Vatican*, no. 3. The program was on August 11, 1940.

142. "Le sens chrétien," in *La Voix du Vatican*, no. 3. The program was on July 13, 1940.

143. "La personne humaine et la liberté chrétienne," in *Fonds André Mandouze*. The program was on July 10, 1940.

144. "Pour reconstruire la foi," in *La Voix du Vatican*, no. 8. The program was on July 27, 1940.

145. See for example the programs of August 18, "Ne pleurez plus" and of August 25, "Ne vous effrayez pas," in *Fonds André Mandouze*.

146. "Le silence," in *La Voix du Vatican*, no. 8.

147. "Vertu actuelle: le silence," signed by V. L., in *La Croix*, August 15, 1940.

148. Emmanuel Mistiaen, *Le Silence* (Bruxelles: Lesigne. 1936). This book had fair success; in 1956 it was translated into German and published with the imprimatur of the archbishop of Vienna and in 1977 it was republished in French by the publisher of religious works, Pierre Téqui; *Das Schweigen*, (Wien: Verlag H. Kapri & Co, 1956); *Le Silence* (Paris: Pierre Téqui, 1977).

149. Jean-Louis Crémieux-Brilhac, et al., "*Époque nouvelle, radio nouvelle? Juin 1940*–avril 1942," in *La guerre des ondes. Histoire des radios de langue française pendant la Deuxième guerre mondiale*, ed. H. Eck (Paris: Communauté des radios publiques de langue française et A. Colin, 1985), 39–49.

150. Claude Lévy, "L'organisation de la propagande," in *Revue d'histoire de la Deuxième Guerre mondiale* 64 (1966), 7–28: 13.

151. "Jugement," in *La Voix du Vatican*. Sheet not numbered. The program was on September 22, 1940.

152. ADSS, vol. IIIa, doc. 172, pp. 272–273; doc. 184, 281; doc. 196, 291; ADSS, vol. IV, doc. 118, 189–190: note 1.

3. Vatican Radio, National Socialism, and Communism

1 *Der Notenwechsel zwischen dem Heiligen Stuhl und der deutschen Reichsregierung*, volume II, *1937–1945*, ed. D. Albrecht (Mainz: Matthias-Grünewald-Verlag, 1969), 35: doc. 33; *Der Notenwechsel zwischen dem Heiligen Stuhl und der deutschen Reichsregierung*, volume III, *Der Notenwechsel und die Demarchen des Nuntius Orsenigo 1933–1945*, ed. D. Albrecht (Mainz: Matthias-Grünewald-Verlag, 1980), 545: doc. 525.

2. Pius XII to von Preysing, April 22, 1940, in ADSS, vol. II, doc. 45, 138–142.

3. Ibid.

4. Ledóchowski to Montini, September 25, 1940, in ARSI, Epistolarum Registra, Epistolae ad Romanam Curiam, IX. Unfortunately, no trace has remained of this archive.

5. Raffaella Perin, *The Popes on Air: The History of Vatican Radio from Its Origins to World War II* (New York: Fordham University Press, 2024), Chapter 1.

6. ARSI, Ex-Ass. Italiae, VII. Domus Scriptorum—Radio Vaticana, Epistolae, 1005, fasc. 4.

7. Ledóchowski to Montini, October 3, 1940, in ARSI, Epistolarum Registra, Epistolae ad Romanam Curiam, IX.

8. Ledóchowski to Montini, October 8, 1940, in ARSI, Epistolarum Registra, Epistolae ad Romanam Curiam, IX. However, apart from some exceptions, the Archive of the Secretariat of State has not kept the scripts.

9. Typed note, in ASRS, *AA.EE.SS.*, Pio XII, parte I, Stati Ecclesiastici, Pos. 694, f. 47.

10. AAV, Segr. Stato, 1943, Stato Città Vaticano, posiz. 171, ff. 9-55.

11. The process of the Germanization of Alsace-Lorraine is summarized in Pierre Rigoulot, *L'Alsace-Lorraine pendant la guerre 1939–1945* (Paris: Presses Universitaires de France, 1997), 32–38; In particular, the dismantling of the Christian institutions, 44–45.

12. "The Church Abroad. From Radio Vatican Broadcasts, in German for Germany," in *The Tablet*, October 7, 1940, 290.

13. *Anlage I zu Bericht A 745 vom 28. Oktober 1940. News Bulletin October 9, 1940. Englisch/Europa*, in PAAA, Botschaft Rom (Vatikan). Akten, bd. 552. *Daily Digest of Foreign Broadcasts*, Vatican City, in Italian for Italy, October 9, 1940, 7:30 p.m.; in Spanish for Spain, October 9, 1940, 8:00 p.m.; in English for India and Ceylon, October 15, 1940, 4:00 p.m. The original in ASRS, *AA.EE.SS.*, Pio XII, parte I, Stati Ecclesiastici, Pos. 694, f. 261.

14. Note by Cardinal Maglione, October 19, 1940, in ASRS, *AA.EE.SS.*, Pio XII, parte I, Stati Ecclesiastici, Pos. 694, ff. 270–273v.

15. Note by Tardini, October 23, 1940, in ASRS, *AA.EE.SS.*, Pio XII, parte I, Stati Ecclesiastici, Pos. 694, f. 268.

16. Note by Tardini, October 25, 1940, in ASRS, *AA.EE.SS.*, Pio XII, parte I, Stati Ecclesiastici, Pos. 694, ff. 266–267v.

17. Note by Tardini, October 27, 1940, in ASRS, *AA.EE.SS.*, Pio XII, parte I, Stati Ecclesiastici, Pos. 694, ff. 258–259.

18. Note by Tardini of October 28, 1940, in ASRS, *AA.EE.SS.*, Pio XII, parte I, Stati Ecclesiastici, Pos. 694, f. 257.

19. See also *Anlage II zu Bericht A 745 vom 28. Oktober 1940. Abschrift.* in PAAA, Botschaft Rom (Vatikan). Akten, bd. 552.

20. Ledóchowski speaks to Montini about it in the quoted letter of October 3, 1940: "So Fr. Coffey, who looked after the American program very well, has left Rome: he is replaced by Fr. McCormick, less experienced than him, but, to my great regret, there was that error in speaking about the law on compulsory enlistment in the United States without taking into account the subsequent amendment." ARSI, Epistolarum Registra, Epistolae ad Romanam Curiam, IX.

21. Note by Tardini, October 27, 1940, in ASRS, *AA.EE.SS.*, Pio XII, parte I, Stati Ecclesiastici, Pos. 694, ff. 258–259.

22. "The World week by week. Axis Attempts to Annex the Papacy," in *The Tablet*, November 9, 1940, 363. From the ADSS, vol. IV, it can be deduced that the program in Spanish was on October 24. See doc. 134, 210, note 5.

23. Note by Tardini, October 25, 1940, in ASRS, *AA.EE.SS.*, Pio XII, parte I, Stati Ecclesiastici, Pos. 694, f. 243.

24. Tardini to Ledóchowski, October 28, 1940, in ASRS, *AA.EE.SS.*, Pio XII, parte I, Stati Ecclesiastici, Pos. 694, f. 201.

25. Ledóchowski to Tardini, October 29, 1940, in ASRS, *AA.EE.SS.*, Pio XII, parte I, Stati Ecclesiastici, Pos. 694, f. 205.

26. Note by Tardini, October 28, 1940, in ASRS, *AA.EE.SS.*, Pio XII, parte I, Stati Ecclesiastici, Pos. 694, ff. 199–200v.

27. See note 7 of doc. 45 in ADSS, vol. II, 141.

28. Letter from Ledóchowski to Maglione, October 28, 1940, in ARSI, Epistolarum Registra, Epistolae ad Romanam Curiam, IX.

29. Ledóchowski gave Tardini the transcription of some letters from Italian listeners from Italy, Albania, and the Arctic Circle, and listeners in English from the US, the Philippines, England, Ireland, and India. See ASRS, *AA.EE.SS.*, Pio XII, parte I, Stati Ecclesiastici, Pos. 694, ff. 314–316.

30. Tardini to Ledóchowski, October 29, 1940, in ASRS, *AA.EE.SS.*, Pio XII, parte I, Stati Ecclesiastici, Pos. 694, f. 194.

31. Note by Tardini, November 2, 1940, in ADSS, vol. IV, doc. 140, p. 216–217.

32. See, in addition to the aforementioned note by Tardini, that of November 3–4, in ADSS, vol. IV, doc. 143, 221.

33. Ledóchowski to Tardini, November 4, 1940, in ARSI, Epistolarum Registra, Epistolae ad Romanam Curiam, IX.

34. Tardini to Ledóchowski, November 5, 1940, in ASRS, *AA.EE.SS.*, Pio XII, parte I, Stati Ecclesiastici, Pos. 694, ff. 202–204.

35. For the epilogue of the affair, see ADSS, vol. IV, doc. 151, 229–231.

36. Ledóchowski to Tardini, November 5, 1940, in ASRS, *AA.EE.SS.*, Pio XII, parte I, Stati Ecclesiastici, Pos. 694, f. 8.

37. See Ennio Di Nolfo, *Vaticano e Stati Uniti 1939–1952. Dalle carte di Myron C. Taylor* (Milano: Franco Angeli Editore, 1978), 9–98: 32–33; and Elena Aga Rossi, "La politica del Vaticano durante la seconda guerra mondiale. Indicazioni di ricerca e documenti inediti sulla missione di Myron Taylor," in *Storia contemporanea* 4 (1975): 881–899: 889.

38. Gerald P. Fogarty, *The Vatican and the American Hierarchy from 1870 to 1965* (Stuttgart: Hiersemann, 1982), 263.

39. Letter from Cicognani to Maglione, January 9, 1941, in ADSS, vol. IV, doc. 224, 327–328.

40. The whole text of the annual message from President Roosevelt to Congress on January 6, 1941, is published on the website of the Franklin D. Roosevelt Presidential Library and Museum, http://www.fdrlibrary.marist.edu/fourfreedoms. For a contextualization, see Robert Dallek, *Franklin D. Roosevelt and American Foreign Policy 1932–1945* (New York: Oxford University Press, 1995), 257–258; and Luca Castagna, *A Bridge Across the Ocean. The United States*

and the Holy See between the Two World Wars (Washington D.C.: The Catholic University of America Press, 2014).

41. Cicognani to Maglione, January 16, 1941, in ADSS, vol. IV, doc. 235, 344.

42. "I presupposti per il nuovo ordinamento dell'Europa," in *L'Osservatore Romano*, December 25, 1940, 1.

43. Attolico to Ciano, December 24, 1940, doc. 348, in ASDMAE, DDI, serie IX, volume 4 (Roma: Istituto Poligrafico e Zecca dello Stato, 1986), 328–329: 329.

44. "Nella giornata della universale supplicazione," in *Discorsi e radiomessaggi di Sua Santità Pio XII*, volume II (Città del Vaticano: Tipografia Poliglotta Vaticana, 1960), 321–327: 323.

45. Attolico to Ciano, December 24, 1940, doc. 161, in DDI, 170–171.

46. "Nella giornata della universale supplicazione," 326.

47. Doc. 161, in DDI, 171.

48. NA, FO 371/30173.

49. *Daily Digest of Foreign Broadcasts*, Vatican City, in English for North America, January 20, 1941, 02:30 a.m.

50. Perin, *The Popes on Air*, Chapter 2.

51. *Daily Digest of Foreign Broadcasts*, Vatican City, in English for North America, February 7, 1941, 2:30 a.m. The pastoral letter bears the date of January 13 but was read in the Dutch churches on January 25. See Robert A. Graham, "Un messaggio del papa Pio XII ai vescovi olandesi nel 1943," in *La Civiltà Cattolica*, April 5, 1980, 133–143: 140–141.

52. "News, Notes and Texts from All Parts," in *The Tablet*, May 3, 1941, 350–351.

53. The three encyclicals were *Mit brennender Sorge* (March 14, 1937), *Divini Redemptoris* (March 19, 1937), and *Firmissimam constantiam* (March 28, 1937). *Daily Digest of Foreign Broadcasts*, Vatican City, in English for North America, February 10, 1941, 2:30 a.m.

54. *Daily Digest of Foreign Broadcasts*, Vatican City, in English for North America, February 17, 1941, 2:30 a.m.

55. *Daily Digest of Foreign Broadcasts*, Vatican City, in English for North America, March 17, 1941, 2:30. a.m.

56. *Daily Digest of Foreign Broadcasts*, Vatican City, in English for North America, April 4, 1941, 2:30. a.m.

57. The text is published in "'Fede nel Primato di Pietro. Fedeltà all'odierno Pietro' nella pastorale parola del Card. Faulhaber," in *L'Osservatore Romano*, April 2, 1941, 1–2.

58. *Daily Digest of Foreign Broadcasts*, Vatican City, in English for North America, April 11, 1941, 2:30. a.m.

59. "Suprema missione," in *L'Osservatore Romano*, April 7–8, 1941, 1–2.

60. James Hennessey, "American Jesuit in Wartime Rome: The Diary of Vincent A. McCormick, s.j., 1942–1945," in *Mid-America* 56 (1974). Unfortunately, the pages of the diary on the last years of the war are full of shortcomings.

61. Philippe Chenaux, "Father Włodzimierz Ledóchowski (1866–1942): Driving Force behind Papal Anti-Communism during the Interwar Period," in *Journal of Jesuit Studies* 5 (2018): 54–70; and David I. Kertzer, *The Pope and Mussolini*, (New York: Random House, 2015), 234-235.

62. Kertzer, *The Pope and Mussolini*, 210-211.

63. Peter Godman, *Hitler e il Vaticano. Dagli Archivi Segreti Vaticani la vera storia dei rapporti fra il nazismo e la Chiesa*, Italian trans. S. Bourlot (Torino: Lindau, 2005), 237.

64. James Bernauer, *Jesuit Kaddish. Jesuits, Jews, and Holocaust Remembrance* (Notre Dame: University of Notre Dame Press, 2020), 85.

65. Quoted in Owen Chadwick, *Britain and the Vatican during the Second World War* (Cambridge: Cambridge University Press, 1986), 88–89.

66. Fogarty, *The Vatican and the American Hierarchy*, 269–270. We do not have the complete text of the telegram; therefore we only report Fogarty's quotation. Tittmann also refers to his meeting with Ledóchowski in his memoirs: Harold Tittmann, Jr., *Inside the Vatican of Pius 12: The Memoir of an American Diplomat During World War 2*, ed. H.H. Tittmann, III (New York: Doubleday, 2004).

67. Di Nolfo, *Vaticano e Stati Uniti*, 39; Charles R. Gallagher, *Vatican Secret Diplomacy: Joseph P. Hurley and Pope Pius XII* (New Haven: Yale University Press, 2008), 114–115.

68. Telegram: Tittmann to Hull, May 28, 1941, in LOC, Myron Taylor's Paper, box 1.

69. Letter from Ledóchowski to Maglione, October 28, 1940, see *supra*.

70. Letter from Maglione to Cicognani, August 11, 1941, in ADSS, vol. V, doc. 41, 139–140.

71. Note from Maglione, September 10, 1941, in ADSS, vol. V, doc. 69, 191–193: 193.

72. *Daily Digest of Foreign Broadcasts*, Vatican City, in English for North America, May 2, 1941, 2:30. a.m.

73. In June 1942, the Vatican wireless quoted from an interview given to *Le Temps* by Cardinal Cerejeira, patriarch of Lisbon, in which the archbishop agreed with Salazar that faith was a spiritual, not political, question and he would not have altered the Church-State separation in Portugal. "News, Notes and Texts, Portugal, Church and State," in *The Tablet*, June 2, 1942, 308. In January 1943, Cerejeira's pastoral letter on the "new State" was read on the German program. *Daily Digest of Foreign Broadcasts*, Vatican City, in German for Germany, January 13, 1943, 8:45 p.m.

74. Perin, *The Popes on Air*, Chapter 2.

75. *Daily Digest of Foreign Broadcasts*, Vatican City, in Spanish for Spain, February 3, 1941, 8:00 p.m.

76. *Daily Digest of Foreign Broadcasts*, Vatican City, in Spanish for Spain, March 19, 1941, 8:00 p.m.

77. *Daily Digest of Foreign Broadcasts*, Vatican City, in Spanish for Spain, March 24, 1941, 8:00 p.m.

78. The program was on March 31, 1941. For the complete script, see *Funk-Abhör-Berichte. Sendungen fremder Rundfunksender.* Band V. *Fremdsprachige Originaltexte*, April 2, 1941, in LOC.

79. See *supra* in this chapter.

80. *Funk-Abhör-Berichte. Sendungen fremder Rundfunksender.* Band V. *Fremdsprachige Originaltexte*, March 28, 1941, in LOC.

81. The passage seems to paraphrase a concept expressed in Paul's *First Letter to Timothy*, when he explained that the profession of a false knowledge had misled the people from the true faith.

82. In this passage, too, the reference to the *Letter to the Galatians* is clear.

83. The program in Spanish was on April 4, 9:00 p.m., in *Funk-Abhör-Berichte. Sendungen fremder Rundfunksender.* Band V. *Fremdsprachige Originaltexte*, April 4, 1941, in LOC; in German in *Daily Digest of Foreign Broadcasts*, Vatican City; in German for Germany, April 4, 1941, 7:45 p.m.; in French in *Radio Vatican. Années 1940–1941–1942–1943. Emissions prises en sténo à Toulon*, program of March 31, 1941, also shown in *La Voix du Vatican*, no. 13. It is probable that all the programs are based on the summary provided by *L'Osservatore Romano* of March 30, 1941, 2.

84. On the controversial passages in which Gröber repeated concepts typical of traditional Catholic antisemitism, see Giovanni Miccoli, *I dilemmi e i silenzi di Pio XII. Vaticano, seconda Guerra mondiale e Shoah* (Milano: Bur, 2007), 376.

85. "Radiomessaggio alla Spagna," April 16, 1939, in *Discorsi e radiomessaggi di Sua Santità Pio XII*, volume I (Città del Vaticano: Tipografia Poliglotta Vaticana, 1955), 49–54.

86. Vicente Cárcel Ortí, *Le missioni diplomatiche*, in *Il cardinale Gaetano Cicognani (1881–1962). Note per una biografia* (Roma: Studium, 1983), 53–233: 163–233. On the Catholic Church in the Spanish Civil War, see, at least, Alfonso Alvarez Bolado, *Para ganar la guerra, para ganar la paz* (Madrid: Universidad Pontificia Comillas, 1995); and Hilari Raguer, *La pólvora y el incienso. La Iglesia y la Guerra Civil española (1936–1939)* (Barcelona: Ediciones Península, 2001).

87. See at least Joaquín Luis Ortega, "La Iglesia española desde 1939 hasta 1975," in *Historia de la Iglesia en España*, volume V, *La Iglesia en la España contemporánea (1808–1975)*, ed. V. Cárcel Ortì (Madrid: Biblioteca de Autores Cristianos, 1979), 665–714.

88. "The Church abroad, Portugal. New Catholic Workers' League," in *The Tablet*, March 29, 1941, 249–250.

89. *Daily Digest of Foreign Broadcasts*, Vatican City, in Spanish for Spain, June 18, 1941, 10:00 p.m. The script was picked up by *L'Osservatore Romano* on June 19, 1–2.

90. *Daily Digest of Foreign Broadcasts*, Vatican City, in Spanish for Spain, July 19, 1941, 10:00 p.m.

91. *Funk-Abhör-Berichte. Sendungen fremder Rundfunksender.* Band V. *Fremdsprachige Originaltexte*, May 9, 1941, 10:00 p.m., in LOC.

92. *Daily Digest of Foreign Broadcasts*, Vatican City, in Spanish for Spain, August 20, 1941, 10:00 p.m.

93. *Daily Digest of Foreign Broadcasts*, Vatican City, in Spanish for Spain, August 25, 1941, 9:00 p.m.

94. *Daily Digest of Foreign Broadcasts*, Vatican City, in Spanish for Spain for Santiago, Chile, November 9, 1941, 5:00 p.m.

95. *Daily Digest of Foreign Broadcasts*, Vatican City, in Spanish for Santiago, Chile, December 15, 8:00 p.m.

96. On August 2, 1940, von Ribbentrop let the Spanish ambassador in Berlin know that his government wanted Spain to rapidly enter the war. The trend of the conflict had played in favor of Franco's playing for time, but the Germans, once again, pressed the *Generalissimo* the following year, ensuring the promise that he would enter the war as soon as possible.

97. Maglione to G. Cicognani, November 29, 1940, in ADSS, vol. IV, doc. 185, 278–279. *Arriba*, in particular, described Hitler as the "most human figure that history has ever known."

98. G. Cicognani to Maglione, January 16, 1941, in ASRS, *AA.EE.SS.*, Pio XII, parte I, Spagna, Pos. 974, ff. 266-271. New Vatican documents show the Holy See's concern about German propaganda in Spain during World War II, especially with regard to news about the situation of the Church in Germany. The Spanish press, both those close to Franco and the Catholic press, published false reports about German Catholics, spreading the idea that they were not persecuted at all by the National Socialist regime. I have reconstructed this story in Raffaella Perin, *La situazione della Chiesa cattolica tedesca nella stampa spagnola durante la seconda guerra mondiale* in *Dal modernismo alla 'Terza Spagna'. Saggi in onore di Alfonso Botti* (Roma: Viella, forthcoming).

99. G. Cicognani to Maglione, January 31, 1941, in ADSS, vol. IV, doc. 250, 369–373: 372.

100. On the English edition, see Perin, *The Popes on Air*, Chapter 2.

101. Wilfred D. Halls, *Politics, Society and Christianity in Vichy France* (Oxford: Berg, 1995), 225; and Dominique Chassard, *Vichy et le Saint-Siège. Quatre ans de relations diplomatiques. Juillet 1940–août 1944* (Paris: L'Harmattan, 2015).

102. ADSS, vol. IV, doc. 35, 97; and Léon Papeleux, "La diplomatie vaticane à l'heure des victoires de Hitler," in *Revue d'histoire de la Deuxième Guerre mondiale* 98 (1975): 27–56: 31.

103. See the reconstruction by Jean-Louis Clément, "La hiérarchie catholique et les principes de la révolution nationale," in *Guerres mondiales et conflits contemporains* 2 (2005): 27–36.

104. See the note from Maglione to Valeri of February 1, 1941, in ADSS, vol. IV, 373.

105. Valeri to Maglione, October 4, 1940, in ADSS, vol. IV, doc. 107, 172–175.

106. On collaboration, see the books by Robert Paxton, including Robert O. Paxton, *La France de Vichy 1940–1944* (Paris: Seuil, 1997), 95 f.

107. Paxton, *La France de Vichy*, 122.

108. Valeri to Maglione, November 13, 1940, in ADSS, vol. IV, doc. no. 164, 241–243.

109. Valeri to Maglione, June 12, 1941, in ADSS, vol. IV, doc. no. 397, 543–545.

110. Cf. Renée Bédarida, *Les catholiques dans la guerre 1939–1945* (Paris: Hachette, 1998), 101–115; Jean-Louis Clément, *Les évêques au temps de Vichy: loyalisme sans inféodation. Les relations entre l'Église et l'État de 1940 à 1944* (Paris: Beauchesne, 1955); and Halls, *Politics, Society and Christianity*, 46 f.

111. "Intégration," in *La Voix du Vatican*, no. 12. The following can be read in the transcription of Toulon: "We were unable to get the rest, the interference was too strong. The Vatican disappeared, drowned out by others." Part of the program, precisely because of the interference, was repeated on March 4. See *Radio Vatican. Années 1940–1941–1942–1943. Emissions prises en sténo à Toulon*, February 24, and March 4, 1941.

112. This sort of diary was written in Limoges, where the Catholic paper *La Croix* had moved shortly before the arrival of the German troops in Paris. Limagne was a political informer for the paper and, although unable to ply his trade any longer, wanted to be a witness. Together with publishers Léon Merklen and Alfred Michelin, he set up a listening service that let them receive European radio stations (especially the BBC and Vatican Radio), but also those from the other side of the Atlantic. In the *Éphémérides* we find, noted down, the contents of the programs and the orders of Vichy to the press, the originals of which were destroyed with the approach of the liberation.

113. Note of March 18, 1942, in Pierre Limagne, *Éphémérides de quatre années tragiques: 1940–1944*, volume I (Lavilledieu: Éditions de Candide, 1987), 117. The text of the lecture was included by mistake in a packet of sheets to be sent to the printers for composition. Once the mistake had been realized, the commander of censorship was informed that he should not take some texts that were about to arrive for consideration. This did not happen, and the text on collaborationism reached the central censorship, together with the remonstrances for the group of "Gaullists" of *La Croix*. See the note of June 5, 1941, 180. On *La Croix* during the war, see Marie-Geneviève Massiani, "'La Croix' sous Vichy," in *Cent ans d'histoire de La Croix 1883–1983. Colloque sous la direction de R. Rémond et E. Poulat, mars 1987* (Paris: Editions Centurion, 1988), 301–321. On the functioning of censorship under Vichy, see Philippe Amaury, *Les deux premières expériences d'un 'Ministère de l'Information' en France, l'apparition d'institutions politiques et administratives d'information et de propagande sous la IIIe République en temps de crise (juillet 1939–juin 1940), leur renouvellement par le régime de Vichy (juillet 1940–août 1944)*, volume 2 (Paris: Librairie générale de droit et de jurisprudence, 1969), 466–488.

114. Limagne, *Éphémérides*, volume I, note of November 13, 1940, 47.

115. "La Catholicité. L'union des corps," in *La Voix du Vatican*, no. 6. It was published, after censorship, by *La Croix*, November 28, 1940, 2.

116. Limagne, *Éphémérides*, volume I, note of December 8, 1940, 62. For the script of the program, see "Une seule vérité," in *La Voix du Vatican*, cit., no. 7. Published by *La Croix*, December 22, 1940, 1.

117. "Reflechir," in *La Voix du Vatican*, no. 9.

118. *Daily Digest of Foreign Broadcasts*, Vatican City, in English for India and Ceylon, November 12, 1940, 4:00 p.m.; "En Pologne!" in *La Voix du Vatican* no. 5, the program was on November 29, 1940.

119. Note of November 29, 1940, in Limagne, *Éphémérides*, volume I, 57.

120. "Les motifs de la condamnation de la doctrine du national-socialisme," in *La Voix du Vatican*, no. 6. The program was on December 16, 1940.

121. This text was read on February 4, 1941, and published as the opening of no. 10 of *La Voix du Vatican*; also repeated on February 19, 1941, published in *Radio Vatican. Années 1940-1941-1942-1943. Emissions prises en sténo à Toulon*.

122. Program of February 18, 1941, in *Radio Vatican. Années 1940-1941-1942-1943. Emissions prises en sténo à Toulon*.

123. A report by the BBC on jamming explains the functioning of the interference, which consists of transmitting from another radio station, on the same frequency, a signal that is high enough to cover the broadcast to be disturbed. Germany usually only interfered with propaganda programs but with an excellent organization, capable of quickly finding even new stations. The fact that the Germans deemed it necessary to interfere with the frequency of Vatican Radio is, as confirmed by the BBC report, direct evidence of the fact that, despite the penalties (which over time became increasingly severe) inflicted on those who listened to foreign radio stations, Vatican Radio and the BBC could still be heard. See BBC Monitoring Service-Organisation and policy, file 1–2, in BBC Written Archives.

124. "Situation religieuse en Allemagne," in *La Voix du Vatican*, no. 13 and *Radio Vatican. Années 1940-1941-1942-1943. Emissions prises en sténo à Toulon*; *Daily Digest of Foreign Broadcasts*, Vatican City, in French for France, March 30, 1941, 11:00 a.m. The perception of a certain insistence by Vatican Radio in French on this topic, expressed by Pierre Limagne in his diary of March 30, is also interesting: "Vatican Radio, after having already, in its broadcast on Friday, denounced the anti-Catholic discriminations in Germany, returns to the question today with much insistence." See Limagne, *Éphémérides*, volume I, 124. It was also quoted in the first *Cahier du Témoignage chrétien* of November 1941, paragraph I, "Le National-Socialisme, mystique anti-chrétienne," 2 f.

125. Note by Tardini, April 3, 1941, ADSS, vol. IV, doc. 306, 437–438.

126. "L'Eglise catholique en Alsace," in *La Voix du Vatican*, no. 13. The program was on April 4, 1941.

127. Program of April 16, 1941, *Radio Vatican. Années 1940-1941-1942-1943. Emissions prises en sténo à Toulon*.

128. Note, in ASRS, *AA.EE.SS.*, Pio XII, parte I, Stati Ecclesiastici, Pos. 694, f. 232.

129. AAV, Segr. Stato, 1943, Stato Città Vaticano, posiz. 171, f. 46.

130. Robert Leiber was born in 1887 in Oberhomberg, Germany. After arriving in Rome in the early 1920s, he collaborated with historian Ludwig von Pastor on his history of the popes. In 1924, he met Nuncio Pacelli and from then on became his close collaborator. He taught History of the Church at the Gregorian University where he lived. He died in Rome on February 18, 1967.

131. Pencil note by Ledóchowski of April 26, 1941, in ARSI, Ex-Ass. Italiae, VII. Domus Scriptorum-Radio Vaticana, Epistolae, 1005, fasc. 4.

132. Ledóchowski to Soccorsi, April 27, 1941, in ARSI, Ex-Ass. Italiae, VII. Domus Scriptorum-Radio Vaticana, Epistolae, 1005, fasc. 4.

133. Leiber to Ledóchowski, April 28, 1941, in ARSI, Ex-Ass. Italiae, VII. Domus Scriptorum-Radio Vaticana, Epistolae, 1005, fasc. 4.

134. Note by Ledóchowski, ARSI, Ex-Ass. Italiae, VII. Domus Scriptorum-Radio Vaticana, Epistolae, 1005, fasc. 4.

135. Letter from Ledóchowski to Maglione, April 30, 1941, in ADSS, vol. IV, doc. 332, 474–477: 474. *La Corrispondenza*, a Catholic newsletter, had let the news arrive in Germany that in the Vatican there was already a change in the air on April 23. The founder of the newsletter was Oreste Daffinà, a Calabrian journalist who enjoyed the protection of Tacchi Venturi and who was a trusted informer of the fascist political police on Vatican affairs. *La Corrispondenza*, April 23, 1941, in PAAA, Akten. Kirchenfragen, bd. 3. On Daffinà see Mauro Canali, *Le spie del regime* (Bologna: il Mulino, 2004), 292. This also explains a note by Tardini of April 30 in which he says that "The French ambassador knows that Vatican Radio is forced not to speak of Germany any longer. He was told—so he writes—by a diplomatic colleague." ADSS, vol. IV, doc. n. 332, n. 1, 474–477: 474–475.

136. ADSS, vol. IV, doc. n. 332, 475. Some summaries of letters from listeners in spring 1941 in ASRS, *AA.EE.SS.*, Pio XII, parte I, Stati Ecclesiastici, Pos. 694, ff. 216–228.

137. Leiber to Ledóchowski, April 30, 1941, in ARSI, Ex-Ass. Italiae, VII. Domus Scriptorum-Radio Vaticana, Epistolae, 1005, fasc. 4.

138. Note by Ledóchowski, May 2, 1941, evening, in ARSI, Ex-Ass. Italiae, VII. Domus Scriptorum-Radio Vaticana, Epistolae, 1005, fasc. 4.

139. Ledóchowski to Pius XII, May 3, 1941, in ARSI, Ex-Ass. Italiae, VII. Domus Scriptorum-Radio Vaticana, Epistolae, 1005, fasc. 4.

140. Note by Ledóchowski, May 4, 1941, at 4.30 p.m., in ARSI, Ex-Ass. Italiae, VII. Domus Scriptorum-Radio Vaticana, Epistolae, 1005, fasc. 4.

141. Leiber to Ledóchowski, May 5, 1941, in ARSI, Ex-Ass. Italiae, VII. Domus Scriptorum-Radio Vaticana, Epistolae, 1005, fasc. 4.

142. *Daily Digest of Foreign Broadcasts*, Vatican City, in French for France, May 4, 1941, 12:00 p.m. The French original is on a typewritten sheet in ARSI, Ex-Ass. Italiae, VII. Domus Scriptorum-Radio Vaticana, Epistolae, 1005, fasc. 4.

143. Extract of May 11, 1941, cut out and included in *Radio Vatican. Années 1940–1941–1942–1943. Emissions prises en sténo à Toulon.*

144. Perin, *The Popes on Air*, Chapter 2.
145. Paul Duclos, *Le Vatican et la Seconde Guerre Mondiale. Action doctrinale et diplomatique en faveur de la paix* (Paris: éditions A. Pedone, 1955), 35. Father Dauchy also reports the episode of the interview in *Les temps héroïques de Radio Vatican*. I have reconstructed the affair in a monograph on Father Mistiaen in preparation.
146. *Harold H. Tittmann, Jr. Papers*, box 1, folder 27, in Georgetown University Special Collections Research Center, Washington D.C.
147. Duclos, *Le Vatican et la Seconde Guerre Mondiale*, 35: footnote 4.
148. Program of May 9, 1941, in *Radio Vatican. Années 1940–1941–1942–1943. Emissions prises en sténo à Toulon*.
149. Programs from May 12–17; 20; 23–24; 26–31, 1941, in *Radio Vatican. Années 1940–1941–1942–1943. Emissions prises en sténo à Toulon*.
150. Statistics of the programs from 1938 to 1941, published by the IBU, confirm that the programming of Vatican Radio in 1941 was divided as follows: 1.6% musical programs; 94.1% spoken programs; and 4.3% religious programs. It also reveals that the musical programs were introduced by Vatican Radio that year. Union Internationale de Radiodiffusion, *Rapport Général sur le développement et la situation actuelle de la Radiodiffusion internationale*, Genève, June 1943, 10.
151. Program of July 26, 1941, in *Radio Vatican. Années 1940–1941–1942–1943. Emissions prises en sténo à Toulon*.
152. Note by Tardini, June 2,1941, in ASRS, *AA.EE.SS.*, Pio XII, parte I, Stati Ecclesiastici, Pos. 694, f. 11.
153. Coded message from London, no. 69, May 26, 1941, in ASRS, *AA.EE.SS.*, Pio XII, parte I, Stati Ecclesiastici, Pos. 694, f. 24.
154. Coded message for London, no. 113, May 27, 1941, in ASRS, *AA.EE.SS.*, Pio XII, parte I, Stati Ecclesiastici, Pos. 694, f. 24.
155. Letter from Godfrey to Maglione, June 6, 1941, in ADSS, vol. IV, doc. 390, 532–535: 535.
156. Memorandum from the British Legation, June 10, 1941, in ADSS, vol. IV, doc. 396, 541–542.
157. Note by Tardini, June 11, 1941, in ASRS, *AA.EE.SS.*, Pio XII, parte I, Stati Ecclesiastici, Pos. 694, f. 102.
158. Letter from La Vallette to the BBC Monitoring Service, January 29, 1941, in NA, INF 1/781.
159. Letter from Grisewood of the BBC to Richard Hope, of the Religious Division of the Ministry of Information, February 16, 1941, in NA, INF 1/781.
160. Letter from Hope to Randall, May 14, 1941, in NA, INF 1/781.
161. Letter from Randall to Hope, May 15, 1941, in NA, INF 1/781. On June 6, the Catholic Section of the Ministry of Information, in agreement with the Foreign Office, sent a letter to James Walsh, editor of the *Catholic Times*, to ask him to publish a cautious reference to the current position of Vatican Radio, regarding the

end of the critical programs of the German anti-religious policy, in a form that would not offend the Holy See.

162. The spy, Achille Villa, worked for Vatican Radio under the pseudonym of "Lavil," providing information to the fascist political police on the espionage and counterespionage activity of the diplomatic seats in the Vatican, sending all of the material possible, especially radio telegrams from England, the Americas, Dublin, and Lisbon. See Canali, *Le spie*, 265.

163. See for example, the report sent on January 8, 1941, from the Italian Embassy to the Holy See in ASDMAE, Embassy by the Holy See, b. 163, Stazione Radio Vaticana.

164. Note by Tardini, June 13, 1941, in ADSS, vol. IV, doc. 401, 548.

165. Radio bulletin. Vatican City (Polish) June 11, 8:45 p.m., in ASDMAE, Embassy by the Holy See, b. 163, Stazione Radio Vaticana. See the original script in ARSI, Allegata Epistolis ad Curiam Romanam, VIII, annex 100.

166. Note by Montini, Ex Aud. SS. mi, June 15, 1941, in ASRS, *AA.EE.SS.*, Pio XII, parte I, Stati Ecclesiastici, Pos. 694, f. 7. According to Tittmann, the fear of the Holy See that the Germans would put pressure on the Italian government so that they denounced the Lateran agreements was influential to the decision. See the draft of the memoirs in the *Harold H. Tittman, Jr. Papers*, box 3, folder 66.

167. Ledóchowski to Maglione, June 16, 1941, in ARSI, Epp. Regg. Ad Curiam Romanam IX.

168. *Extraordinary meeting in the Sala delle Consulte* 19.6.1941 1:30 p.m., in ARSI, Ex-Ass. Italiae, VII. Domus Scriptorum-Radio Vaticana, Epistolae, 1005, fasc. 3.

169. The Jesuit Dauchy, in the already quoted interview, confirms that the scripts were submitted to the Secretariat of State before they were broadcast. Called back to work for Vatican Radio in February 1942, he said: "When they were not mere documents of the Holy See or the translation of an article from the O.R. [*L'Osservatore Romano*], the written script had to be presented in the morning, before 10, to receive the approval of the Secretariat of State." *Les temps héroïques de Radio Vatican*, interview with Father Albert Dauchy S.J., October 16, 1976, in ASRV.

170. This is what Fr. Soccorsi wrote in a memo of September 1943: "So far, our brother would bring the scripts for censorship to the Vatican every day at 10:30 am (also bringing the radio newspaper bulletins); and if there was any response from the censor, he would bring it back from the Vatican when he brought the radio bulletin at 3:00 pm. [...] Every day at least four copies of all censored broadcasts were made in the Curia: three were taken daily by Brother to the Vatican, one remained here in the radio archives." AAV, Segr. Stato, 1943, Stato Città Vaticano, posiz. 134, ff. 3-4.

171. Tittmann also stated that "it was well known in the Vatican that it did not matter to Pius XII whether Vatican Radio was in trouble now and again

because he had never really liked it." He then added that Vatican Radio, run by the Jesuits, was difficult to control.

172. Letter from Attolico to Pavolini, June 27, 1941, in ASDMAE, Embassy by the Holy See, b. 163, Stazione Radio Vaticana.

173. Letter from Maglione to Valeri, September 3, 1941, in ADSS, vol. IIIa, doc. 302, 450–452: 451. On the complaints of the Polish bishops regarding the pope's silence about Poland, see Alessandro Duce, *Pio XII e la Polonia (1939–1945)* (Roma: Edizioni Studium, 1997), 197–208; Robert A. Ventresca, *Soldier of Christ. The Life of Pope Pius XII* (Cambridge: Harvard University Press, 2013), 173–176; and Andrea Riccardi, *La guerra del silenzio. Pio XII, il nazismo, gli ebrei* (Bari-Roma: Laterza, 2022), 87 f.

174. For a summary with examples taken from the Italian and French press see Chenaux, *L'ultima eresia*, 22–27, and for an overview of the antisemitic stereotypes in the Italian diocesan press between 1937 and 1939 see Elena Mazzini, *Ostilità convergenti. Stampa diocesana, razzismo e antisemitismo nell'Italia fascista (1937–1939)* (Napoli: Edizioni scientifiche italiane, 2013). For how the antisemitic and anti-Protestant stereotypes grew closer between the two World Wars see Raffaella Perin, "La Chiesa veneta e le minoranze religiose," *Chiesa cattolica e minoranze in Italia nella prima metà del Novecento*, ed. R. Perin (Roma: Viella, 2011), 133–223.

175. There are many works that have dealt with the subject. To be recalled: Maxime Mourin, *Le Vatican et l'URSS* (Paris: Payot, 1965), 29–136; Emilio Gentile, *Contro Cesare. Cristianesimo e totalitarismo nell'epoca dei fascismi* (Milano: Feltrinelli, 2010), 77–78, 262–292; Giorgio Petracchi, "I gesuiti e il comunismo tra le due guerre," in *La Chiesa cattolica e il totalitarismo. Atti del convegno Torino, 25–26 ottobre 2001*, ed. V. Ferrone (Firenze: Olschki, 2004), 123–152; Andrea Riccardi, *La Chiesa cattolica, il comunismo e l'Unione Sovietica*, ibidem, 79–92; Laura Pettinaroli, *La politique russe du Saint-Siège* (Rome: EFR, 2015), and Giuliana Chamedes, *A Twentieth Century Crusade. The Vatican's Battle to Remake Christian Empire* (Cambridge: Harvard University Press, 2019).

176. Some books: Hubert Wolf, *The Pope and the Devil: The Vatican's Archives and the Third Reich* (Cambridge: Harvard University Press, 2008), Chapter III, especially on the phases that led to the Concordat; Alessandro Bellino, *Il Vaticano e Hitler. Santa Sede, Chiesa tedesca e nazismo (1922–1939)* (Milano: Guerini e Associati, 2019); Giovanni Sale, *Hitler, la Santa Sede e gli ebrei* (Milano: Jaca Book, 2004), 36 f.; Miccoli, *I dilemmi*, 118 f., to which reference should be made for a more detailed analysis of the events and the climate; and Guenter Lewy, *The Catholic Church and Nazi Germany* (New York: McGraw-Hill, 1964).

177. Miccoli, *I dilemmi*, 127, 135. On March 4, 1933, Pius XI said: "Hitler is the first and only statesman to speak publicly against the Bolsheviks. Until now it had been solely the pope."

178. Miccoli, *I dilemmi*, 494, n. 14. See also Father Ledit's position on this in Daniele Menozzi, "Regalità di Cristo e politica nell'età di Pio XI: i congressi internazionali di Cristo re," in *Chiesa, laicità e vita civile. Studi in onore di Guido Verucci*, eds. L. Ceci and L. Demofonti (Roma: Carocci, 2005).

179. On *Mit brennender Sorge* see at least: Wolf, *The Pope and the Devil*, 264–271; Thomas Brechenmacher, "La preparazione dell'enciclica Mit brennender Sorge (21 marzo 1937)," in *Le gouvernement pontifical sous Pie XI. Pratiques romaines et gestion de l'universel*, ed. L. Pettinaroli (Rome: École française de Rome, 2013), 545–560; and Fabrice Bouthillon and Marie Levant, eds., *Pie XI. Un pape contre le nazisme? L'encyclique Mit Brennender Sorge (14 mars 1937). Actes du colloque international de Brest, 4–6 juin 2015* (Brest: éditions dialogues, 2016). On the *Divini Redemptoris* see Chenaux, *L'ultima eresia*, 70–75; and Emma Fattorini, *Pio XI, Hitler e Mussolini. La solitudine di un papa* (Torino: Einaudi, 2007), 64–70.

180. Chenaux, *L'ultima eresia*, 72.

181. Miccoli, *I dilemmi*, 162. See also what Pope Pius XI is alleged to have said to Osborne at the audience on December 29, 1938, as the chargé d'affaires refers to in a letter to Foreign Secretary Lord Halifax: "There is no doubt that Nazi Germany has taken the place of communism as the Church's most dangerous enemy." Quoted in Chadwick, *Britain and the Vatican*, 25.

182. This is the case, for example, of the bishop of Padua, Monsignor Carlo Agostini who, taking a cue from the encyclical *Mit brennender Sorge* said that the situation of the clergy in Germany "is a real tragedy no less tremendous of hatred and dispersion" than the one in Spain. "Sulle condizioni della Chiesa in Germania. Al Ven. Clero e Diletti Figli della Città e Diocesi," in *Bollettino Diocesano di Padova*, 1937, no. 6, 376.

183. For the diocesan press, see the examples given in Mazzini, *Ostilità convergenti*, 48 f.

184. On Vatican Radio between 1936 and 1937 see Perin, *The Popes on Air*, Chapter 1.

185. Marie Levant, "'Facendo nostra la parola di nostro Signore.' Pio XI di fronte alla politica della mano tesa in Francia," in *Pius XI: Keywords*, eds. A. Guasco and R. Perin (Berlin: LIT Verlag, 2010), 325–338.

186. Miccoli, *I dilemmi*, 175 f.; David I. Kertzer, *The Pope at War: The Secret History of Pius XII, Mussolini, and Hitler* (New York: Random House, 2022), Chapter 3. In particular, Kertzer unearthed a secret dialogue between Hitler and Pius XII with the intermediary of Prince Philipp von Hessen from 1939 to 1941.

187. Note by Tardini, November 27, 1941, in ADSS, vol. V, doc. 151, 316–318.

188. Note by Tardini, September 5, 1941, in ADSS, vol. V, doc. 62, 182–184.

189. Note by Tardini, September 17, 1941, in ADSS, vol. V, doc. 85, 227–229.

190. Note by Tardini, June 29, 1941, in ADSS, vol. IV, doc. 433, 593.

191. Note by Tardini, September 12–13, 1941, in ADSS, vol. V, doc. 74, 202–206: 205.

192. *Radiomessaggio al IX Congresso eucaristico nazionale degli Stati Uniti,* June 26, 1941, in *Discorsi e radiomessaggi di Sua Santità Pio XII,* volume III (Città del Vaticano: Tipografia Poliglotta Vaticana, 1960), 123–127: 125–126. *Daily Digest of Foreign Broadcasts,* Vatican City, in English for North America, June 26, 1941, 8:00 p.m.

193. *Radiomessaggio pasquale al mondo,* April 13, 1941, in *Discorsi e radiomessaggi,* volume III, 39–45: 42–43.

194. Raczkiewicz to Pius XII, April 6, 1941, in ADSS, vol. IV, doc. 312, 442–446.

195. According to a note by the editors of the ADSS, the letter was put back in the first section of the Secretariat of State on June 3, with a note by Montini: "Ex Aud. SS.mi: To the 1st section, because I want to study how to answer." See ADSS, vol. IV, footnote 5, 446.

196. Pius XII to the Polish president, June 25, 1941, in ADSS, vol. IV, doc. 421, 569–571.

197. This is what he wrote in the 1960s to a confrere, to whom he told the different positions in the Vatican regarding the war and the attitude that Vatican Radio should have had. Quoted in Renée Bédarida, "La Voix du Vatican (1940–1942) Bataille des ondes et Résistance spirituelle," in *Revue d'histoire de l'Église de France,* 173 (1978): 215-243: 228.

198. "Le bonheur de l'homme et le regime sovietique," program of January 9, 1941, in *La Voix du Vatican,* no. 8.

199. *Daily Digest of Foreign Broadcasts,* Vatican City, in German for Germany, August 11, 1941, 8:45 p.m.

200. *Daily Digest of Foreign Broadcasts,* Vatican City, in Spanish for Spain, August 20, 1941, 9:00 p.m.

201. *Daily Digest of Foreign Broadcasts,* Vatican City, in German for Germany, October 24,1941, 7:45 p.m. The script of the program picks up some subjects dealt with by Fr. Pellegrino in two articles in *La Civiltà Cattolica*: "L'«attacco a fondo» dell'ateismo sovietico," of July 23, 1941, volume III, 169–181, and "Sopravvivenza religiosa nella Russia sovietica," of September 26, 1941, volume IV, 25–34. The July article had a *post scriptum* in which it said that the text had already been written when the "inevitable conflict with Russian Bolshevism broke out," and dwelled on observing how Stalin needed communist ideology in support of Russian nationalism to be able to fight. Pellegrino's article was also the object of a report by Attolico to Ciano, in which the ambassador commented: "It seems to me very precisely that the article is of Vatican inspiration." DDI, serie IX, vol. 7, doc. 450, 429–430.

202. *Daily Digest of Foreign Broadcasts,* Vatican City, in French, Italian, German, English, and Spanish for Europe, November 5, 1941, 7:00–8:30 p.m.; in Dutch for the Netherlands, November 13, 1941, 7:15 p.m. "L'ateismo bolscevico," in *L'Osservatore Romano,* October 26, 1941, 2.

203. Program in Italian on November 6, 1941, 8:30 p.m. in LOC, *Funk-Abhör-Berichte. Sendungen fremder Rundfunksender.* Band VI. *Fremdsprachige*

Originaltexte. "Le nuove idee," and "Il catechismo dei credenti in Dio," in *L'Osservatore Romano*, October 26, 1941, 2. The article "Le nuove idee" was also read in Polish on November 11, and in Dutch on November 20. *La Voix du Vatican* confirms that the articles were also translated into French and published by the clandestine newssheet no. 19, postponing the publication of the program on atheist communism, which was circulated in no. 20.

204. *Daily Digest of Foreign Broadcasts*, Vatican City, in Polish for Poland, October 10, 1941, 7:15 p.m.

205. *Daily Digest of Foreign Broadcasts*, Vatican City, in German and Spanish for Germany and Spain, November 4, 1941, 7:45 p.m.

206. *Daily Digest of Foreign Broadcasts*, Vatican City, in Spanish for Spain, December 30, 1941, 8:00 p.m.

4. Vatican Radio, Racism, Antisemitism, and the Shoah

1. It must be recalled here, at least, the internal study by the Congregation of the Holy Office that should have led to the condemnation of nationalism, racism, and totalitarianism (1934–1937); the ban of Alfred Rosenberg's *Mythus des 20. Jahrhunderts* (1934) and Giulio Cogni's, *Il razzismo* (1937) in the Index of Forbidden Books; the publication of the book by ethnologist and Catholic priest Wilhelm Schmidt, *Rasse und Volk: ihre allgemeine Bedeutung, ihre Geltung im deutschen Raum*, in 1935 on which John La Farge's book, *Interracial Justice* of 1937 was based, and which was well-known in the Roman Curia; and the order that Pius XI gave in 1938 to Theologian of the Pontifical Household Mariano Cordovani o.p. to draw up a report on the "race" question, and to the Jesuit La Farge to draw up a draft of an encyclical on racism and antisemitism.

2. See the answer of the Congregation of the Sacraments to the Lessona Decree in 1937 which prohibited marital relations between an Italian man and an Ethiopian woman; see Lucia Ceci, *Il papa non deve parlare. Chiesa, fascismo e guerra d'Etiopia* (Roma-Bari: Laterza, 2010), 160–169. In Italy, the Catholic press distinguished between German racism and Italian racism, defining the former as intrinsically anti-Christian and the latter acceptable insofar as it was intended for the physical and moral improvement of the "race," without such action being carried out in hatred of "other races." For an analysis over the long term, see Matteo Caponi, "Antirazzismo cattolico e questione nera nell'Italia del secondo dopoguerra," in *Italia contemporanea* (2021), https://journals.francoangeli.it/index.php/icoa/article/view/13406, where the author argues that the cliché of a natural Catholic anti-racism is challenged by investigating interracialism as a third way, opposed to both racism and militant, humanitarian, and egalitarian anti-racism, and that the notion of anti-racism struggled to be incorporated within Catholic mass culture until the 1960s. See also Tommaso Dell'Era *Cogni Giulio* and *Razza* in *Dizionario storico dell'Inquisizione*, eds. A. Prosperi, J. Tedeschi, and V. Lavenia (Pisa: Edizioni della Normale, 2010), volume 1, 343–346, and volume 3, 1300–1302; and Tommaso Dell'Era, "Chiesa cattolica, razzismo,

antisemitismo e fascismo. Le lettere dell'agosto 1938 tra Giovanni Cazzani, vescovo di Cremona, e Roberto Farinacci, gerarca fascista," in *Giornale di storia* (28) (2018): 1–129.

3. In Italy, the most prominent personality dealing with these issues was Agostino Gemelli o.f.m., future founder of the Catholic University of Milan, who in 1915 and 1916, in the journal *Vita e Pensiero* blamed the "interbreeding of the races" for the decline in fertility in marriages. Moreover, at the conclusion of the conference on eugenics, held in Naples in 1924, an order of the day was voted in which it was recognized that "the proposing of the perfecting of the race is a laudable intent, but that it must be achieved only by wide social and hygienic provisions, by instructive propaganda, and above all by the diffusion of a profound Christian education." See Roberto Maiocchi, *Scienza italiana e razzismo fascista* (Firenze: La Nuova Italia, 1999), 25–26.

4. On the first statement of the concept of monogenism see the article "La scienza e la genealogia trasformistica," in *La Civiltà Cattolica*, 1879, volume X, 291–301. On the relationship of the Catholic Church with eugenic theories and practices, see, regarding the Italian case, Maiocchi, *Scienza italiana e razzismo fascista*; and, with regard to Portugal, Richard Cleminson, *Catholicism, Race and Empire. Eugenics in Portugal, 1900–1950* (Budapest-New York: CEU Press, 2014). See also Marius Turda and Aaron Gillette, *Latin Eugenics in Comparative Perspective* (London: Bloomsbury, 2014); and Sarah Walsh, *The Religion of Life: Eugenics, Race, and Catholicism in Chile* (Pittsburgh: University of Pittsburgh Press, 2021).

5. John Connelly, *From Enemy to Brother. The Revolution in Catholic Teaching on the Jews, 1933–1965* (Cambridge: Harvard University Press, 2012), 16–18.

6. See Isacco Turina, *Chiesa e biopolitica. il discorso cattolico su famiglia, sessualità e vita umana da Pio XI a Benedetto XVI* (Milano-Udine: Mimesis, 2013), 101 f.; and Lucia Pozzi, *The Catholic Church and Modern Sexual Knowledge, 1850–1950* (London: Palgrave Macmillan, 2021).

7. "Decretum de «educatione sexuali» et de «eugenica»," in *Acta Apostolicae Sedis*, 1931, 118–119.

8. Connelly, *From Enemy to Brother*, 92.

9. Hubert Wolf, *The Pope and the Devil: The Vatican's Archives and the Third Reich* (Cambridge: Harvard University Press, 2008), 264, 271.

10. For a detailed overview see Connelly, *From Enemy to Brother*, Chapter 2. On the birth and the reception of the document see Raffaella Perin, "Insegnare la religione contro il razzismo. Le istruzioni della Santa Sede," in *La religione istruita nella scuola e nella cultura dell'Italia contemporanea*, eds. L. Caimi and G. Vian (Brescia: Morcelliana, 2013), 167–189.

11. In the summer of 1938, Pius XI repeated several times that "exaggerated nationalism" was contrary to the faith, that "Catholic means universal, not racist, not nationalistic, in the separatist sense of the two attributes." See Domenico Bertetto, ed., *Discorsi di Pio XI*, volume III (Vatican City: Libreria Editrice Vaticana,

1985), 769–770, 775, 777–784. Also see Gabriele Rigano, "'Spiritualmente semiti'. Pio XI e l'antisemitismo in un discorso del settembre 1938," in *Römische Quartalschrift für Christliche Altertumskunde und Kirchengeschichte* 3–4 (2014): 281–308.

12. Georges Passelecq and Bernard Suchecky, *L'encyclique inaboutie de Pie XI* (Paris: La Découverte, 2019); David I. Kertzer, *The Pope and Mussolini* (New York: Random House, 2014), Chapters 22 and 25.

13. Raffaella Perin, *The Popes on Air: The History of Vatican Radio from Its Origins to World War II* (New York: Fordham University Press, 2024), Chapter 2.

14. Raffaella Perin, "Pio XI e la svolta di fine pontificato: verso una condanna dell'antisemitismo," in *Pio XI nella crisi europea/Pius XI. im Kontext der europäischen Krise* (Venezia: Edizioni Ca' Foscari, 2016), 37–56. http://doi.org/10.14277/978-88-6969-092-1.

15. ASRS, *AA.EE.SS*, Pio XII, Stati Ecclesiastici, Pos. 581 B, ff. 217–223 (Razzismo italiano), 225–230 (Azione Cattolica). In the report on racism, Pacelli pointed to the publication of the *Manifesto of Racist Scientists* (July 15, 1938) as the beginning of the regime's racial policy; cited Pius XI's speech to the students of Propaganda Fide on July 28, 1938, in which he "refuted some racist statements, explained in what sense one could speak of different races, and above all hinted at the painful consequences to which racist policy practiced on a large scale, without regard to charity and justice and not intended only to safeguard imperial interests by avoiding dangerous crossbreeding, that is, to that false nationalism carried to excess which then flows into hatred and revenge, would lead." In the same report, he emphasized the broad acceptance of the papal address in all countries except Italy and Germany, and the particular "exultation" with which "it was received in Israelite circles, which, numerous, sent respectful addresses of homage. The Italian government, on the other hand, was irritated by the clear and energetic papal expressions." See also Giovanni Coco, "Writing and rewriting history. The opening of the Vatican archives covering the pontificate of Pius XII," in *War and Genocide, Reconstruction and Change: The Global Pontificate of Pius XII, 1939–1958*, eds. S. Unger-Alvi and N. Valbousquet (New York: Berghahn Books, forthcoming).

16. "Decretum" (February 24, 1940), in *Acta Apostolicae Sedis* (1940), 73. On the topic, see Robert Graham, "Il 'diritto di uccidere' nel Terzo Reich. Preludio al genocidio," in *La Civiltà Cattolica*, 1975, volume I, 557–576.

17 Ruggero Taradel and Barbara Raggi, *La segregazione amichevole: 'La Civiltà Cattolica' e la questione ebraica 1850-1945* (Roma: Editori Riuniti, 2000), 122.

18. *Daily Digest of Foreign Broadcasts*, Vatican City, in Spanish for Spain, February 3, 1940, 8:00 p.m.

19. *Daily Digest of Foreign Broadcasts*, Vatican City, in French for France, February 11, 1940, 10:00. a.m.

20. *Daily Digest of Foreign Broadcasts*, Vatican City, in German for Germany, January 6, 1941, 7:45 p.m.

21. *Daily Digest of Foreign Broadcasts*, Vatican City, in German for Germany, May 24, 1940, 8:30 p.m.

22. *Daily Digest of Foreign Broadcasts*, Vatican City, in German for Germany, February 20, 1941, 7:45 p.m.

23. Mariano Cordovani, "Cura della razza e cristianesimo," in *L'Osservatore Romano*, February 27, 1941, 1–2; *Daily Digest of Foreign Broadcasts*, Vatican City, in German for Germany, March 5, 1941, 7:45 p.m. The previous year, on February 27, 1940, the news was spread concerning the decree of the Holy Office against sterilization. *Daily Digest of Foreign Broadcasts*, Vatican City, in German for Germany, February 27, 1940, 8:30 p.m.

24. *Radio Vatican. Années 1940–1941–1942–1943. Emissions prises en sténo à Toulon*, February 27, 1941.

25. NA, INF 1/781, Telegram from NCWC for the Catholic Section, March 14, 1941.

26. *Daily Digest of Foreign Broadcasts*, Vatican City, in German for Germany, November 20, 1941, 7:45 p.m.

27. *Daily Digest of Foreign Broadcasts*, Vatican City, in German for Germany, November 28, 1941, 7:45 p.m. Pius XI said, in audience with the students at Propaganda Fide College: "Catholic means universal, not racist, not nationalistic, in the separatist sense of the two attributes. [. . .] There is no other way of thinking Catholic, and this is not a racist, nationalistic, separatist thinking [. . .]. One forgets that humankind, all humankind, is one, great, universal human race. [. . .] The Holy Father himself recalls having heard an old scholar [. . .] who to the expression human race [. . .] preferred the term humankind."

28. "L'unité du genre humain," in *La Croix*, December 12, 1940; "L'unité du monde," in *La Voix du Vatican*, no. 7, 1–2.

29. "L'égalité des hommes," in *La Voix du Vatican*, no. 12, 1–2. I have been unable to date this program, but it was probably in the first few months of 1941.

30. The unabridged text is published in E. Leclef, ed., *Le Cardinal van Roey et l'occupation allemande en Belgique* (Bruxelles: Goemaere, 1945), 299–307.

31. "Démission catholique à aucun prix," program of April 16, 1942, in *La Voix du Vatican*, no. 23, 2–3.

32. The Dominican Joseph Thomas Delos theorized the conditions, without which it was not possible to assure and respect individual rights, at the International Catholic Conference held in the Hague in August 1938. See the pages that Daniele Menozzi has dedicated to the question in *Chiesa e diritti umani. Legge naturale e modernità politica dalla Rivoluzione francese ai nostri giorni* (Bologna: il Mulino, 2012), 118 f.

33. *Radio message for Pentecost*, https://www.vatican.va/content/pius-xii/it/speeches/1941/documents/hf_p-xii_spe_19410601_radiomessage-pentecost.html.

34. *Acta Apostolicae Sedis*, 1905–1906, 321–327.

35. Raffaella Perin, "Benedict XV: The 'Children of Israel' and the 'Members of Different Religious Confessions,'" in *Benedict XV. A Pope in the World of the "Useless Slaughter" (1914–1918)*, volume 1, dir. A. Melloni, eds. G. Cavagnini and G. Grossi (Turnhout: Brepols, 2020), 739–762.

36. Toward the end of his pontificate, Pius XI turned to personalism "as the foundation of the Church's spiritual alternative to totalitarianism." In the encyclical *Mit brennender Sorge*, he said that "Man as a person possesses rights that hold from God and which must remain, with regard to the collectivity, beyond the reach of anything that would tend to deny them, to abolish them, or to neglect them." Personalism became the foundation for the Church's defense of human rights. See Samuel Moyn, *Christian Human Rights* (Philadelphia: University of Pennsylvania Press, 2015), 75.

37. There is now an abundant bibliography on these subjects. See at least: David I. Kertzer, *The Popes Against the Jews: The Vatican's Role in the Rise of Modern Anti-Semitism* (New York: Alfred A. Knopf, 2001); Connelly, *From Enemy to Brother*; Giovanni Miccoli, *Antisemitismo e cattolicesimo* (Brescia: Morcelliana, 2013), this is a collection of essays by the Italian historian, a forerunner as far as studies on anti-Judaism in relation to antisemitism are concerned; and A. Riccardi and G. Rigano, eds., *La svolta del 1938. Fascismo, cattolicesimo e antisemitismo* (Milano: Guerini e Associati, 2020).

38. Numerous studies were published after a rich essay by Giovanni Miccoli in 1989, "Santa Sede e Chiesa italiana di fronte alle leggi antiebraiche del 1938," now in Miccoli, *Antisemitismo e cattolicesimo*, 265–369. Among these, the most recent are Taradel and Raggi, *La segregazione amichevole*; Annalisa Di Fant, "Stampa cattolica italiana e antisemitismo alla fine dell'Ottocento," in *Les racines chrétiennes de l'antisémitisme politique (fin XIX-XX siècle)*, eds. C. Brice and G. Miccoli (Rome: École française de Rome, 2003), 121–136; Cristiana Facchini, "Antisemitismo delle Passioni. La 'Palestra del clero' e il tema del deicidio," in *Storicamente* 7 (2011): http://storicamente.org/facchini_antisemitismo; Raffaella Perin, "Antisemitismo nella stampa diocesana negli anni trenta del Novecento,": http://www.storicamente.org/07_dossier/antisemitismo/perin.htm.; and Elena Mazzini, *Ostilità convergenti. Stampa diocesana, razzismo e antisemitismo nell'Italia fascista (1937–1939)* (Napoli: Edizioni scientifiche italiane, 2013).

39. The Apostolate of Prayer was founded by French Jesuit François Xavier Gautrelet in 1844 to promote devotion to the Sacred Heart of Jesus among the masses of the faithful. Members of the association pledged to offer their prayers and actions daily in a spirit of reparation for the sins of humanity. Beginning in the 1860s, Fr. Henry Ramière joined Gautrelet in directing the Apostolate and reorganized it: the goals became the promotion of the cult of the Sacred Heart and the promotion of a crusade of prayers to achieve the salvation of souls and the Christianization of society. The internationality of the Society of Jesus gave the association a strong impetus with a worldwide spread. The list of twelve prayer intentions (plus twelve others of a missionary nature that Ledóchowski

wanted to add starting in 1928), was approved by the Society's general and the pope about midway through the previous year.

40. ARSI, AdP, Varia, Israel.

41. Susan Zuccotti, "*L'Osservatore Romano* and the Holocaust, 1939–1945," in *Holocaust and Genocide Studies* 2 (2003): 249–277; David I. Kertzer and Roberto Benedetti, "Italian Catholic Press and the Racial Laws (1938–1943)," in *Holocaust and Genocide Studies* 4 (2021): 65–181. From the analysis I made on the Italian diocesan weeklies from 1922 to 1945, it clearly emerges that during the years of the Second World War, although with less frequency compared to the previous years, antisemitic articles were proposed. See Raffaella Perin, "L'atteggiamento della Chiesa cattolica verso gli ebrei nella stampa diocesana (1920–1945). Il caso triveneto," in *Ventunesimo secolo* 17 (2008): 79–107.

42. *Daily Digest of Foreign Broadcasts*, Vatican Radio, in Italian for Italy, May 13, 1940, 8:30 p.m.

43. "Notiziario," in Francesco Pellegrino, *Discorsi alla Radio. Alla Radio Vaticana dal 1939 al 1949. All'EIAR dal 1942 al 1943*, January 8, 1940, in ASRV; *Daily Digest of Foreign Broadcasts*, Vatican City, in English for Great Britain and elsewhere, January 9, 1940, 3:00 p.m.

44. "Notiziario."

45. On the Holy Cross Society see Zoltán Vági, László Csősz, and Gábor Kádár, *The Holocaust in Hungary: Evolution of a Genocide* (Walnut Creek: Altamira press, 2013), 405. See also "Catholics Form Group to Aid Converts Hit by Law," in *Jewish Telegraphic Agency*, December 24, 1939.

46. See Paul A. Hanebrink, *In Defense of Christian Hungary. Religion, Nationalism, and Antisemitism, 1890–1944* (Ithaca: Cornell University Press, 2006), 172–174.

47. Raul Hilberg, *The Destruction of the European Jews* (Chicago: Quadrangle Books, Chicago, 1961), 509 f.

48. Hilberg, *The Destruction of the European Jews*, 509 f.

49. ASRS, *AA.EE.SS.*, Pio XII, parte Asterisco, Stati Ecclesiastici, Pos. 575*, f. 765.

50. "Le leggi ebraiche approvate dalla camera ungherese," in *L'Osservatore Romano*, March 26, 1939, 2.

51. "Dopo i colloqui italo-ungheresi," in *L'Osservatore Romano*, January 8–9, 1940, 6.

52. "Notiziario," November 20, 1939.

53. *Daily Digest of Foreign Broadcasts*, Vatican City, in English for Great Britain, January 16, 1940, 7:00 p.m.

54. *Daily Digest of Foreign Broadcasts*, Vatican City, in English for Great Britain, April 23, 1940, 8:00 p.m. The name of the newspaper was not specified by the BBC monitor.

55. *Daily Digest of Foreign Broadcasts*, Vatican City, in English for Great Britain, April 23, 1940, 4:00 p.m.

56. *Daily Digest of Foreign Broadcasts*, Vatican City, in Spanish for Spain, April 24, 1940, 9:00 p.m.

57. See at least the recent book by Francesca Trivellato, *The Promise and Peril of Credit: What a Forgotten Legend about Jews and Finance Tells Us about the Making of European Commercial Society* (Princeton: Princeton University Press, 2019).

58. "Notiziario," March 11, 1940; *Daily Digest of Foreign Broadcasts*, Vatican City, in Spanish for Spain, March 2, 1940, 9:00 p.m.

59. Sergio I. Minerbi, *The Vatican and Zionism: Conflict in the Holy Land, 1895–1925* (Oxford: Oxford University Press, 1990) is still valid. See also Agathe Mayeres-Rebernik, *Le Saint-Siège face à la question de Palestine. De la declaration Balfour à la creation de l'État d'Israël* (Paris: Champion, 2015); Paolo Zanini, "La questione della Palestina: la difficile difesa degli interessi cattolici di fronte all'affermarsi dei nazionalismi," in *Il pontificato di Pio XI nella crisi europea*: https://edizionicafoscari.unive.it/media/pdf/books/978-88-6969-096-9/978-88-6969-096-9-ch-04.pdf.; and Maria C. Rioli, *A Liminal Church Refugees, Conversions and the Latin Diocese of Jerusalem, 1946–1956* (Leiden: Brill, 2020).

60. *Daily Digest of Foreign Broadcasts*, Vatican City, in German for Germany, June 15, 1940, 8:30 p.m.

61. *Daily Digest of Foreign Broadcasts*, Vatican City, in German for Germany, April 27, 1940, 8:30 p.m.

62. See Michael R. Marrus and Robert O. Paxton, *Vichy et les Juifs* (Paris: Calmann-Lévy, 1981), 17 f.; and Laurent Joly, *L'État contre les juifs: Vichy, les nazis et la persécution antisémite (1940–1944)* (Paris: Grasset et Fasquelle, 2018).

63. See Wilfred D. Halls, *Politics, Society and Christianity in Vichy France* (Oxford: Berg, 1995), 100 f.; Jean-Louis Clément, *Les évêques au temps de Vichy. Loyalisme sans inféodation: les relations entre l'Église et l'État de 1940 à 1944* (Paris: Beauchesne, 1999); and Sylvie Bernay, *L'Église de France face à la persécution des Juifs 1940–1944* (Paris: CNRS Edition, 2012).

64. "Un seul Dieu. . .," program on November 17, 1940, in *La Voix du Vatican*, no. 5; "Les causeries de Radio-Vatican. Catholicité: 'Je crois en un seul Dieu,'" in *La Croix*, December 7, 1940, 2.

65. Note of December 17, 1940, in Pierre Limagne, *Éphémérides de quatre années tragiques*, (Lavilledieu: Éditions de Candide, 1987), volume I, 49, footnote 1.

66. *Daily Digest of Foreign Broadcasts*, Vatican City, in French for France, November 30, 1940, 7:00 p.m.

67. For a detailed reconstruction, see Hilberg, *The Destruction of the European Jews*, 190 f.

68. For a summary see Renato Moro, *La Chiesa e lo sterminio degli ebrei* (Bologna: il Mulino, 2002), 129 f.; Michael Phayer, *Pius XII, the Holocaust, and the Cold War* (Bloomington: Indiana University Press, 2008).

69. Program in German quoted in "German Paganism and Christianity," in *The Tablet*, February 15, 1941.

70. *Daily Digest of Foreign Broadcasts*, Vatican City, in German for Germany, September 5, 1941, 8:45 p.m.

71. "6° giorno: Il ravvedimento e la conversione del popolo ebraico," in *L'Osservatore Romano*, January 24, 1941, 4; *Daily Digest of Foreign Broadcasts*, Vatican City, in Italian for Italy, January 24, 1941, 7:30 p.m.

72. On the history of the prayer of Good Friday, see Daniele Menozzi, *"Giudaica perfidia". Uno stereotipo antisemita fra liturgia e storia* (Bologna: il Mulino, 2014).

73. The whole program was published in *L'Osservatore Romano*, January 18–19, 1943, 2.

74. *Daily Digest of Foreign Broadcasts*, Vatican City, in Italian for Italy, January 23, 1943, 7:30 p.m. Carlo Alberto Ferrero di Cavallerleone (1903–1969) became the military ordinary of Italy in 1944.

75. *Daily Digest of Foreign Broadcasts*, Vatican City, in Italian for Italy, July 20, 1942, 9:30 p.m.; in English for India, July 21, 1942, 5:00 p.m.; in Polish for Poland, July 28, 1942.

76. The text of the pastoral letter in Italian translation in ASRS, *AA.EE.SS.*, Pio XII, parte I, Olanda, Pos. 97, ff. 68–71 sent from Giobbe to Maglione, October 9, 1942, here, ff. 78–79.

77. Orsenigo to Montini, July 28, 1942, in ADSS, vol. VIII, doc. 438, 607–608.

78. See Giovanni Miccoli, *I dilemmi e I silenzi Pio XII* (Milan: Rizzoli, 2007) 361–366; and Lieve Gevers, "Catholicism in the Low Countries During the Second World War. Belgium and the Netherlands: a Comparative Approach," in *Religion under Siege*, volume I, *The Roman Catholic Church in occupied Europe (1939–1950)*, eds. L. Gevers and J. Bank (Leuven: Peeters, 2007), 205–242.

79. *Daily Digest of Foreign Broadcasts*, Vatican City, in French for France, September 14, 1942, 8:00 p.m.

80. "Ne trahissons pas nos frères," in *La Voix du Vatican*, no. 28, 3–4.

81. See Marrus and Paxton, *Vichy et les Juifs*, 319 f.

82. See the detailed description in Marrus and Paxton, *Vichy et les Juifs*, 351 f.; and Laurent Joly, *La rafle du Vel d'Hiv. Paris, juillet 1942* (Paris: Grasset, 2022).

83. Marrus and Paxton, *Vichy et les Juifs*, 362 f.

84. Dominique Chassard, *Vichy et le Saint-Siège* (Paris: L'Harmattan, 2015).

85. Letter from Suhard to Pétain, quoted in Jacques Duquesne, *Les catholiques français sous l'Occupation* (Paris: Grasset et Fasquelle, 1996), 274. As Orsenigo noted in a letter to Montini of July 28, 1942, any intervention whatsoever on behalf of the Jews, even only converted Jews, with the authorities of the Reich, was always rejected. See ADSS, vol. VIII, doc. 438, 607–608.

86. Valeri to Maglione, July 29, 1942, in ADSS, vol. VIII, doc. 440, 610.

87. Valeri to Maglione, in ADSS, vol. VIII, doc. 443, 613–615.

88. Letter from Saliège of August 23, quoted in Duquesne, *Les catholiques français*, 275. On the protests of the prefect and the countermeasures of censorship, see 275–278.

89. Duquesne, *Les catholiques français*, 279.

90. The text by Saliège, which arrived in the Curia together with a letter of the nunciature of Paris dated August 27, was not read by Pius XII until September 17, after Mistiaen's program had been broadcast. However, Mistiaen could have received Saliège's letter through other channels as it was already circulating outside the French borders, as shown by an article in *The Tablet*. See ADSS, volume VIII, doc. 454, 625–62, and "News, notes and texts," in *The Tablet*, September 12, 1942, 7.

91. Miccoli, *I dilemmi*, 359–361.

92. Nevenko Bartulin, *Honorary Aryans: National-Racial Identity and Protected Jews in the Independent State of Croatia* (New York: Palgrave Macmillan, 2013), 62.

93. For a summary of the ideological components of the regime of the Ustaša, see Bartulin, *Honorary Aryans*, 49–56.

94. Muslims, on the other hand, had to present a declaration signed by two reliable witnesses that could certify their "Aryan" descendance.

95. For the details on the Roma and on the "half Jews," see Bartulin, *Honorary Aryans*, 69.

96. See the letters of April 23 and May 22 and 30, 1941, in Richard Pattee, *The Case of Cardinal Aloysius Stepinac* (Milwaukee: The Bruce Publishing Company, 1953), 299–305.

97. Pattee, *The Case of Cardinal Aloysius Stepinac*, 305–306. See also ADSS, vol. VIII, doc. 216, 368–370.

98. Letter from Stepinac to Artuković of March 7, 1942, in Pattee, *The Case of Cardinal Aloysius Stepinac*, 306.

99. Peter Longerich, *Holocaust. The Nazi Persecution and Murder of the Jews* (Oxford: Oxford University Press, 2012), 365–366; and Jozo Tomasevich, *War and Revolution in Yugoslavia 1941–1945. Occupation and Collaboration* (Stanford: Stanford University Press, 2001), 392. About 80,000 to 100,000 people died in the Jasenovac concentration camp, half of whom were Orthodox Serbs and then Jews and Roma.

100. On Marcone's mission to Croatia, see Miccoli, *I dilemmi*, 67 f.; and Andrea Riccardi, *La guerra del silenzio: Pio XII, nazismo, gli ebrei* (Roma-Bari: Laterza, 2022), 240–255.

101. Maglione to Marcone, February 21, 1942, in ADSS, vol. VIII, doc. no. 289, 442–443.

102. Maglione to Ujčić, May 1, 1942, in ADSS, vol. VIII, doc. no. 363, 523–524.

103. *Daily Digest of Foreign Broadcasts*, Vatican City, in English for England and Ireland, June 12, 1942, 9:15 p.m. From the original transcription by the monitor, it can be noted that the reception was not good.

104. Maglione to Marcone, March 30, 1943, in ADSS, vol. IX, doc. no. 123, 214.

105. A. Cicognani to Maglione, March 26–27, 1943, in ADSS, vol. IX, doc. no. 117, 206–207.

106. Maglione to Marcone, April 2, 1943, in ADSS, vol. IX, doc. no. 130, 218–219.

107. Marcone to Maglione, May 8, 1943, in ADSS, vol. IX, Annex I, 219–221.

108. ADSS, vol. IX, Annex II, 221–224. On Stepinac's covering letter, in which he highlights the positive attitude of the Croatian government in relation to the Catholic Church, and on the tendency of the archbishop to use anti-Jewish stereotypes to justify antisemitic measures, see the comments of Menachem Shelah, "The Catholic Church in Croatia, the Vatican and the Murder of the Croatian Jews," in *Holocaust and Genocide Studies* 3 (1989): 323–339: 335–336; and Miccoli, *I dilemmi*, 80.

109. Annex III, May 31, 1943, in ADSS, vol. IX, doc. no. 130, 224–229.

110. Letter from Stepinac to Pavelić of March 6, 1943, in Pattee, *The Case of Cardinal Aloysius Stepinac*, 310–312.

111. Sermon by Stepinac, March 14, 1943, in Pattee, *The Case of Cardinal Aloysius Stepinac*, 271–276: 273.

112. Shelah, *The Catholic Church in Croatia*, 334. On the limits of the protest by Stepinac, who ascribed the responsibility for the racial legislation to "unresponsible people" or "unresponsible and unwanted elements," see the observations in Miccoli, *I dilemmi*, 413 f.

113. *Daily Digest of Foreign Broadcasts*, Vatican City, in German for Germany, May 12, 1943, 9:45 p.m. The script was reproduced in "News, Notes and Texts, Yugoslavia. An Archbishop and the Jews," in *The Tablet*, May 22, 1943, 247.

114. Hilberg, *The Destruction of the European Jews*, 453 f.

115. The original German text is in AAV, Segr. di Stato, Comm. Socc., b. 302. There is also an account in the *Daily Digest of Foreign Broadcasts*, Vatican City, in German for Germany, July 6, 1943, 9:45 p.m.; and "News, Notes and Texts, Yugoslavia. The Archbishop of Zagreb and the Jews," in *The Tablet*, July 17, 1943, 31.

116. Homily pronounced in Zagreb on October 25, 1942. For the whole text, see Pattee, *The Case of Cardinal Aloysius Stepinac*, 276–281.

117. Phayer, *Pius XII, the Holocaust and the Cold War*.

118. On this a comparison with what was published by *L'Osservatore Romano* is also interesting. Between August and September 1941, the newspaper of the Holy See published three articles on the situation of the Jews and Serbs in Croatia, implying, however, that each case showed that the reprisals of the Croatian authorities against them were due to acts of sabotage. "La situazione in Croazia," August 13, 1941, 1; "Esecuzioni ed arresti nei Balcani," August 15, 1941, 1; and "Condanne del tribunale speciale croato," September 25, 1941, 1.

119. Telegram from Cicognani to Maglione, March 26–27, 1943.

120. Note by Maglione, April 1, 1943, in ADSS, vol. IX, doc. 127, 216–217.

121. ASRS, *AA.EE.SS.*, Pio XII, parte I, Stati Ecclesiastici, Pos. 694, f. 384.

122. See the contributions by C. Gubbins, E. Barker, S.W. Bailey, and F.W.D. Deakin on the region in *British Policy towards Wartime Resistance in Yugoslavia and Greece*, eds. Ph. Auty and R. Clogg (New York: Macmillan, 1975).

123. See Robert Graham, "La riabilitazione del cardinale Stepinac. Un primo passo," in *La Civiltà Cattolica*, 1992, volume II, 1992, 546–555: 552; and Esther Gitman, "Archbishop Alojzije Stepinac of Zagreb and the Rescue of Jews, 1941–45," in *The Catholic Historical Review*, 3 (2015): 488–529: 508.

124. See the analysis in Miccoli, *I dilemmi*, 386 f. On the Slovakian case, see Hilberg, *The destruction of the European Jews*, 458 f.; James Mace Ward, *Priest, Politician, Collaborator: Jozef Tiso and the Making of Fascist Slovakia* (Ithaca: Cornell University Press, 2013). On the antisemitism in Slovakian Catholicism, see Miloslav Szabó, "Catholic racism and anti-Jewish discourse in interwar Austria and Slovakia: the cases of Anton Orel and Karol Körper," in *Patterns of Prejudice*, 3 (2020): 258–286.

125. See for example the note by Maglione of November 12, 1941, to the minister Sidor, in ADSS, vol. VIII, doc. 199, 345–347.

126. Note by Tardini, July 13, 1942, in ADSS, vol. VIII, doc. 426, 597–598. The appeal by Osborne, here, doc. 328, 480.

127. Burzio to Maglione, March 9, 1942, ADSS, vol. VIII, doc. 298, 453.

128. Note by Maglione, March 25, 1942, ADSS, vol. VIII, doc. 322, 475; Burzio to Maglione, March 31, 1942, here, doc. 334, 486–489.

129. *Daily Digest of Foreign Broadcasts*, Vatican City, in French, English, and German, respectively June 7 and 21, 1943, 9:00 p.m., 9:15 p.m., and 9:45 p.m. Also published by *The Tablet*, "News, Notes and Texts, The Jews and the Natural Law," July 3, 1943, 8.

130. See the letter from Burzio to Maglione of April 27, 1942, and the Annex, in ADSS, vol. VIII, doc. 360, 515–519.

131. Burzio to Maglione, April 10, 1943, in ADSS, vol. IX, doc. 147, 245–251.

132. ADSS, vol. IX, footnote 5, 246–247.

133. See Miccoli, *I dilemmi*, 397.

134. Maglione to the Slovakian Legation, May 5, 1943, in ADSS, vol. IX, doc. 176, 275–277.

135. Note the smug reaction of the Slovakian Minister for Internal Affairs on the reassurances by the auxiliary bishop of Trnvo, in ADSS, vol. IX, doc. 147, 246.

136. Hilberg, *The Destruction of the European Jews*, 509 f.

137. Only a few Hungarian bishops dared to speak out in public. For details see Randolph L. Braham, *The Politics of Genocide. The Holocaust in Hungary* (New York: Columbia University Press, 1994), 222.

138. According to Rev. Albert Bereczky, the sentence had already been said by Serédi at a meeting discussing the need for possible joint action by the Christian churches. See Randolph L. Braham, *The Christian Churches of Hungary and the Holocaust*. https://www.yadvashem.org/download/about_holocaust/studies/Braham ENGPRINT.pdf.

139. Rotta to Tardini, September 16, 1944, in ADSS, vol. XI, doc. 354, 541–542.

140. Hilberg, *The Destruction of the European Jews*, 511; table 64.

141. Tardini to Cicognani, September 23, 1944, in ADSS, vol. XI, doc. 367, 553–554.

142. Quoted by Robert A. Ventresca, *Soldier of Christ: The Life of Pope Pius XII* (Cambridge: The Belknap Press, 2013), 216.

143. Horthy to Pius XII, September 19, 1944, in ADSS, vol. XI, doc. 360, 546–547.

144. Pius XII to Horthy, October 18, 1944, in ADSS, vol. XI, doc. 393, 576.

145. *Daily Digest of Foreign Broadcasts*, Vatican City, in Spanish, August 24, 1944, 10:00 p.m.

146. *Daily Digest of Foreign Broadcasts*, Vatican City, in Spanish, August 29, 1944, 10:00 p.m.

147. Telegram from Cicognani to the Secretariat of State, October 19, 1944, in AAV, Segr. di Stato, Comm. Socc., b. 286, f. 5.

148. Telegram from Tardini for Rotta, October 21, 1944, in AAV, Segr. di Stato, Comm. Socc., b. 286, f. 6.

149. ASRS, *AA.EE.SS.*, Pio XII, parte I, Ungheria, Pos. 100, f. 61.

150. ASRS, *AA.EE.SS.*, Pio XII, parte I, Ungheria, Pos. 100, f. 62. On October 26, Pius XII sent a telegram to Serédi, answering a plea from Rotta so that the Holy See participated in a collection called by the Hungarian primate "in favor of the many Israelite (?) refugees." The telegram opened saying that appeals were continuing to arrive from Hungary to implore the pope "in the defense of people exposed to persecution due to their religious confession, descendance and political reasons" and were pleased that the Cardinal had devoted a day of prayer and help for them. See ff. 80 f. However, it appears that the Ufficio Cifra [Coding Department] had incorrectly understood Rotta's telegram which telegraphed "very many refugees [numerosissimi rifugiati]" not "Israelites refugees," who, Tardini noted, had nothing to do with this. Tardini commented: "Card. Serédi's initiative did not concern them [the Jews]. By fortune the text of the Holy Father's telegram can be explained: having His Holiness learned that Card. Serédi was doing his best for the refugees he [the pope] took the opportunity to recommend to him all those who are suffering etc. etc. But it is disheartening that the Coding Department functions so poorly!"

151. Apparently, Tardini informed the two diplomats concerned that Pius XII might make some declaration against the Soviet occupation that the pope had no intention of publicly denouncing the state of the Hungarian Jews because he would have been forced to condemn the behavior of the Russians as well. See the documents quoted by Ventresca, *Soldier of Christ*, 217.

152. Moro, *La Chiesa e lo sterminio degli ebrei*, 163. For years now there has been no doubt about the Vatican's knowledge of the ongoing extermination of the Jews but documentation made available after the opening of the archives to the pontificate of Pius XII made the discovery of a letter from Jesuit Lothar König to Fr. Leiber dated December 14, 1942, possible. In the letter, he reported that there was an "SS blast furnace in the Belzec extermination camp, where up

to 6,000 people, mostly Poles and Jews, are killed every day." As the archivist who oversaw the reorganization of the Pius XII papers explains, it is unclear when König's letter reached the pope's desk, but it is speculated that this occurred before December 24, 1942. See *Le "Carte" di Pio XII oltre il mito. Eugenio Pacelli nelle sue carte personali. Cenni storici e Inventario*, ed. G. Coco (Città del Vaticano: Archivio Apostolico Vaticano, 2023), 119-123.

153. I have examined the question of Pius XII's silences in Raffaella Perin, "Note a margine di un libro recente: *La guerra del silenzio. Pio XII, il nazismo, gli ebrei* di Andrea Riccardi" in *Mondo Contemporaneo*, 304 (2024), forthcoming.

154. Roncalli to Maglione, in ADSS, vol. IX, doc. 22, 87-90.

155. Maglione to Hughes, February 23, 1943, in AAV, Nunziatura Apostolica Egitto, pos. XX acattolici ed infedeli, E) Ebrei 1942-1945, f. 6. Letters to Arthur Hughes from Jewish personalities to ask the Holy See for help are kept in this position. On the reasons that prevented the Holy See from consenting to the emigration of the Jews to Palestine, which emerge from the correspondence of Maglione and Tardini, see Miccoli, *I dilemmi*, 89 f.

156. See Raffaella Perin, "Une diplomatie désarmée dans la Seconde Guerre mondiale: un bilan historiographique," in *Monde(s)* 2 (2022): 35-56.

157. I am referring to the debates which arose around the play *The Deputy* by Rolf Hochhuth in the Sixties, and after the publication of the book by Daniel J. Goldhagen, *A Moral Reckoning. The Role of the Catholic Church in the Holocaust and its Unfulfilled Duty of Repair* (New York: Alfred A. Knopf, 2002). Giovanni Miccoli defined the controversies on the silence of the "pro-Nazi Pope" as twisted and misleading because they eluded the historically central question, i.e., the need to understand why the pope had not spoken, and what the deep and inextricable reasons that came into play were. See the considerations of Renato Moro on the historiography of Miccoli on antisemitism and the Shoah in "L'antisemitismo cattolico," in *Una storiografia inattuale? Giovanni Miccoli e la funzione civile della ricerca storica*, eds. G. Battelli and D. Menozzi (Roma: Viella, 2005), 229-250. For a summary of the historiographical debates on the "silences" of Pius XII, see Alessandro A. Persico, *Il caso Pio XII. Mezzo secolo di dibattito su Eugenio Pacelli* (Milano: Guerini, 2008); and Muriel Guittat-Naudin, *Pie XII après Pie XII. Histoire d'une controverse* (Paris: éditions EHSS, 2015).

158. *Al Sacro Collegio nel giorno onomastico di Sua Santità*, in *Discorsi e radiomessaggi di sua Santità Pio XII*, volume VII (Città del Vaticano: Tipografia Poliglotta Vaticana, 1964), 67-78. For a more in-depth analysis of the other topics dealt with in this speech, see Ventresca, *Soldier of Christ*, 219-222.

159. *Daily Digest of Foreign Broadcasts*, Vatican City, in Italian, January 24, 1945, 08:30 p.m.

160. The initiative of Archbishop of the Church of England William Temple and Rabbi Joseph H. Hertz to found the *Council of Christians and Jews* in 1942, in which Cardinal Arthur Hinsley as "Joint President" also took part, must at least be mentioned. Its aim was to fight racial and religious intolerance. Rabbi Hertz

recalled the words of Pius XI to the representatives of the Belgian Catholic radio in September 1938, on the inadmissibility for Christians to be antisemites. See Marcus Braybrooke, *Children of One God: A History of the Council of Christians and Jews* (London: Mitchell, 1991).

161. It must also be recalled how important these were in the lack of an overall condemnation of antisemitism during the wars, and how much this still influenced Pius XI in the course of 1938, although he had strong doubts that led him to take some major steps toward a stronger opposition of antisemitism. For a discussion of these issues see Perin, "Pio XI e la svolta di fine pontificato"; http://doi.org/10.14277/978-88-6969-092-1.

5. Toward the Axis Defeat: Vatican Radio, the Occupation of Rome, and the End of the War

1. *Reichsgesetzblatt*, 1939, Teil I, 1683.

2. Ansgar Diller, *Rundfunkpolitik im Dritten Reich*, Band. 2, *Rundfunk in Deutschland*, ed. Hans Bausch (München: Deutscher Taschenbuch Verlag, 1980), 309 f.

3. Robert Graham, "La Radio Vaticana tra Londra e Berlino. Un dossier della guerra delle onde: 1940–1941," in *La Civiltà Cattolica*, 1976, volume I, 136: footnote 5.

4. Diller, *Rundfunkpolitik im Dritten Reich*, 310.

5. As Ansgar Diller writes, quoting a document published by Boberach in Diller, *Rundfunkpolitik im Dritten Reich*, 311. See also *Berichte des SD und der Gestapo über Kirchen und Kirchenvolk in Deutschland 1934–1944*, ed. H. Boberach (Mainz: Matthias-Grünewald-Verlag, 1971), doc. 44, 389.

6. Diller, *Rundfunkpolitik im Dritten Reich*, 313.

7. Ulrich von Hehl, *Priester unter Hitlers Terror. Eine biographische und statistische Erhebung*, volume 1, eds. U. von Hehl, et al. (Paderborn: Schöningh, 1996), 119–120.

8. ASRS, *AA.EE.SS.*, Pio XII, parte I, Stati Ecclesiastici, Pos. 694, ff. 379–382.

9. See the analysis by Giovanni Miccoli, *I dilemmi e i silenzi di Pio XII. Vaticano, seconda Guerra mondiale e Shoah* (Milano: Bur, 2007), 181–212.

10. See what Orsenigo wrote to Maglione on January 17, 1941, in ADSS, vol. IV, doc. 238, 347–351: 350.

11. Miccoli, *I dilemmi*, 204.

12. L. Volk, ed., *Akten Kardinal Michael von Faulhabers 1917–1945*, volume II, *1935–1945*, Reihe A, Bd. 26, Mainz, 1978, doc. n. 912, 983.

13. See Miccoli who lists the series of letters from Pius XII to the German bishops in which he clarifies his position, Miccoli, *I dilemmi*, 207 f.: footnote 317.

14. *Daily Digest of Foreign Broadcasts*, Vatican City, in German for Germany, January 13 and 14, 1942, 7:45 p.m.

15. The script of the program was also published in "News, Notes and Texts, Germany, Dark Times Ahead," in *The Tablet*, January 24, 1942, 47.

16. *Daily Digest of Foreign Broadcasts*, Vatican City, in German for Germany, March 10, 1942, 7:45 p.m. The letter was published in the diocesan bulletin on February 5 and also sent to the pope. Pius XII answered the tribute of the archbishop on March 1, 1942. ADSS, vol. II, doc. 84, 255–260.

17. Miccoli, *I dilemmi*, 185; and bibliography in note 228.

18. The letter is dated June 14, 1942, and is quoted by Miccoli, *I dilemmi*, 7.

19. *Daily Digest of Foreign Broadcasts*, Vatican City, in German for Germany, April 13, 1942, 8:45 p.m.

20. "News, Notes and Texts. Germany," in *The Tablet*, August 8, 1942, 67.

21. L. Volk, ed., *Akten deutscher Bischöfe über die Lage der Kirche 1933–1945*, volume V, *1940–1942* (Mainz: Matthias-Grünewald-Verlag, 1983), doc. 769, 754–761: 755.

22. *Daily Digest of Foreign Broadcasts*, Vatican City, in German for Germany, July 2, 1942, 9:45 p.m.

23. The pastoral letter was published in full in *Akten Deutscher Bischöfe*, doc. 788, 913–918.

24. *Daily Digest of Foreign Broadcasts*, Vatican City, in German for Germany, September 18, 1942, 8:45 p.m.; "News, Notes and Texts. Germany," in *The Tablet* September 26, 1942, 155.

25. "News, Notes and Texts, Germany. Four Fulda Pastorals," in *The Tablet*, December 19, 1942, 300–301.

26. *Daily Digest of Foreign Broadcasts*, Vatican City, in German for Germany, December 21, 1942, 8:45 p.m.; "News, Notes and Texts. Germany," in *The Tablet*, January 9, 1943, 18.

27. *Daily Digest of Foreign Broadcasts*, Vatican City, in German for Germany, March 3, 1943, 8:45 p.m.

28. *Daily Digest of Foreign Broadcasts*, Vatican City, in German for Germany, March 10, 1943, 8:45 p.m.

29. Confirming the fact that Vatican Radio did not read the collective pastoral letter of March 22, 1942, *The Tablet*, unlike its usual habit, took the text from a different source, ascribing it to the bishop of Würzburg, one of the few to read the original text before the halt by Bertram. See "The battle raging in Germany," in *The Tablet*, June 20, 1942, 306–307.

30. *Akten Deutscher Bischöfe*, doc. 732, 651–658. A copy had been sent to Nuncio Orsenigo, asking him to have it delivered to the Holy See. Maglione to Orsenigo, March 6, 1942, in ADSS, vol. V, doc. 278, 464, in which the secretary of state acknowledged receipt of the account, and note 3, 464–465.

31. See the letter from Pius XII to Faulhaber of February 2, 1942 in ADSS, vol. II, doc. 78, 235–241: 236.

32. *Daily Digest of Foreign Broadcasts*, Vatican City, in German for Germany, March 22, 1943, 8:45 p.m.

33. *Der Sieg des Kreuzes in der Weltgeschichte*. Vatican Radio program, March 17, 1942. German, in ASRS, *AA.EE.SS.*, Pio XII, parte I, Stati Ecclesiastici, pos. 694, ff. 54–55.

34. For the details, see the account by Augustin Rösch of April 23, 1942, in L. Volk, ed., *Akten Kardinal Michael von Faulhabers 1917–1945*, volume II, *1935–1945* (Mainz: Matthias-Grünewald-Verlag, 1978), doc. 886, 914–921: 917. The original text of the pastoral letter is in *Akten Deutscher Bischöfe*, doc. 751/I, 700–704. The original letter was read in full only in the dioceses of Bamberg, Speyer, and Würzburg and in some parishes of Regensburg and Passau. The revised text and its circulation in *Akten Deutscher Bischöfe*, doc. 751/II, 705–708.

35. *Akten Deutscher Bischöfe*, doc. 751/I, 702–703.

36. "Il radiomessaggio natalizio al mondo," in *Discorsi e radiomessaggi di Sua Santità Pio XII*, volume IV (Città del Vaticano: Tipografia Poliglotta Vaticana, 1960), 325–346: 339–340. On the limits of the rights of the human person expressed in the radio message of Pius XII, see Daniele Menozzi, *Chiesa e diritti umani. Legge naturale e modernità politica dalla Rivoluzione francese ai nostri giorni* (Bologna: il Mulino, 2012), 138–139; for a different interpretation see Samuel Moyn, *Christian Human Rights* (Philadelphia: University Pennsylvania Press, 2015). On the drafting stages of the speech see Giovanni Coco, "Gli scritti di Pio XII e il radiomessaggio del Natale 1942," in *Rivista di Storia della Chiesa in Italia*, 1 (2020): 217–241.

37. *Daily Digest of Foreign Broadcasts*, Vatican City, in Italian and English for the world, December 24, 1942, 11:00 a.m. and 3:15 p.m.; in Italian, French, English, and German, December 28, 1942.

38. "This vow is owed by humanity to hundreds of thousands of people, who without any fault of their own, at times only due to nationality or descent, are destined to death or to a progressive perishing." "Il radiomessaggio natalizio," 345.

39. See the different reactions collected by Renato Moro, "I cattolici italiani di fronte alla guerra fascista," in *La cultura della pace dalla resistenza al Patto Atlantico*, eds. M. Pacetti, M. Papini, and M. Saracinelli (Bologna: Il lavoro editoriale, 1988), 119: footnote 45; Paolo Pombeni, *Il gruppo dossettiano e la fondazione della democrazia italiana (1938–1948)* (Bologna: il Mulino, 1979), 117.

40. Carlo Colombo, "Nel ventennio di un messaggio natalizio," in *Vita e Pensiero* 2 (1963): 78–89.

41. See Anthony Rhodes, *The Vatican in the Age of the Dictators 1922–1945* (London: Hodder and Stoughton, 1973), 272–273.

42. On the reactions, see Owen Chadwick, *Britain and the Vatican during the Second World War* (Cambridge: Cambridge University Press, 1988), 218–220.

43. As the Italian historian Andrea Riccardi explains in the "Introduction" to *La guerra del silenzio. Pio XII, il nazismo, gli ebrei* (Bari-Roma: Laterza, 2022), the problem of Pius XII's "silences" is not only about the Jews but more generally about the crimes committed by fascist regimes during the war, and is an issue raised by his contemporaries, even members of the ecclesiastical hierarchy (e.g., Msgr. Roncalli). See Raffaella Perin, *The Popes on Air: The History of Vatican Radio from Its Origins to World War II* (New York: Fordham University Press, 2024), Chapter 2.

44. *Daily Digest of Foreign Broadcasts*, Vatican City, in German for Germany, December 28, 1942, 8:45 p.m. The comment of the German announcer was also published in "News, Notes and Texts, Vatican City, No 'Peace at any Price'" in *The Tablet* of January 9, 1943, 19.

45. Osborne to Maglione, September 14, 1942, in ADSS, volume V, doc. 467, 676–677; note by Tardini on the conversation with Myron Taylor of September 22, 1943, in ADSS, volume V, doc. 480, 704–706.

46. ASRS, *AA.EE.SS.*, Pio XII, parte I, Germania, Pos. 847. The title of the collection is *Invitation to the Holy See by the Allied governments to protect against the German barbarities.*

47. The *New York Times*, December 18, 1942. https://www.nytimes.com/1942/12/18/archives/11-allies-condemn-nazi-war-on-jews-united-nations-issue-joint.html.

48. *Daily Digest of Foreign Broadcasts*, in German for Germany, August 3, 1942, 9:45 p.m.

49. ASRS, *AA.EE.SS.*, Pio XII, parte I, Germania, Pos. 830, ff. 99–101.

50. ADSS, vol. IIIa, doc. 287, 418–422.

51. Perin, *The Popes on Air*, Chapter 3.

52. Sapieha to Maglione, November 3, 1941, in ADSS, vol. IIIa, doc. 323, 489–491.

53. Maglione to Sapieha, November 29, 1941, in ADSS, vol. IIIa, doc. 329, 496–498.

54. *Daily Digest of Foreign Broadcasts*, Vatican City, in Polish for Poland, March 17, 1942, 7:15 p.m.

55. "News, Notes and Texts, Vatican City. A History Lesson," in *The Tablet*, March 14, 1942, 135.

56. *Daily Digest of Foreign Broadcasts*, Vatican City, in Polish for Poland, May 8, 1942, 8:15 p.m.

57. *Daily Digest of Foreign Broadcasts*, Vatican City, in Polish for Poland, July 14, 1942, 8:45 p.m.

58. *Daily Digest of Foreign Broadcasts*, Vatican City, in Polish for Poland April 16, 1943, 8:45 p.m.

59. See documents 508–510, in ADSS, volume IIIb, 796–802.

60. *Daily Digest of Foreign Broadcasts*, Vatican City, in Polish for Poland, June 4, 1943, 8:45 p.m. The unabridged script "Al Sacro Collegio nel giorno onomastico di Sua Santità," June 2, 1943, in *Discorsi e radiomessaggi*, volume V, 71–80: 77–78.

61. See Riccardi, *La guerra del silenzio*.

62. James Hennessey, "American Jesuit in Wartime Rome: The Diary of Vincent A. McCormick, s.j., 1942–1945," in *Mid-America* 56 (1974): 46.

63. Ibidem. McCormick criticized Pius XII's silence since he did not apply the doctrine of the just war *in bello* toward the Nazi occupations and crimes.

64. For a broader explanation of this hypothesis of interpretation, see the pages dedicated to it by Miccoli, *I dilemmi*, 239–253; in particular, 247–253.

65. Miccoli, *I dilemmi*, 247.

66. In his audience with Pius XII on December 26, 1943, the ambassador of Poland asked the pope that Polish broadcasts be increased from two to four and that in the dissemination of papal documents the Polish language be considered among the main ones and that their translation be disseminated promptly. AAV, Titoli (Pio XII), 1943, Stato Città del Vaticano, pos. 173, f. 2.

67. *La Voix du Vatican*, no. 15.

68. Note of September 2, 1941, in Pierre Limagne, *Éphémérides de quatre années tragiques*, volume I (Lavilledieu: Éditions de Candide, 1987), 238.

69. "Ce coin d'horizon pourquoi le cachez-vous?" program of September 1, 1941, in *La Voix du Vatican*, no. 15. See also those on patience and the ability to smile even in the face of difficulties of October 13 and 14. *Radio Vatican. Années 1940–1941–1942–1943. Emissions prises en sténo à Toulon*, and *La Voix du Vatican*, no. 18.

70. "Être honnête dans ses pensées," program of September 3, 1941, in *La Voix du Vatican*, no. 15. The quoted passage was also included in the first issue of the *Cahiers du Témoignage chrétien*.

71. "Agir sans penser c'est marcher sans voir," program of September 5, 1941, in *La Voix du Vatican*, no. 15.

72. "Quelques préceptes à l'usage de la vie quotidienne. Penser dans agir voir sans marcher," program of September 9, 1941, in *La Voix du Vatican*, no. 17.

73. Program of September 29, 1941, in *La Voix du Vatican*, no. 16.

74. Program of October 3, 1941, in *Radio Vatican. Années 1940–1941–1942–1943. Emissions prises en sténo à Toulon*.

75. Thérèse of Lisieux had been canonized by Pius XI on May 17, 1925. Emma Fattorini has underlined the particular devotion of Achille Ratti to "Teresina," who became a support for the pope especially during the years of his illness. See Emma Fattorini, *Pio XI, Hitler e Mussolini. La solitudine di un papa* (Torino: Einaudi, 2007), 39–44.

76. "News, Notes and Texts from All Parts, Vatican City. V for Vatican," in *The Tablet*, October 25, 1941, 267. The italics are mine.

77. *Daily Digest of Foreign Broadcasts*, Vatican City, in French, Dutch, Italian, German, Spanish and English for Europe, October 30, 1941, 7:00 p.m.

78. The announcement was made in the program of November 25, but some anticipation was obviously given earlier as well if Limagne spoke about it in his diary as early as October 7.

79. From October 1, 1941, laws were passed to codify the political role and legal status of radio broadcasting in France, making it increasingly an instrument of propaganda at the government's disposal. See Philippe Amaury, *Les deux premières expériences d'un 'Ministère de l'Information' en France, l'apparition d'institutions politiques et administratives d'information et de propagande sous la*

IIIe République en temps de crise (juillet 1939–juin 1940), leur renouvellement par le régime de Vichy (juillet 1940–août 1944), volume 2 (Paris: Librairie générale de droit et de jurisprudence, 1969), 409–422. Over the years the Listening Centre under the *Groupement des contrôles radioélectriques* (GCR) became increasingly efficient. The English, American, Soviet, and German radios, and in some cases Vatican Radio too, were monitored but the interest was above all on the pope's radio messages. See at least the collections AN, 65AJ/1177 e F/41/784 on Radio Vatican; for the Listening Centre AN, F/41/130 a 155.

80. Note of January 25,1942, in Limagne, *Éphémerides*, volume I, 386.

81. AAV, Nunziatura Parigi, b. 564, fasc. 34, f. 23. The attachments are in ASRS, *AA.EE.SS.*, Pio XII, parte I, Stati Ecclesiastici, Pos. 649, ff. 324–335.

82. "Une grande date dans l'histoire de Fourvière," in *La Croix*, September 10, 1941, 4.

83. See the biographical note in Claudie Brunel, *Antoine Lestra, un catholique social dans la tradition légitimiste. Cent ans de catholicisme social à Lyon et en Rhône-Alpes*, eds. J. D. Durand, et al. (Paris: Les Éditions Ouvirères, 1992), 181–186.

84. "Rectification: France. 15 Septembre 1941," in *La Voix du Vatican*, no. 16. Limagne also noted it on September 15, in *Éphemerides*, volume I, 249: "Vatican Radio carefully blames this sentence that *La Croix* has accidently let pass in an article of Antoine Lestra [. . .]."

85. AAV, Arch. Nunz. Parigi, b. 564, fasc. 34, ff. 30–31.

86. Quoted in Renée Bédarida, "La Voix du Vatican (1940–1942). Bataille des ondes et Résistance spirituelle," in *Revue d'histoire de l'Église de France* 173 (1978): 215–243: 234.

87. In Aix there was a group of *jécistes* (*Jeunesse étudiante chrétienne*) led by Rémy Montagne who published the listening notes of Vatican Radio. See Jacques Duquesne, *Les catholiques français sous l'Occupation* (Paris: Grasset et Fasquelle, 1996), 139.

88. AAV, Arch. Nunz. Parigi, b. 564, fasc. 34, f. 34.

89. Jacques Sémelin, *Sans armes face à Hitler. La résistance civile en Europe 1939–1943* (Paris: Payot, 1989), 39. For a broader view of the Resistance in Europe, see Olivier Wieviorka, *Une histoire de la Résistance en Europe Occidentale* (Paris: Perrin, 2017); and Giorgio Vecchio, *Il soffio dello Spirito. Cattolici nelle Resistenze europee* (Roma: Viella, 2022).

90. Anna Bravo has emphasized how the civil Resistance was also characterized by the capacity to act "while the things happen." See Anna Bravo, *La conta dei salvati. Dalla Grande Guerra al Tibet: storie di sangue risparmiato* (Roma-Bari: Laterza, 2013), 93.

91. Bédarida, "La Voix du Vatican," 242; 236–239.

92. Manuscript letter (illegible signature) of April 10, 1942, in ASRS, *AA.EE. SS.*, Pio XII, parte I, Francia, Pos. 923, f. 45.

93. ASRS, *AA.EE.SS.*, Pio XII, parte I, Francia, Pos. 923, f. 46.

94. Maglione to Valeri, April 15, 1942, in ASRS, *AA.EE.SS.*, Pio XII, parte I, Francia, Pos. 923, f. 44.

95. Valeri to Maglione, June 1, 1942, in ASRS, *AA.EE.SS.*, Pio XII, parte I, Francia, Pos. 923, f. 43.

96. Some extracts of these letters were published in the 1950s. Paul Duclos, *Le Vatican et la Seconde Guerre Mondiale. Action doctrinale et diplomatique en faveur de la paix* (Paris: éditions A. Pedone, 1955), 219. Mistiaen gives an account of this to Tittmann in the 1960s. Letter from Mistiaen to Tittman of August 10, 1966, in *Harold H. Tittmann Jr. Papers*, box 1, folder 27. Many letters from listeners are kept in ASRS, *AA.EE.SS.*, Pio XII, parte I, Stati Ecclesiastici, Pos. 694, f. 216f.

97. Quoted in Bédarida, "La Voix du Vatican," 238.

98. Letter from Mistiaen to Tittmann of July 18, 1966, in *Harold H. Tittmann Jr. Papers*, box 1, folder 27.

99. This is what can be inferred from a letter from the vicar general of the Jesuits, Alessio Ambrogio Magni, to Montini of April 4, 1944: "I had already authorized the Father to leave Rome and go to England; but I no longer had this transfer carried out only to uphold the august wish of the Holy Father to keep Father Mistiaen in his position." ARSI, Epistolarum Registra, Epistolae ad Romanam Curiam, IX.

100. AAV, Arch. Nunz. Parigi, b. 564, fasc. 34, ff. 32–33.

101. *Les temps héroïques de Radio Vatican*, interview with Father Albert Dauchy S.J., October 16, 1976, in ASRV.

102. Ledóchowski to Maglione, November 21, 1941, in ARSI, Epistolarum Registra, Epistolae ad Romanam Curiam, IX.

103. AAV, Segr. di Stato, Comm. Soccorsi, b. 6, f. 2rv.

104. For the details on drawing up the final document, see Jean-Louis Clément, *Les évêques au temps de Vichy* (Paris: Beauchesne, 2000), 184 f.

105. *Daily Digest of Foreign Broadcasts*, Vatican City, in French for France, November 12, 1942, 8:00 p.m.

106. *Daily Digest of Foreign Broadcasts*, Vatican City, in French for France, November 13, 1942, 8:00 p.m.

107. *Daily Digest of Foreign Broadcasts*, Vatican City, in French for France, November 16, 1942, 8:00 p.m.

108. *Daily Digest of Foreign Broadcasts*, Vatican City, in French for France, December 7, 1942, 8:00 p.m.

109. The last program that the Resistance were able to circulate was that of October 15, 1942, "Le courage chrétien," in *La Voix du Vatican*, no. 30.

110. Program of February 2, 1943, in *Radio Vatican. Années 1940–1941–1942–1943. Emissions prises en sténo à Toulon.*

111. Program of February 12, 1943, in *Radio Vatican. Années 1940–1941–1942–1943. Emissions prises en sténo à Toulon.*

112. Michèle Cointet, *L'Église sous Vichy 1940–1945. La repentance en question* (Paris: Perrin, 1998), 287 f.

113. Wilfrid D. Halls, *Politics, Society and Christianity in Vichy France* (Oxford: Berg, 1995), 312.

114. Quoted in Clément, *Les évêques au temps de Vichy*, 209–210.

115. Cointet, *L'Église sous Vichy*, 289.

116. Halls, *Politics, Society and Christianity*, 313.

117. *Daily Digest of Foreign Broadcasts*, Vatican City, in French for France, April 26, 1943, 9:00 p.m. The monitor was unable to understand all the words well.

118. Cointet, *L'Église sous Vichy*, 290–291. The text said: "Submitted to a constriction that the French government tries to make more human but which is not an obligation of conscience for them, if they want to be strong, they will give to this ordeal all its value of redemption, they will be a support for their brothers." Quoted in Clément, *Les évêques au temps de Vichy*, 212.

119. *Daily Digest of Foreign Broadcasts*, Vatican City, in English for Great Britain, June 18, 1943, 9:15 p.m.; in German for Germany, 9:45 p.m.

120. Program of February 19, 1943, in *Radio Vatican. Années 1940–1941–1942–1943. Emissions prises en sténo à Toulon*.

121. Bérard to Montini, February 20, 1943, in ADSS, vol. IX, doc. 61, 138–139: footnote 1.

122. Montini to Bérard, February 23, 1943, in ADSS, vol. IX, doc. 61, 139.

123. The dots in the original indicate the parts of the program that were not received.

124. Program of February 22, 1943, in *Radio Vatican. Années 1940–1941–1942–1943. Emissions prises en sténo à Toulon*. The subject was also dealt with in the programs of February 23 and March 2.

125. Ennio Di Nolfo, *Vaticano e Stati Uniti 1939–1952. Dalle carte di Myron C. Taylor* (Milano: Franco Angeli, 1978), 250–257. Despite the diplomatic activity by Pius XII to avoid Rome being bombed, from July 1943 there were fifty-one air raids which claimed almost 7,000 victims. See Umberto Gentiloni Silveri, *I bombardamenti alleati su Roma*, https://www.senato.it/application/xmanager/projects/leg17/file/Umberto_Gentiloni_Silveri.pdf.

126. See the letter from President Roosevelt to Pius XII of July 10, 1943; the letter of the delegate in Washington, Cicognani, to Maglione; the notes commenting on the letter from Roosevelt made by Tardini and the planned reply; the request of intercession with the Spanish government by Maglione to the nuncio in Madrid to preserve Rome from the bombings, in ADSS, vol. VII, doc. 285–288, 479–484.

127. Andrea Riccardi, *Roma "città sacra"? Dalla Conciliazione all'operazione Sturzo* (Milano: Vita e Pensiero, 1979), 213–215. See all the reports by the fascist spies to the Ministry of Internal Affairs which note the expressions of attachment to the pope and disaffection for Mussolini. On the bombings in Italy, see also the

contributions in Nicola Labanca, ed., *I bombardamenti aerei sull'Italia. Politica, Stato e società (1939–1945)* (Bologna: il Mulino, 2016).

128. "Il Santo Padre tra i fedeli della Sua Diocesi di Roma colpiti dall'incursione aerea," in *L'Osservatore Romano*, July 21, 1943, 1.

129. *Daily Digest of Foreign Broadcasts*, Vatican City, in Italian and in English for Great Britain, July 20, 1943, 8:30 p.m. and 9:15 p.m.

130. "La Lettera del Sommo Pontefice al Cardinale Vicario di Roma," in *L'Osservatore Romano*, July 22, 1943, 1; *Daily Digest of Foreign Broadcasts*, Vatican City, in English, Italian, and German, July 21, 1943, 9:15 p.m., 9:30 p.m., and 9:45 p.m.

131. A note by the curators of the ADSS clarifies the phases of the writing of the letter: on July 15, the pope had decided to answer; the draft prepared by Tardini on July 11 was taken up by Fr. McCormick who presented his draft on the morning of July 19, shortly before the start of the bombings, and corrected it on July 20. The pope was able to review the draft the following days and give it to Montini on July 25, signed it on July 26, and on July 27 the letter was given to Tittmann, who sent it via Berne. The letter bears the date of July 20. See ADSS, doc. 303, footnote 1, 502–504: 502. In his diary, McCormick confirms that he was the main writer of the letter, under the supervision of Tardini. The American Jesuit continued to be convinced that the pope should have taken the side of the Allies since, if the Axis had proclaimed Rome an open city, there would have been no need to bomb it. See Hennessey, *American Jesuit In Wartime Rome*, 48–50.

132. *Daily Digest of Foreign Broadcasts*, Vatican City, in German for Germany, July 24, 1943, 9:45 p.m.

133. M. Piccialuti Caprioli, ed., *Radio Londra 1940–1945. Inventario delle trasmissioni per l'Italia*, volume II (Roma: Ministero per i beni culturali e ambientali, 1976), 391.

134. Note from Montini, July 25, 1943, in ADSS, vol. VII, doc. 313, 520–522.

135. Note from Maglione, July 31, 1943, in ADSS, vol. VII, doc. 321*, 532–533.

136. Note from Tardini (who summarizes the meeting of the Secretary of State), August 4, 1943, in ADSS, vol. VII, doc. 327, 537–539.

137. The observations are by Francesco Traniello, in the study made by Renato Moro which goes over the historiography of the forty-five days of Badoglio's government and analyzes the positions of the Holy See, of the Catholic Action of the press, and of the Catholic hierarchy in "I cattolici italiani e il 25 luglio," in *Storia contemporanea* 6 (1993): 967–1017: 973 footnote 21.

138. Moro, "I cattolici italiani," 979.

139. *Daily Digest of Foreign Broadcasts*, Vatican City, in Italian for Italy, August 2, 1943, 8:30 p.m. On the Allied landing in Sicily, see Rick Atkinson, *The Day of Battle. The War in Sicily and Italy 1943–1944* (New York: Henry Holt and Company, 2007), part I; and Manoela Patti, *La Sicilia e gli Alleati. Tra occupazione e liberazione* (Roma: Donzelli, 2013).

140. *Daily Digest of Foreign Broadcasts*, Vatican City, in Italian for Italy, August 4, 1943, 8:30 p.m.

141. NARA, FBIS, Southern European Analysis, RG 262, entry no. 41, October 22, 1943.

142. AAV, Segr. Stato, 1943, Stato Città Vaticano, posiz. 134, f. 5.

143. The difficulties encountered after the landing in Sicily are described in the report of the *Sezione radio* of the Vatican Information Office of November 23, 1943, in AAV, Uff. Inf. Vat., 549, fasc. 59, 1–2.

144. Francesca Di Giovanni and Giuseppina Roselli, eds., *Inter arma caritas. L'Ufficio Informazioni Vaticano per i prigionieri di guerra istituito da Pio XII (1939–1947)*, 2 volumes (Città del Vaticano: Archivio Segreto Vaticano, 2004).

145. Sergio Pagano, *Una rilevante 'apertura' dell'Archivio Segreto Vaticano: il fondo Ufficio Informazioni Vaticano, prigionieri di guerra (1939–1947)*, in *Inter arma caritas*, p. IX-XXXIV: IX.

146. Di Giovanni and Roselli, "Introduzione," in *Inter arma caritas*, 1–37: 6.

147. *Inter arma caritas*, volume I, "Inventario," 18.

148. *Inter arma caritas*, volume I, "Inventario," 19.

149. Maglione to Evreinov, December 2, 1943, in ADSS, vol. IX, doc. 450, 587.

150. ADSS, vol. IX, doc. 450, 587; footnote 1.

151. The report by the head of the Information Office of December 21, 1943, states: "Continental Italy occupied by the Anglo-Americans. To the previous requests and solicitations, Mons. Godfrey communicated on November 25 that that Government has replied that the messages from the Holy Father to the episcopate had been sent some time ago, but that it did not deem being able to grant a regular service between the Holy See ad the Italian bishops, until the military situation is defined. It remains agreed that no possibility of correspondence is allowed with Continental Italy occupied by the Anglo-Americans and with Sardinia and Corsica." AAV, Uff. Inf. Vat., 549, fasc. 61, 7. In the meeting of the Information Office of May 9, 1944, it can be read: "Southern Italy. In view of the very great opposition expected by the British Government to our service for civilians, it is decided: a) to study how to use the International Red Cross. b) to then telegraph to Madrid and to Algiers to suspend sending messages for civilians, already sent in the previous mails. c) to see whether it is not necessary to suspend sending from our office." AAV, Uff. Inf. Vat., 553. See Leon Papeleux, *L'Action caritative du Saint-Siège en faveur des prisonniers de guerre (1939–1945)* (Bruxelles-Rome: Brepols, 1991), 62–80.

152. Papeleux, *L'Action caritative du Saint-Siège*, 80.

153. *Daily Digest of Foreign Broadcasts*, Vatican City, in Italian for Italy, August 10, 1943, 8:30 p.m.

154. *Daily Digest of Foreign Broadcasts*, Vatican City, in Italian for Italy, August 6, 1943, 8:30 p.m. "Il Sommo Pontefice indice pubbliche preci per impetrare da Dio la pace fra le nazioni," in *L'Osservatore Romano*, August 7, 1943, 1.

155. *The Daily Telegraph* of August 17, 1943, quoted in Umberto Gentiloni Silveri and Maddalena Carli, *Bombardare Roma. Gli Alleati e la «città aperta» (1940–1944)* (Bologna: il Mulino, 2007), 9.

156. *Daily Digest of Foreign Broadcasts*, Vatican City, in English, German, and French, August 14, 1943.

157. *Daily Digest of Foreign Broadcasts*, Vatican City, in German for Germany, August 18, 1943, 8:45 p.m. To confirm that the news was not given in English *The Tablet*, which normally picked up Vatican Radio, had relied on *L'Osservatore Romano* and the Stefani Agency for the chronicle of the bombing, whereas it went back to quoting Vatican Radio on the question of the declaration of Rome as an open city. See "The Italian Situation. The Raiding of Rome," in *The Tablet*, August 21, 1943, 90.

158. AAV, Segr. Stato, 1943, Stato Città Vaticano, posiz. 134, ff. 3-4.

159. AAV, Segr. Stato, 1943, Stato Città Vaticano, posiz. 134, ff. 11-12.

160. AAV, Segr. Stato, 1943, Stato Città Vaticano, posiz. 134, f. 6.

161. AAV, Segr. Stato, 1943, Stato Città Vaticano, posiz. 134, f. 9.

162. Soccorsi to Montini, September 15, 1943, in AAV, Segr. di Stato, 1943, Stato Città Vaticano, pos. 123, ff. 5–6.

163. AAV, Segr. di Stato, 1943, Stato Città Vaticano, pos. 123.

164. *Daily Digest of Foreign Broadcasts*, Vatican City, in German for Germany, September 7, 1943, 8:45 p.m.

165. Miccoli, *I dilemmi*, 200, 489–490: footnote 292.

166. Bertram to Orsenigo, October 5, 1943, in ASRS, *AA.EE.SS.*, Pio XII, parte I, Stati Ecclesiastici, Pos. 694, ff. 80–81.

167. "A Pastoral Letter of the German Bishops," in *The Tablet*, September 25, 1943, 149–151.

168. *Daily Digest of Foreign Broadcasts*, Vatican City, in French for France and in French for Europe, September 11, 1943, 7:45 p.m. and 8:00 p.m.

169. "News, Notes and Texts, Routine Continues in the Vatican," in *The Tablet*, September 18, 1943, 139.

170. NARA, FBIS, Southern European Analysis, RG 262, entry no. 41, September 24, 1943.

171. NARA, FBIS, Southern European Analysis, RG 262, entry no. 41, October 1, 1943.

172. Ibid.

173. Note of September 15, 1943. P. Limagne, *Éphémérides*, vol. III, 1452.

174. Limagne, *Éphémérides*, vol. III, 1455.

175. Soccorsi to Montini, September 20, 1943, in AAV, Segr. di Stato, Comm. Soccorsi, b. 318, f. 57.

176. NARA, Records of the Office of War Information, RG 208, entry 352, Items from Wire File (Foreign Information Digests), October 29,1943.

177. For a detailed account, see Miccoli, *I dilemmi*, 254–261.

178. For a reconstruction that casts doubt on this probability, see Robert A. Ventresca, *Soldier of Christ. The Life of Pope Pius XII* (Cambridge: Harvard University Press, 2013), 193–194. But the historiographical discussion remains open because it was Maglione himself who anticipated to the cardinals, resident in Rome, the possibility that the Nazis would occupy Rome and take Pius XII to Munich. See the already quoted document: Note by Tardini, August 4, 1943, in ADSS, vol. VII, doc. 327, 537–539.

179. Rome, September 22, 1943. ASRS, *AA.EE.SS.*, Pio XII, parte I, Stati Ecclesiastici, Pos. 739, f. 55.

180. Highly confidential informative report number 7, in AAV, Segr. di Stato, Comm. Socc., b. 328, f. 73.

181. *Confidential. Memoranda on Axis-controlled Europe*, in Research Department, Foreign Office, Whitehall, *Review of the Foreign Press*, Series A, October 19, 1943. Transmitted by the apostolic delegate in London, Godfrey to Maglione. ASRS., *AA.EE.SS.*, Pio XII, parte I, Stati Ecclesiastici, Pos. 627, ff. 295 f.

182. Draft reply from Maglione to Godfrey, November 19, 1943. ASRS., *AA.EE.SS.*, Pio XII, parte I, Stati Ecclesiastici, Pos. 627, f. 294.

183. In addition to the pages by Miccoli already indicated, see Susan Zuccotti, *Under His Very Windows. The Vatican and the Holocaust in Italy* (New Haven: Yale University Press, 2000), 150–170; and the contributions in the book M. Baumeister, A. Osti Guerrazzi, and C. Procaccia, eds., *16 ottobre 1943. La deportazione degli ebrei romani tra storia e memoria* (Roma: Viella, 2016).

184. Note by Maglione, September 27, 1943, in ADSS, vol. VII, doc. 415, 651–652.

185. "Carità civile," in *L'Osservatore Romano*, December 3, 1943, 1.

186. "News, Notes and Texts," in *The Tablet*, December 18, 1943, 295–296.

187. It was noted that Pius XII himself "seemed to many to be more attentive to Italian than to universal considerations," *Confidential. Memoranda on Axis-controlled Europe*.

188. "News, Notes and Texts, Vatican City. The Right of Sanctuary," in *The Tablet*, February 12, 1944, 80.

189. Note by Tardini, February 4, 1944, in ADSS, vol. XI, doc. 25, 117–118.

190. Note by Tardini, February 7, 1944, in ADSS, vol. XI, doc. 32, Annex 2, 129.

191. "Senza titolo," in *L'Osservatore Romano*, February 7–8, 1944, 1; "News, Notes and Texts. The Right of Sanctuary," in *The Tablet*, February 12, 1944, 7.

192. "News, Notes and Texts, The War approaches Rome. Bombs on Castel Gandolfo," in *The Tablet*, February 19, 1944, 90, which picked up Vatican Radio of February 14, which in turn repeated *L'Osservatore Romano* of February 10.

193. "News, Notes and Texts, The Osservatore Romano in the Bombing of Rome," in *The Tablet*, March 11, 1944, 128, which repeats a Vatican Radio program, in turn repeated by *L'Osservatore Romano* of March 3.

194. Note by Tardini, March 20, 1944, in ADSS, vol. XI, doc. 108, 223.

195. Note by Tardini, April 2, 1944, in ADSS, vol. XI, doc. 144, 261–262: footnote 1.

196. Proposals to give the Vatican Radio programs greater utility and interest in AAV, Segr. di Stato, 1944, SCV, pos. 33.

197. See "News, Notes and Texts, Vatican City. The Battle Approaches," in *The Tablet*, June 3, 1944, 272; *Daily Digest of Foreign Broadcasts*, Vatican City, in French, June 5, 1944; in Italian, in German, and in Spanish, June 7.

198. It must also be taken into account that the myth of Pius XII in opposition to the one of the Duce had begun to take shape in 1942, also thanks to the distribution of the film *Pastor Angelicus*.

199. Federico Chabod, *L'Italia contemporanea (1918–1948)* (Torino: Einaudi, 1961), 125.

200. For an analysis of the relationship between the ecclesiastical hierarchy and the civil population, conducted at the diocesan level in Italy, see the first part of the book by Jean-Dominique Durand, *L'Église catholique dans la crise de l'Italie (1943–1948)* (Rome: École française de Rome, 1991); and Santo Peli, *Storia della Resistenza in Italia* (Torino: Einaudi, 2015), 155–158. On the Church in the two years, 1943–45, see Gabriele de Rosa, ed., *Cattolici, Chiesa, Resistenza* (Bologna: il Mulino, 1997); some local cases, but with considerations that can be extended to the majority of the Italian clergy, Silvio Tramontin, "La Chiesa veneziana dal 1938 al 1948," in *La Resistenza nel Veneziano. La società tra fascismo, resistenza, repubblica*, volume I, eds. G. Paladini and M. Reberschak (Venezia: Stamperia di Venezia, 1985), 451–501; Giovanni Miccoli, "Chiesa e società nella diocesi di Udine. Fra occupazione tedesca e Resistenza (1943–1945)," in *Fra mito della cristianità e secolarizzazione* (Casale Monferrato: Marietti, 1985), 338–370; Alessandro Santagata, *Una violenza "incolpevole". Retoriche e pratiche dei cattolici nella Resistenza veneta* (Roma: Viella, 2021); and Vecchio, *Il soffio dello Spirito*.

201. *Daily Digest of Foreign Broadcasts*, Vatican City, in Italian, June 7, 1944, 8:30 p.m.

202. *Daily Digest of Foreign Broadcasts*, Vatican City, in Spanish, October 17, 1944, 9:00 p.m.

203. *Daily Digest of Foreign Broadcasts*, Vatican City, in French, August 12, 1944, 9:00 p.m.

204. On September 8, the council of the bishops of the Russian Orthodox Church met in Moscow; Sergij was elected patriarch, and they began to grant spaces of legality for religious activity. See Adriano Roccucci, *Stalin e il patriarca. Chiesa ortodossa e potere sovietico 1917–1958* (Torino: Einaudi, 2011), 173 f.

205. *Daily Digest of Foreign Broadcasts*, Vatican City, in German, January 10, 1945, 8:45 p.m.

206. *Daily Digest of Foreign Broadcasts*, Vatican City, in German, January 26, 1945, 8:45 p.m.

207. "Il radiomessaggio natalizio ai popoli del mondo intero," in *Discorsi e radiomessaggi*, vol. VI, 235–251.

208. "Il radiomessaggio natalizio," 236–243.

209. *Daily Digest of Foreign Broadcasts*, Vatican City, in German, December 30, 1944, 8:45 p.m.

210. *Daily Digest of Foreign Broadcasts*, Vatican City, in Spanish, January 11, 1945, 9:00 p.m.

211. *Daily Digest of Foreign Broadcasts*, Vatican City, in English, May 7, 1945, 8:15 p.m.

212. *Daily Digest of Foreign Broadcasts*, Vatican City, in Italian, May 7, 1945, 8:30 p.m.

213. *Daily Digest of Foreign Broadcasts*, Vatican City, in French, May 7, 1945, 9:00 p.m.

Epilogue: The 1950s

1. Encyclical letter *Miranda prorsus* of September 8, 1957, in "Acta Apostolicae Sedis," 1957, 765–805.

2. https://www.vatican.va/content/pius-xii/it/speeches/1944/documents/hf_p-xii_spe_19441203_lavoratori-rai.html.

3. ASRS, *AA.EE.SS.*, Pio XII, parte I, Santa Sede, Pos. 36, f. 7.

4. ARSI, Ex-Ass. Italiae, VII. Domus Scriptorum-Radio Vaticana, Epistolae, 1005, fasc. 3.

5. Letter of November 17, 1951, here.

6. AAV, Segr. Stato, 1950 segg., Stato Città del Vaticano, pos. 41, fasc. 4, ff. 14–20.

7. AAV, Segr. Stato, 1950 segg., Stato Città del Vaticano, pos. 41, fasc. 20, f. 5.

8. Here, f. 19.

9. Here, f. 24.

10. Here, ff. 27–28.

11. Here, ff. 46–64. See also the news given in the German specialized magazine. "Acht Richtfunkantennen für den Vatikan" in *Funkschau*, 1956, 296.

12. Note of February 9, 1957, in AAV, Segr. di Stato, 1950 sgg., Stato Città del Vaticano, pos. 41, fasc. 1, f. 124.

13. Meeting of the Commission of Programs of March 5, 1958, in AAV, 1950 segg., Stato Città del Vaticano, pos. 91, ff. 26–30.

14. AAV, Segr. Stato, 1950 segg., Stato Città del Vaticano, pos. 41, fasc. 20, ff. 46–64.

15. Mario Marazziti, "Cultura di massa e valori cattolici: il modello di 'Famiglia Cristiana'" in *Pio XII*, ed. A. Riccardi (Roma-Bari: Laterza, 1984), 307–333: 312.

16. As Stefanizzi writes in the report of 1955 on the situation of the Italian program. AAV, Segr. Stato, 1950 segg., Stato Città del Vaticano, pos. 41, fasc. 20, ff. 46–64.

17. Daniele Menozzi, *"Crociata." Storia di un'ideologia dalla Rivoluzione francese a Bergoglio* (Roma: Carocci, 2020), 165–166; Francesco Malgeri, "La

società italiana negli anni '50. Convegno tenuto a Roma dal 14 al 16 ottobre 1982," in *Sociologia. Rivista di scienze sociali* (January/August 1984): 101–107: 102–103.

18. Federico Ruozzi, "The arrival of television in Us and Italy: a new Catholic "holy crusade" or something else?" in *Annali di scienze religiose* 14 (2021): 101–140: 110–111.

19. Federico Ruozzi, *"L'audiovisivo come fonte storica. Il Centro Televisivo Vaticano e la fine del monopolio Rai sull'immagine del Papa,"* in *Telecamere su San Pietro. I trent'anni del Centro Televisivo Vaticano*, ed. Dario E. Viganò (Milano: Vita e Pensiero, 2013), 39–67.

20. Enrico Menduni, *Il mondo della radio. Dal transistor ai social network* (Bologna: il Mulino, 2012).

Index

Adam, 122
Adler, Jacques, 185n5
Agostini, Carlo, 222n182
Airoldi, Sara, 188n27
Albrecht, Dieter, 209n1
Alfieri, Dino, 52, 204n87
Alvarez Bolado, Alfonso, 214n86
Amaury, Philippe, 216n113, 241n79
Ambord, Beat, 3, 27, 112–113, 177, 197n109
Ambruzzi, Luigi, 27, 196n105
Amorth, Antonio, 150
Apor, Gábor, 138
Artuković, Andrija, 129, 232n98
Aspinall, Arthur, 187n19
Atkinson, Rick, 245n139
Attolico, Bernardo, 76–77, 100, 102, 104–105, 212nn43,45, 221n172, 223n201
Audoin-Rouzeau, Stéphane, 199n11
Augustine of Hippo, 53–54, 121, 186n14
Auty, Phyllis, 233n122
Azéma, Jean-Pierre, 206n104

Badoglio, Pietro, 165, 167, 245n137
Bafile, Corrado, 180
Bailey, S. W., 233n122
Balfour, Arthur, 230n59
Bank, Jan, 231n78
Baragli, Enrico, 188nn25,26, 190n13
Barbas, Jean-Claude, 205n98
Barbera, Mario, 112
Barfield, Ray, 198n127
Barker, Elisabeth, 233n122
Barlas, Chaim, 139
Barral, Henri, 62
Barrès, Maurice, 207n115
Bartulin, Nevenko, 232nn92,93,95

Battelli, Giuseppe, 236n157
Baudoin, Paul, 62, 197n114
Baumann, Ferdinand, 28, 198n115
Baumeister, Martin, 248n183
Bausch, Hans, 237n2
Bea, Fernando, 189n32, n2
Becker, Annette, 199n11
Bédarida, François, 206n104
Bédarida, Renée, 158, 186n14, 206n103, 207nn129,130,131, 208nn133,136, 216n110, 223n197, 242nn86,91, 243n97
Beethoven, Ludwig van, 155–156
Bellino, Alessandro, 193n63, 195n79, 221n176
Benedetti, Marina, 187n19
Benedetti, Roberto, 229n41
Benedict XV, 7, 30, 34, 59, 61, 115–116, 189nn30,4, 199nn10,11, 200n11, 204n84, 207n118, 228n35
Benedict XVI, 225n6
Bérard, Léon, 58, 163, 244nn121,122
Berdjaev, Nikolaj, 19
Bereczky, Albert, 234n138
Bergen, Diego von, 50, 68, 102, 150
Bergey, Daniel, 91
Bergoglio, Jorge. *See* Francis, Pope
Bernardini, Filippo, 191n23
Bernauer, James, 213n64
Bernay, Sylvie, 230n63
Bertetto, Domenico, 189n1, 225n11
Bertoye, Georges, 59, 206n113
Bertram, Adolf, 143, 148, 169, 238n29, 247n166
Besson, Marius, 37, 79
Bijsterveld, Karin, 188n24
Blet, Pierre, 185n3, 199n3
Boberach, Heinz, 194n66, 237n5

Boelke, Willi A., 186n10
Boniface, Xavier, 199n11
Bosca, Gianni, 190n5
Botti, Alfonso, 193n51
Bottoni, Riccardo, 204n81
Boubée, Joseph, 27, 196n107
Bourlot, Susanna, 213n63
Bouthillon, Fabrice, 222n179
Bouvier, C., 158
Braham, Randolph L., 234nn137,138
Bravo, Anna, 242n90
Braybrooke, Marcus, 237n160
Brechenmacher, Thomas, 222n179
Brice, Catherine, 228n38
Briggs, Asa, 188n23, 198n123
Brunel, Claudie, 242n83
Brunello, Aristide, 124
Buchberger, Michael, 148
Bürckel, Joseph, 70
Burke, Edmund, 187n19
Burzio, Giuseppe, 134–136, 234nn127, 128, 130, 131

Caimi, Luciano, 225n10
Caliò, Tommaso, 200n16
Calles, Plutarco Elías, 19
Campbell, Paul B., 188n27
Canali, Mauro, 218n135, 220n162
Canali, Nicola, 180
Caponi, Matteo, 200nn16,20, 224n2
Cárcel Ortí, Vicente, 214nn86,87
Carli, Maddalena, 247n155
Caruso, Pietro, 172
Castagna, Luca, 211n40
Casula, Carlo Felice, 205n87
Catherine of Siena, 35
Cavagnini, Giovanni, 200n11, 228n35
Cavalli, Fiorillo, 180
Cavarocchi, Francesca, 199n3
Cavatorta, 62
Cazzani, Giovanni, 225n2
Ceci, Lucia, 199n10, 222n178, 224n2
Cerejeira, Emmanuel, 88, 213n73
Chabod, Federico, 173, 249n199
Chadwick, Owen, 213n65, 222n181, 239n42
Chaillet, Pierre, 63, 208n133
Chamedes, Giuliana, 190n15, 221n175

Charles-Roux, François, 33, 42, 52, 202n44
Charlier, Prosper. *See* Chaillet, Pierre
Chassard, Dominique, 215n101, 231n84
Chenaux, Philippe, 190n15, 199n3, 204n85, 213n61, 221n174, 222nn179,180
Chirico, Adriana, 187n18
Chollet, Jean-Arthur, 90
Ciano, Galeazzo, 76, 212nn43,45, 223n201
Cicognani, Amleto, 76, 84, 130, 133, 137–138, 212n41, 213n70, 232n105, 233n119, 235nn141,147, 244n126
Cicognani, Gaetano, 89, 93, 211n39, 214n86, 215nn97,98,99
Ciriaci, Augusto, 14
Clément, Jean-Louis, 206n103, 215n103, 216n110, 230n63, 243n104, 244nn114,118
Cleminson, Richard, 225n4
Clogg, Richard, 233n122
Clovis, King of the Franks, 59
Cochet, François, 199n11
Coco, Giovanni, 111, 226n15, 236n152, 239n36
Coffey, Edward, 16, 27, 47, 55, 72, 192n37, 210n20
Cogni, Giulio, 224nn1,2
Cointet, Michèle, 244nn112,115,118
Colli, Carlo, 49
Colombo, Carlo, 239n40
Confalonieri, Carlo, 7, 189n34
Connelly, John, 225nn5,8,10, 228n37
Conrad, Frank, 188n22
Cooper, Alfred Duff, 98
Corkery, James, 189n30
Cordovani, Mariano, 113, 224n1, 227n23
Crémieux-Brilhac, Jean-Louis, 209n149
Crozier, 156
Cruvillier, Louis, 63
Csősz, László, 229n45
Curley, Michael, 83

D'Almeida, Fabrice, 188n23
Daffinà, Oreste, 218n135
Dallek, Robert, 211n40
Daniel, Ute, 187n20

Darlan, François, 91
Dauchy, Albert, 159–160, 204n85, 219n145, 220n169, 243n101
De Carolis, 189n32
De Giorgi, Fulvio, 193n47
De Lubac, Henri, 63, 208n132
De Rosa, Gabriele, 249n200
De Staercke, Anton, 15
Deakin, F.W.D., 233n122
Decius, Emperor, 92
Delaire, Jean, 10
Delaney, John Patrick, 16, 26–30, 192n38, 196nn94,95,96,98,100, 198n123
Delaney, Thomas E., 22, 194n73
Delannoye, George, 28, 197n109
Dell'Acqua, Angelo, 138, 180
Dell'Era, Tommaso, 224n2
Delporte, Christian, 188n23
Delos, Joseph Thomas, 227n32
Demofonti, Laura, 222n178
Di Fant, Annalisa, 228n38
Di Febo, Giuliana, 193n47
Di Giovanni, Francesca, 246nn144,146
Di Nolfo, Ennio, 211n37, 213n67, 244n125
Di Nucci, Loreto, 192n42
Dieguez, Alejandro M., 187n19
Diller, Ansgar, 237nn2,4,5,6
Domínguez, Joaquín M., 190n4
Dossetti, Giuseppe, 150
Dostoevskij, Fëdor, 108
Dreyfus, François-Georges, 205n99, 206n104
Duce, Alessandro, 199n6, 221n173
Duclos, Paul, 97, 219nn145,147, 243n96
Duquesne, Jacques, 206nn101,103, 231nn85,88, 232n89, 242n87
Durand, Jean-Dominique, 242n83, 249n200
Dutoit, Henri-Edouard, 91

Eck, Hélène, 209n149
Evangelista, Oscar L., 192n38
Evreinov, Alexander, 166, 246n149

Facchinetti, Vittorino, 36, 188n27
Facchini, Cristiana, 228n38

Fanfani, Amintore, 150
Farinacci, Roberto, 105, 225n2
Farusi, Francesco, 190n5
Fattorini, Emma, 193n52, 195n80, 206n109, 222n179, 241n75
Faulhaber, Michael von, 80, 144–145, 169, 194n64, 212n57, 237n12, 238n31, 239n34
Feltin, Maurice, 58, 60, 206n108
Feltrinelli, Giangiacomo, 193n62
Ferrero di Cavallerleone, Carlo A., 124, 231n74
Ferro, Marc, 206nn100,104
Ferrone, Vincenzo, 190n15, 221n175
Fickers, Andreas, 188n24
Finney, Robert G., 188n23
Flaubert, Gustave, 40
Foch, Ferdinand, 59–60, 207n115
Fogarty, Gerald P., 211n38, 213n66
Fortner, Robert S., 188n22
Fouilloux, Étienne, 193n53, 206n105
Franc [François d'Assise Bertoye]. *See* Bertoye, Georges
Francis of Assisi, 35–37, 200nn15,16,17,18
Francis, Pope, 1, 185nn1,2, 250n17
Franck, Hans, 48, 203n74
Franco, Francisco, 88, 215nn96,98
Frangioni, Filippo, 190n14, 193nn52,55
Franzinelli, Mimmo, 204n81
Frédénucci, L., 157
Frings, Josef, 147
Führer. *See* Hitler, Adolf

Galen, August von, 145
Galeazzi, Enrico, 180
Gallagher, Charles R., 205nn94,97, 213n67
Galletto, Albino, 180
Galli della Loggia, Ernesto, 192n42
Gallo, Salvatore, 27, 196n106
Gambetta, Léon, 66
Gasparri, Pietro, 7, 116
Gautrelet, François Xavier, 228n39
Gemelli, Agostino, 150, 225n3
Gentile, Emilio, 192n45, 193n56, 221n175

256 | Index

Gentiloni Silveri, Umberto, 244n125, 247n155
Gerlier, Pierre-Marie, 58, 90, 158
Gevers, Lieve, 231n78
Gianfranceschi, Giuseppe, 7, 10, 189nn3,4
Gillette, Aaron, 225n4
Giobbe, Paolo, 125, 196n102, 231n76
Gitman, Esther, 234n123
Giusti, Maria Teresa, 192n42
Glatterfelder, Gyula, 119
Glorieux, Achille, 180
Godfrey of Bouillon, 64–65
Godfrey, William, 98, 171, 219n155, 246n151, 248nn181,182
Godman, Peter, 213n63
Goebbels, Joseph, 142–143, 204n77
Goldfarb Marquis, Alice, 187n21
Goldhagen, Daniel J., 236n157
Gombrich, Ernst Hans, 186n7
Goncourt, Edmond *and* Jules, 40
Graham, Robert A., 185n5, 196n108, 197n109, 198n121, 203n62, 212n51, 226n16, 234n123, 237n3
Gregory XV, 4, 108–109, 187n16
Grisewood, Harman, 219n159
Gröber, Conrad, 20, 87, 144–145, 214n84
Grossi, Giulia, 200n11, 228n35
Grover, Andrea, 204n75
Gruber, Hubert, 190n14
Guasco, Alberto, 190n15, 222n185
Gubbins, Colin, 233n122
Guittat-Naudin, Muriel, 236n157
Gundlach, Gustav, 24, 25, 195nn83,91

Haarselhorst, Johannes, 28, 197n112
Hackelsberger, Albert, 20
Halls, Wilfred D., 215n101, 216n110, 230n63, 244nn113,116
Hanebrink, Paul A., 229n46
Hankart, Maurice, 15, 191n30
Hehl, Ulrich von, 237n7
Heidegger, Martin, 109
Heintz, Joseph-Jean, 70
Hennessey, James, 197n109, 212n60, 240n62, 245n131
Hertz, Joseph H., 236n160
Hessen, Philipp von, 222n186

Hilberg, Raul, 229nn47,48, 230n67, 233n114, 234nn124,136,140
Hinsely, Arthur, 46, 236n160
Hitler, Adolf, 21, 23, 35, 52, 70, 72, 74–75, 82–83, 89–91, 99, 103–104, 123, 134, 136, 142–143, 193n63, 194n63, 195nn79,80, 199n3, 204nn77,87, 213n63, 215nn97,102, 221nn176,177, 222nn179,186, 237n7, 241n75, 242n89
Hlond, August, 33–34, 42, 46–47, 151, 199nn7,8, 201n41
Hochhuth, Rolf, 185n3, 236n157
Hope, Richard, 99, 219nn159,160,161
Horthy, Miklós, 136–137, 235nn143,144
Huener, Jonathan, 201n39
Hughes, Arthur, 139, 159, 236n155
Hull, Cordell, 82–83, 213n68
Hurley, Joseph, 3, 55, 56, 205n94, 213n67

Ilarino da Milano, 185n5, 189n3
Immer, 195n83
Innocent XI, 197n111
Isola, Gianni, 188n27
Iturrio, Jesus, 109

Janssens, Jean-Baptiste, 179, 197n109
Jenkins, Philip, 200n11
Joan of Arc, 59–60, 207nn114,115
John XXIII. *See* Roncalli, Angelo Giuseppe
John Paul II, 189nn3,2, 190n15
John the Evangelist, 127
Johnston, Gordon, 186n9
Joly, Laurent, 230n62, 231n82
Jong, Johannes de, 125
Joy, Francis, 27, 118–120, 197n109
Junk, Nikolaus, 191n17

Kádár, Gábor, 229n45
Kertzer, David I., 185n4, 199n3, 213nn61,62, 222n186, 226n12, 228n37, 229n41
Kirby, Dianne, 204n77
König, Lothar, 235n152, 236n152
Kordač, František, 6
Körper, Karol, 234n124
Krumeich, Gerd, 207n114
Kubowitzki, Leon, 137

La Farge, John, 224n1
La Fontaine, Pietro, 10
La Malfa, Ugo, 199n10
La Vallette, John de, 219n158
Labanca, Nicola, 245n127
Lagrée, Michel, 188n28
Lakatos, Géza, 136
Lason, Felix, 27, 50, 196n108
Laval, Pierre, 56, 90–91, 127, 157, 160
Lavenia, Vincenzo, 224n2
Lazzati, Giuseppe, 150
Leclef, Edmond, 227n30
Ledit, Joseph, 11, 16, 18, 222n178
Ledóchowski, Włodzimierz, 3, 28, 30, 47, 50–51, 62, 69–70, 72–75, 81–83, 95–97, 101, 103, 158–159, 178, 191n16, 197nn110,113, 203n66, 209n4, 210nn7,8,20, 211nn24,25,28,29,30, 33,34,36, 213nn61,66,69, 218nn131,132,133,134,135,137,138,139,140,141, 220n167, 228n39, 243n102
Leiber, Robert, 20, 47, 49, 95–97, 101, 158, 177, 218nn130,133,137,141, 235n152
Lenin, Vladimir, 190n15
Leo XIII, 5, 40, 79, 102, 187n17
Lesourd, Paul, 64
Lessona, Alessandro, 224n2
Lesti, Sante, 206n113
Lestra, Antoine, 157, 242nn83,84
Leto, Guido, 16
Levant, Marie, 195n80, 222nn179,185
Lévy, Claude, 209n150
Lewy, Guenter, 193n63, 221n176
Liénart, Achille, 161
Limagne, Pierre, 91–92, 123, 154, 156, 170, 216nn112,113,114, 217nn116,119,124, 230n65, 241nn68,78, 242nn80,84, 247nn173,174
Lo Biundo, Esther, 198n124
Lombardi, Riccardo, 181
Longerich, Peter, 232n99
Lopez, Veneziano, 85
Lovell, Stephen, 198n124
Lubowidzka, Laureta, 100–102, 151
Ludin, Hans, 136
Luke the Evangelist, 54
Lutterbeck, Alfred, 16, 192n40

Mach, Alexander, 135
Mackone, Peter, 28, 198n116
Maddalena, Robert, 63, 208n135
Maglione, Luigi, 26, 47, 62, 71–72, 74–76, 82, 84, 89–91, 95, 97–98, 100–102, 104, 128–130, 132–135, 139, 150–151, 157–159, 165–166, 171–172, 201n41, 210n14, 211nn28,39, 212n41, 213nn69,70,71, 215nn97,98,99,104,105, 216nn108,109, 218n135, 219n155, 220n167, 221n173, 231nn76,86,87, 232nn101,102,104,105, 233nn106,107,119,120, 234nn125,127,128,130,131,134, 236nn154,155, 237n10, 238n30, 240nn45,52,53, 243nn94,95,102, 244n126, 245n135, 246n149, 248nn178,181,182,184
Magni, Ambrogio, 168, 243n99
Mahomet, 18
Maiocchi, Roberto, 225nn3,4
Malgeri, Francesco, 250n17
Mandouze, André, 63, 186n14, 208n140, 209n145
Marani, Alessandra, 187n17
Marazziti, Mario, 250n15
Marchandeau, Paul, 122
Marchetti Selvaggiani, Francesco, 164
Marcion, 123
Marcone, Giuseppe Ramiro, 129–130, 132, 232nn100,101,104, 233nn106,107
Marconi, Degna, 7, 189nn31,33
Marconi, Guglielmo, 3,7, 9–10, 188n22, 189nn31,33,34, 190n8
Marrus, Michael R., 230n62, 231nn81,82,83
Marshall, Bernhard, 191n27
Martin, Jacques, 70, 95
Marx, Karl, 19
Marzano, Arturo, 198n124
Massiani, Marie-Geneviève, 216n113
Matelski, Marilyn J., 185n5
Mathias, Ludovico, 15
Maurras, Charles, 205n99
Mayeres-Rebernik, 230n59
Mayor, Mateo Domingo, 28, 85, 197n112

258 | Index

Mazzini, Elena, 221n174, 222n183, 228n38
McCormick, Vincent A., 3, 27, 55, 72–73, 78, 81, 153, 177, 197n109, 210n20, 212n60, 240nn62,63, 245n131
McNicholas, Timothy, 82–83
Melloni, Alberto, 191n27, 200n11, 228n35
Menduni, Enrico, 251n20
Menozzi, Daniele, 187n17, 199n10, 200nn12,16,17,18, 204n81, 207n119, 222n178, 227n32, 231n72, 236n157, 239n36, 250n17
Menshausen, Fritz, 30, 46, 49, 67–68, 71–75, 94, 102
Merklen, Léon, 216n112
Messineo, Antonio, 112
Miccinelli, Carlo, 28, 197n111
Miccoli, Giovanni, 193n51, 204nn81,87, 214n84, 221nn176,177, 222nn178, 181,186, 228nn37,38, 231n78, 232nn91,100, 233nn108,112, 234nn124,133, 236nn155,157, 237nn9,11,13, 238nn17,18, 241nn64,65, 247nn165,177, 248n183, 249n200
Michael the Archangel, 155
Michelin, Alfred, 216n112
Minerbi, Sergio I., 230n59
Mistiaen, Emmanuel, 3–4, 27–28, 61–67, 91–97, 107, 113–114, 122, 126–128, 154–161, 163, 173–175, 177–178, 209n148, 219n145, 232n90, 243nn96,98,99
Młodochowski, Josef, 27, 101, 196n108
Molotov, Vjačeslav, 105
Montagne, Rémy, 242n87
Montclos, Xavier de, 185n5
Monteleone, Franco, 188n23
Monticone, Alberto, 185n5, 189n3, 190n6, 199n8, 200n13
Montini, Giovanni Battista, 14, 27, 30, 33, 46–47, 69, 75, 101, 150, 163–165, 167, 169–170, 191n25, 198n1, 199n4, 202nn43,61, 203nn66,67, 204nn85,86,87, 209n4, 210nn7,8,20, 220n166, 223n195, 231nn77,85, 243n99, 244nn121,122, 245nn131,134, 247nn162,175
Moro, Renato, 193nn47,57, 230n68, 235n152, 236n157, 239n39, 245nn137,138
Morozzo della Rocca, Roberto, 207n119
Moses, 140
Mourin, Maxime, 221n175
Moyn, Samuel, 228n36, 239n36
Muckermann, Friedrich, 11, 20–21, 190n14, 191nn16,17,34, 193n63
Murphy, Joseph, 27, 196n98,100
Murray, John, 45, 202n52
Mussolini, Benito, 36–37, 52, 81, 96, 99, 105, 149, 165, 167, 192n45, 199n3, 213nn61,62, 222nn179,186, 226n12, 241n75, 244n127

Napoleon, 70, 152, 156
Neri Serneri, Simone, 199n10
Neveu, Pie Eugène, 196n102
Nietzsche, Friedrich, 109
Nora, Pierre, 207n115

O'Connell, William, 82–83
O'Neill, Charles E., 190n4
Orel, Anton, 234n124
Ormesson, Wladimir d', 60, 62, 197n114, 207nn116,126,127,128
Orsenigo, Cesare, 25, 42, 68, 73, 143, 169, 202n54, 209n1, 231nn77,85, 237n10, 238n30, 247n166
Ortega, Joaquín Luis, 214n87
Ortiz de Urbina, Ignacio, 16, 27–28, 58, 85, 159, 177, 192n39
Osborne, Francis D'Arcy, 33, 77, 98, 100, 134, 139, 222n181, 234n126, 240n45
Osti Guerrazzi, Amedeo, 248n183

Pacelli, Carlo, 180
Pacelli, Eugenio. *See* Pius XII
Pacetti, Massimo, 239n39
Pagano, Sergio, 203n61, 246n145
Paladini, Giannantonio, 249n200
Papeleux, Léon, 215n102, 246nn151,152
Papini, Massimo, 239n39

Index | 259

Passelecq, Georges, 194n76, 195n81, 201n29, 226n12
Pastor, Ludwig von, 218n130
Pattee, Richard, 232nn96,97,98, 233nn110,111,116
Patti, Manoela, 245n139
Paul the Apostle, 92, 140, 214n81
Pavelić, Ante, 128–131, 133, 233n110
Pavolini, Alessandro, 102, 221n172
Paxton, Robert O., 206n102, 215n106, 216n107, 230n62, 231nn81,82,83
Pedroni, Angelo, 180
Peli, Santo, 249n200
Pellegrino, Francesco, 28, 35–41, 43, 51, 108, 118–119, 180, 197n110, 200nn13,14,15,21,23, 201nn32,33,34,35, 202n45, 204n82, 223n201, 229n43
Pérez García, Enrique, 28, 85, 197n109
Perin, Raffaella, 185n6, 187n15, 190nn12,15, 194n74, 200n14, 209n5, 212n50, 213n74, 215nn98,100, 219n144, 221n174, 222nn184,185, 225n10, 226nn13,14, 228nn35,38, 229n41, 236nn153,156, 237n161, 239n43, 240n51
Perrin, Jules Xavier, 62–63
Persico, Alessandro A., 236n157
Pertici, Roberto, 192n42
Pétain, Philippe, 56–61, 64, 84–85, 90–92, 122, 127–128, 157, 160, 205n98, 206nn99,100,104,111, 207n117, 231n85
Peter the Apostle, 40, 212n57
Petracchi, Giorgio, 190n15, 192n42, 221n175
Pettinaroli, Laura, 190n9, 196n102, 221n175, 222n179
Phayer, Michael, 199n6, 230n68, 233n117
Piccialuti Caprioli, Maura, 245n133
Pignatti Morano di Custoza, Bonifacio, 24, 26, 82, 195n87
Pinch, Trevor, 188n24
Pirozzi, Felice, 180
Pitt, William, 187n19
Pius VI, 152
Pius VII, 70, 152

Pius IX, 102, 187n16
Pius X, 5, 41, 115, 187n17, 187n19, 201n36
Pius XI, 6–7, 9–11, 13, 15–17, 20, 24–25, 27, 30–31, 36–37, 39–40, 55, 58, 79, 81, 103–104, 110–111, 113, 120, 188n29, 189nn30,32,34,36,37,39,1,2, 190nn7,11,15, 191nn18,19,21,23,24,27, 28,29,35, 192n45, 193nn52,53,58, 194nn76,77,78, 195nn82,83,84,85,86,87,90, 201nn28,29,36, 221n177, 222nn178,179,181,185, 224n1, 225nn6,11, 226nn11,12,14,15, 227n27, 228n36, 230n59, 237nn160,161, 241n75
Pius XII, 1–3, 27–28, 30–31, 33–35, 37, 39–43, 46–53, 56, 68–69, 71–83, 85, 87, 90, 95–96, 98–102, 104–107, 111–112, 115–116, 120, 125, 130, 132–134, 136–141, 144–146, 148, 149–154, 158–160, 163–165, 167, 169–170, 172–175, 177–178, 181–182, 185nn3,4, 193n51, 198nn1,2, 199nn3,6,7,10, 200nn17,20, 201n31, 202nn45,46,47,49,56,58,59, 60,61, 203nn62,63,64,65,67,74, 204nn81,85, 205nn87,94, 209n2, 210nn9,13,14,15,16,17,18,21, 211nn23,24,25,26,29,30,34,36, 212nn44,51, 213n67, 214nn84,85, 215n98, 217n128, 218nn136,139, 219nn152,153,154,157, 220nn166,171, 221n173, 222n186, 223nn192,193, 194,196, 226n15, 227n33, 229n49, 230n68, 231nn76,78, 232nn90,100, 233nn117,121, 235nn142,143,144,149, 150,151,152, 236nn152,153,157,158, 237nn8,9,13, 238nn16,31,33, 239nn36,43, 240nn46,49,63, 241n66, 242nn81,92,93, 243nn94,95, 96, 244nn125,126, 246n144, 247n166, 248nn178,179,181,182,187, 249n198, 250nn2,3,15; secretary of State, 14, 25, 58, 103, 111, 194nn77,83, 196n107, 206n107; nuncio in Germany 145–146, 195n80, 218n130
Pivato, Stefano, 188n28
Pizzardo, Giuseppe, 13

Pollard, John, 189n30, 199n11
Pombeni, Paolo, 239n39
Potter, Robert W., 205n90
Poulat, Émile, 216n113
Poverello. *See* Francis of Assisi
Pozzi, Lucia, 225n6
Preda, Daniela, 204n84
Preysing, Konrad von, 68–69, 143, 209n2
Procaccia, Claudio, 248n183
Prometheus, 188n28
Prosperi, Adriano, 224n2
Pucelle d'Orleans. *See* Joan of Arc

Raboy, Marc, 189n34
Raczkiewicz, Władisław, 106, 223n194
Raggi, Barbara, 226n17, 228n38
Raguer, Hilari, 214n86
Ramière, Henry, 228n39
Randall, Alec W.G., 99, 219nn160,161
Rarkowski, Franz J., 74
Ratti, Achille. *See* Pius XI
Ready, M. J., 22, 194n73
Reberschak, Maurizio, 249n200
Reginek, Thomas, 203n62
Rémond, René, 206n104, 216n113
Renan, Ernest, 40
Renier, Olive, 186n7
Respighi, Luigi, 189n32
Reynaud, Paul, 56
Rhodes, Anthony, 239n41
Ribbentrop, Joachim von, 52, 105, 150, 204n87, 215n96
Riberi, Antonio, 159
Riccardi, Andrea, 50, 198n2, 199nn6,10, 204n79, 221nn173,175, 228n37, 232n100, 236n153, 239n43, 240n61, 244n127, 250n15
Rigano, Gabriele, 199n10, 204n84, 226n11, 228n37
Rigoulot, Pierre, 210n11
Rioli, Maria Chiara, 230n59
Ritter, Saverio, 101
Robertson, Emma, 186n9
Roccucci, Adriano, 249n204
Roche, Jean, 62–63, 207n129, 208n135
Rollo-Koster, Joëlle, 187n15
Roncalli, Angelo Giuseppe, 139, 189n30, 236n154, 239n43
Roop, Joseph E., 186n11
Roosevelt, Franklin Delano, 56, 75–77, 81, 84, 97, 99, 150, 164–165, 173, 211n40, 244n126
Roosevelt, Theodore, 56
Rosa, Enrico, 39
Rösch, Augustin, 239n34
Roselli, Giuseppina, 246nn144,146
Rosenberg, Alfred, 94, 224n1
Rossi, Elena Aga, 211n37
Rotta, Angelo, 136, 137, 234n139, 235nn148,150
Rousso, Henry, 206n102
Rubinstein, Vladimir, 186n7
Ruffini, Ernesto, 111
Ruozzi, Federico, 191n27, 251nn18,19
Ruy, Louis, 62

Salazar, António de Oliveira, 84, 88, 213n73
Sale, Giovanni, 221n176
Saliège, Jules-Géraud, 128, 231n88, 232n90
Sapieha, Adam Stefan, 151, 240nn52,53
Santagata, Alessandro, 249n200
Saracinelli, Marisa, 239n39
Saresella, Daniela, 187n19
Sarnoff, David, 188n22
Schlesinger, Rudolf, 193n62
Schmidt, Johannes, 147
Schmidt, Wilhelm, 110, 224n1
Schurmans, Maurits, 28–29, 61, 95, 197n109
Schwarte, Johannes, 195nn83,91
Sémelin, Jacques, 157, 242n89
Semkowski, Ludwik, 27, 196n108
Serédi, György, 119, 136–138, 234n138, 235n150
Sergij, Patriarch of Moscow, 249n204
Shapiro, Robert M., 204n75
Shelah, Menachem, 233nn108,112
Shirer, William, 27, 196n99
Sidor, Karol, 134, 234n125
Sigismondi, Pietro, 69, 95, 148
Sigismund III, 108

Silva, Ramon, 186n7
Smith, Richard Lorenz, 10
Soccorsi, Filippo, 10–11, 13–15, 24,
    27–31, 46, 71–72, 74–75, 95, 166, 168,
    170, 178, 191nn25,31,32,33, 192n36,
    204n85, 218n132, 220n170,
    247nn162,175
Spicer, Kevin, 194n63
Stahl, Friedrich, 171
Stalin, Joseph, 249n204
Stefanizzi, Antonio, 180–181, 250n16
Stepinac, Aloysius, 129–134,
    232nn96,97,98, 233nn108,110,
    111,112,116, 234n123
Sterling, Christopher H., 185n7,
    188nn22,23,27
Stevens, Harold, 45, 202n50
Stroothencke, Wolfgang, 113
Sturzo, Luigi, 244n127
Suchecky, Bernard, 194n76, 195n81,
    201n29, 226n12
Suhard, Emmanuel C., 128, 160, 162,
    174, 231n85
Szabó, Miloslav, 234n124
Szalasi, Ferenc, 137
Sztojay, Döme, 136

Tacchi Venturi, Pietro, 29, 96,
    218n135
Taradel, Ruggero, 226n17, 228n38
Tardini, Domenico, 24–25, 49, 69,
    71–75, 82, 94, 98, 101, 103–106, 134,
    136–137, 151, 165, 172–173, 180,
    191n23, 195nn84,87, 198n122, 199n5,
    201n41, 202n61, 203nn61,67,
    204n76, 205n87, 210nn15,16,17,18,21,
    211nn23,24,25,26,29,30,31,32,33,34,
    36, 217n125, 218n135, 219nn152,157,
    220n164, 222nn187,188,189,190,191,
    234nn126,139, 235nn141,148,150,151,
    236n155, 240n45, 244n126,
    245nn131,136, 248nn178,189,190,194,
    249n195
Taylor, Myron, 52, 55, 75–76, 81, 84,
    138, 150, 205nn88,93, 211n37,
    213n68, 240n45, 244n125
Tedeschi, John, 224n2

Temple, William, 236n160
Testa, Gustavo, 97
Théas, Pierre-Marie, 128
Thérèse of Lisieux, 155, 241n75
Tiso, Jozef, 134, 234n124
Tittmann, Harold Jr., 81–83, 97, 158,
    164, 213nn66,68, 219n146,
    220nn166,171, 243nn96,98,
    245n131
Tittmann, Harold H. III, 213n66
Tomasevich, Jozo, 232n99
Török, Sándor, 136
Tramontin, Silvio, 249n200
Traniello, Francesco, 245n137
Trivellato, Francesca, 230n57
Tuka, Vojtech, 134
Turda, Marius, 225n4
Turina, Isacco, 225n6
Tworek, Heidi J.S., 187n20, 188n23

Ujčić, Josip, 232n102
Unger-Alvi, Simon, 226n15

Vági, Zoltán, 229n45
Valbousquet, Nina, 226n15
Valeri, Valerio, 58, 90–91, 102, 128,
    151, 157–158, 215nn104,105,
    216nn108,109, 221n173, 231nn86,87,
    243nn94,95
Vallette, John de la, 99
Valsangiacomo, Nelly, 198n125
Valvo, Paolo, 193n58, 194n76, 195n88
Van Roey, Jozef Ernest, 114–115,
    227n30
Vaughn, Joseph Louis, 27, 196n104
Veca, Ignazio, 207n120
Vecchio, Giorgio, 242n89, 249n200
Ventresca, Robert A., 221n173,
    235nn142,151, 236n158, 248n178
Venturini, Galileo, 28, 197n111
Verucci, Guido, 222n178
Vian, Giovanni, 187n19, 225n10
Viganò, Dario E., 251n19
Villa, Achille, 220n162
Vittorio Emanuele III, 167
Volk, Ludwig, 194n64, 237n12, 238n21,
    239n34

Voog, Roger, 185n5
Vries, Wilhelm de, 174
Walker, Andrew, 185n7
Walsh, James, 219n161
Walsh, Sarah, 225n4
Ward, James Mace, 234n124
Ward, Marilyn S., 205nn91,92
Weizsäcker, Ernst von, 68, 165
Wieviorka, Olivier, 242n89
Willaert, Ferdinand, 61
Winock, Michel, 207n115
Wolf, Hubert, 195n80, 221n176, 222n179, 225n9

Wolfe, Kenneth, 198n129
Wood, Edward, Earl of Halifax, 222n181
Wood, James, 188nn22,23
Worcester, Thomas, 189n30
Wyszynski, Stefan, 179

Zanini, Paolo, 230n59
Zeij, Jacob, 117
Zichy, Gyula, 118, 119
Zola, Émile, 40
Zuccotti, Susan, 204n75, 229n41, 248n183

Raffaella Perin is Associate Professor of History of Christianity at the Catholic University of the Sacred Heart of Milan.

World War II: The Global, Human, and Ethical Dimension
G. Kurt Piehler, *series editor*

Lawrence Cane, David E. Cane, Judy Barrett Litoff, and David C. Smith, eds.,
  *Fighting Fascism in Europe: The World War II Letters of an American Veteran
  of the Spanish Civil War*
Angelo M. Spinelli and Lewis H. Carlson, *Life behind Barbed Wire: The Secret
  World War II Photographs of Prisoner of War Angelo M. Spinelli*
Don Whitehead and John B. Romeiser, *"Beachhead Don": Reporting the War from
  the European Theater, 1942–1945*
Scott H. Bennett, ed., *Army GI, Pacifist CO: The World War II Letters of Frank and
  Albert Dietrich*
Alexander Jefferson with Lewis H. Carlson, *Red Tail Captured, Red Tail Free:
  Memoirs of a Tuskegee Airman and POW*
Jonathan G. Utley, *Going to War with Japan, 1937–1941*
Grant K. Goodman, *America's Japan: The First Year, 1945–1946*
Patricia Kollander with John O'Sullivan, *"I Must Be a Part of This War": One Man's
  Fight against Hitler and Nazism*
Judy Barrett Litoff, *An American Heroine in the French Resistance: The Diary and
  Memoir of Virginia d'Albert-Lake*
Thomas R. Christofferson and Michael S. Christofferson, *France during World
  War II: From Defeat to Liberation*
Don Whitehead, *Combat Reporter: Don Whitehead's World War II Diary and
  Memoirs*, edited by John B. Romeiser
James M. Gavin, *The General and His Daughter: The Wartime Letters of
  General James M. Gavin to His Daughter Barbara*, edited by Barbara Gavin
  Fauntleroy et al.
Carol Adele Kelly, ed., *Voices of My Comrades: America's Reserve Officers
  Remember World War II*, foreword by Senators Ted Stevens and Daniel K.
  Inouye
John J. Toffey IV, *Jack Toffey's War: A Son's Memoir*
Lt. General James V. Edmundson, *Letters to Lee: From Pearl Harbor to the War's
  Final Mission*, edited by Dr. Celia Edmundson
John K. Stutterheim, *The Diary of Prisoner 17326: A Boy's Life in a Japanese Labor
  Camp*, foreword by Mark Parillo
G. Kurt Piehler and Sidney Pash, eds., *The United States and the Second World
  War: New Perspectives on Diplomacy, War, and the Home Front*
Susan E. Wiant, *Between the Bylines: A Father's Legacy*, Foreword by Walter
  Cronkite
Deborah S. Cornelius, *Hungary in World War II: Caught in the Cauldron*
Gilya Gerda Schmidt, *Süssen Is Now Free of Jews: World War II, The Holocaust,
  and Rural Judaism*

Emanuel Rota, *A Pact with Vichy: Angelo Tasca from Italian Socialism to French Collaboration*

Panteleymon Anastasakis, *The Church of Greece under Axis Occupation*

Louise DeSalvo, *Chasing Ghosts: A Memoir of a Father, Gone to War*

Alexander Jefferson with Lewis H. Carlson, *Red Tail Captured, Red Tail Free: Memoirs of a Tuskegee Airman and POW, Revised Edition*

Kent Puckett, *War Pictures: Cinema, Violence, and Style in Britain, 1939–1945*

Marisa Escolar, *Allied Encounters: The Gendered Redemption of World War II Italy*

Courtney A. Short, *The Most Vital Question: Race and Identity in the U.S. Occupation of Okinawa, 1945–1946*

James Cassidy, *NBC Goes to War: The Diary of Radio Correspondent James Cassidy from London to the Bulge*, edited by Michael S. Sweeney

Rebecca Schwartz Greene, *Breaking Point: The Ironic Evolution of Psychiatry in World War II*

Franco Baldasso, *Against Redemption: Democracy, Memory, and Literature in Post-Fascist Italy*

G. Kurt Piehler and Ingo Trauschweizer, eds., *Reporting World War II*

Kevin T Hall, *Forgotten Casualties: Downed American Airmen and Axis Violence in World War II*

Chad R. Diehl, ed., *Shadows of Nagasaki: Trauma, Religion, and Memory after the Atomic Bombing*

Raffaella Perin, *The Popes on Air: The History of Vatican Radio from Its Origins to World War II*

www.ingramcontent.com/pod-product-compliance
Lightning Source LLC
Chambersburg PA
CBHW020400080526
44584CB00014B/1102